THE LIFE OF
MATTHEW SIMPSON

THE MACMILLAN COMPANY
NEW YORK • CHICAGO
DALLAS • ATLANTA • SAN FRANCISCO
LONDON • MANILA

**THE MACMILLAN COMPANY
OF CANADA, LIMITED**
TORONTO

The Life of

MATTHEW
SIMPSON

by

ROBERT D. CLARK

NEW YORK
The Macmillan Company
1956

FOREWORD

MATTHEW SIMPSON, nineteenth century Methodist preacher and bishop, was a political figure of some importance, a friend of Lincoln, Grant, Hayes, and others. Among his admirers great claims have been made concerning his influence on Lincoln, particularly in the writing of the Emancipation Proclamation. Much less is said of the resolution he forced through the General Conference of 1868 designed to aid in the impeachment of Andrew Johnson. And scarcely noted at all is the amazing transition of the Methodism he served from a body which, in 1830, disdained politics and preached only a simple theology of salvation or damnation, to a denomination which, in 1870, was proud of the political influence of its leading bishop.

Altogether, Matthew Simpson was a remarkable man. Born on the Ohio frontier, denied an opportunity for formal study, he acquired a measure of learning that evokes admiration and prompts reappraisal of the rudeness of our forefathers. Trained in medicine, he practiced religion. Awkward and uncouth, so unsure of himself in the presence of people that he dared not study law, he won distinction as one of the most eloquent preachers of his country and his times.

Much of the writing on nineteenth century American Methodism has been antiquarian in its emphasis—an exploitation of the public's interest in the eccentric Peter Cartwright and his fellows, or in the strange phenomena of camp meetings and love feasts. Matthew Simpson might be forced into this stereotype: he was converted in a camp meeting, inducted into the ministry as a circuit rider, and widely acclaimed for the sensational effects of his sermons.

But the story of Matthew Simpson is more than remarkable incident or phenomenal success. It is as much the story of Methodism as it is of Simpson, for it is in a large measure an account of his fight for the status of his church.

In early nineteenth century America the Methodists were the youngest but the largest of the denominations. Less favored economically, socially, educationally, politically, than their fellows, they were drawn together by the common bond of religion. They preached no election of the saints but a "full and free" salvation. Through conversion, classmeetings, and love feasts they built a common religious experience and terminology, and through an itinerant ministry, they strengthened "connectional bonds." The older, better established denominations scorned and ridiculed their uneducated ministry, their heretical doctrines, and their emotional forms of worship, but the criticism served only to intensify Methodist loyalty and Methodist unity.

Against this background Simpson, steeped in the classics, in science, in the Bible and Wesley, fought his battles. In his youth, in a frontal attack on Presbyterianism, he defied the "bulls eminating from Geneva." As the young president of Indiana Asbury University, enamored as he was of learning, he was equally motivated by the fear that the Presbyterians would preempt all higher education. He was antislavery in sentiment, but he viewed Abolitionism, not simply as an abstract right but as a threat to the church he loved; and so, for twenty-five years he sought to temper the extremists of North and South, or North and Border.

For the most part, he was not a narrow polemicist or a rabid partisan. But he could never forgive the South for the breaking up of the "Old Church" over the slavery issue, and in the post-war reconstruction he led the northern Methodists in their aggressions against the Church, South. He was jealous, too, of Methodist claim to distinction, and when the Republicans, flush with victory, began the distribution of the spoils, he accosted them to demand political preferment for the leaders of his church.

In all his battles eloquence was his strength—not eloquence of language only, or of action, but the eloquent optimism of his age. He preached the ultimate triumph of Christianity, the destiny of the American people, and the greatness of the Methodist church. If he were chauvinistic and sectarian at times, he was also the champion of learning and of tolerance, and of the magnanimity and inclusiveness of the gospel he preached. Courageous, generally farsighted, and intellectually far above most of his contemporaries in the church, he helped to prepare the way for men like the late Francis J. McConnell and present-day liberals of the Methodist church. A far cry, all this, from Matthew Simpson, the simple, evangelical itinerant of 1833.

The most important single source for this study has been the Bishop Matthew Simpson Papers in the Manuscripts Division of the Library of Congress. Of almost equal importance have been the official Methodist newspapers, the several Christian Advocates, and the two unofficial papers, *Zion's Herald* and *The Methodist,* all but the latter of which were published during almost the entire period of Simpson's ministry. Of the large number of writers of biography and general history to whom I have turned for both interpretation and facts, I owe most to William Warren Sweet, the historian of the church in American history.

I am chiefly indebted to William Best Hesseltine who suggested the topic, gave valuable advice in the course of preparation, and read and criticized parts of two drafts of the manuscript. I wish also to thank Professor Hesseltine's graduate seminar which, in the spring of 1951, allowing the intrusion of an outsider, read the entire manuscript and offered unsparing and valuable criticisms. The late Bishop Francis J. McConnell read parts of the manuscript and, in conversation and correspondence, offered encouragement and made many helpful suggestions. I am indebted also to Professor Alan Nichols and the late Professor Frank Garver, both of the University of Southern California, to Mrs. Dolores Renze of the Colorado Historical Society, to Dr. Wallace Smeltzer, historian of the Pittsburgh Conference of the Methodist Church, to H. B. McConnell and Milton Ronsheim of the Cadiz (Ohio) *Republican,* and to a host of others.

I cannot here mention all of the libraries which rendered service to me: chief among these, in addition to the Library of Congress, are the libraries of Allegheny College, the Colorado Historical Society, Drew Theological Seminary, Emory University, Johns Hopkins University, the University of Oregon, West Virginia University, the Enoch Pratt Free Library of Baltimore, and the libraries of the Baltimore and Pittsburgh conferences of the Methodist Church, and of the Methodist Publishing House at Nashville, Tennessee.

The generosity of the John Simon Guggenheim Memorial Foundation made it possible for me to spend one year, free from academic responsibilities, in study and writing. The Graduate School Research Fund of the University of Oregon provided me with funds for the purchase of microfilm and photostats and for clerical services in the collection of data and the typing of the manuscript.

The *Mississippi Valley Historical Review* and the *Indiana Magazine of History* have permitted me to incorporate parts of articles into chapters IX and XX.

Finally, I owe much to Opal Routh Clark for her sympathetic and critical reading, her protective regard for research and writing, and her good-natured tolerance of my neglect of domestic duties.

R. D. C.

CONTENTS

THE LIFE OF
MATTHEW SIMPSON

I

LIFE IN CADIZ

MATTHEW SIMPSON, young doctor of medicine in Cadiz, Ohio, closed his office and discontinued his practice late in March, 1834. On April 5, astride a horse, his saddle-bags behind him, he rode from the village as a Methodist itinerant to the first of thirty-four appointments on a six-weeks' circuit. For several months he had been preaching alternate Sundays at Cadiz and St. Clairsville; but this day marked a signal decision. Against the advice of many friends and neighbors, he had renounced his original profession and yielded with inner satisfaction to a peculiar develop-ment of circumstances which he called "Providence." Henceforth, no ordinary physician, he was to be a healer of souls.

Fifteen miles from Cadiz, on a hill overlooking Perrine's mill and farmhouse, he pulled up his horse before the small stone house where he had arranged his first appointment. Poised there on the hill-side, he may have weighed once again his recent decision, painfully balancing his growing success as a physician—the financial security, the high esteem, the contribution which a Methodist doctor could make to his church—against the homeless life of the itinerant minis-ter, the hardship and danger of the western saddle trails and the backwoods roads, the meager and uncertain income, and above all the fear of failure, of moving lips that could not speak.

Or he may have dreamed of success—of camp meetings and re-vivals, of the messenger of God confronting a multitude, and of a torrent of words, a flood of eloquence, a surging emotional tide en-gulfing the awe-stricken people.

He was aware that he had more than usual talents, but he knew also of his limitations. Not one of the young men of Cadiz could match him in ciphering and spelling, in rendering Latin into Eng-lish, or in explaining the wonders of natural science. But he lacked social graces. He was tall—over six feet—gangling, and stoop-shouldered. His low forehead, made lower by the deep V of his hair-line, his high cheekbones, his thin, serious lips, his small pointed face—these features, his neighbors said, did not suggest great ora-tory. He was timid—so timid that he sometimes crossed the street to avoid meeting people, so nervous in the presence of strangers that his small hand trembled when he passed the collection plate at quarterly conference. Even after he had become a young physician, he wore clothes that fitted him so oddly that Cadiz could not forget the awkward boy who had slouched along its streets, his short panta-loons hitched up by one gallus.

Only the sudden impetuous rush of his speech, or the bright-ness of his blue eyes—now sparkling with animation, now flashing in anger, now moist with sympathy—caught the attention of his neighbors and stayed their judgment. Long years of surprised ob-servance of the development of his talents made them wary. Still they shook their heads over the closing of the doctor's office. He scarcely looked the part of a preacher. He could write, they ad-mitted. But could he speak?

As he sat now overlooking Perrine's, he himself would have been astonished at his own dream had it projected the man he was to become: college professor and president, editor, bishop, friend of Presidents and statesmen, shrewd politician, patriotic orator, the most eloquent preacher in Methodism, and chief architect of the century in building America's largest Protestant church.

He would have smiled in amusement had his reverie included the men he was to know: President Lincoln, General Grant, Secre-tary Stanton, and a host of others. His brows would have drawn together in quick self-reproach had his dreams anticipated, even fleetingly, the role he was to play in changing the frontier ways of his church, in chipping away and leveling the barrier between the united cause of Methodism and the American people.

Whatever thoughts may have troubled him on that April after-noon, he did not long heed. Simple in his faith, he believed only that the providence of God was plainly written for him in the unfolding of events, and that his responsibility was to obey. Dig-ging his heels into the ribs of his horse, he rode down into the valley to the first of his appointments.

That night, after preaching to four men and eleven women

on the text, "Are the consolations of God small with thee? is there any secret thing with thee?" he wrote at some length in his journal: marking the route he had taken from Cadiz to Perrine's, describing the wooded hills and the smiling meadow, the creek and the "handsome mill" that ran three pair of stones, and noticing the household's "sprightly young damsel . . . just seventeen, neat in her person . . . and amiable in her manners." But he had no word for his thoughts of the day.[1]

Matthew Simpson was born in the little village of Cadiz, Ohio, in 1811, to parents who a decade earlier, with their respective families, had slashed and chopped their way into the frontier wilderness. The Simpsons were Scotch-Irish. James, the father, had been a boy in his early teens, the youngest member of his family, when he sailed in 1793 with his widowed mother, his sister, and his older brothers from Londonderry to Baltimore. They had lived briefly in eastern Pennsylvania and then had joined the westward-moving horde to cross the Alleghenies to Pittsburgh and settle finally in Harrison County, Ohio.

James suffered from sciatic lameness and was troubled by a recurring hacking cough. Frontier farming and outdoor life did not appeal to him. Genial and warm-hearted, he liked to talk, and he was quick at driving a bargain. So he clerked in a store at Pittsburgh until he was able to persuade his employer to set him up in business on a partnership basis.

As a likely place, he selected Cadiz, the county seat of Harrison County. It was but a clearing in the forest, a village of a dozen houses, mostly of log chinked with yellow clay; but it was strategically located at the juncture of two of the principal roads from the east: one from Pittsburgh by way of Steubenville, and the other from Washington, Pennsylvania, by way of Wellsburg, (West) Virginia. The roads joined on the Cadiz hillside, near the courthouse square, and proceeded thence to Zanesville. James, with his brother Matthew, opened a store and began to sell and trade and to manufacture weavers' reeds.

In 1806 at Short Creek, Jefferson County, James met and fell in love with Sarah Tingley. She also was a Methodist, and listened with the same subdued but eager feeling to the exciting tales and the stirring exhortations of the itinerant preachers. The first of the

Tingley family to experience conversion in a frontier meeting, she was the first also to join the Methodist Church.

James and Sarah were married that year and went at once to Cadiz to share the log house and store building with his mother and his brother Matthew. Their daughters Hetty and Elizabeth were born in 1807 and 1809; young Matthew, in 1811.

Shortly after the birth of his son, James Simpson became seriously ill. His face flushed with fever and his body convulsed with coughing, he went with his family to Pittsburgh to seek the aid of physicians. "Consumption," they said, diagnosing his illness with a term which in early Ohio was more literal than figurative in its certain fate. The frontier remedies were not equal to the need. A few weeks later James Simpson died. But first he and Sarah, distraught by worry and grief yet ruled by one dominant purpose, consecrated young Matthew to their God and prayed that he might become a preacher.

Sarah Simpson took her three children back to the small log house in Cadiz which James had built for her, and which she continued to share with her husband's aging mother and his unmarried brother Matthew.

Young Matthew's earliest memories were of the roaring fire on the stone hearth, the menacing shadows on the wall, and the stories of Grandma Simpson. On long winter evenings she told the children of her girlhood experiences in northern Ireland, of the simple ways of the Irish village, of the exacting standards of the Scotch Presbyterians; of her marriage, her family, and the tragic accident which had resulted in the death of her husband. She told them of Mr. Wesley and his visit to Ireland—how he stood before the people and talked to them about knowing God, and how she, a widow of a few months, felt her heart strangely moved. She recounted in vivid and angry detail the persecution of the Protestants by the Catholics, the abuse heaped upon Mr. Wesley, the threats and violence, and the burning of Methodist chapels. And with these stories she interspersed those of fairy and elf and ghost, told with such realism that Matthew, in the half-dark room, could feel his hackles rising and panic seizing him as he was sent from the fireside to his bed.

He was three years old when he learned to read. His sisters

Hetty, who was seven, and Elizabeth, five, had their books, and he must have his. So they taught him, painfully spelling out the letters, and demanding that he spell them back. They taught him simple arithmetic, too. When he was five his mother and uncle moved from the log house to a new frame building down the street from the courthouse square. In gathering up his belongings he ran across an old multiplication table his sister had set for him—which seemed, as he reviewed it, a task long since mastered and half forgot.

Matthew was embarrassed and astonished when the itinerant preachers, who frequently stopped overnight at his mother's house, asked him, a boy of six, if he could read. But in general he liked them. His spirit might grow faint and wilt in the thick miasma of religious talk, but it revived again at night by the fireside. For even the preacher—when the solemn prayers and the preaching were done—had wonderful stories to tell: of riding into the wilderness, his trail marked only by the blazes on the trees; of swimming his horse across the churning, rain-swollen rivers; of the wildcat's scream, or the bear's great bulk blocking his trail; of camp meetings in the brush arbor, and the flickering torches, the singing and shouting and moaning of the people, the rough, boastful talk of the drunken rowdies; and fights, battles for the Lord, not with prayers only, but with clubs and fists. Preaching was a good life for those who were called.

Only a little less vivid than the stories of Grandma Simpson and the preachers were his mother's teachings about the God above the skies who heard all his words, even saw every one of his thoughts. If he loved God and served him, she said, he would go to heaven; but if he did not love God he would be forever separated from Him, and from his own mother and all of his friends and loved ones. If there was food on the table God had given it to him; and if the larder ran low he was comforted by his mother's assurance that God would provide. When a cousin sickened and died he heard from his mother that it was God's will; and when another drew close to death but recovered he learned that God in His providence had spared the boy for a special purpose.[2]

After they moved to the new house Matthew began to study with his uncle. Scarcely any one in Harrison County knew so much as Uncle Matthew. A small, frail man, he shunned the vigorous outdoor life of the frontier; but he read a great deal, books on history, law, and religion. People said he was a walking encyclopedia. He even owned a German New Testament which he taught young Matthew to translate by comparing it with the English. James had left him a growing business, more than one man could handle. Because he was not so genial as James, nor so ready in bargaining, he closed out the store; but he continued to make the weavers' reeds. Clever and inventive, he put together a crude machine which did a much better job of splitting and shaping the canes than a man could do by hand. The work was heavy, however, and he was in "feeble" health and not able to turn the crank of his machine very regularly.

In order to increase the meager income on which his brother's family depended, Uncle Matthew built a small addition to the frame house and opened a common school. He was meticulous as well as scholarly, and stern despite his kindly face. The boys in his school thought him a strict disciplinarian.

The people of the town respected him, not only for his learning and his practical, inventive skill, but for his character. For twenty-five years he lived in the same house with his brother's widow, and prompted no tongues to wag. He was a quiet man, but he could argue like a lawyer when he was put to it. So his neighbors sent him to the Ohio senate, and returned him for ten out of twelve years; and one year they elected him associate judge of the county court.[3]

For two brief terms young Matthew attended a "select" school where he learned to chant the rules of grammar, the tables of arithmetic, and the elements of geography. But he studied for the most part with Uncle Matthew: answered his questions on books read; puzzled out in his mind the arithmetic problems that his uncle set (it was silly and childish to do them on paper); walked with his uncle in the woods and told back to him the orders and classes of the plants and trees which crowded the hillside and pressed in upon the little village; learned to point out and name the stars which hung close and brilliant in the Cadiz sky.[4]

As soon as he was old enough he had to help in the small factory. The work was hard for a boy, dressing and smoothing the long strips of wood, stacking them in neat piles, even turning the heavy crank of the reed-making machine for what seemed hours on end. Uncle Matthew was exacting, and the boy had to do the work laid

out for him before he was allowed to turn to his books. Then he
read voraciously, poring over the volumes of biography, history,
travel, and science which he was able to borrow from the lawyers
and the preachers, or from the small public library of which Cadiz
was so proud.

In the Puritan Methodist household there was little opportunity to play for play's sake. Uncle Matthew did not believe in it at all;
but oftentimes the exasperated mother, worried over her boy's
poor health, drove him out of doors, away from his books. Once
outside, he delighted in running, jumping, wrestling with his fellows, and striving constantly to outdo them. He made kites in the
spring of the year, and felt the exciting tug of the March winds; he
ran with the boys to the bottom of the hill and paddled about in
the shallow waters of Short Creek; he made a bow and arrow—
stripped the bark from the branch of an ash; carefully shaped and
notched the elastic wood; balanced and feathered his arrow—and
practiced on targets in a forest quite as primeval as that of the
stories to which he had listened.

Even more than the play, he liked to walk alone in the woods,
or with his Uncle Matthew, to hear the sound of the wind in the
trees, to fling himself down in a clearing, to pull and chew the
long stems of the blue grass, and to think. To drink in the beauty
of the woods—the pale spring greens of the beech, the linden, and
the maple; to wonder at the trunk of the great white oak which
lightning had shattered; to marvel at the late afternoon sun and
its way, after it had dropped behind the hill, of lighting up the
tops of eastern trees. And, prompted by Uncle Matthew, to moralize
a little, to begin to apprehend the goodness and greatness of God and
marvel at it. To retrace the argument of the preachers in his mother's
house, and to wonder what he must do to be saved, but to think, also,
of the stirring drama he had witnessed in the county court, and to
picture young Matthew Simpson, attorney at law, pleading for the
life of his client.[5]

Nothing pleased Matthew so much as the shop where Uncle
Joseph Tingley every week published the four-page *Harrison County
Telegraph*. He could swagger a little at the shop. It gave him a
kind of status he could never claim from turning the crank of
Uncle Matthew's machine. He loved the acrid smell of the ink; the
tedious, yet amazingly fast, picking out and setting of the type

against his composing stick; the hard pressure of the locked form of type against the heel of his hand; the rapid drumming on the type with the leather inking balls; the heavy lever of the hand press, and best of all, perhaps, the thrill that came in taking the printed page from the tympan.

He knew the secrets of the town and of the nation, most of them before they were broadcast by word of mouth—the names of the people whose letters lay unclaimed in the post office at Cadiz or Freeport, the notices of the sheriff's sales, the theft of a horse at Jefferson, the date of the general muster and the tax collection, the new law partnership at Cadiz, the latest items in the stock of goods at Thomas Bingham's store; he read and sometimes set the national news, stories of floods and fires and other disasters, excerpts from foreign papers, the President's message to Congress, the arguments of Webster and Clay, news of the campaign for President, and arguments on the merits of Clay, Jackson, and John Quincy Adams. He learned, from strong-minded Uncle Tingley, to hate slavery as inconsistent with American principles of "liberty, freedom, justice and equality," and to favor Mr. Adams for the Presidency (even though he was not a western man), because he had never been connected either with slavery or with dueling.[6] He wrote some "pieces" for the paper himself, mostly verses which Uncle Joseph or his successor, David Christy, published in the poetry column.

In addition to the common school of Uncle Matthew, Cadiz soon had an academy where young frontiersmen learned to translate the classical languages, to write orations, and to declaim. Matthew, not yet twelve years old, was determined to attend, to study Latin and Greek. He was encouraged by two boys from the country, students at the academy, who boarded with his Uncle Matthew's partner. Following them about, he often went up to their room, questioned them concerning their studies, and fondly thumbed through the pages of their Latin books. After a time he tried his hand at translation, and so amazed them with his facility that they went to his mother and Uncle Matthew to urge that he be enrolled in the academy. Uncle Matthew demurred, mindful of the cost.

Some weeks later, illness of their hostess brought the two

students into Matthew's own home, to remain until she should recover. Eagerly welcoming them, Matthew again turned over the pages of his friends' Latin books, pausing now and then to try his skill at rendering a sentence into English. Again he begged his uncle's permission to study the language. If he could not attend the academy, he could get the boys to help him. He could learn to translate by comparing the text to the English, as he had done with the German. No cost was involved; it was late in November, the days were short, and the evenings long. Besides, Uncle Matthew was about to leave for the session of the legislature, and could not supervise the boy's study himself. It looked like the working of Providence. So the uncle yielded, provided that his nephew would first do half a man's work each day in the shop. The boy quickly agreed, and began at once to memorize the Latin declensions and conjugations.

It was extraordinary how easily he could fix the Latin words and forms in his mind. Bending over his books night after night, unmindful of the fire as it flamed or died down on the hearth, or of the flicker of the candle on the fine print of the page, he sought only to learn—and to excel; to satisfy in some manner his gnawing desire for knowledge—and recognition.

In the weeks before his uncle's return in February, he completed the study of the grammar, read *Historica Sacra* (a collection of Latin essays), four books of Caesar, and a large part of Sallust's *Catiline*—in short, he overtook the friends who had begun some eighteen months before.

Uncle Matthew wanted to know at once what his nephew had learned, and demanded that he read for him. Amazed at the boy's progress, he agreed to send him to the academy.

During the remainder of the four months, young Matthew finished the first volume of *Graeca Majora* (bristling with its Latin notes, some of them as tough for a boy as the Greek itself), a part of the poetry of the second volume, and a number of books of Homer. He completed in the three terms all that was required in the entire Greek and Latin courses of the neighboring colleges.

In the months that followed he studied advanced algebra, French, Spanish, a little Italian, botany, geology, and chemistry. All the while he worked in his uncle's shop; and as soon as he was large enough he began to assist in the common school. So he busied himself until his seventeenth year, in the summer of 1828. That year he became acquainted with Charles Elliott.

II

Mr. Elliott had come to Cadiz in the interest of Madison College, the newly established Methodist institution at Uniontown, Pennsylvania, where he was professor of languages. Young Matthew looked on him with awe and admiration. He was a college professor; and he was one of the two classically educated preachers in the entire Pittsburgh Conference of the Methodist Episcopal Church. A stockily built Irishman, thirty-six years of age, with a huge blond head and friendly blue eyes, Professor Elliott was impressive. He abounded in good humor, pithy sayings, and learned saws. His thick Irish brogue, straight from county Donegal, his pious sentiments, and his deep suspicion of the Catholic Church made him quite at home in a family reared at the fireside of Grandma Simpson.[7]

Passionately devoted to the Methodist church, and jealous of the welfare of Madison College, Mr. Elliott was in search of just such young men as Matthew Simpson. They were needed for the college and church alike. So he listened attentively to Uncle Matthew's recital of the boy's accomplishments. Questioning young Matthew himself, he noted his skill in Latin and Greek. A boy like that ought to be in college, in a Methodist college. A way could be found. He would listen to no objections, financial or otherwise. He himself needed an assistant (how little he could afford one, he well knew); he would take Matthew into his home and let him help with the instruction in Latin and Greek. There was no resisting Professor Elliott, especially, as Uncle Matthew said, when it was such a clear case of the working of Providence.

On the first Monday in November, 1828, young Matthew, with $11.25 in cash, and with his clothes and a few books rolled into a bundle, set out on foot for Uniontown, some ninety miles away. Uncle Matthew, reluctant at last to see him go, this boy whom he loved like a son, walked down the road with him an hour's distance, to Craig's Plantation.

A quick goodbye at Craig's, and Matthew went on alone down

the pike toward Uniontown. Ahead of him as he swung along rapidly and steadily, he could see at any moment only a short stretch of the road before it turned left or right into the wooded ridge or dropped over the hillside into the narrow valley beyond. Short distances, those, to a boy whose head was filled with thoughts of college. Underfoot the road was rough with November frost, the caked earth resistant to the weight of a man's foot. But he walked all the way—save a few miles' ride on horseback out of Wellsburg, Virginia.

At half-past four on Wednesday afternoon of the third day he reached Uniontown and went to Mr. Elliott's home. The professor came in a few minutes later and welcomed him warmly. The next morning Matthew enrolled as student number 46 in the classical department. He paid $4.62½ on his tuition, $1.00 for a Greek book, and 62½ cents for a Latin grammar, 9¼ cents for paper. He spent also 37½ cents for stockings, 18¾ cents for a penknife, and 6¼ cents for a comb.[8]

At the Elliotts' he had a bed in a room with four other students and a place at the family table. He received his "victuals" free for assisting Mr. Elliott; but he paid for everything else—his coal, candles, washing, and the sleeping room. He found the boarding good, and Mr. and Mrs. Elliott "quite agreeable." He was delighted with the arrangement for family prayers. Professor Elliott and the students, each taking his turn, read and compared the Vulgate, Septuagint, Hebrew, French, and German Bibles.

Mr. Elliott put him to work at once reviewing Latin, Greek, Euclid, and Hebrew, the latter of which he had hastily studied at home. In addition to his own studies, he heard Mr. Elliott's classes in Cicero and the Greek New Testament, and on rainy days and days when the professor was away from home on business, he conducted the classes in Latin and Greek grammar, "Mair's Introduction," *Virgil,* and *Graeca Majora.*

For his own reading in Latin, he was, at the end of the first month, half through Livy ("fine print, about 300 pages").

"Read as much and as rapidly as you can," Mr. Elliott said, "and you will become perfect by practice. You will need no instruction from me in Latin and Greek." [9]

Matthew was strongly inclined to agree with him. The passages in Livy which he found difficult for himself were scarcely less so for Mr. Elliott. And he soon discovered that his professor knew little if any more Hebrew than he did himself.

Mr. Fielding, the instructor in mathematics, was a little more skeptical about Matthew's abilities.

"What progress have you made in the sciences?" he asked.

"I read Euclid at home, with Uncle Matthew," Simpson replied, "and studied some algebra and learnt surveying."

That sounded a little like boasting to Mr. Fielding. "Which did you study first, Euclid or surveying?" he asked.

"Surveying."

"Surveying? I'm afraid you haven't studied it to so good an advantage as had you read Euclid first. I advise you to commence with Euclid again."

He began with Euclid; but after two or three lessons Mr. Fielding put him into an advanced class which was reviewing the text in preparation for the term examination. With no little satisfaction Matthew discovered that he could easily keep pace with the class. On the instructor's advice, he then began the study of algebra at home, reporting only when he was confronted by a problem he could not solve.

As the Christmas holidays and the end of the fall term approached, the rumor spread that the college tutor was going to resign. The position paid eighty dollars for the year, forty dollars for each of the five-month terms. Matthew did not doubt for a moment that he could get the appointment, but he was not at all certain that he should apply. On the whole he had found college disappointing. Expecting to meet young men of "superior minds and large attainments," and professors who "would take me by the hand as a giant would lead a child," he had discovered instead that "teachers are but men, and if the United States can parade no smarter young men than what comes to this college, Alas for the times." [10]

None the less, he would like to stay if he could do so without causing undue hardship to the family at home. His expenses would be considerable. With boarding at $1.50 per week (high because of the cost of grain) and washing twenty-five cents, the costs for a month of four and one-half weeks would be $7.87½, "leaving only twelve and a half cents for incidental expenses, such as shoe-blacking, mending, &c." The family then would have to pay for such items as shoes, hat, stockings, coat, pantaloons, vests, about fifty dollars for the year, of which he could earn only a part during the summer.

He doubted that he could enjoy or profit from college if it were to work a hardship at home. He had already gained much, including confidence in his own ability. Besides, he had paid strict attention to all the forms and rules, and he had learned something about both studying and teaching. If he had a good common school with a few Latin or Greek scholars, could he not advance as much in real learning as he could as tutor?

Classes were dismissed on Christmas Day. Matthew rose early, before daybreak, to attend prayer meeting. The day was beautiful—clear and crisp and cold. At eleven o'clock Matthew went to the chapel to hear the preaching of Dr. Henry Bascom, former president of the college and now occasional lecturer on belles-lettres. But Matthew's mind was not on the sermon. He was to be tutor—Matthew Simpson, tutor, Madison College. All the eloquence of Dr. Bascom could not crowd that fact out of his thinking. A few days later, the fall term having ended, he started for home, walking over the same road he had taken two months before.

When the excitement of his return had subsided he surveyed the situation at home. Uncle Matthew was unwell, and his sister Betsey was suffering again from the disease which had taken their father's life. Hetty, who had been teaching in Uncle Matthew's school, was soon to be married. There was no doubt about it—he was needed at home. He resigned the tutorship, and so, after two months at Madison, concluded his college student days. He and his uncle, before the opening of the winter term, moved the school to the old academy building and added higher classes in languages and mathematics.

II

AMONG THE LITERATI

MATTHEW SIMPSON did not mind going back to Cadiz. It was a town to be proud of. Eastern nabobs might suppose that they were intellectually superior to backwoodsmen who were fed on corn pone and skimmed milk, or who could lie in bed at night and look up through apertures in their roofs at the laughing stars. Some of the westerners themselves might tamely stand with their hats under their arms worshiping eastern excellency and saying "Please your honor & I mean no offence." [1] But in general the spirit of independence had been at work. Ohio was throbbing with energy and power. Thirty years ago a wilderness, it stood in 1829 fourth in population among the states—with more people than Massachusetts and Connecticut combined.

Harrison County with a population of 20,000 was, next to Cincinnati, the most densely settled area of the state. Coal and limestone were plentiful, corn and wheat grew rank in the clearings, the peach and apple orchards every summer and fall were heavy with fruit, and great numbers of sheep grazed on the hillsides. Cadiz had a large brick courthouse, only a block from Matthew's home, a printing office, ten stores, six taverns, two large brick Presbyterian churches, a Methodist meetinghouse (how well he knew that plain, unpainted, rectangular hall, stained a nut-brown with age!), a steam gristmill, about 140 dwelling houses, and 820 inhabitants.[2]

The National Road went through St. Clairsville, a dozen miles to the south, but the Cadiz route was well traveled. From early spring until late fall families poured through the little town on their way west. Great freighters, creaking and groaning with their loads, drawn by four or six or even nine head of horses, ground to a stop before the crowded taverns; and drovers, raising thick clouds of dust, herded their cattle and sheep and hogs along the road to the eastern market.

There was already some talk of a railroad in this bustling town; and young men, too impatient to wait for steam and rail, had built a trial road on the hillside. Passengers could ride down, but they had to walk up! Uncle Matthew had invented a new machine for making men's neckties, an ingenious device to weave the bristles into the high stock; Hetty and her husband, taking over the business of manufacturing the stocks, were making a great success. The village had organized a volunteer fire company and purchased a new engine—Matthew Simpson was assigned to the crank. The young men of the town interested in intellectual pursuits had banded together to form the Juvenile Literary Society; and New Athens, a half-dozen miles away, boasted of its new Franklin College.[3]

For Matthew it was the library and the Juvenile Literary Society that gave variety to the village life and the routine of Uncle Matthew's school. He dug into volumes on natural science, astronomy, and botany, read poetry, history, and biography, pored over the almanacs and the newspapers; and out of them all he sifted odd nuggets of information, short bits of history, explanations for the wonders of things—whatever would satisfy the ravenous appetite of the literary society. He wrote essays, stories, verse, and was in turn erudite, clever, melodramatic, and pious. He discussed conductors and nonconductors, Franklin's experiments, the invention of the lightning rod, and he gave advice on what to do in case of an electrical storm. He described in detail the movement of the earth and its relation to other planets and the sun, and he reviewed the history of astronomy. He explained at length the laws of reflection and refraction, and the workings of spectacles; he described the human eye and the telescope and the microscope.[4]

On the occasion of the falling of stars in 1833, when much of the American continent was frightened into a frantic calling upon God and temporary repentance, the people of Cadiz gathered around him for an explanation. That morning he had arisen earlier than usual, about four o'clock, awakened perhaps by the shouts of his neighbors, and had stepped out into the yard to look up into the sky. The sight was "truly sublime." From the upper reaches of the heavens the meteors "appeared to flow without cessation in all directions towards the horizon . . . some quite faint, others extremely brilliant. There was no cross shooting . . . or flying from one point of the compass to another."

A few neighbors pressed about him, anxious to hear what he had to say. There was no cause for alarm, he assured them—the phenomenon had occurred before in history, according to books on astronomy. It was "phosphuretted hydrogen-gas," he said, giving the explanation he had read. The gas, he went on, was generated on the earth and rose in long columns; it took fire spontaneously in the air after having passed through water or vapor, and then the flames descended along the column.

When he came to write up the incident for the literary society, he was not so sure that the scientists were right. Why, he asked, if the phenomenon were caused by the igniting of columns of gas, did it occur so infrequently? [5]

Writing was good for a young man, Matthew told the society. Certainly, it was good for him. Tall, thin and stooped, and frail-looking, he was so painfully self-conscious he could scarcely talk with strangers or young women. Public speaking? Quite out of the question. He could not declaim, his friends said; but he could write. Writing was good for a man: it improved his style. As politeness and good manners made a man attractive and popular, so good style made matter more readable; without it the writing might lie "neglected and forgotten, to slumber in the archives of oblivion." A man's style ought to be "sententious and not obscure, explicit & not prolix, pointed and not inelegant, polished & not spiritless, sublime & not turgid, familiar & not vulgar." Difficult ends, those, to be achieved only by a study of language, a "careful perusal of those eminent authors whose style is considered the Model," and practice. Practice was especially important, for there were always critics to attack the best of writers; and, no matter how finely polished the writing, there would be errors which "the glasses of Jealousy will magnify & distort beyond description."

Matthew's own style was frequently grandiose, embellished by figures calculated to "excite an interest which could never be produced by an unornamented narration." "Perhaps you may remember," he said to the young literati of the frontier, "the beauty of the evening, how the moon's pale beams quivered through the nocturnal atmosphere & the stars disappearing to add variety and beauty to the scenery. . . . Virgil happily expresses the stillness which prevails on such occasions by saying, 'Omnia Noctis Erant,' All was night." And he described an ambitious but unsuccessful writer who had hindered his prospects by too great a devotion to his domestic responsibilities as "chained with the adamantine hands of affection to the wheel-barrow of matrimonial life."

He wrote for the sheer joy of writing. No matter if the subject was trivial. Pens? Good! Ideally suited for digression, display of erudition, and declamation. A treatise on any subject ought to begin with a concise history of ancestors or antecedents. So with pens: how introduce the topic save with detailed observations on the use of the quill to the goose and a denunciation of man's tendency to describe that noble bird with "ridiculous epithet"? Then to the main disquisition, the importance of the pen in conveying ideas: the "scientific writings of Euclid, Pythagoras & Achimedes . . . the Histories of Thucydides, Herodotus, Livy & Sallust; the orations of Demosthenes, Lyscious & Cicero, & the poems of Homer & Pindar, of Horace, Virgil & Ovid."

Was it with such a simple instrument as the pen that he held in his hand that all of the late celebrated authors had written? Were their pens any better than his? Might his pen, too, prove "as volatile as Sterne's, as satiric as Swift's, & as easy as Scott's?" If time but allowed, could he not with that remarkable pen "write essays as polished & instructive as the [Illinois] Rambler, translate the yet untranslated poems of the ancients into verse as smooth & agreeable as Pope's Homer and write original Poems as Luxuriant in thought, in imagery, and in language as the Paradise lost . . ." He would indulge his fancy in descriptions of nature "as wild and fascinating as the Lady of the Lake, or Don Juan," he would write upon scientific subjects "with the ability of Newton, or Cavallo, Hutton, Bonnycastle, or Ryan," and describe the vegetable kingdom "with the attention of Linneus, Smith or Barton." He would—but already he had "planned too much!" [6]

He could not declaim, but he could write—and he could read what he had written. The words came easily enough when he could look down and see them clearly engrossed in brown ink. Even sentiments of love were easy on paper. "Dunce," the Cadiz boys called him, making fun of his bashful attempts at romance. "Plague on them." They were "fit for nothing but to bray." They could not understand his feelings of "honour," his embarrassment and self-consciousness—how in spite of himself in company his eyes would "roll in quest of hers," and yet how "unwilling diffident and shy" he became when it was his lot to speak. But he could put his feelings down on paper; he could write about star-eyed Susan, haughty Nancy, and "sweet Matilda Jane," her on whom he could not gaze (save now and then a stolen glance) lest he meet her eye. If only he were a painter! But that would not do, either, for

> canvass never can delight
> Like her bright eyes of blue
> They look like crystal windows
> Her soul is peeping through.

He had his revenge with the village dandy, however, in a thinly disguised and rollicking narrative of the "Courtship of Burd." Burd, having preened himself and groomed his horse, called upon three sisters who

> like the ships whose keel outweighs
> The masts & cordage which they raise
> So they are heavier everywhere
> Than in their head, for little's there.

They were, nevertheless, clever enough to plot a vicious prank to play on Burd. When

> Miss Jane the pretty girl
> Had caught his heart within a curl

one of the others slipped out into the night and loosened the girth of the saddle of the young gallant's horse. At last the swain arose to depart. The girls accompanied him to his horse and invited him to return, to which he quickly cried, "I will, I will."

> While in his ear such music rung
> Into the air himself he flung
> Upon the saddle firmly lands
> The reigns & whip are in his hands
> And then to show his horsemanship
> He flourishes then cracks his whip
> The noise resounded through the air
> The horse swings off & he goes—where!

How should a poet remember what then happened—save that the "strong rebuff and laughter of the girls" sounded like thunder in the hero's head? [7]

I I

In the summer of 1829 Matthew decided to walk to Wheeling, (West) Virginia, to the session of the Pittsburgh Annual Conference of the Methodist Episcopal Church. The conference was for preachers, but Mr. Elliott, and Dr. Bascom, and other members of the Madison College faculty would be there. William McKendree, first of the western men to be elected to the episcopacy, would preside over the deliberations and appoint the men to their churches and circuits; and, barring sickness or accident, all the preachers would be present—men who had preached in his mother's parlor and in the meetinghouse at Cadiz, and even the great Dr. Martin Ruter of Pittsburgh.

Matthew was surprised to discover how old and frail Bishop McKendree was. White-haired and stooped, he could scarcely bear his sixty-nine years. Twenty-one years he had been a bishop, elected from the great Western Conference which once had embraced the circuits of Kentucky, Ohio, Tennessee, and western Virginia. Like Bishop Francis Asbury, he had made all Methodism his circuit and, like Asbury, he had sought to unite Methodism into one family. In a voice which was low but seemed to Matthew to be exceptionally sweet and musical, he told of the work in the other conferences which he had visited, of the revivals which were in process, of the joy and victory and peace he found in preaching Christ; and at last, in climax, he pleaded with his brethren to give their entire devotion to spreading the gospel. Matthew was stirred deeply. Following this frail old man on the long, hard trail from conference to conference, he caught for the first time a glimpse of the vastness and the oneness of Methodism.[8]

Charles Elliott preached the ordination sermon on Sunday afternoon, and again Matthew was strangely moved. The sermon was not addressed to him but to the candidates for the ministry; and yet he felt oddly uncomfortable, quite as if it were spoken directly to him. Afterward, he talked with Mr. Elliott and Dr. Bascom, who told him that there had been a great revival at the college, and that students who had been uninterested in religion or the church had become marvelously converted and gave promise of "deep piety" and of "great usefulness." Turning the matter over in his mind on the way home, he found it peculiar that he had rejoiced to hear the good news about the students when he himself was not a Christian, nor a member of the church.

Reared in a Methodist family, under the influence of a widowed mother, two older sisters, and a deeply religious uncle, he had early acquired the outward accouterments of religion, a heavy and dark garment which he rarely put off. Even as a child he had felt a "deep reverence for God," and often when "conscious of any error or act of impropriety, did . . . pass through seasons of severe mental sufferings." He had learned from his mother the habit of prayer; he regularly read "God's holy word" and attended "God's house"; and, though he had "a heart as prone to evil as any other," he "was restrained from every word or act of either profanity or licentiousness, and never engaged in what are termed by Christians sinful amusements." But he had not been "saved." He had grown to young manhood, attended a Methodist college, and returned home without the experience of conversion.[9]

In the fall of 1829 the preachers on the circuits announced a camp meeting for Dickerson's grove, three miles south of Cadiz. On Sunday morning Matthew and his sister Betsey walked to the camp. The scene was a familiar one: the tents and wagons ranged in rows like streets; the dust rising above the milling crowds and settling, a gray stain, on leaves already turning from green to yellow; the rude square platform for the preacher, the stumps and hewn trunks of the trees where the people sat; the sound of exhortations, prayers, shouts, issuing from several of the tents, the swelling chorus of Wesleyan hymns; the low nasal voice of the preacher, gaining strength and resonance as he warmed to his subject; the simple argument, the gripping stories, and the dramatic climax of the sermon, a veritable struggle with the powers of hell; the awful stillness, broken only by an occasional sob, or a suppressed amen, or the groaning of the wind in the trees; and presently, like a rushing night wind, the screaming of sinners for mercy, the loud exhortations of a score of ministers and class leaders, and the shouts of the saints.

All day long Matthew and Betsey went from public meeting to prayer circles in the tents and back to public meeting, stopping now and then at the little clusters of people to talk about the progress of the camp, the most recent "awakenings," and the comparative "power" of the preachers. It was not particularly exciting; but Betsey desired to remain overnight with friends who had pitched a tent on the grounds, and her brother agreed to return after school the following day to walk home with her.

On Monday, Matthew found that the camp had been stirred by a "remarkable religious interest." Several boys and young men, some of whom had been the wild boys of Cadiz, had been marvelously awakened and converted. He talked with some of them, and was amazed at their forthright declarations of religious experience and purpose. These boys, village dandies and no-goods—why should they, who had never been subjected to Christian influences, be so deeply moved when he, who had been reared in a Methodist home, felt no conviction of sin, no prompting to repentance? And how, going back to Cadiz, could they escape falling into the old ways?

The questions troubled him all through the sermon that followed. As the preacher developed his text the darkness gathered in the grove and moved out into the clearing. Men tossed pine boughs and knots on the fires near the platform, and the leaping flames lighted the faces of the people as they sat hunched on the logs. The preacher's voice rang out, but Matthew scarcely heard what he had to say. He could not get away from the question, Why should these boys be so stirred and wrought upon and awakened when he was not moved at all?

At last the preacher ceased his preaching and began to plead, to call the people to repentance. The effect was hypnotic. The great crowd surged toward the railing which set aside a space for "mourners." Matthew followed, mechanically, and stood with his hand on the rail, absorbed in his own thoughts. A short distance away he saw a friend, a boy who like himself had been reared in a Christian home but had never "professed" to be a Christian. Impulsively, Matthew edged his way through the crowd to the young man, put his hand on his shoulder, and asked, "Would you like to go forward for prayers?"

The boy dropped his head, and the tears started from his eyes. "I will go," he said, "if you will go with me." [10]

They went together, stooping to crawl under the rail. Stepping over or around the people who knelt or lay prostrate on the ground, they found an open spot and dropped to their knees. All about them people were sobbing and crying, and the preachers were exhorting them to pray on; but Matthew had no desire to weep or pray. For him the matter was settled. Without any special "feeling," he purposed to be religious and resolved to join the church at the first opportunity.

At the next visit of the circuit rider to Cadiz, some four weeks later, Matthew "gave in" his name for membership. He immediately felt a new sense of obligation, an increased concern for the new converts, and an intense anxiety to participate in the affairs of the church. He suggested that the young men, converts at the recent camp, organize a special prayer meeting; and, driven by feelings of duty and doubts of his own ability to extemporize, he wrote out, memorized, and promptly forgot his first public prayer. He organized a Sunday school, against some resistance from older Methodists who doubted that teaching on the Sabbath was proper, or that boys should be allowed to mess up the building; he taught the pupils himself, and he solicited some sixty dollars to purchase a library of religious books for the pupils. In all this he found a new satisfaction, a sense of worthiness and accomplishment that he had never experienced in Uncle Matthew's school or in the exercises of the Juvenile Literary Society.

By the summer of 1830, absorbed in his religious activities, his literary society, and his reading, and exhausted from teaching in Uncle Matthew's school and studying or attending meetings late at night, he fell ill, his health "seriously affected." It was time, Uncle Matthew said, for him to halt some of these diverse activities, and to begin to expend his energies more purposefully.[11]

III

Matthew was inclined to agree with his uncle that he should study with more purpose. Teaching in a subscription school certainly was not a satisfactory lifelong profession. It was too irregular, too tedious, and it did not pay well enough.

Law appealed to him: for years he had attended the sessions of the county court, where Uncle William Tingley was clerk, and had listened with rapt attention while the lawyers harangued the jury. But his mother and uncle and the preachers who visited them doubted how far a good Methodist could engage in the practice of law. Even more important to his mind was the knowledge that he could not speak, that he never would be able to face a jury and plead for a client's life, or to wrangle with opposing counsel over the points of the law.

At last he decided upon medicine and entered upon the study in the office of Dr. McBean, under whom he had studied the classics in the academy. For the next three years he pored over medical books, memorizing the terms, the medical descriptions, definitions, and remedies. He studied Cooper's *Principles and Practice of Surgery* and *Surgical Dictionary,* Hufeland's *Treatise on the Scrofulous Disease,* Gibson's *Surgery,* Good's *Study of Medicine,* and Dewees's *A Compendious System of Midwifery.* Now and then he noted in his diary the volume he was studying, and for a brief period he took extensive notes to assist his memory; but he stopped the notetaking when his eyes began to trouble him—it was unnecessary labor, anyway, when he could remember without the notes. Occasionally he walked into the woods to gather medicinal herbs, boneset and lobelia, or simply to "botanize." Periodically, he rode six miles to Dr. McBean's home in Freeport, to be examined on the books he had studied.

Long before he completed his course he plugged teeth for his brother-in-law, attended a friend who was ill with the bilious fever, repaired the galvanic battery "electric machine" for his sister Betsey, and prescribed powders for an aunt. To build up his body he walked frequently, and worked summers in the harvest fields. One September he bought a horse—for forty dollars, payable in April—so that he might ride for his health.

To pay his tuition and the cost of the expensive medical books, he taught school and turned the big crank in the factory until Uncle William Tingley offered him twenty-five dollars a month for three months to copy records in the county court. He accepted the offer gratefully. There were exciting cases in the Harrison Court of Common Pleas: indictments for the selling of spirituous liquors without license, for unlawfully "playing with each other at cards at a certain game called seven up," for assault and battery; suits for the recovery of debts, for collection of property damages, for slanderous accusations of unchaste and immoral conduct. So day by day, in the hours he could take from his medical studies, Matthew sat at the high counter in the courthouse, copying the records his Uncle Tingley had laid out for him. "This," he said, "I would prefer to school-keeping." [12]

In general he adhered to the more conservative medical theories of the period. After the manner of Dr. Benjamin Rush and the Philadelphia school, he employed the lancet, prescribed calomel, and applied "blisters." But, like other frontier doctors confronted with the high cost of drugs, he also depended upon herbs and folklore. He even gathered a few prescriptions from that arch adversary of physic, the founder of patent medicines, Dr. Samuel Thomson: "Spear Mint," he noted, after Thomson, is "good to stop vomiting—sits pleasantly on the stomach." "Penny Royal—may be used in all sickness—good for the stomach & warming & cleansing & sweetening." For cough powder: "four tea spoons of Skunk cabbage, two of hoarhound, one of Wake Robbin, one of No. 1, one of No. 2, one of Bay Berry, one of bitter Root & one of . . . powder—make fine mixture. Take half a Teaspoon before going to bed." [13]

In April of 1833 Matthew went to Freeport for the last two or three months of his study with Dr. McBean. He traveled with the doctor on his rounds, reviewed his studies with him, and finally, as required by the state law, appeared before and was approved by a local board of examiners. Dr. McBean issued the certificate in his own handwriting, a small scrap of paper dated at Cadiz, July 25, 1833:

Mr. Matthew Simpson Jr has studied the science of medicine under my direction, for the period prescribed by the state medical law; and I have no hesitancy in saying that I consider him an eminently qualified member of the medical profession, and altogether deserving of the public patronage.

John McBean [14]

Matthew immediately opened an office at Cadiz.

III

CROWS AND METHODIST PREACHERS

WHILE Matthew studied medicine he practiced religion. He read the Methodist weekly newspaper, the New York *Christian Advocate and Journal,* the sermons and *Journal* of John Wesley, the letters of John Fletcher, and such other volumes as he could put his hands on. He attended Sunday school teachers' meetings, and prayer meetings; gave his testimony at class meeting and answered the prodding questions of the leader. On Fridays he fasted, being careful to record in his journal, "Usual abstinence." He visited other communities for the quarterly conferences of his church, fasting before he went. At one such session he was "particularly struck" by the testimony of a young man, a confirmed Deist on Monday last, who had been "awakened and convinced" on Tuesday at a prayer meeting. At the same conference he saw a pair of celestial maps, and gazed for the first time on the wonders of a Miltonic heaven.[1]

His thoughts on religion spilled over into his study and practice of medicine. "How striking a difference," he said, noting the calm suffering of his sister Hetty when she was ill, "exists between the religious and the thoughtless." Called to military muster at near-by Rumley, he deplored the "strange habits, outlandish customs; licentiousness, drunkenness, and blasphemy . . . everywhere prevalent." "Fiddling and dancing," he said, documenting his charge, "were going on at almost every wagon of provisions." When a "powerful stir broke out" among the three or four thousand present at a camp meeting, he yielded a little to the emotional tide; and, if he did not experience the ecstatic joy of some of the others, a sense of peace flowed over him.

Uncle Matthew looked on and was pleased. Often he had heard

from Sarah Simpson's lips how James and she, in the last days before his death, had consecrated the baby Matthew, and had prayed
that he would become a preacher. But neither Sarah nor Uncle
Matthew would tell the boy of their hope, lest they interfere with
the divine call. Matthew had thoughts on the subject himself, even
before his conversion. As he worked in the church he felt a growing
conviction that he must preach. It was a despairing thought, a
haunting fear. How could he preach when he could not speak? [2]

Yet he could not shake the sense of responsibility; it pursued
him into his medical studies as well as into the prayer meeting;
it seemed to be indissolubly connected with his own salvation. He
longed for some one to tell him his duty; he fasted, and prayed,
and begged for divine direction, but he found no rest. Now and
then, when he had spoken well at class meeting, or when the words,
molten with his own need, had flowed freely at public prayers, he
felt an awareness of God, an assurance of His approval—the same
awe-stricken sense of the presence of God that he had felt as a boy
when, lying on a hillside, he had seen the western sun reach over
the shadows to light up the tops of the trees.

But hope quickly turned to despair. He did not have the heart
cleansed from sin so clearly described in Mr. Wesley's *Journal*.
Uncle Tingley, even when he was ill, might be cheerful, and hopeful, and gentle of spirit; but he himself was not dead to the world
as he ought to be, he did not feel the continual fervency of spirit
that he had once felt, he had not put away all his old evil days. Week
by week, month by month, his life was a continual inward searching,
a morbid probing, a despairing cry, " 'O God! create a clean heart
and renew a right spirit within me.' " How could he preach when
he had neither the ability to speak nor the grace to do God's will?

In the agony of conflict, he suddenly discovered the key to all
the problems which confronted him. It lay in his abiding belief in
Providence. "Trust in the Lord with all thine heart," he read in
the Scripture; "and lean not unto thine own understanding. In all
thy ways acknowledge Him, and He shall direct thy paths." The
verse seemed to have been written especially for him. It was the
proof of his mother's simple faith, of his uncle's reliance on the
mysteries of God. It was to trust God and events, not arguments—
blindly if necessary. He could preach if Providence clearly indicated that he must.

To others he gave no intimation of his intended course of action; but in a short time he had opportunity to test his faith. One Sunday, when no preacher was present and a prayer meeting was scheduled for the evening, he felt strongly impressed that he should speak. But he dreaded the opinions of his friends—those who knew that he could not speak—and even more the keen appraisal of Uncle Matthew.

As he sat debating the matter with himself, his uncle entered the room and said, after a moment of silence, "Matthew, don't you think you could speak to the people tonight?"

Surprised and startled, he replied hesitatingly, "Do you—think that I ought to?"

"Yes," said his uncle simply. "I think you might do good."

That settled the matter for Matthew. It was clearly the working of Providence. That night, by some strange coincidence, he thought, the meetinghouse was crowded as he rose to make his first religious address. He had not written out what he had to say, nor had he thought it through very well; but he was deeply stirred, and the words came easily, gushing forth from some inner resource he had not hitherto tapped. The people, amazed by his performance, began to press upon him to preach; but he evaded all conversation on the subject.

None the less, more responsibilities were heaped upon him. He was called upon with increasing frequency to speak at prayer meetings and other functions; and much to his surprise, and in spite of his protests and embarrassment, he was named leader of a "female" class. "If it be the will of the Lord," he said resignedly, "I pray him to enable me to perform my duty."

His successes or failures in speaking, he equated with his religious experience. When he was able to talk freely and with liberty he praised God for His goodness; but when he searched for words that would not come, when he stood perspiring with fear, his tongue cleaving to the roof of his mouth, he condemned himself for his little religion, for his lack of power in prayer, and he begged for the "awakening energy of the Holy Spirit."

Whatever his own misgivings, the people of Cadiz thought well of his efforts. They named him an officer in the local Temperance Society and called upon him to deliver an address on temperance at the Presbyterian church. Matthew was not a little pleased when the editor of the *Harrison County Telegraph* published his remarks. His church gave him charge of a class of new converts and Sunday school teachers and pupils; and in the spring of 1833, when he was absent from meeting, it voted him a license to exhort. If he would not enter the ministry of his own accord, the people would at least make a lay preacher out of him.

So, possessed of an exhorter's license, he went down to Dr. Mc-Bean's at Freeport for his final medical examinations.

There, Charles Elliott found him. Professor Elliott had not been able to get his mind off Matthew, the awkward boy with the brilliant mind who had passed so brief a time in his home and at college. When family interests took him to Ohio in the spring of 1833 he rode over to Cadiz to call on the Simpsons. Uncle Matthew related to him the succession of events which had crowded his nephew's life: his independent study and the exercises in the literary society; his three-year study of medicine; his conversion; and his activities in the church.

That was enough for Elliott; he must ride over to Freeport. He arrived early in the morning and was just alighting in front of the inn when Matthew saw him from across the street and hurried over to greet him. For an hour they talked, chiefly of Madison College and the educational need of the Methodist Church. Elliott outlined his hopes and dreams, his vision for Methodism and Christian education. He talked earnestly of Matthew's talents, praised him for his activities in the Juvenile Literary Society and in the church, and at last begged him to devote his life to learning and the church.

When the talk had run out and it was time to go, Elliott turned impulsively, his voice and his deep blue eyes pleading as much as his words: "Matthew," he said, "don't you think you are called to preach?"

"Well," Matthew replied, a little uneasily, "I've had thoughts on the subject." After a moment he went on. "But if the church wants me to preach, I believe the way will open without any agency of mine. I design simply to follow the openings of Providence."

Charles Elliott had no hesitation about becoming an agent of Providence; he had played the role before. Hurrying back to Cadiz, he stopped to see the preacher and arranged for Matthew to be examined for license by the next quarterly conference.

At the conference the presiding elder precipitated a crisis by demanding a trial sermon.

"You must excuse me," Matthew said, "but there is no rule in the Discipline authorizing persons to preach before they are licensed, and I don't wish to take any step toward the ministry unless called out by the church."

The elder, not at all impressed by this modestly clothed arrogance, opposed the license. Some of the people voiced their fears that Matthew's health was not strong enough for the rigors of the circuit, and others doubted that his speaking would be satisfactory. But in the end the quarterly conference granted the license and recommended that he be admitted on trial to the Pittsburgh Annual Conference. Perhaps, said a layman from Cadiz, God had work for him to do: "He has always been the child of Providence."

The action of the quarterly conference served only to intensify Matthew's inward struggle. Was his health equal to the rough, itinerant life? Could he preach? How could he abandon the practice of medicine before he had fairly begun? How could he support his mother on the $100 annual salary allowed to a preacher? What would his mother say? With both his sisters married and gone, how could he leave her alone? Would he not break her heart?

He dreaded the necessity of talking to her; but one day, finding her alone, he went into the room and dropped to the floor beside her chair. His speech was scarcely coherent—the recounting of his long struggle, the fears and the doubts; but at last he blurted out his purpose plainly. He could not help it—he did not want to preach—but he believed God required it of him.

He paused, waiting for her to speak. She turned toward him, her eyes suffused with tears even as she smiled.

"My son," she said, "I have been looking for this hour since you were born." [3]

Matthew's mind was at rest. He must and would preach—if not at once, then as soon as the way opened. For the present, however, the difficulties seemed to be insuperable: he had just begun medical practice; he was still employed in the county court; his mother needed his support; and his sister Betsey had come home, dying from consumption. He therefore wrote to the presiding elder that he would not be able to accept an appointment, and requested that the elder withhold the recommendation of the quarterly conference.

Elliott would have none of it. The presiding elder, he told the conference, had no right to withhold the recommendation; and he went to the bishop to argue the point and to set forth the unusual merits of young Simpson. A way could be found to overcome the family difficulties. Matthew could be made third preacher on the circuit, assigned to pulpits close to his home until he could better arrange his personal affairs. A heated discussion ensued; but in the end the bishop and the conference agreed, and Matthew Simpson was admitted on trial to the Pittsburgh Annual Conference. His presiding elder directed him to preach at Cadiz and St. Clairsville on alternate Sundays until he could close out his practice of medicine and devote full time to the ministry.

The action of the conference seemed to be providential, and Matthew resolved to get ready as soon as possible.

I I

In the spring of 1834, after eight months of practicing medicine through the week and preaching on Sundays, Matthew Simpson closed his office and joined the ranks of itinerant preachers. His sister Hetty McCullough and her family had come to live with their mother and Uncle Matthew. And the younger sister, Betsey, racked by a consumptive cough until her frail body could no longer bear the struggle, had died late in 1833. Matthew was free to enter the ministry.

There was something relentless, as certain as Providence itself, about the life of a Methodist circuit rider. In the early settlement of the trans-Allegheny West no more romantic figure had appeared. With his Bible, his saddlebags, and his horse he rode the frontier trails, a challenger of nature's wilderness and man's unbelief.

The trails were often dim, sometimes indicated only by notches in the bark of trees; but he followed them to the very edge of settlement, where not infrequently he encountered men who had moved there "especially to get rid of those wretched people called Methodists," but who scarcely had completed their rude cabins before "here was the Methodist preacher preaching hell fire and damnation, as they always did." The bad-weather proverb of the Ohio River valley was, "There's nobody out today but crows and Methodist preachers." [4]

When Matthew Simpson strapped the bags on his saddle and rode out of Cadiz one April day in 1834, the severe hardships of the circuit in eastern Ohio had largely disappeared. The Methodists, with more than 70,000 communicants and nearly 500 meeting-houses, had grown to be the most numerous religious body in the state, and Harrison and Belmont counties, in which the circuit lay, boasted a population of 50,000.[5] Matthew and his two colleagues had thirty-four appointments on their circuit, the farthest of which was less than twenty-five miles from Cadiz. None the less, the romance of the circuit rider lingered on. The preacher was still engaged in an endless battle with nature and a relentless pursuit of sin. So Matthew rode forth in the manner and tradition and with the trappings of the forefathers.

Most of his preaching places were small meetinghouses in villages or on a Methodist brother's farm; but now and then he met his congregation in a home, and on one occasion, the "congregation being very large," he preached to them out of doors and "had considerable liberty." He introduced preaching into Morristown, speaking in the schoolhouse and attracting the lodgers from a near-by hotel, some of them "tipsy" and controversial. He was once misdirected and traveled thirteen miles instead of seven, over "a very bad road"; but he amused himself by "examining the strata of limestone, coal, etc.," and arrived at his appointment in time for preaching.

He preached only for results, believing that, at the peril of his soul, he must get men converted. His texts were imperative. At St. Clairsville one Sunday evening he preached on "He that is not with me is against me: and he that gathereth not with me scattereth." The next day in the home of James Eaton he chose the text, "But the scripture hath concluded all under sin, that the promise by faith of Jesus Christ might be given to them that believe." Tuesday, Wednesday, and Thursday he was preaching from the solemn themes: "For God sent his only beloved son, that whosoever believeth on him might be saved"; "In whom we have redemption through his blood, even the forgiveness of sins"; and "Being now justified by his blood, we shall be saved from wrath through him."

The most discouraging point in his whole ministerial career

came in these first few weeks. An eminent minister, called in for the dedication of a church, preached a series of five sermons, "full of thought most forcibly expressed, and accompanied with a divine unction." There was a stirring as of a mighty wind, and the people felt a strange sense of the presence of God in their midst.

Simpson, comparing the eloquent visitor's preaching to his own, became discouraged and humiliated. As the series continued his humiliation deepened. What right had he to stand in the sacred desk and utter "feeble thoughts like the lispings of childhood" when the services of such men could be secured? He resolved to quit the circuit, support himself by medicine, and continue his speaking only as a local preacher. A prominent layman, a class leader and steward, in whom he confided his intentions was utterly astonished and urged him not to think of making the change.

His depression was relieved in a manner not unlike that in which it had come on. At an appointment where he had a very large congregation, he was visited by another minister of the conference, a little older and more experienced than himself. Simpson invited him to preach. The young visitor's thoughts were "crude and disjointed," he mispronounced words, violated the commonest rules of grammar and in general gave such an exhibition of ignorance that Simpson was "deeply mortified," but cured of his own discouragement.

Following the tradition of the saddlebags, he carried with him his books and writing materials, diligently continued his studies, and prepared for his conference examinations. Sometimes he was so exhausted that he "would have lain down"; but, steeped in the *Journal* of John Wesley, he sought to emulate Wesley's rigorous itinerancy and so denied himself rest until he had spent some time in reading and writing. The "way of duty," he moralized, after climbing a hill above one of his preaching places, was "steep and arduous, but the effect delightful."

From April until July, when the Annual Conference met at Washington, Pennsylvania, Simpson traveled the circuit. For his services he was able to collect only $17.75 of the $25 allotted for the quarter's work.

At the conference he passed his examinations, preached at one of the morning sessions, and mingled with his fellows to discuss the probable appointments for the next year. Prompted by Uncle Matthew and by his own fears, he consulted with his presiding elder.

"I would prefer an appointment in a healthy region," he said, citing Uncle Matthew's concern, "and not far from home."

He hastened to add, however, that he wished "to take his place among his brethren," and that he sought no special favors.

The presiding elder assured him that he had "just such a circuit as would be best" for him, and Matthew, as was the custom, went home to await the announcement of the appointments. The bishop, far from giving him a healthy, out-of-door circuit, assigned him to a station, as junior minister to the largest church in the conference, in smoky, soot-filled Pittsburgh!

He received the news of his appointment with objections which he enumerated in his journal: "1st. My little experience in the ministry; 2d. My health might not suit confinement; 3d. I feared that I could not please the people." None the less, he sold his horse, laid aside his saddlebags, and after preaching a sermon in the Presbyterian church took the stage for Pittsburgh.[6]

IV

STATIONED AT PITTSBURGH

THE traveler en route to Pittsburgh in 1834 could locate the city by the cloud of thick brown smoke which hung above it, long before he could discern shops and dwellings. When he alighted from the packet or stage, he stepped into a smoke-filled atmosphere. The black soot drifted down in flakes, settled on the people, and clung to the exterior of the dingy and ancient-looking dwellings and business houses. The "dirtiest town in the United States," a Frenchman wrote of it.[1] The streets were half darkened by the heavy pall, and men read by candlelight in hours that should have been lighted by the sun.

But the smoke was a symbol of activity. "Nowhere in the world," wrote the critical Frenchman, "is everybody so regularly and continually busy as in the city of Pittsburgh." He found "no interruption of business for six days in the week, except during the three meals, the longest of which occupies hardly ten minutes."

The Birmingham of America already boasted a population of thirty thousand. Steamboats lined the two sides of the Golden Triangle which marked the confluence of the Allegheny and Monongahela rivers. Boxes, bales, and barrels were piled six feet high all along the cobblestone wharf. The city was proud of its rolling mills, forges, and foundries, as well as of its cotton mills, glass factories, distilleries, and scores of other small manufactories. At night the row of coke ovens at the base of Coal Hill glared into the darkness, giving off more light than the sperm-oil lamps along the streets. The Pennsylvania Canal system and two trans-state turnpikes emptied their traffic into the city and carried the western produce to eastern markets. Only recently the town pump had given way to a great reservoir from which water was piped into houses.[2]

Matthew Simpson reached the bustling city on August 1, 1834. Stepping from the stage at a point not far from the Golden Triangle, he made his way to the home of James Verner on Penn Street. Verner, an immigrant from Scotland, was a prosperous lumberman and brewer. A stanch Methodist and a church steward, he maintained an elegant home and supplied generous hospitality to itinerant preachers. Matthew found him warm-hearted and genial and eager to discuss the affairs of the church.

Even more diverting than Verner was his sixteen-year-old daughter Ellen. Tall and slender, her light brown hair tightly rolled in braided coils at the side of her head, she was quick to blush, yet ready to question or challenge with her flashing blue eyes. Her speech was free yet modestly pious. Ellen Holmes Verner —the name was as well poised and stately as its owner.[3]

Matthew learned quickly that Methodism and the city of Pittsburgh were at one in enterprise and growth. Although divided in 1828 by a disastrous quarrel which had led to the formation of the Methodist Protestant Church, the Pittsburgh station in 1834 had more than 800 members, with two churches and two other regular preaching places, requiring the services of three preachers.[4] Moreover, Dr. Charles Elliott was in the city as the editor of the newly established weekly newspaper, the *Pittsburgh Conference Journal*.

The other preachers arrived within a few days: Thomas Hudson, senior minister in charge of the station, a man of middle age, a revivalist, and an exhorter of unusual ability; and William O. Hunter, a man of Simpson's age and, like him, a student of the classics and of Hebrew. The official board decreed that the two junior preachers should live with Mr. Hudson. They were to receive the $100 per year allowed by the conference; Mr. Hudson $600 for the support of his family and for the board and room of the younger preachers.[5]

The men began at once to arrange their appointments. The two larger churches, Smithfield and Liberty, regularly held three services on Sunday; Birmingham had preaching morning and evening, and Bayardstown in the afternoon. Each minister must preach two or three times on Sunday as well as conduct other exercises of the day and week. By the third Sunday Matthew had adjusted himself to the new routine. He walked that day to Birmingham, preached at eleven, had dinner, read "fifty or 60 pages" from the biography of the "first female missionary from America to Burmah," spoke to the "Sabbath scholars" at two, held class at three, preached at Liberty Street at night. It was, he said, "a sabbath day to my soul."

The heavy demands of the pulpit called for a strictly imposed self-discipline. With his overacute sense of duty Matthew was soon prescribing a rigid daily routine and lashing himself for failures. In the manner approved by John Wesley, he arose early, from four to five o'clock, studied biblical and theological matters until ten, and then busied himself with calling on the people. For formal sermon preparation he had little time, and Saturday night or Sunday morning frequently found him with "comparatively slight preparation." [6]

His preaching was an overflow of his emotions, a venting of the fears and hopes, of the struggles and triumphs he had experienced himself or had encountered in his daily talks with the people. His words came with an impetuous rush; and as his excitement increased, flecks of foam gathered at the corners of his mouth. He had only one thought: to reconcile men to God. If the people were deeply stirred he knew himself in the will of God; if they were indifferent he was sure that he had failed, and sought relief in penitence. [7]

In the intensity of his emotion he soon fell into the preacher's habit of sustaining his words with the pious suffix "uh": "Shall we do evil-uh, that good may come-uh?"

Dr. Henry D. Sellers, brother-in-law of Bishop John Emory and a prominent layman, sent for him and discoursed on the evils of the habit. "You must quit it," he said. Matthew agreed, and arranged to return for further criticisms. In a short time he was reporting every Monday morning to discuss the sermon of the preceding day. [8] He was a little discouraged, however, by his poor preaching, and Uncle Matthew comforted him with the thought that "very few of those popular orators will rate high in God's account when the day of reckoning comes." [9]

His colleague William Hunter was quite as eager for self-improvement and quickly accepted the proposal that they write skeletons of sermons on the same text and compare notes. Matthew began to jot down outlines of the sermons he preached, simple ideas in topical sequence. He sometimes employed major divisions, rhetorical categories he had borrowed from John Wesley: *Nature of, Design of, Precepts for, Examples of, Duration, Manner.* More often he used a simple listing of points, a series of pictures, a sequence of situations. Aroused by the derelicts on the streets and fortified by the growing temperance sentiment of the conference, he preached one night to the Drinker. Every argument was etched clearly and vividly on his mind. He had no need in the pulpit for an outline, nor for a scrap of paper, but he jotted down a skeleton, a list of arguments, warnings, pictures, each one direct and blunt, clearly designed to make the intemperate see themselves in a most unfavorable light.

1. Where are you going?
2. Do you not *believe* there is poison in the glass?
3. Look, first, at your *companions.*
4. Look at your *property.*
5. Look at your *money.*
6. Look at your *wife.*
7. Look at your *children.*
8. Look at yourself.
9. Look at your poor soul.
10. Do you ask, what shall I do?
11. Do you answer 'I would so if [I] was only able' (stop from this moment). You are able through Divine strength.[10]

When he enlarged upon a simple theme he did so with a blunt urgency, a naïve directness. When he called his congregation to repentance he warned, "Time shall be no longer," and asked, "Are we prepared?"

Remember time shall soon be no longer— This year is nearly gone and with it have fled many hopes & joys. Should this year close your life how would it be with you? God may soon say to you Time shall be no longer. Thou fool this night shall thy soul be required of thee. The lady dying at her toilette— Sargent fell in the pulpit. Where will you be in another year, some here, some abroad, some sick, some dying, some in heaven, some in hell—I every second, then in 2 hours 24/60/1440 2880 have died since we came here. Hundreds have fallen while [I] have been exhorting, listen to their voices, one cries Glory to God—another . . . Oh God I can't die—I won't die & dies with the words in his mouth. Oh! Sinner Time shall be no more . . . now you may repent, now you may be saved. Oh! be saved to night.[11]

Some of his sermon ideas, he took directly from Uncle Matthew, who often had criticized the preachers on the circuit, not for their poor grammar only, but for their poor exegesis. So he wrote to Uncle Matthew, begging for interpretations of the Scriptures. "Query . . . does the expression 'the stones should cry out,' etc. mean any more than that it was impossible for the Jews to be silent—like the camel & needle's eye?" And how should he interpret such stories as that of Saul and the witch of Endor? [12]

Uncle Matthew answered the inquiries and suggested interpretations of the Scripture in long exegetical accounts. He believed that a naturalistic interpretation of Saul and the witch was "attended by fewer difficulties than any other." He cautioned against using a text to prove what it did not say. "Remember how Euclid would argue." He warned against the error of "philosophical theologians" who turned to the Bible in a vain attempt to establish "every principle of geology and natural philosophy." He praised knowledge and argued the importance of learning for the preacher, and he suggested as a proposition for a missionary sermon, "Those nations who have not the Scripture are more sunk in ignorance and crime than those who have it." [13] The union of learning and Christian piety was a tempting theme to young Matthew Simpson, enamored as he was of both books and pulpit.

I I

When Charles Elliott learned that the bishop had put down Matthew Simpson as junior preacher for Pittsburgh, he was delighted. It was good to have the most brilliant and best educated young preacher in the conference stationed in Pittsburgh where he, Elliott, could look after him. "My boy, Mattie," he liked to call him, and was pleased when Simpson reciprocated with "Father Elliott." [14] He thought it regrettable, however, that Matthew had not been able to finish at Madison College. A young man so gifted in languages and mathematics, and trained likewise as a physician, ought to have a college degree. It would make him more useful to the church. Moreover, with all his learning, he was entitled to it. Some day he might make a college president or a Methodist editor.

In the months that Matthew was still practicing medicine at Cadiz, Elliott had talked with Dr. Martin Ruter, president of Allegheny College, the Methodist school at Meadville. Allegheny ought to do something for Simpson. Ruter had first responded, some weeks before Matthew went on the circuit, by offering him a tutorship. Elliott was disgusted. "The best professorship they have there or elsewhere is not too good for you," he wrote, "and I would regret much to place you a kind of underling under persons who will require 7 long years study . . . to accomplish what you, through God's blessing, have accomplished." Matthew immediately declined the offer.[15]

Once aroused over the importance of the degree, Matthew was not satisfied to let the matter rest. The conference, having recently undergone an exciting campaign which led to the acquisition of Allegheny College from the Presbyterians, was astir over the importance of education. College graduates began to have a prestige which was new to Methodism. Ruter, said to be the best educated man in the Methodist denomination, had also been the first to receive the doctor of divinity degree. Simpson, mingling with these men, felt keenly the need for recognition of his own studies.

Shortly after his removal to Pittsburgh, Matthew applied to the faculty of Allegheny College for the privilege of qualifying for the degree by examination. Dr. Ruter promptly offered him an honorary degree of master of arts. Matthew, after consulting with Elliott, refused. He preferred to take the regular degree. Ruter consented, suggesting that he visit the campus for two weeks at the end of the fall term of 1834 to be examined on the senior courses. He stipulated that Simpson should deliver a commencement oration in Hebrew.[16]

Matthew began at once to review his Greek and Latin and Hebrew. He reflected on a theme for the oration. It must be of the most solemn kind, a description of the attributes of God, or of his wonderful works of nature, of Providence, or perhaps a scriptural account of the Messiah's kingdom. He would write it in English, in his best style, and translate it into Hebrew. He ought, advised Uncle Matthew, to deliver it slowly and impressively, pronouncing each word in a manner which would seem as natural as possible.[17]

The review for the examinations and the writing of the oration proved to be more difficult than Matthew had expected. He had too many sermons to preach, too many calls to make. He was here, there, and almost everywhere, with the well and with the sick, and had no time to compose an oration and translate it into Hebrew. Besides, it was so many years since he had studied the Hebrew that he had to start afresh. Uncle Matthew advised him to discuss the situation frankly with Dr. Ruter, even at the risk of damaging his reputation.[18]

Dr. Sellers thought the whole matter of his going to Meadville a waste of time and money. The Presbyterians had a good college, Western University, in Pittsburgh. Why should he not take his degree there? It was a good idea, Matthew thought.

The interview which Dr. Sellers arranged with the president of Western University quickly became an examination. President Bruce discussed the course of study, inquired what branches of knowledge Matthew had pursued, and questioned him on what he had mastered.

At last he said: "You have learned much more than our college requires. If you will enroll as a student and attend my lectures in moral science twice a week until the end of the term, you shall receive the degree at the next commencement." [19]

Matthew was jubilant. Mr. Elliott and Dr. Sellers agreed that he must accept the proposition. He wrote at once to Dr. Ruter, explaining that camp meeting, quarterly conference, and other church duties made it impossible to go to Meadville for his examinations, and he had therefore, on the advice of others, arranged to enroll at Western University.

A few days later a letter from Dr. Ruter reported that the Board of Trustees of Allegheny College had met and, without delay, had conferred on him the honorary degree *Magister Artium.* "I felt dissatisfied with the plan of your going to the Pittsburgh Seminary," he wrote, "for reasons I have not time to mention in this communication." [20]

Matthew was indignant. He did not want an honorary degree when he was entitled to an earned one. Dr. Sellers thought that he should pay no attention to it, and Charles Elliott advised him to continue his study at Western University. When the word came that Allegheny College had bestowed the same honorary degree upon Alfred Brunson, rustic Methodist preacher of the saddlebags and muscle era who was serving as agent for the college, Matthew was even more disturbed. He did not care to have his name "coupled along with *Alfred Brunson*—a man in no way qualified." [21]

But Matthew Simpson was not one to deal lightly with the workings of Providence. Was it not to the interest of the church to sustain the work of its own seminary? Would he not discourage other young men of his church conference by showing scorn for the honor of a Methodist institution? He had not sought the honor, but the duties of which he had written had interfered with his going to Meadville; and now that he was offered a higher degree he would not have to take the examinations or prepare the Hebrew oration. Might it not after all be the working of Providence? When Uncle Matthew, although stating his preference for the earned degree, chided his nephew for his contempt for Alfred Brunson (who after all was a self-educated man of considerable ability as a preacher and a pamphleteer, and was the one most responsible for the acquisition of Allegheny College by the Methodists), Matthew suddenly made up his mind. He would accept the degree.[22]

And so he became Matthew Simpson, *Magister Artium.*

In a short time Dr. Ruter invited him to join his faculty at Allegheny: "What would you think of coming as professor of chemistry on a partial salary, and depending for the rest upon your lancet? You would have plenty of business, as there is no Methodist physician at Meadville."

"I do not think much about it," Matthew wrote back.

He had closed the door on his life as a physician and he did not propose to open it again. "I charge you before God," Charles Elliott had said, "not to think of being any thing else than a travelling Preacher." He still must serve nearly three years of his itinerancy before completing the four years his church required of elders; and not until then could he think of the classroom.[23]

He was busy enough in a church which approached its task with all the enterprise that characterized Pittsburgh. Early in the fall he and his colleagues had conducted a camp meeting which, despite considerable opposition, had resulted in a large number of conversions. The revival thus begun spread to other churches in the city and continued week after week until some three hundred members were added to the rolls.

Matthew had only one objection to the constant round of religious activity: it interfered with his reading and study. A man who was a sincere follower of John Wesley must study not the Bible only, and religious matter, but literature and natural science. "The bible," wrote Uncle Matthew, "being the most learned of all books those who wish fully to understand it must become the most learned." [24]

So, in addition to his study of the Hebrew Bible and the Greek Testament "in regular order," the nephew, complaining to his diary that he had no time for it, read books on travel, theology, mental philosophy, and natural science. He discovered Locke's *Essay Concerning Human Understanding* and read and reread it. He studied French and German pronunciation ("You ought not to hesitate about the expence," wrote Uncle Matthew); and he gathered together a group of young men with whom he met each week, endeavoring to "direct them in their course of reading and to inspire them with a thirst for knowledge." At the suggestion of Charles Elliott, he opened a book depository for the Methodist Publishing House; and he began the collection of materials for a history of Methodism in Pittsburgh (which activity his Uncle Matthew thought a bit unnecessary with all the other responsibilities he had).[25]

Encouraged by Dr. Ruter and Charles Elliott (who needed articles to fill his *Journal*), Matthew organized the Preacher's Lyceum of the Pittsburgh Annual Conference: Dr. Martin Ruter, president; M. Simpson, first vice president. The Lyceum was to meet for the reading of essays, for examinations, discussions, and devotion, on the occasion of annual conferences. Between these, members were to write essays, limited to "two pages of ruled or letter paper," and submit them to the editor of the *Journal*, signed —in that day of acrimonious anonymity—with "proper signatures." [26] Matthew Simpson, although not a frequent contributor, wrote on music in olden times, attacked the Baptist theory of immersion, appealed for a more appropriate celebration of Easter than the current fad of eating colored eggs, and propounded a series of questions which should serve as a guide for the leaders' reports at quarterly conference.[27]

Not given to controversy, he rarely participated in the journalistic warfare which filled the columns of the *Conference Journal* and other religious newspapers; but when the issue was Methodism or the conference course of study he lashed out with biting ridicule in a sudden exhibition of temper which was in strange contrast to his generally even disposition.

The course of study for young preachers, planned by Charles Elliott and Dr. Ruter, was rigorous—much more so than that generally required in Methodism. Each year the candidate for ordination must study the Bible, with commentaries and notes; at various times he must read Wesley's sermons, and Watson's *Bible Dictionary* and *Theological Institutes;* he must study church history, Bible history, and the discipline of the Methodist Church; he must master Blair's *Rhetoric* and, to prove his ability in composition, must submit each year a written sermon. Simpson's topic for 1835 was "The Intellectual and Moral State of the Heathen World"; and the following year he wrote a practical homily on "Self-Denial." [28] In addition to these studies immediately related to the pulpit, the candidate must read books in geography, zoology, botany, "moral and political philosophy," "moral science," logic, natural philosophy, and chemistry. On all of these studies he was supposed to undergo "a strict examination, not merely on . . . having read, but having carefully *studied* them." [29]

Johannes, anonymous writer in the *Conference Journal,* complained of the burdensomeness of the course of study for young preachers. Too much reading was required. It interfered with the more important business of saving souls. Besides, it was un-Methodistic. What was needed was a return to "old Methodism," where the circuit riders read as they rode, and composed their sermons from their experiences and not from books which other men had written.

Simpson was indignant. Writing under the name Fenelon, he held up Johannes's complaint to ridicule and scorn: The course of study was little enough to expect of the Methodist preacher. Estimating the required reading for the first two years at 2,920 pages (without allowance for the fine print and the double columns), he calculated that in the 730 days of two years the preacher would have to read only four pages per day, and that local preachers, who had four years to complete the course, would have only two pages to read per day!

As for "old Methodism": what was "old" but the Methodism of John Wesley? Wesley's Methodism was simply this: *"That no man may administer the ordinances without a collegiate education, and Theological instruction."* If perhaps Johannes did not mean Wesley's Methodism but simply referred to the discipline then in use, very well: there he would find "every minister enjoined to read 5 hours per day—now allow him one hour to read the Bible. Here is 4 hours left, that is 1 page to the hour— Oh, tell it not in Gath— publish it not in Askelon that a Methodist preacher can be found who thus opposes duty." [30]

V

SENTIMENTS HAVE NO BLOOD

ALL through that first year old Uncle Matthew worried about his boy in Pittsburgh: his sermon preparation, his relations with the people and with the other preachers, his study program, and, above all, his health. Almost every letter admonished him to be careful. "Use charcoal," the uncle advised, or "Continue to sponge skin dayly"; "Be sure to wear your over coat and over socks," and "Warm your feet before the fire before going to bed at night." He fretted when there was no letter— "You promised to write soon, but your mother thinks it is a long soon"—and begged the young man, if he could not find time to write, to mark an *H* or an *S* on the copies of the *Conference Journal* sent home—to show whether he was in health or was sick.[1]

The bond of affection was strong, but Uncle Matthew complained once of unappreciativeness or forgetfulness. Stung to the quick, the younger man replied with impassioned avowal of love and fidelity. Surely his uncle could not think that, "while this heart beats or this mind acts," he would forget one who had been so long the object of his warmest regard: that uncle who had held him frequently in his arms, had sung to him in gleeful mood, had turned his infant mind to science, had given him books, had filled his mind with "moral & religious sentiments"! No, not " 'while life or thought or being lasts, or immortality endures.' "[2]

As the end of the conference year approached, Uncle Matthew became increasingly concerned over the younger man's relations with the other preachers and the people. It was a critical time in a Methodist minister's career, especially a young minister's. The itinerant system, which required the bishop to limit all appointments to one or two years, was highly competitive. There was no open bidding; but the larger stations and circuits, by devious means, sought the best preachers, and the better preachers expected the bishop to reward them for their abilities and their years of service. Tensions mounted, whisperings and speculations increased, the people criticized this minister and praised that one, and the preachers themselves forgot their high calling. Did young Matthew remember what he had been taught in his youth, that one who excelled in piety or learning would become an especial object of envy? that others would find and impute sinister motives to any man who did more than the common drones? that even men who were above character detraction would countenance it in the belief that young men frequently needed a taking down? "You are to expect all this from preachers of the gospel of your own order, and that, too, from men who really do love you," and must watch diligently and pray much: "Be meek and patient under opposition." [3]

However, the young minister was not particularly anxious. He had no thought of seeking a return to Pittsburgh. Dr. Sellers might call him "bishop" among friends, and praise him for his preaching; and his friend and colleague William Hunter might bemoan the fact that he was doomed "like a wounded snake" to drag his slow length along while Matthew drove ahead; and parishioners might praise the sweet sound of his voice; but he had preached himself out and knew it. He looked forward to a change in pulpits.[4]

Long before the meeting of the conference, however, he began to speculate on the place to which he should be sent. The presiding elder told him that there had been requests for him in Blairsville and Williamsport. Birmingham was to be set off from Pittsburgh as a separate station, and he knew that the people there wanted him. What did Uncle Matthew think? As for himself, he felt sure that the presiding elder intended to send him to Blairsville, a small place forty-nine miles away.[5]

The conference met in July at Pittsburgh. In the great buzz of speculation Matthew soon learned that he had been set down for Williamsport (now Monongahela City), a station not far from Pittsburgh. With its 200 members it was a good church—an exceptionally good church for a young preacher; but Dr. Sellers would have none of it. The people at Liberty Street church in Pittsburgh wanted Simpson and must have him, and they petitioned the presiding bishop, James A. Andrew. Dr. Sellers, a brother-in-law to Bishop John Emory, presented the petition. Both the presiding elders and the Smithfield church, however, were opposed. Matthew was set down for Hudson, a little place on Lake Erie, damp and cold, "109 miles from this place . . . where nearly all are Presbyterians."

When the word reached the Liberty Street officials they dispatched a note which the bishop received just before the reading of the appointments. He hurriedly called together the presiding elders, retired for consultation, and returned in a few minutes to read off Simpson's name for Liberty Street. He arranged that an older man, Charles Cooke, should be in charge of the Pittsburgh churches, unless the two congregations chose to divide, and he recommended that there be a frequent exchange of pulpits.[6]

Simpson at once became the center, if not the victim, of a bitter and prolonged church quarrel. The congregations voted to divide; but Smithfield, hoping to place the rival church at a disadvantage, refused to receive the younger man into its pulpit. None the less, the division of members proved to be about equal, and in a few weeks Matthew was enumerating to his uncle his reasons for bright prospects: First, he had received more members than he had anticipated, "2d . . . my congregations are as large as ever. 3d, I have many warm & attached friends . . . 4th, my officiary is said to be superior to any ever in the city . . . 5th, our class & prayer meetings are lively and profitable. 6th, my own liberty in preaching is very good." [7]

In one matter, at least, Matthew was glad to be returned to Pittsburgh. From the day when he had arrived, in the previous summer, he had felt irresistibly attracted to the home of James Verner on Penn Street. Ellen Holmes Verner! How often he had tasted her name on the tip of his tongue. Ellen, tall, slender, almost regal in bearing, quick to blush, reserved, sometimes shy, and yet how free and easy in speech among those whom she knew.

Winter nights, he had gone to her house often to dine or sit in the parlor and talk with the family, and to gaze on Ellen. Her very presence shocked him like a galvanic battery, and the sensation, a strange warmth diffused over his whole being, lingered long after he left her home. Back in his room he could see her still, hunched close to the fire on the hearth, warming her feet, or half reclining against the black cushion of the sofa, her blushes deepened by the flame of the fire; or he could feel her presence beside him on the sofa, the rhythm of her breathing disturbing the pattern of his own.[8]

The church frowned on the marriage of young preachers until they should complete four years in the ministry and receive ordination. Marriage made them less available for the more difficult circuits: it increased the cost of maintaining the preacher, and there were not stations enough to bear the burden.

None the less, Simpson determined to marry, once he was settled at Liberty Street. On September 19, a little over a month after his return to Pittsburgh, he proposed marriage, and Ellen accepted. Jubilant and yet somewhat fearful, he wrote to Uncle Matthew. Dared he marry right away? What would his brethren, and the officiary in the church, and the people say? Would it be better to wait? [9]

Uncle Matthew was delighted to learn that his nephew had at last come to his moorings. There would be no further cause for fear or anxiety on that subject! The news would no doubt create some little sensation in the society; but to delay the marriage would not decrease the sensation, unless he waited until the end of the conference year. Luther and Wesley had married and had displeased some of their people, but soon all went on as before; and so it would be with Matthew.[10]

There was no doubt about Uncle Matthew's wisdom when he concurred in a matter on which young Matthew felt so keenly! So, on Tuesday November 3, 1835, he and Ellen were married. A little group gathered in the parlor of the Verner home at six o'clock to see them stand together and repeat the vows: Matthew, tall, awkward, and self-conscious, and Ellen, trembling beside him.[11]

On Wednesday they took passage on the *Beaver* down the Ohio River to Wellsville, where his mother and Uncle Matthew were living with Hetty and her family. After two short days they returned to Pittsburgh on Friday afternoon, ecstatically happy even though they arrived at the Golden Triangle in a shower of rain. Matthew held his quarterly conference at five o'clock the next morning, an hour so early that the thoroughly disgusted presiding elder refused to attend.[12]

On Sunday he preached twice; and rarely had he "enjoyed more liberty." For that he was thankful—it should prevent any one's thinking that his marriage might make him "less useful and devoted than formerly." [13]

After some months at the Liberty Street church, Matthew Simpson was greatly encouraged. He had secured more than half the members in the division; and although the quarrel with Smithfield continued an occasional exchange had been allowed. His own preaching was much improved, and Dr. Sellers had said that if marrying had that effect on preachers he wished they all would get married. Matthew modestly confessed, however, that he thought it would be better for the congregation if he preached only twice on Sunday! [14]

As the winter wore on, a few were converted and added to the church roll. "The Spirit of the Lord came down," and a growing seriousness prevailed in the congregation. Matthew called in another young preacher to assist him in a protracted meeting. The altar was crowded with mourners, many were converted, and fifty-four joined the church, bringing the total to more than a hundred new members since conference.

"To God be all the glory," said Matthew. But he was not unaware that he himself had played a major role in God's success. Providence had surely designed a very short life for him, he thought, "or else one marked with peculiar incidents of an arduous and responsible character." [15]

There was no doubt that Matthew Simpson, in his many enterprises, was highly successful; but through all of his success ran a tiny rivulet of despair which sometimes, as he sat writing in his diary, rose to flood and overflowed. His writing was a catharsis, a purging of the faults and shortcomings consequent upon the rigorous standard he had set. He scourged himself not only for failures in the pulpit but for failing to live enough in the "spirit of prayer and self-examination." He conversed "too freely respecting the imperfections of absent persons," he did not visit enough from house to house, he did not talk enough "upon religious subjects." Occasionally he enumerated his "hinderances": "First, indolence—I do not fill up my time as carefully as I ought. Secondly, Timidity—I suffer myself for fear of offending people to have my time run away with as it ought not to be. I pray too little, & visit too little, and when I do first do not converse as closely as I ought." [16]

With all his self-abasement, however, he was still the child of
Providence. He did not expect ever to become a Calvinist, but he
was more and more satisfied that he could detect the "government of God" even in the smallest matters. Lightning struck the
house in which he boarded, and that portion of the house in which
he lived; but "providentially" he was not in. He was returning
from camp meeting when the driver of his hack, challenged by another driver, began racing his horses. The rear axle broke and
dropped the hack to the ground, but "providentially the horses
stopt & no injury was sustained by us—*Deo gratio*." [17]

Providence failed him, however, in regard to a wrongly exe-
cuted marriage. The father of the young man brought suit and
won the decision, and Matthew was fined one hundred and forty
dollars and twenty-five cents. "A pretty considerable sum for one
marriage scrape," he confessed to his diary.[18]

I I

After the quarrel with Johannes in the Pittsburgh *Conference
Journal,* Matthew had resolved not to engage again in journalistic
controversy. Some of his brethren had reproved him for dealing
too severely with the unlettered Johannes. Such sharp words about
so small a matter as the correct use of Latin and English might
prove to be divisive. Even Uncle Matthew feared that his nephew
had been saucy, and that his display of superior learning might
"abate that brotherly love which ought to subsist between preachers." [19]

But it was one matter to quarrel with a Methodist colleague
and quite another to defend his Methodism against the onslaughts
of the Calvinists. In the West the Presbyterians found it difficult
to defend the strict Calvinist doctrine of election against the Meth-
odistic preaching of a "full and free salvation." Humiliated by the
success which accompanied the illiterate and theologically perverse riders of the Methodist circuit, they poured their anger and
contempt into the columns of several religious weeklies, among
them, the Pittsburgh *Christian Herald.*

In the winter of 1836, William Annan, a Presbyterian preacher,
announced his determination to hold up Methodism to "public
scorn" until he should "break down its influence." A particularly

vicious attack on one of Wesley's tracts accused the founder of
Methodism of having selected passages which not only exhibited
Calvin in an unfavorable light but actually misrepresented him. By
"foreordination" Calvin meant "permission," Annan argued.[20]

The editor of the *Conference Journal* selected Matthew Simpson to reply. For weeks Matthew studied Wesley and Calvin, compared the Latin texts and the standard editions of Calvin's *Institutes* with Wesley's translated passages, and finally wrote a series
of articles that he signed, "A Wesleyan." He quoted extensively
from the *Institutes* to show that Calvin really believed in foreordination, and that Wesley had cited the passages honestly. The conclusion seemed to be "irresistible" that Wesley was much better
acquainted with the works of Calvin and had stated their substance
more fairly than Annan had done with all his pretense at research! [21]

Warfare in the religious press, as in the political, was often
waged not to demolish the enemy but to improve the morale of
the faithful. Annan, therefore, did not hear of the attack in the
Conference Journal for six months. When he did, he challenged
"A Wesleyan" to meet the charges which he straightway would
sustain: that Wesley was guilty of *"false reference, false translation,
pious fraud,* &c. with other things 'so palpable and scandalous as
should redden with shame the cheeks of their advocates.'" Ig-
noring Wesley, he proceeded at once to discuss the "palpable and
scandalous" conduct of some of the "intolerant and arrogant"
Methodists whom he knew.[22]

Because his statement was published in the Presbyterian *Herald,*
it did not meet his opponent's eye for another month. Time did not
cool the burning words, however, and Matthew, his own temper ignited by what he read, went home to write a reply. In what manner
had the Methodists ever been intolerant? Had they, he asked (distributing his argument over four centuries), "ever been accused of
burning their enemies," had they *"ever made laws compelling others
to support* them," had they "ever advanced the idea of carrying
their religion into politics"? Knowing that these arguments constituted a strong appeal in the democratic West, he pressed the
point. The intolerance which worried Mr. Annan was that the
Methodists preached the Gospel "in the same neighborhood with
himself" and, despite the "bolts of Geneva logic which he has

hurled," had "dared to proclaim that Jesus Christ by the grace of God tasted death for *every* man not just the elect and have invited even the *reprobate* to come and be saved." [23]

He never published his reply. When he pointed out to the *Herald* that Annan's attack had appeared in its columns, and demanded that they be opened to him for defense, the editor demurred, stating that the controversy was too personal: its merits depended too much upon the correct use of language and the fairness of translations, and it would afford little "advantage to souls, or to the cause of Christ."

However, he did not hesitate to attack in turn. The argument was then transferred to the editorial columns of the two papers. The charges of the Presbyterian editor, wrote William Hunter in the *Journal,* could not injure Matthew Simpson—he was "too extensively, and too favorably known for that." In fact, the editor of the *Herald* could scarcely injure anyone. He had attacked too often and too indiscriminately. "His pen, like some people's tongues, has ceased to be a scandal." [24]

I I I

On moving to Pittsburgh in the summer of 1834, Matthew had been quite unconcerned with the problem of slavery or the growing agitation in the North for emancipation. He subscribed heartily to the antislavery position of the Methodists and had done so since childhood, when Uncle Joseph Tingley had denounced the evil in the pages of the *Harrison County Telegraph.* Uncle William Tingley, Uncle Matthew, Charles Elliott, and all the Methodist preachers whom he knew held the same views.

The church, from its first organization in 1784, had forbidden the "buying or selling the bodies and souls of men, women, or children, with an intention to enslave them": a rule which reflected not only the opinion of John Wesley, but the Revolutionary doctrines of liberty and equality and the non-slaveholding status of the early Methodists.

In no great time the church, yielding to the demands of its members, made all its legislation on slavery "conformable to the laws of the state." This provision was of no great importance in 1800, when emancipation was almost universally permitted; but it was of first significance a generation later, when many southern states forbade the freeing of slaves. Ministers as well as laymen became owners of slaves, and the church increasingly shifted its emphasis from emancipation to evangelization.

In the early 1830's the radical Abolitionist movement sprang up almost simultaneously in New England and the West—incited in New England by the fanatical and acrimonious pen of William Lloyd Garrison, inspired in the West by the evangelical preaching of Theodore Weld. Among the converts of Weld's revival in 1834 was Orange Scott, firebrand evangelist and a presiding elder of the Methodist Episcopal Church in New England. Like Weld and the antislavery men of the West, Scott fused abolitionism and salvation into one persuasive appeal; and, like Garrison, he vilified men who did not agree with him. Scott's approach was simple: he pleaded for men to be saved, and he argued that when they had, by the grace of God, become brothers in Christ they could no longer endure the enslavement of their brethren. To the alarm of the church officials Scott's doctrine infected Methodist societies from New England to Ohio.[25]

Shortly after Matthew went to Pittsburgh, some one placed in Uncle Matthew's hand a copy of Garrison's attack on the American Colonization Society. Uncle Matthew was moved, but not quite convinced by his argument for equal privileges and amalgamation. He advised young Matthew to say very little for or against either the Colonization Society or Garrison's American Anti-Slavery Society. If duty called, he should present his own views on what ought to be done for the unfortunate blacks.[26]

In October, 1834, an agent of the American Anti-Slavery Society spoke at Cadiz and organized a society of twenty-two members. Uncle Matthew was secretly pleased. If the society conducted itself prudently, and stuck to the main question, he might join. A few weeks later he handed in his name, and so did Uncle William Tingley; but young Matthew held his own counsel.[27]

Meanwhile, Orange Scott's vigorous campaigns vexed the church greatly. The South, which had been silent on the question for many years, raised an angry protest, and the church began to pull apart along the Mason-Dixon line. The bishops admonished Scott and his fellows not to disturb the peace of the church. The New York weekly *Christian Advocate and Journal*, the chief organ of

Methodism, closed its columns to all agitation on the subject, and the publishing house, while abusing the abolitionists and printing accounts of the happiness of the slaves, refused to publish anti-slavery tracts or books. When the publishing house burned in a disastrous fire in the spring of 1835 Uncle Matthew thought it the judgment of God on the editors for their abuse of the abolitionists. "I tell you, my son," he wrote, "it is not safe to rail at such men to slander or oppose them or ill treat them." [28]

At the quadrennial General Conference in Cincinnati in 1836 the whole church was in a high fever over the abolitionist issue. Angered by the vituperation heaped upon them and alarmed at the threat to their institutions, the southern delegates came breathing threats of disunion. There were only two abolitionists among more than a hundred delegates, and so the alarm of the southerners was out of proportion. The South and the conservative North, in complete control of the deliberations, exhorted the ministers of the church generally to abstain from abolition movements and associations and to refrain from encouraging their publications; they declared that slavery was beyond the control of ecclesiastical and federal government, that only the state legislatures could deal with it. Shocked by Orange Scott and his agitations, and outraged by his attendance at an abolitionist rally in Cincinnati, the conference denounced his published defense as "palpably false," and his conduct as meriting "unqualified reprehension." [29]

William Lloyd Garrison, looking on the proceedings from his retreat in Boston, pronounced the conference "a cage of unclean birds and a synagogue of Satan." [30]

Uncle Matthew was scarcely less outraged by the incident, and Uncle William Tingley resigned all his offices in the church. When preachers went so far as to apologize for slaveholding members and rail at men who thought it their duty to say that slavery was wrong, Uncle Matthew thought it time that all men, "preachers as well as others," must either accept slavery as compatible with religion, or speak out against it. There could be no middle course.[31]

Young Matthew agreed. Prodded by his uncle, he had begun to reflect on the question. He was impressed by the fact that Cicero, Jefferson, Franklin, Wesley, Clarke, and Watson (the latter three, Methodists), all were opposed to slavery. Santo Domingo seemed to be proof enough of the "capability of the blacks for improvement and self government." As for threats of open warfare, ridiculous! The abolitionists had nothing to fight with but sentiments and words. Sentiments had no blood, words had none, paper had none. Abolitionists would spill no blood; if it were spilled, it would be spilled by their opponents. The fact was that the slaveholders were afraid—afraid of moral force. They were afraid that public opinion would force the repeal of the slave laws, afraid that they would have to live by the sweat of their own brows.[32]

Once persuaded, Matthew wrote to La Roy Sunderland, editor of Orange Scott's *Zion's Watchman*, praising the course of the editor and condemning the action of the General Conference. He spoke out boldly: The church should be held together if possible, but if the South continued in its course the North must "let them go." [33]

In the meantime, the bishops, fortified by the action of the General Conference, began to take strong measures against the abolitionists. They outlawed discussion of the slavery question in the sessions of the annual conferences, they refused to admit petitions against slavery, they removed Orange Scott from his presiding eldership, and swept other abolitionists out of places of influence. We must not, said Bishop Beverly Waugh, "hazard the unity of the Methodist Episcopal Church . . . by agitating those fearfully exciting topics." [34]

Uncle Matthew was caustic. He thought the tyranny of the bishops would do little to promote harmony in the church, but he had no doubt that the South would regard it as a defense of slavery. If any person heretofore had scruples about holding slaves, he would be "eased of his doubts." [35]

Young Matthew, however, was somewhat shaken. He still could not bring himself to approve of the proslavery extremists of the South; but with his friend William Hunter, who had succeeded Charles Elliott as editor of the *Conference Journal*, he began to believe that the bishops were right, or partly so—it was not necessary, or good for the church, for the abolitionists to agitate the question so vigorously.

He began to believe, also, that abolitionism was essentially un-Methodistic, that it was a tool of the Presbyterians and the Congregationalists for interference in the affairs of the state. Theodore Weld, eloquent evangelist who had pleaded so recently in

Pittsburgh and western Pennsylvania for emancipation, with the same fervency that he might have pleaded for the salvation of their souls, was one of the Lane Seminary rebels, turned out in Cincinnati by Dr. Lyman Beecher. Weld preached his antislavery sermons in Presbyterian churches; his converts were chiefly Presbyterian preachers and laymen, and his colleagues were fellow rebels from Lane Seminary.

To Matthew it soon became perfectly clear that abolitionism was cut from the same cloth, dominated by the same leadership, as the anti-Methodist benevolence societies of the Congregationalists and the Presbyterians. The Calvinists had been very sly in their benevolences: the Home Missionary Society, the American Tract Society, the American Bible Society, and others, all bore general names to "excite the public liberality," but were conducted by and for the benefit of Congregationalists and Presbyterians. Having failed to enlist the Methodists in support of their enterprises, they had labeled them schismatics and denounced them for their uneducated preachers and their popish government.[36]

Matthew did not doubt the evil of slavery, and he suspected with his friend William Hunter that the South itself might be conspiring to split the church. But he feared the abolitionists even more than the fire-eating southerners. The longer he studied the subject the more he came to see that sentiments, far from being bloodless, were ruddy and sanguine, eager for the fight. And so he came to believe that the only hope for the glory of God and the unity of the church lay in the conservative party. When La Roy Sunderland cordially invited him to write a second time for the abolitionist *Zion's Watchman* he did not accept.[37]

Early in 1837 Dr. Martin Ruter, in offering Matthew a position at Allegheny College, probed carefully to learn his view on slavery. Abolitionism had caused great excitement at the Presbyterian Church in Meadville, but the authorities were trying to keep it out of the college. "I should be glad to be able to say—not what your *sentiments are*," he wrote to Matthew, "for every one has a right to his own—but that you are not a member of any abolition, or anti-slavery society." [38]

No, he was not a member of any such society. That much he could say, at least.

IV

In the summer of 1836 Simpson, Hunter, and Charles Elliott, all received new appointments. Elliott became editor of the denominational weekly at Cincinnati, the *Western Christian Advocate*. Hunter, with the vigorous support of Simpson, won election to the editorial chair of the *Conference Journal* at Pittsburgh, succeeding Elliott. Simpson, having served his limit of two years in Pittsburgh, succeeded Hunter at Williamsport and moved there late in the summer.

Houses were scarce, but Matthew and Ellen found a small one-story place with a sitting room, two very small bedrooms, and a kitchen at fifty dollars a year. It was badly run down, but they swept and scrubbed and painted, and brought in their scanty furnishings.[39]

In the fall Matthew went back to Cadiz, alone, for the dedication of a new church. It was the first time he had returned since his marriage, but he did not take Ellen with him. His friends were displeased and slightly suspicious. He had been married a year, and they had not met his wife.

Matthew, hugely amused over their sly inquiries, reported to Ellen in great glee: "They wanted to know if you were *unwell!* but I thanked them all that you were in good health." Then they wanted to know "how my *family* were." "All well," he told them, and "left them just as wise as they were before for they did not like to ask plainly what I saw they wanted to know." [40]

At Williamsport he entered upon his duties with the vigor he had exhibited at Pittsburgh. He drew up a plan to relieve the church of its debt, arranged a cancellation of a part of it and pledges for the rest; he reestablished the Sunday school, scheduled prayer meetings in different parts of the town, one for each night in the week, preached twice on Sunday at Williamsport, and filled two appointments in the country on Sunday afternoons.

Lest he not be faithful to his responsibilities, he drew up a scheme of moral discipline, listing first what he should refrain from, and second what he should do. He should "never injure the feelings of any person"; he should "speak evil of no one"; nor should he "give

way to a jesting or jocose spirit, or to talk upon unimportant subjects," or to "lengthy conversations with my family and intimates."
On the other hand, he should:

Rise at 4 every morning . . . Dress as expeditiously as possible . . . Fill
up all my leisure hours with useful reading . . . Visit & pray from house to
house, & talk pointed and faithfully . . . Always endeavor . . . to give a
religious direction to every conversation . . . never suffer conversation to
turn upon me . . . If commended to pray for humility . . . if apparently
successful, be thankful to God.

As if this were not burden enough for mortal man, he proposed to examine himself regularly on such questions as:

Do I feel the Spirit of prayer? . . . Can I think of any plan which will
enable me to live more holy? . . . Am I using all the means of improvement? . . . Is my heart given to God? Am I placing my affections upon
anything on the earth? . . . Do I feel humbled under a view of my un-
worthiness & unfaithfulness? [41]

In the spring of 1837, when Simpson was about to complete his
fourth year in the ministry, Allegheny College again importuned
him to join its staff. Dr. Ruter was leaving to accept a commission
as missionary to the Indians of Arkansas and Texas. Competently
trained professors were few in the Methodist church. The college
regarded its need as desperate. Simpson had traveled his four years
in the conference and would be ordained at the next session. If he
were ever to join the faculty, he no longer had reason to delay.

He pondered the question at length. The decision was a critical one. Among Methodists, honor and preferment heretofore had
been with the church, not with the educational institutions. No
other major religious denomination in America had been so slow
to recognize the value of education, no other had been so suspicious
of a learned ministry. To preachers reared on the frontier and
schooled in saddlebag theology, the fear of the Lord was the beginning and the end of wisdom.

Progress, however, was in the direction of learning and through
the institutions. For Methodists it would be a difficult struggle; but
the battle against the old ways and ideas had already well begun.
Matthew Simpson's preferences and sympathies were overwhelmingly on the side of learning. From his youth up, he had had "an
insatiable thirst for knowledge" and an anxiety to "improve every

opportunity." [42] The call of the college was irresistible. Therefore he accepted a professorship in natural sciences and stepped out of the pulpit, never again to be a pastor. Four months he had spent on the circuit, three years at a station. It was not merely to the college classroom that he was now moving. He had discovered the vanguard of his church; he was exchanging the pulpit of the local society for the rostrum of the conference.

VI

ALLEGHENY PROFESSOR

FROM the time of his appointment until the opening of the summer term at Allegheny College in May, Matthew Simpson had two and one-half months to prepare for his classes. Uncle Matthew was not in the "least doubtful" that his nephew would rise in eminence "equal to any in the U.S.," but he thought he should have at least a month's practice in chemistry. How else he could demonstrate the experiments with credit, Uncle Matthew was at a loss to know.[1]

Young Matthew read feverishly and made extensive notations. He listed the "instruments" he must have: "Prism-lamps, thermometer, glass tubes, concave tin mirrors, Ball & ring, pyrometer, tubes with balls, fine tube with ball, differential thermometer, cryophorus wire with copper & zinc pieces—electro magnetic rotation."

With an eye to the wizardry of the test tube and the flame, he jotted down experiments, such sleight-of-hand performances as would quicken the pulse of his students as well as illustrate the characteristics and properties of cohesion, color, oxygen, hydrogen, and other phenomena and elements of natural philosophy. "Blow out lighted candle and it will catch in oxygen," he noted. "Fill a jar with nitrogen, dip a taper it is extinguished." "Pour a few drams of colored ether into thin glass tube of half inch. Mix one or two parts sulph acid with 5 of water, dip the tube & ebullition [bubbling up]." [2]

Leaving Ellen in Pittsburgh to await the birth of their first child, Matthew went to Meadville early in May of 1837. He tramped about the streets, keeping an eye out for a house and noting the relation of town to college; but he was listless. He could not get his mind off Ellen. He knew that she was better off with her parents in Pittsburgh; but, Providence permitting, in two weeks he would make the hundred-mile trip down to see her.[3]

He found most of the fifteen hundred people of the village scattered about the floor of the valley along French Creek. Allegheny College was on a hill above the town, and a half-mile from it. Following the slender path through the woods from the town to the college, Matthew came quickly to the crest of the hill. Bentley Hall was visible through the trees before he reached the campus: a handsome three-story, red brick building ornamented with white cut stone. Of colonial design, one hundred and twenty feet long and sixty feet wide, topped with a lofty bell tower, it was a monument to the labor and the taste of Timothy Alden, the founder of the college. The first story contained classrooms; the second, a chapel, a library, and a laboratory with chemical and "philosophical" apparatus. The third floor consisted of two large and well furnished halls for the literary societies. To the rear, visible from the window, two low wooden sheds stretched as left and right wings from the main building to house the college steward and to provide rooms for the self-boarding students.[4]

Matthew examined the philosophical apparatus and found it good; but he was more interested in the library. The collection of books amazed him: eight thousand volumes, "well selected" and containing many "rare and valuable works" that Timothy Alden had persuaded New England friends to give to his western college: Isaiah Thomas, founder of the American Antiquarian Society, Dr. William Bentley of Salem, and Judge James Winthrop of Cambridge. Thomas Jefferson had praised Dr. Alden for his collection of books, and the words were written down for every man to see: "I had not expected that there was such a private collection in the U.S." [5]

In the opening days of the term Matthew met his classes, assigned readings in the textbooks, and heard recitations; he re-examined the philosophical apparatus and conducted a few simple experiments. The college had scarcely fifty students, and the preparatory school only a few more. His own classes were small and informal. He could easily go to Ellen when the time came.

Late in June he received the word and hurried down to Pittsburgh to be present when Ellen gave birth to a son. He proudly held in his arms the small warm bundle of his own flesh, and named him James, for his own father, James Simpson, dead these many years.

Ellen recovered rapidly, and Matthew returned to Meadville to prepare for his family. Once more he was all energy, his mind crammed with the work of the college and the details of moving. He rented the house of Dr. Ruter, president, who had resigned to go as a missionary to Texas. He bought a carpet that was on the floor and arranged to have his own household goods moved in as soon as the house was vacant. He instructed Ellen to purchase some additional carpets and rugs and smaller items of furniture, but no dishes or looking glasses. The box of cupboard ware that they had shipped from Williamsport was pretty badly broken, and they had better buy in Meadville whatever more they wanted. She should get some Chinese cement, however, for they might be able to repair a few of the pieces.

He knew that the fifty dollars he had left would not go far, especially after she paid William Hunter the twenty dollars they owed him. He had drawn on the treasury at the college about as heavily as he could, but if she needed it he would find more money in some way. He was sensitive to the contrast between his own low financial estate and the comfortable income of Ellen's parents, especially when her brother, who was not sympathetic to the church, taunted her. Matthew warned her that she *must not* ask her father for help, nor discuss the particulars of their circumstances. But if her father *offered* help *voluntarily,* she need not refuse.

It was impossible to put into words his happiness at knowing that she was up and around. Only a short while, and they would be together at Meadville. In the meantime, he missed her very much, and could be solaced only by hearing from her. She must sit down the *very* same day she received his letter and answer him. *"Do-do-do-do* write," he begged.[6]

In a few days Ellen was ill again, prostrated by fever. Matthew, who had already arranged to be absent from the campus for his ordination at the annual session of the Conference, stopped over at Pittsburgh until she showed signs of recovery. Then he returned to his duties at Meadville, reluctantly. He conjured up a thousand fears. Perhaps she had had a relapse, or caught cold in the rainy weather, or eaten something that disagreed with her, or was again sick—and yet perhaps, perhaps, it was not so. Thus between fear and hope he passed the days waiting to hear from her.[7]

A week after his return to Meadville there was still no word from Ellen. Her father had promised to write on Thursday, and he should have had the letter by Monday; but here it was Thursday a week, and still he had not heard. Three days of restless anxiety. He felt both perplexed and grieved: perplexed because he feared that she might be ill, grieved because his happiness was so unimportant to her. Could she not relieve his agony by a single line? If she was well he wanted to know it, and be relieved of his fears; if she was sick he wanted to know it, so that he might sympathize and weep and pray. Would she keep him longer in suspense?[8]

Her letter came at last. She was mending rapidly, was nearly well. Soon she and James would join him at Meadville. Relieved, Matthew turned with vigor and enthusiasm to his classes and his study.

He taught chiefly from textbooks: Cavallo on natural philosophy for the freshmen; Keith on the globes for sophomores; Turner on chemistry for the juniors; and, for the seniors, Jameson on rocks and minerals, and astronomy with globes.[9]

Cavallo was an old acquaintance to whom Matthew turned with affection. Many hours he had spent in Cadiz thumbing the pages of *The Elements of Natural or Experimental Philosophy* and exploring the meanings of the physical universe. Heat, said Cavallo, was a "subtile and elastic" fluid called *caloric*, definite quantities of which were added to or subtracted from bodies when they became hot or cold. Temperature was simply the measure of the quantity of caloric. Light, as Newton taught in his corpuscular theory, was the sensation produced when minute particles, issuing from a luminous body, entered the eyes. Magnetism and electricity, like heat, were subtile and "imponderable" fluids, having no weight.[10]

From Keith the student learned the use of the globes, not merely by twirling them around and working a few problems, but by understanding the principles of geography and astronomy. Keith began, therefore, with definitions. The student must know the meaning of the Terrestrial Globe, the Celestial Globe, the Axis of the Earth, the Poles of the Earth, the Zodiac with its spring, summer, autumnal, and winter signs, an apparent solar day, a mean solar day, the astronomical day, the artificial day, the civil day, and the sidereal day. He must be able to define "horizon" and to distinguish between the Sensible, or visible, horizon and the Rational, or true, horizon, and so on through 123 terms in the first chapter.[11]

All knowledge was of God, Matthew believed; and to learn was to know God more fully. All knowledge when properly understood would confirm the Scriptures. It was therefore incumbent upon the student to learn as much of science as his program would permit, and on the teacher to relate science to God. In the hands of the proper teacher the textbooks, premised upon the ultimate authority of the Bible, could be made to subserve the purposes of religion. Keith was especially clear and forceful in his recognition of the hand of Providence. Did he wish to prove that the mountains had existed from the foundations of the world? He cited as proof the argument that they were needed *before* as well as *after* the flood "to display the goodness and beneficence of the Deity." Uncle Matthew was right: the schools ought to have Christian men to teach the principles of science. How else could a class get a satisfactory answer to the question which one of Matthew's geology students raised: Where did the waters of the Deluge come from? [12]

On Saturdays he met his students in the laboratory for experimentation with the electrical machine, the air pump, the test tube. He generated gas, activated the galvanic battery, mixed prussiate of potash and sulphate iron to produce a deep blue color, pasted bits of white paper to the globes which he then twirled in an unforgettable exhibition of changing geographical relationships.[13]

Matthew regularly taught six classes—not only natural philosophy, but mathematics or Latin or French or German, as the need might arise. Because of the distance of the campus from the town, and the long and severe winters, the faculty scheduled only one daily session of six hours, from early morning until early afternoon. To him, after his years in the ministry, the teaching day was short, and the library down the hall from his classroom was most inviting. He read particularly from the church fathers, translating rapidly from the Latin or the Greek; he took copious notes on Origen's *De Principiis* and his reply to Celsus, and on Sale's *Koran*. He read from George Whitefield, Francis Asbury's *Journal,*

Jonathan Edwards, Lyman Beecher. Greatly intrigued by Josiah Priest's *American Antiquities and Discoveries in the West,* he carefully turned over in his mind the author's speculation concerning the origin of the American Indian, as well as of the Negro and the White. Shem, Ham, and Japheth—Brown, Black, and White, Shem the father of the American Indian as proved by the derivation of the word! [14]

From his reading and conversation he continued to collect odd facts of science, noting that a "razor shell, found in Italy, bores into rocks, must be dug out," and that the thermometer in Sweden on Feb. 1, 1571, was 57° below zero." He heard it said that orchardists in Ohio had proved that apples "pulled" in the dark of the moon decayed less quickly. Not much truth in that old wives' tale, he guessed. Dissatisfied with his lack of system, he began to paste clippings into scrapbooks under such titles as "Medical Scraps," "Botany," "Chemistry," "Mineralogy," "Geology," "Geography," "Astronomy," "Ornithology," "Zoology," "Biography," "Theological," "Classical Ancient," "Classical Modern," "Mechanical," "Theological Anecdote," "Wit and Repartee." He purchased an *Index Rerum* for 1837 and began minute listings of unusual facts and details:

Anabasis—not written by Zenophon, but by Themistogines of Syracuse—
    Prideaux Con. Vol 1 p. 33.
Academy of Sciences at Paris—formed 1666. Hallam, His. Lit. v. 2.
Arcadians pretend they existed before the moon. Herodotus Note to V
    3 p. 177.[15]

As a student of science Matthew modestly admitted to himself that he was "advancing tolerably well." However, he could not say so much of his progress in religion. "I am indeed in religion, a mystery of mysteries," he lamented. His chief reason for flailing himself was his "slothfulness," or "procrastination," or inability, when he was impatient to get at his studies, to excuse himself from the tedious and unprofitable company which often ran away with his time. "It seems," he said, "impolite to leave, and it murders time to sit and hear them whining." [16]

Some of the distraction from study arose from his administrative responsibilities. He had not been at the school six months when he was named vice president and made a member of the board of trustees. The board, chiefly concerned with problems of finance, devised plans to raise money, through the legislature and through the Methodist conferences. It charged the new vice president with the responsibility of writing reports, visiting conferences and churches, and otherwise representing the institution; it also instructed him to supervise the college commons, which had been instituted on his recommendation. He was a member of numerous committees: one to look into establishing a "primary department" to be located in the "Borough" of Meadville; another to consider "the propriety" of erecting a new building; others still to supervise the painting of window frames, to keep the grounds in order, and to discipline the two rival literary societies when their interrelations reached such a pitch of animosity that the professors could not conduct classes.[17]

Matthew's teaching, reading, and administrative duties did not interfere with his preaching, despite his self-scourging. He visited "charges" from six to twenty miles from Meadville, assisted in quarterly and protracted meetings, in the founding and dedication of churches, introduced Methodism into Seagerstown, and was called upon to preach one of several funeral sermons at the death of the former president, Martin Ruter. He had not yet, however, attained any great powers as a preacher, as is indicated by the cryptic comment of Bishop Beverly Waugh. "Heard Prof. Simpson preach in the evening," confided the bishop to his journal; "it was only a tolerable performance." [18]

II

All his life, Simpson had identified himself with the interests of Methodism. When others lashed at the church he shrank from the cutting sting; when they praised it he grew warm with the sense of achievement. He took his bearings for his own destiny by the star of John Wesley, and he sailed, if somewhat unsteadily, in the course which the founder of Methodism had marked out. He kept a diary because Wesley had done so; he read Wesley's sermons and *Journal;* he defended him vigorously against the attacks of the Presbyterians; and he championed the conference course of study on the basis that John Wesley had honored scholarship.

At Allegheny College he gained a new perspective of Methodism. As a boy at Cadiz, as a circuit rider, and as a preacher at Pittsburgh, he had seen chiefly the immediate responsibility of the church: the saving of souls. Only now and then had he caught a brief glimpse of the vastness and diversity of Methodism. The college rose like a pinnacle above local interests and differences. Gordon Battelle and F. H. Pierpoint, outstanding young men from western Virginia, Calvin Kingsley, promising young student and tutor from Lake Erie, a score of men from western Pennsylvania and New York, and a like number from the region south of the Ohio—these students, some Whigs, some Democrats, might quarrel over politics or differ on issues of slavery and the national bank, but they were one in their devotion to Methodism.

Quizzing students on their textbooks, tramping through the woods with them in search of specimens, or repairing the electrical machine for the Saturday morning experiments, Matthew Simpson felt a new devotion—a dedication of himself to the cause of learning among Methodist youth. He began to understand as never before the importance of Methodist unity. The Pittsburgh Annual Conference, stretching out into three states, partly free, partly slave, if it divided over political issues, could not support its college or attend to the central responsibility of saving souls. So he began to reassess the problem of slavery and the activities of northern abolitionists.

Soon he began to imbibe some of the antiabolition spirit of the faculty and the students. He sharpened his conviction that abolitionism was allied with the Presbyterian Church, and was inimical to the unity and mission of Methodism. He began to look upon the abolitionists as a little bit ridiculous and upon their tactics as quite transparent. Slightly amused, he mockingly drafted a prospectus for a society of his own—an "Anti-Cannibal Society." Ought there not be one? There were societies concerned with Sabbath breaking, intemperance, slavery. Why not with cannibalism? He would draw up a prospectus and launch a seven-point program: 1) collect facts; 2) employ agents; 3) distribute tracts with pictures; 4) get cooperation of ecclesiastical bodies; 5) use no force but moral suasion; 6) have both male and female join; 7) brand those who do not join as pro-cannibals.[19]

He let some months pass before mentioning the subject to Uncle Matthew. He sensed a storm brewing and sought to steer

clear of it as long as possible. Then he protested the political tactics of the abolitionist preachers in the Methodist church. He
thought it strange that they should openly campaign for their
own delegates to the next General Conference, selecting men not
for their ability but for their willingness to vote for abolitionist
measures.

Uncle Matthew did not think it strange at all. The abolitionists
believed that slaveholding was a great sin. They loved the old
church. Ought they not, therefore, to seek to turn her from her
evil ways?

The issue was clearly joined. That slavery was a great evil,
Matthew did not doubt for a moment. Often, perhaps usually, it
was a sin, a great sin. But the Bible sanctioned it. Was slavery,
therefore, always wrong in itself?

Uncle Matthew, totally unprepared for defection in his own
family, was humiliated, crushed. "Slavery not wrong in its self,"
he exclaimed, weeping as he wrote. "No words ever brought so many
tears to my eyes. . . . I abhor them on the paper before me my
tears would wash them out. In some weak moment the enemy gained
an advantage over your intellect." Surely God in whom were all
the treasures of wisdom could save him from such delusion.[20]

Matthew was deeply hurt, not so much by the reproof on
slavery as by his uncle's manifest lack of confidence. Never in the
long years of close association had he brought his uncle to such
pain. Ought not Uncle Matthew to have confidence in him? Ought
he not to trust his intellectual integrity? It was not, he wrote, that
he favored slavery; he was in fact much closer to his uncle's position than to that of the antiabolitionist, but he did believe that
slavery was sanctioned by the Bible and therefore could not be
"wrong in itself." [21]

Uncle Matthew carefully separated the issues: he had not for
a moment lost confidence in his nephew; but surely young Matthew
would not ask him to believe that he was incapable of erring in
sentiment on a moral or religious subject. "And if in my judgment,"
wrote Uncle Matthew, "you had fallen into an error highly injurious . . . ought my tears . . . not be considered evidence of never
failing confidence?"

On slavery's not being wrong in itself, he argued from the
premise of *higher law*. The Bible countenanced some things that

were wrong in themselves—killing, for example, which was condemned by the law of Moses but was permitted, even commanded, of Saul when he held the Amalekites prisoners. Why these things were countenanced, he did not know, for they were "justifiable only for reasons known to God and not always obvious to us."

On the whole, the old man wrote, his grief was assuaged by his nephew's letter: "You are far nearer to us than to our opponents. . . . If you act on your principles you will be a pretty good Abolitionist." He was glad to know that Matthew and Ellen and little James planned to visit the family at Wellsville. He would be glad to see little James, who would not be an antiabolitionist; and he would be glad to see James's papa and mamma "just as they are." [22]

The exchange prompted young Matthew to further reflection on slavery. Slavery as it existed generally in the South was a sin. That much he would grant; but some men living in this legalized system might hold slaves without criminality. Therefore, the abolitionist doctrine that slavery was sin *per se* was false. However, he should like to see slavery in the South cease immediately. Northerners might, if they could hit upon the right plan, exercise some influence over the South "by reasoning and expostulation," but it would have to be without bitterness. On the other hand, there certainly ought to be no interference with the political rights of free men, such as petitioning of Congress; and the power of Congress to regulate trade ought to be interpreted as permitting control of the interstate slave traffic. The rules of the Methodist discipline against buying or selling slaves ought to be strictly enforced. He was inclined to accept some of the principles of abolitionism "without approving of the *shaking* or *agitating* part of it." [23] He favored abolishing slavery so long as it did not injure the institution of Methodism.

In the summer of 1838 the Pittsburgh Conference, paying lip service to the disciplinary doctrine that slavery was a great evil, declared it incompatible with the duties and obligations of Methodist preachers for them to deliver abolition lectures, attend abolition conventions, or circulate abolition papers. In the East the gag rule of the bishops was effectively silencing the abolitionist agitation.

Young Matthew, still uneasy of conscience in the presence of his uncle, took refuge in the action of the church: he would not, himself, have dealt so severely with the abolitionists, but as a Methodist preacher he had the duty to uphold and defend the institution of the church. Uncle Matthew taunted him: he had better take heed to himself and his doctrine. "To defend the powers that be whether in Church or State so far as they go right is patriotic and commendable: To defend their wrong doing is mean and servile (mark well my words)." [24]

III

The years at Allegheny College were fruitful and profitable to Matthew Simpson, but they were not altogether happy.

The severity of the first winter was such that in February and March Ellen and little James returned to Pittsburgh for the warmth and comfort of her parents' home. Again Matthew suffered from loneliness. Things went badly in his housekeeping. The girl who was helping quit, and Eliza, the "black woman," could not come for ten days. He and the students who lived with him were boarding at the college for breakfast and dinner and eating "a piece" at home at night. He sold the cow for $15, a dollar less than he had paid for her, but he had made a bargain of it even so! It cost him $1.50 to mend the sleigh. The weather was bitterly cold, nineteen degrees below zero. Nearly everything in the cellar froze, and the ice on the creek was two feet thick. The winter dragged on, and some snow remained on the ground until the middle of May. His health was poor; he suffered much from a cough and trouble with his chest.[25]

Even more disturbing was the problem of personal finances. Matthew had gone to the college with the promise of a salary of $550; but he was unable to collect it. At the same time he was proud. He did not care to have Ellen embarrassed in the presence of her family—her brother especially. There was only a "dull chance" of sending any money to her: the treasury was empty. He had tried in vain to borrow. Therefore she should "make a bill" wherever she was acquainted, get whatever things she wanted to be "perfectly independent." [26]

There were also troubles at the college. The president appeared to be a poor administrator; some of the students were guilty of bad conduct, and there was general dissatisfaction with one of the professors. More than half the students had threatened to leave the school, and three had already withdrawn. He thought that one of the professors would be removed, and that he would have to give up his own classes in science to take over the instruction in mathematics. After a few days the trouble blew over, and the students settled down with only minor notes of dissatisfaction. But Matthew could not forget the incident and wrote to Ellen, "I felt dissatisfied with myself and almost every body else." [27]

Meanwhile, Charles Elliott, editor of *Western Christian Advocate* in Cincinnati, had been made Doctor of Divinity by Allegheny College. To the leaders of the Indiana Conference who were establishing a college, he praised Simpson mightily. In consequence, the board of trustees elected him professor of mathematics at a salary of $800, and tempted him with the promise: "Some two or three years hence we shall want a president, and if you are the man that Dr. Elliott represents you to be, I see no reason, why you may not be promoted to that station." [28]

Uncle Matthew and other friends counseled against going. The position was no great advancement, and he still might be forced to play second role. None the less, after refusing the offer, Matthew was soon lamenting to Ellen that he had not gone: "I long for greater pecuniary freedom. It is exceedingly trying on my feelings to endure insinuations such as are occasionally used from some quarters." [29] The allusion to Ellen's "unsaved" brother was perfectly clear.

The following winter, the Indiana officials notified Matthew that he had been elected president and professor of mathematics at a salary of eleven hundred dollars. Again the winter had been severe; his health was poor and his finances "precarious." His friends advised him to accept the offer, and he concurred. The board of trustees at Allegheny College expressed its appreciation and its regrets. Each of the literary societies voted to have his portrait painted—an honor which he declined. He arranged for subsequent payment of his Allegheny salary, and contracted to have his household goods sent as quickly as possible to Terre Haute, by way of the Allegheny, Ohio, and Wabash rivers. He and his family took the boat to Cincinnati and the stage to Indianapolis. His new duties were to begin with the spring term.

VII

THE MIND'S THE MEASURE

MATTHEW SIMPSON had a fight on his hands when he moved to Indiana, and he knew it; but it was the kind of battle he loved—for God and Methodism. The Presbyterians controlled both the board of trustees and the faculty of the state university at Bloomington, which had opened in 1828. In addition, the New School and Old School Presbyterians had established colleges at Wabash and Hanover.

The first generation of American Methodists had opposed higher education as a matter of self-defense; hearty yeomen, come-outers from the established church, they had found their commission to preach in the grace of God and not in book learning. But by 1830, although still opposing "manufactories for preachers," they perceived that higher education was indispensable to their church. How else were Methodist lawyers, Methodist teachers, Methodist doctors, and Methodist sons in general to get their college training without endangering their Methodist faith?[1] Moreover, some of the circuit riders themselves, fed upon the rich journals of John Wesley and the commentaries of Adam Clarke, were as hungry for knowledge as they were for power.

Protesting against the domination of the state university by "one religious sect," the Methodists sought to gain representation on the board and the faculty. Outnumbering the Presbyterians in Indiana four to one, they attempted in 1834 the stratagem of placing the election of the hitherto self-perpetuating university board in the hands of the legislature. In the angry debate which ensued Samuel Bigger, a Presbyterian lawyer from Rushville, laughed the Methodists out of court. He doubted their competence to manage a "literary institution." When Ohio University wished to get a Methodist professor, he said, "they had to send to Europe for him."[2]

Bigger's contempt was not altogether unfounded, for there was not one Methodist preacher in Indiana who was a college graduate. And he secured the overwhelming support of his fellow legislators in moving to lay the Methodist proposal on the table.

The Methodists, however, were considerably stirred up. "Why don't we start a school of our own?" demanded "Indiana Itinerant" in the *Western Christian Advocate*. The Presbyterians of Indiana had 4,000 members, he argued, and controlled three schools; the Methodists had 24,000 members and "no voice in any." [3]

The Indiana Annual Conference, formed in 1832, had in fact recommended at its first session the establishment of a college. Next to the religion of the Son of God, said the committee on education, the "lights of Science" were "best calculated to lessen human woe and to increase the sum of human happiness"; moreover, in an institution of their own, Methodists could exclude doctrines which they considered "dangerous" and "incompatible with . . . revelation." [4]

After the defeat in the legislature, the Methodists hesitated no longer; they ordered the establishment of a college, chose a site at Greencastle, secured a charter, and, in 1837, established a grammar school. The following year they opened a preparatory department. In the spring of 1839 the board elected Matthew Simpson to the presidency and announced that college classes would begin in the summer term.

I I

From Cincinnati to Indianapolis and Putnamville, President elect Simpson, with his wife and two-year-old son James, traveled overland. The National Road was "execrably bad." When it rained in Indiana, said a friend, the land did not "flow with milk and honey so much as with mud." [5] The stage jolted over long stretches of corduroy turnpike and occasionally, where much travel had broken or wrenched the logs out of place, a wheel would drop suddenly and jarringly into a mudhole. Once the stage upset, shaking up the Simpsons considerably, although without any serious consequence to Ellen or James.

Greencastle, a village of five hundred, was not on the National Road, and so the Simpsons took a "private conveyance" at Putnam-

ville for the last six miles. They arrived on a Saturday afternoon
in late April. Court was in session; the village was crowded with
lawyers and their clients, and no rooms were available in the two-
story log hotel. Ellen, who was soon to bear her second child, was
exhausted; little James was tired and cross, and Matthew himself
was depressed by the long ride and the drab town. He went unhappily to a second hotel, a small frame building on the public
square. It was full also; but several guests were to leave that evening, and the landlord promised a room. The floors were being
scrubbed, however, and so the family was shown to the back porch
to wait for the court to adjourn and the floors to dry.

Fretful with the delay, he pressed his claims; and, learning that
a lawyer from a near-by town occupied one of the better rooms,
he commandeered it after promising the reluctant landlord that he
would assume the responsibility for entrance. Having found a
place for Ellen to rest, he returned to the porch to await the lawyer.

Before him, as he sat there that afternoon and evening, were
the unpainted houses of the town, and the irregular clearings still
cluttered with ugly stumps and fallen logs. Beyond was the intense
beauty of the Indiana countryside. Late in April the gently rolling hills were already dark green with underbrush; the willows were
in the first pale green leaf, and the sycamores stood white-trunked
and stark against the great elms and beeches. The crisp, fresh evening air bore the "bass hootings of the night-owl and the weird
treble of the whippoorwill," even the lyrical note of the mockingbird. But Matthew Simpson had no eyes or ears for beauty. Despondent, he saw only the small, one-story frame houses and heard
only the harsh tones of the hotel's cracked dinner bell.[6]

Restlessly, he walked about the village, down the muddy, un-
graded streets, seeking the university. The fifteen-acre campus offered no salve for his depression. Covered with underbrush and
scattered locust trees, bounded on one side by dense woods and
cut off from the village by a deep gully, it was still unimproved, save
for the partially raised brick walls of one building.[7]

The university was temporarily in a small two-story brick
house with two rooms below and one above—the building to which
young Tommy Goodwin had been directed a year and a half earlier
when he arrived at Greencastle with dreams of a stately campus
presided over by a corps of learned men.

"I don't know for certain," a local resident had said in answer to Tommy's question about the university. "It was, last summer, at the deestrict schoolhouse, but I have hearn that they have moved it to the county siminary. . . . You will not find it much of a university, I reckon." [8]

It was not much of a university; but it was the kind Matthew Simpson understood and could fight for, once he recovered from fatigue and depression. As the day wore on, word that the new president of Indiana Asbury University was at the hotel got about. The lawyer, when he at last came in from the court, proved to be "exceedingly polite" and kind. A little later, a trustee of the university learned of the Simpsons' arrival and hurried over to insist that they come to his house and live with his family until they could find a place to rent. In the friendly atmosphere of a Methodist home, filled with Methodist talk and Methodist hope, Matthew and Ellen Simpson's spirits began to rise.

Matthew heard in detail the story of the opening of the school and the report of the forty or fifty boys in the preparatory department. In a few days, at the opening of summer term on the first Monday of May, nearly eighty students enrolled in the preparatory school, and eleven in the college. The new president, much encouraged, took over the upper room of the academy building for the advanced students and began "to lay a foundation for the future." [9]

III

While young Matthew Simpson surveyed the prospects of his university with none too light a heart, his Methodist brethren were carefully taking his measure. Before electing him they had, with high aspiration, invited the two most prominent Methodist educators to the presidency of their new college; but both had declined. Even with the fulsome praise of Charles Elliott, they had chosen Matthew Simpson somewhat reluctantly.

Now they shook their heads with surprise and disappointment. He was but twenty-seven years of age, and younger in appearance. Tall, slender, and slightly stooped, he moved awkwardly and with a certain shyness. His face was rather thin and small, and his reddish brown hair lay low on his forehead. To men who, influenced by phrenology, equated high foreheads and intelligence, he did not look much like a college president.

The handsome Edward R. Ames, later bishop and long-time friend and frequent competitor of Simpson, took one look at him and said, "We'll have to discount Elliott's recommendation twenty percent." [10]

One trustee said to another, "I thought to see in the new president a man, but found only a stripling." [11]

The blunt Allen Wiley, one of the older members of the conference, and the man delegated to carry on the correspondence which had led to the selection of a president, frankly said to Simpson himself that he was "disappointed." "You look much younger than I thought you would," he said.

Simpson, his blue eyes sparkling with good humor, replied, "That is a difficulty which time will help to cure." [12]

One Sunday morning after his arrival in Greencastle, he stood trial before his first Indiana congregation. The people had flocked in great numbers to their places on movable benches in the unfinished, unpainted Methodist chapel. The men, if they were typical Methodists of their era, crowded together on one side of the aisle, rolled their quids about in their mouths, and spat quizzically as they took the measure of the new president. The women, across the aisle, peered out from under their bonnets in critical appraisal. They all had seen him before the service, and already there were whispers that "he won't do." But from the rostrum, where his tall frame towered above the roughhewn pulpit, his high musical voice rang out in praise to God and in confidence for the future, his face lighted up—aglow, men said, with the spirit of God—and his peculiar eloquence laid a spell on the congregation. The questioning looks changed to smiles, and the whisperings to murmurs, "He will do," "He will do." [13]

All that summer Matthew Simpson taught at the university and preached in and near Greencastle. Once he met a few of the preachers at Indianapolis and preached to the people there. His first major test with Methodists generally was in the fall at Lawrenceburg during the Indiana Annual Conference. The preachers, about one hundred and fifty in number, gathered from all over the state and from southern Michigan. The majority came on horseback, and many traveled more than two hundred miles.

A few had heard the new university president at Greencastle, and the word of his eloquence was abroad. When both Bishop Robert R. Roberts and Thomas A. Morris, presiding officers at the conference, declined the request to make the address celebrating the hundredth anniversary of John Wesley's foundation of the Methodist society, the young president, as the next highest official of the church in attendance, received the call. No theme was more to his liking than the one hundred years' march of Methodism.

The exercises were held on Friday morning in the little brick church, with two aisles and a narrow, high pulpit. The Methodists of the surrounding communities, excluded from the business meetings of the conference, crowded into the chapel with their preachers, making an audience of about five hundred. The occasion was dramatic—the centennial of the founding of Methodism; and it was the first opportunity many of them had had to hear the new president of their college. Moreover, they were aroused by the rapid spread of "Millerism," and were interested in the prospect of some great moral victory, perhaps even the triumphant second coming of Christ.[14]

Matthew Simpson chose for his discourse the first nine verses of the forty-seventh chapter of Ezekiel. The chapter records a part of the vision of the prophet, who as a captive in Babylon dreamed that the Lord escorted him through a temple newly erected on the site of the old one. When the prophet reached the door and looked to the east he saw a stream of water issuing from the threshold. A man with a line in his hand measured out the waters, and after each measurement of a thousand cubits he led the prophet through the stream. At first the water reached only to the prophet's ankles; then, to his knees, to his loins; and at last they were a mighty river that he could not pass over. The stream poured forth into the desert, and all that it touched was healed; and "every thing shall live whither the river cometh."

To Simpson the Scripture was a symbol, a flash of insight, a spark struck by the juxtaposition of the prophet's words and the history of Methodism. The meaningless fragments of his own knowledge and experience, thus illuminated, fell into their place in the Great Design. He perceived the force of Uncle Matthew's argument that the operations of God were not confined to the salvation of souls and the providential decisions of humble Christians, but were manifest in history, in the discovery of America, and in the march of Methodism. God had opened up a new land of Canaan and raised up a new Chosen People.

He painted in vivid pictures the humble beginnings of Christianity and of Methodism, the first tiny trickles of the stream, the struggles against persecution and hardship, the gradual increase, and then the unbelievable growth and spread of Methodism and its life-giving institutions.

He had a "wonderful expression" as he seemed to take onto himself the role of the prophet and to wade into the waters to his ankles, to his knees, to his loins. "His great soul came into his face . . . Light seemed to flash from side to side." The tide of emotions quickly rose to "an uncontrollable pitch." He had scarcely finished his introduction when a woman, the wife of one of the wealthiest citizens of the community, could stand the emotion no longer. She rose, stepped to the middle aisle, and waved her hand above her head, exclaiming, "Sun, stand thou still and let the moon pass by." Simpson paused, and another preacher began the singing of a hymn while friends led the woman from the church.

When Simpson resumed his theme the resistance of the audience was broken, and emotion was at a new high level. With every "fresh unfolding of the subject," every new interpretation of the symbol, came a "fresh gust of tears and shouting." The preachers were so overcome as almost to drown out the voice of the speaker. The circuit rider beside James Hill could not keep quiet. He stamped on the floor and shouted, "Did you ever hear the like?" Hill, distressed, tried to quiet the fellow by pressing on his knees. At last he forced the man's head down between the seats and pounded him on the back.

On went the stream, and Simpson from the mountain top pointed out its course to the congregation. It was at last a mighty torrent, "sweeping everything before it, cutting for itself a deep and wide channel, carrying huge rocks and giant trees in its course," spreading over the plains, where it left its healing waters, its rich verdure and fruitage.

With one voice the Methodists of Indiana voted Professor Simpson the "prince of pulpit orators." As for himself, Simpson had found both the theme and the method to suit his needs and to move the people.

IV

No less important to Matthew Simpson in establishing himself with Indiana Methodists was his inaugural address as president
of Indiana Asbury University. The event was postponed in order to
allow the completion of a part of the building.

Before the summer was half gone, Uncle Matthew was worrying: "Don't forget the inaugural address; your duty and reputation
both require attention to that."

Young Matthew worried too. Ellen and James and baby
Charles, who had been born shortly after their arrival in Indiana,
were visiting in Pittsburgh, and he had to add household tasks to
his college teaching and administrative duties.

It was too bad, Uncle Matthew thought. He had no doubt that
others who had made such "luminous addresses" had had leisure for
preparation. None the less, he was confident. His nephew might not
rate so high as other educators in speech making (the family had
had no first-hand report of the conference sermon), but there were
very few men, if any, who had had "greater facility in acquiring a
knowledge of literature, languages, and science than yourself." He
had no doubt that the address would be "good and fully equal to
what the best of them at your age and experience could have
made." [15]

By late July the first draft of the address was completed, and
sent to the uncle for criticism. It was good, Uncle Matthew said, save
that some generalizations ought to be qualified and some definitions made clear. The nephew carefully noted these as he began the
process of refining.

The commencement and the inauguration were set for September 13, 1840, just before the Indiana annual conference was to
meet at Indianapolis. Methodist preachers and members, friends of
the college, officials of the school and state, gathered at Greencastle for the exercises. Henry Ward Beecher, the twenty-six-year-old pastor of the Second Presbyterian Church in Indianapolis, who was
scheduled to address the literary society in the evening, came early
for the commencement and inaugural exercises. Governor David
Wallace, in a highly embellished address of welcome, praised the
work of Indiana pioneers and Methodist circuit riders, and then
turned the keys of the institution over to President Simpson.

The young president stepped forward to deliver his address. The chapel of the new building was packed: most of the preachers who had been at last year's conference were present, and members of the Board of Trustees had a prominent place; friends of the institution, men who had struggled to place Methodism in the front ranks of western education, eagerly waited to hear what he had to say. There were still some who were a little suspicious— Indiana Methodists who, nurtured by the circuit riders and still unweaned from frontier ways, looked with doubt upon higher education and "larnin" among preachers, even though the committee of the conference had promised that the college should not be a "manufactory in which preachers are made."

Uncle Matthew had warned that the effect of the address would determine the people's judgment of the college. "Speak as if you are perfectly sure of the correctness, propriety, and importance of every sentence," he wrote. "If the speaker . . . is sure he is right, the hearers will be so too." [16]

The president began with the story of an ancient Greek artist to whom a visitor expressed wonder that he should work so hard to perfect his productions. He answered, "I paint for eternity." Why, the speaker asked now, had so much time and effort been spent in erecting this edifice, why was there on this day "such a congregation of the talents and beauty of our enterprising, though youthful state—and why such a deep interest . . . in the exercises of this day? . . . 'We paint for eternity.' " [17]

The critical question, to which he addressed himself, was: Why should these efforts be devoted to education? In the manner of John Locke, he answered that in the first place man is the creature of his education. A beaver might build a dam like his sires, without alteration or improvement; but man, according to his learning, built for himself a hovel, or a wigwam, or the "rock-hewn palaces of Petra, or the hundred-pillared domes of Thebes." Not only was he a creature of education, but he was continually receiving an education. Whether he was a child at play, a student at his books, or a young man at work, he was subject to lessons which would determine his future. Man had an insatiable desire to learn, an unquenchable thirst implanted by God. The only power of the parents, then, was to choose in what the youth should be educated. The negligent parent allowed his child to learn the science of wickedness—the "foolish jest, the impure song, and the profane exclamation." The responsible parent directed his son's desire for knowledge toward the proper objects.

He insisted further that individual character depended upon the kind of instruction received, that national character was similarly determined, and that "true fame and prosperity" were dependent upon "intellectual and moral culture." He cited the instances of Washington, of Hannibal, of the Indian stalking his game or his enemy; he contrasted Sparta and Athens, Carthage and Rome, Egypt and Israel, Russia and Britain, and extolled the wisdom of the Pilgrim Fathers in planting church and school on the American continent.

Having thus argued, generally, the importance of education, he turned to a consideration of colleges and universities. He praised them first because they supplied the outlines of general knowledge. They taught the student the principles of chemistry, of mineralogy, of geology. They instructed him in natural philosophy, in the motions of nature—from the movements of the birds in the air to the ships upon the sea—the propagation of sound, the flash of the lightning, "the colors that sparkle in the dewdrop as it glistens on the trembling leaf."

But colleges taught the student not only the nature of the world in which he lived, but the history of man, the principles which had raised and overthrown nations, the actions of the good and the great as opposed to the conduct of the bad; they explained to him the strange phenomena of the mind, the laws of being, and taught him to think with accuracy and precision. And above all, in thus leading him through every department of nature, they showed him the "grand design of the Supreme Creator."

He praised the colleges, again, because one of their grandest objects was to teach students to write and speak, to communicate interestingly and successfully. In America every man was by birthright an orator; he was at birth "invested with the attributes of sovereignty." Few men were orators by nature. Few there were who would not profit from the periodic exercises in writing and declamation, the studies in logic, in structure and analysis of language, in style, and more especially in foreign languages. However popular it was to declaim against study of the classics, no man, he said, could obtain a mastery of his own tongue, or aspire to true scholarship without studying Latin and Greek.

He praised the colleges because they taught students to seek amelioration of the condition of man. "Moral Science shows that man to be a criminal who does not employ himself in labors of benevolence." He praised them also because they elevated the standards of professional achievement, and because they contributed largely to the effectiveness of the common schools.

His greatest praise for the colleges was that they had always been precursors of great improvements, of the progress of mankind, whether in government or in the arts of civilization. He eulogized Charlemagne and King Alfred for their encouragement of learning; he traced the early history of universities, and found in them the awakening mind of the Renaissance, the spread of the ideas of justice and liberty, the crumbling and decay of tyranny. In the advancement of knowledge through the universities, he saw the rise of the idea of popular rights, the signing of the Magna Charta, and the formation of the American Constitution, "that noblest work of man."

"Yet," he said, rising to a brief but scornful denunciation of those who opposed education, "some there are, even in this favored land, so ignorant of history, and so grovelling in all their conceptions, that they publicly declaim against colleges as fostering aristocracy." Such men would, in other days, have been the first "to strangle liberty in her cradle, and, bowing their own neck to the foot of the despot, to swear allegiance to his throne."

He thought the universities likewise instrumental in bringing about the Reformation in religion. Luther, Calvin, Wesley, Whitefield, all were university men. The college in America, far from being the nursery of vice and infidelity as some men supposed, was favorable to religious instruction. Students were required to observe the Sabbath; they listened daily to the reading of the Scriptures, and their preceptors were men of "irreproachable habits and unblemished piety." Even more important, an enlargement of knowledge gave a clearer idea of the greatness of Deity. Man's only concept of infinite holiness, of spotless purity, was inseparably associated with infinite wisdom. How did man, at the time of creation, differ from the animals? Not that he was purer, but simply that he was wiser. If then man, within his sphere, should seek to be like God, "he must seek not only for spotless purity, but also for extensive knowledge."

President Simpson now had spoken for nearly two hours, with

an amazing display of erudition. He had laid down the premises of his argument carefully and clearly, and had heaped upon them an abundance of illustration from history, biography, science, and the Bible. He had relieved the argument with a score of sharp, vivid pictures: Luther casually taking the Scriptures from the shelves of a library for the first time; the Carthaginians scaling the mountain heights of Italy and pouring down upon the fair plains, only to be checked by their ignorant fear of a storm; the dust of a plant carelessly brushed away, but seen through the microscope as a crowded city of living beings.

Considering in conclusion the argument that Indiana already had too many literary institutions, and therefore ought not to establish another for sectarian purposes, he denied it. A new institution would not damage those already existing. "A star hitherto invisible, when it suddenly shines brightly in the heavens, robs not other luminaries of their glory, but only augments the splendor of the sky." Indiana, with a great deal more territory and more than twice the population of Connecticut, had but one-fifth the number of college students. Parents of the West wished their sons to be educated in Western institutions where they could become attached to the customs and be identified with the interests of their own people.

As for the cry of "sectarianism," young men enrolled at Indiana Asbury University would be subject to no proselyting. However, if the critics meant by sectarianism that the professors were religious men and, as such, had "settled views upon Christian character and duty," then he hoped the institution would ever be sectarian. "Education without morals is pernicious, and to have morals without religious instruction is impossible."

Ardent as he was for Methodism and its schools, he was not unmindful of the fact that many potential patrons of the school were not affiliated with any church. Praising, therefore, the projectors and founders of the college, he referred to them as "friends of this university," and "people in all parts of the state." His flights of eloquence and periods of approbation had been for his country and his state, not for his denomination. He had mentioned religion, but he had eulogized learning.

The people were profoundly moved. John Hammond was so highly delighted that he immediately decided to send his son to

Indiana Asbury University; Henry Ward Beecher said that a copy of the address should be sent to every family in Indiana; the board of trustees directed the printing of a thousand copies; and Edward R. Ames, who was not easily excited over the achievement of others, insisted on "quick publication," and said that he would look after arrangements even though he had already been criticized for meddling. "By the help of God," he declared, "we will scatter it to every nook and corner of the State." The address, printed with that of Governor Wallace, was distributed in pamphlet form to the people.[18]

Uncle Matthew reported some weeks later that Charles Elliott thought the inaugural was "great": in some places "it might have been improved, but it was such as he could not make." Leonidas L. Hamline, who was soon to be elected bishop, believed it "upon the whole . . . the best inaugural made by any Methodist preacher at the head of a college." Uncle Matthew himself was "exceedingly joyful at the success of performance," but he admonished young Matthew to remember in deep humility "whence cometh thy strength." Nor should he forget that "popularity of any kind is uncertain." [19]

Nearly a year after the address William Hunter, the former editor of the Pittsburgh *Conference Journal,* who had long meditated upon "epistleizing" his old friend, wrote that it was not a "slow speech." "If I had been an editor I would have given it a 'puff.' I am not surprised to hear that you are marvellous popular out there." [20]

As L. L. Hamline said, the address, although not above criticism, was of a sort to "command an unbounded respect." It brought to the young president the substantial reputation he needed in launching upon an educational career. A year and a half before, the Methodists of Indiana had looked doubtfully upon the tall, slightly stooped youth who had come to head their university; but now the reputation of Matthew Simpson, preacher and educator, was secure. As a layman said, after mistaking the older and much more handsome college agent, Samuel Cooper, for the president and Simpson for some young itinerant, "Ah, I see the wisdom of Dr. Watts's saying, 'The mind's the measure of the man.' " [21]

VIII

HOOSIER SCHOOLMASTER

IN August, 1839, President Simpson's first catalogue of courses, a twelve-page leaflet with a bright yellow cover, listed the twenty-five trustees of the University, the nine members of the visiting committee, the three professors, including himself, and the 86 students, only twelve of whom were in the college. It itemized the student expenses, outlined entrance requirements and the course of study for each year, and set forth the general rules and regulations governing conduct.[1]

The school year, two terms of twenty-one weeks each, opened on the first Monday of November, and ran, with a spring vacation of four weeks, until mid-September. Tuition per term in the college was $12, in the preparatory department, $8.50. Janitor's fees, including fuel, were $1.50 for the winter session, $1 for the summer. Boarding in private families cost from $1.50 to $2 per week, exclusive of light, fuel, and washing. Parents were not to furnish their sons with pocket money. Such funds should be placed in the care of a faculty member or a citizen of the community, to be dispensed as needs for stationery, clothing, and books might arise.

Students, to be admitted to the freshman class, must demonstrate a knowledge of geography, English grammar, arithmetic, first lessons in algebra, Latin grammar, *Historica Sacra,* Caesar's Commentaries, Virgil, Greek grammar, and Greek Testament. Only eight men qualified for freshman status in the summer of 1839; twenty-four others, designated "irregular," were making up their deficiencies while they pursued a "partial College course."

Once a student was admitted he followed a neatly arranged course of study, three classes per term with no elections. His first two and one-half years were devoted to language and mathematics. He studied Greek and Latin history, poetry, oratory, and philoso-

85

phy, all from the original texts. He continued in algebra and geometry and advanced to trigonometry, mensuration, surveying, differential and integral calculus. At the beginning of his junior year he entered the study, in translation, of ancient and modern history with chronology, and at mid-year he delved into the mysteries of experimental philosophy and chemistry, and learned the artifices of rhetoric-logic-criticism. Not until his senior year did he turn to political economy and grammar, the law of nations, and the capstone to all of his studies, Paley's *Theology*, moral science, evidences of Christianity, and astronomy, which, although a natural science, served but to confirm the omniscience of the God whom he had studied in Paley.

President Simpson was especially proud of one radical departure from the traditional curriculum: he had convinced the members of the board of the practical value and the wide appeal of scientific training. The catalogue announced, therefore, that Indiana Asbury University would award the degree of Bachelor of Science to students who became "thoroughly acquainted with the Scientific and Literary course," embracing all the collegiate requirements except Latin and Greek.

The university had three instructors, the Reverend Matthew Simpson, A.M., president and professor of mathematics and natural science, the Reverend Cyrus Nutt, A.B., professor of the Latin and Greek languages, and the Reverend John W. Weakley, A.B., principal of the preparatory department. Of the 86 students enrolled in the summer of 1839, 50 were in the preparatory school, 24 in the irregular course, and the remaining 12 in the college proper. Enrollment climbed steadily, and by the opening of the fall term in 1840 the president was able to add another instructor.

William C. Larrabee, professor of mathematics and natural science, was an important addition to the faculty. The best trained of Simpson's appointees, he had received his A.B. from Bowdoin College in 1828, and had served as teacher and principal in several Methodist academies in New England and New York. He had once been state geologist in Maine and had acquired a large private collection of mineral specimens which he brought with him.[2]

President Simpson, happy to yield the test tubes, equations, triangles, conic sections, and differentials, attended to the mental and moral needs of the students. He heard recitations in logic, rhetoric, moral science, political economy, mental philosophy, natural theology, and evidences of Christianity. On Sunday afternoons at three o'clock, acting on a directive from the board, he lectured to the entire student body on topics as various as anatomy and physiology, envy, errors of thinking and how to guard against them, beauty, the value of national days of celebration, and the ministry. The lectures constituted one of his more important contributions to student thinking.

Speaking for twenty or thirty minutes, he ranged as widely in his materials and proofs as he did in his choice of topics. He alluded to classical mythology, to biblical narratives, to ancient history, and to modern literature. He cautioned the student about the necessity of exercising, keeping clean, watching the diet; he warned that emotions often arise because of the condition of the body, and that many a man had alienated friends because his liver excreted "a little more bile one day than it did another." He recognized that there might be some truth in phrenology—respecting functions of various parts of the brain—but declared that "it must ever be impossible to tell from the external form of the cranium the . . . internal development." [3]

He enlarged upon his favorite educational theme: knowledge is requisite to happiness. "Man must know where he is, and what are his instruments before he can acquire contentment or success." Students must learn to act upon evidence, not impressions, they must get over childhood dependence upon others for their conclusions. He accepted the authenticity of the Old Testament without question, and he regarded "revelation" as a sound test of subjects suitable for the student to think upon; but he lashed out at the fanciful thinking of religious people, ridiculing those who wrote learned articles on the kind of fruit Eve plucked from the tree and stated their reasons as confidently as if they "had stood in the garden and beheld the beautiful fruit or tasted its luscious sweets." No subject, he insisted, was suitable for serious reflection unless the student could answer affirmatively the question, "Have I any powers by the exercise and attention of which I can acquire any knowledge of it?" He cautioned against the tendency of some "overly eager persons" to read too rapidly, and thus to fail in digesting what they had read; and he warned equally against the desire of others to have an opinion on every topic and "so to circumvent careful thinking."

He praised his age as one of active enterprise ("The good old days of leisure are forever gone"); he lauded the constitution, which "contains so many of the elementary principles of liberty and order"; and in impassioned frontier oratory he eulogized the flag:

that cluster of stars—of equal, beautiful, brilliant stars . . . undying, unchangeable, unextinguishable stars that smile on in their own inherent brightness without even a twinkling of jealousy at the thousand other bright orbs that are beaming all around them.

He advised the students to be simple and plain in manners, to avoid select associations, to feel themselves "identified with the body of the Community." He charged them to labor for "the elevation of the masses." It was an object unknown to Athens, "the Paradise of Antiquity," with its thirty-one thousand citizens and four hundred thousand slaves, but was the "legitimate design of Christianity"; it was "in peculiar harmony with American Institutions," and it reflected the "tendency of the improvements and discoveries of the age." This great object, once realized, would "employ the wealth of the world productively . . . effectually remove all causes of war," and be "the crowning glory of humanity."

He adapted his lectures to student audiences. His divisions were sharp and clear, with the "first," "secondly," and "thirdly" usually called out unabashedly, and the framework well supported with illustration. With humor he was generous and natural. Did the lecture on the cranium seem abstract? He lightened it. There was an ancient theory, he said, which supposed that ideas were like little particles floating around in the back of the brain: when stirred up they were in consciousness, when settled like sediment they were in memory. The theory must yet be much more widely accepted than is commonly believed, for the schoolmaster—thinking the ideas of his pupil settled—makes his head fairly ring with a brisk cuff and so sets the particles into motion until they dash against one another so furiously as to shine like stars. He, of course, would omit reference to that other process of "stirring them up with a long rod" because he could not "anatomically trace any very great connection between the ideas and the parts to which the rod is applied." He chided the students who, rather than study, put forth their efforts in cultivating a hearing sharp enough to catch the whisperings of their classmates, and warned them that if Lamarck's "philosophical theory" that animal organs, like the elephant's trunk, the hog's nose, the squirrel's forelegs and claws, develop to meet their needs, then these students, by their great desire to hear would "by and by give rise to a race of animals with most *dreadful long ears*." [4]

It was the duty of the university, President Simpson believed, not only to impart knowledge but to teach the students to speak to others. "Few can be writers, but all may be orators." He expected Indiana Asbury graduates to achieve eminence; and every man who aspired to eminence must seek such a mastery of language as should enable him "to pour forth truth in all its strength and beauty." He therefore set up, in addition to the classroom readings in oratory and rhetoric, a rigorous system of exercises in speaking. At chapel service every morning three or four students, taking turns in alphabetical order, delivered declamations, and thus in the early years declaimed about once a month. Each month, on the "Public Saturday," selected students declaimed; and each week every college student had to read an original essay before one of his professors.

Simpson highly approved of the two literary societies which the students had organized before his arrival: the Platonian and the Philological. They were "well calculated to improve young men in public speaking, and also to familiarize them with the forms of the transactions of most deliberative assemblies." The societies met regularly, held public "exhibitions" on occasion, and debated such topics as "Should Roman Catholics be admitted into our Republic?" "Is the extension of territory opposed to the prosperity of this Union?" and "Are writings addressed chiefly to the imagination injurious in their tendency?" The faculty approved dialogues and colloquies as a variant of the traditional debate but frowned upon all "theatrical" representations and forbade "the wearing of female attire." [5]

The principal speech occasion of the year was commencement day. Friends of the university gathered from far and near; preachers arranged their circuits so as to be at the college and yet save themselves long rides and "severe tax on horse flesh"; and people of Greencastle were asked to make "large arrangements for men and horses." Each member of the graduating class was required to deliver an oration. The people would sit from eight o'clock in the morning until twelve, then eat lunch in their seats in the chapel so as not to lose their places. One year when the president was absent Professor Larrabee wrote an enthusiastic letter describing the exercises: "The audience was chained down by their deep interest till past one o'clock. A slight catastrophe happened, but nobody was hurt. A yard or two of plastering tumbled on some dozen heads . . . Dickerson was speaking . . . We thought it likely some of the great high sounding words which Dickerson so freely uses proved too much for the plastering." [6]

I I

To the founders of Indiana Asbury University the practice of religion was quite as important as the acquisition of knowledge. Daily chapel services were a matter of course. President Simpson and his staff led in the prayers and delivered brief exhortations. At intervals the college altars were crowded with penitents. Students wrote to their parents whenever a revival occurred, and the word spread quickly. The news "meets me everywhere," wrote William Daily, presiding elder and Simpson's close friend. "May God bless you and the University . . . and may the culture of the heart keep pace with the culture of the head." Professor Caleb Mills of the New School Presbyterian Wabash College rejoiced with Simpson on learning "that God has visited your institution with the blessed influences of his Spirit"; his own school had been "refreshed from the same source." [7]

One year, during a "wonderful season," the faculty suspended classes, some of the Greencastle stores closed, and college and town united in three public services each day. No one was more active than President Simpson, who wept like a father with the penitent or mounted the pulpit to pour forth his eloquence.

Revivals and daily chapel meetings, however, failed to satisfy the board of trustees, who in the year of the big revival decreed that students should rise a half-hour before sunrise to attend public prayers. The rule, adopted in July, was mercifully amended in October to read five o'clock for summer, eight-thirty for winter! [8]

The faculty required students seeking admission to present testimonials of "good moral character." The discipline of the school was "mild but strict," for the faculty desired "to gain the affections of the students, and . . . to manifest the kindness of friends, rather than the cold attention of mere instructors." So said Matthew Simpson in his first catalogue. However, he warned that any student "disposed to indulge in immoral or disorderly habits" would be "dismissed with as little disgrace as possible."

The students thought him a rigid disciplinarian and early dubbed him "old Doc." Some "strongly suspected" that he had a well developed system of espionage. Certainly he was ingenious in finding out their faults.

One dark night one of the students, son of a prominent citizen, being slightly in his cups, failed to recognize the president and accosted him gruffly at a muddy street crossing.

"Buck up here and carry me across the street."

Without a word, the president obeyed. On the other side of the street, he called the student by name and said, "I think you have ridden far enough." Recognizing the voice, the student hurried to his room and gave no further cause for disciplinary action!

On another occasion Simpson shocked the students in chapel by a dramatic reprimand for the "rude disorder" which had occurred on the streets the night before and had caused him deep "mortification." He would not investigate to learn the names of the guilty. He knew who they were. He had gone with them, and he knew their names as well as their deeds. But he would not expose them. He would trust to their honor that there would be no repetition.

Recognizing the keen sense of humor which lay behind the president's austere exterior, students sometimes took liberty with him that they dared not take with others. One day, before the third story of the building was completed, a group of preparatory school boys, disobeying an express faculty rule, crawled up to inspect the area. Simpson, coming upon them unexpectedly, seized a lath and applied it to the boy nearest him while the rest scampered to safety.

A few days later, Simpson, the boy, and several of his companions sat together at dinner.

"Dr. Simpson," said the boy, with sudden impudent politeness, "you lathed me the other day; I'd like to know when you are going to plaster me."

The color rose on Simpson's face as he fought briefly for composure, and then he yielded to the boys and joined them in hearty laughter.[9]

The students liked the president and his wife. Lonely and embarrassed farm boys, away from home for the first time, they went reluctantly to the door of the imposing two-story brick house where the Simpsons lived, after the first two or three years. They were astonished and then pleased when the president met them in his blue homespun suit and his shock of uncropped hair, looking quite as much a farmer as they. They never forgot his hearty greeting and insistence that they come in; the quiet friendliness of the tall and slender young wife who at his call hurried in from the kitchen to meet the new students; the talk about Asbury and the studies they would pursue; the president's sparkling manner and his lively wit mixed in with pious sentiments; and finally the warm invitation to come again. If they thought Mrs. Simpson a little reserved, somewhat overnice in manner and dress, they soon learned that she was a good cook, given to heaping the food on the plates of guests, and was thoughtful of students who were ill, to whom she would often carry hot cornbread and steaming rice.[10]

Parents, anxious for the well-being of their sons, sought the president's personal supervision. Would he see to it that the boy boarded with a "religious family who would have special regard to his morals"? Would it be possible for a boy from Washington, D.C., to live in the Simpson home? Would he talk to Allen Wiley's son about one thing: "he sits in a kind of doubled up posture, which will injure him, for as he is now growing he will become permanently crooked." [11]

Matthew Simpson loved the boys of his school, but he had favorites, chief among them John Wheeler and James Harlan.

Wheeler, who had followed him from Allegheny College, lived with the family and became one of the three graduates of the first class. He went to Indianapolis after his graduation and opened a common school, delivered public lectures on natural philosophy, began the publication of a meteorological journal, and, with the help of equipment borrowed from Indiana Asbury, delivered public lectures on natural philosophy. To the great displeasure of Henry

Ward Beecher, he also fell in love with Mary Yanders, member of a prominent family in the Second Presbyterian Church. Mr. Beecher preferred to have his young parishioners marry within their own congregation, especially when the alternate choice was a Methodist. When the girl's father inquired about the young man Simpson wrote reassuringly of his religious and intellectual character, his amiability, energy, and industry. The father consented to the marriage. A year later, Wheeler became professor of Latin at Indiana Asbury. He was on the way to a college presidency in his own right.[12]

Harlan, an Indiana farm boy, entered the university in 1841. In homespun cotton clothes and homemade shoes without stockings, he had walked the eighteen miles from his father's farm with his belongings, including a few books, tied in a bundle and carried on a stick over his shoulder. He sought out the president and inquired, "Are you the man who keeps school here?"

Simpson, his blue eyes dancing, answered in the affirmative. Quizzing the new scholar, he found him alert and well informed but deficient in some prescribed courses. He therefore placed him in the preparatory department and recommended that he board at a farm home three miles from the campus, so that he could walk back and forth for his health.

Even the pittance required for his room and meals was, however, more than Harlan could afford, and so he begged permission to live in one of the unused rooms on the third floor of the college building and to cook for himself.

Harlan was no country bumpkin. Although his formal schooling was limited, he had borrowed books on history, geography, natural philosophy, and mechanics from the Park County Public Library at Rockville; and he had studied surveying and logarithms under a lawyer who boarded with his parents. He had even taught the district school for several terms. In the exciting political campaign of 1840 he had joined the pilgrimage to the battlefield of Tippecanoe and had listened eagerly to the great Whig orators. He had taught school one year in Rockville, had noted the superior air of the town-bred boys, and had felt discomfort in their presence.

At Indiana Asbury, after tremblingly surviving the first ordeal of declaiming in chapel, Harlan rapidly acquired self-confidence and poise, and skill in public speaking. Soon chosen for the public debate between the literary societies, he was twice named the president of his own society; he was much in demand as a speaker at Whig political rallies, and was active in the organization and instruction of Sunday schools. An outstanding student, he graduated with honors in 1845.

When Simpson promptly offered to name him as agent to collect funds for the college, Harlan declined. A year later a delegation of Methodists from Iowa appeared on the campus, seeking a principal for the new school and college they were establishing, and Simpson recommended Harlan. The committee offered him a position, which he accepted. The next year the people of Iowa elected him as the first state superintendent of public instruction, and he was launched on a political career which led precipitantly to the United States Senate and in 1865 to Abraham Lincoln's cabinet.[13]

III

As was his manner, Simpson crowded his Indiana hours and days with activities and new undertakings. Did he have a trip to make? He tucked a book into his saddlebags or satchel and read or journalized along the way. A preacher of camp-meeting sermons and an observer of the excited behavior of people at religious revivals, he was absorbed in Benjamin Rush's discussion of the effects of excessive joy, which, he noted, "produced madness in many of the successful adventures in the South Sea speculation in England in the year 1720," and sometimes caused Swiss soldiers in foreign countries to become "deranged" when they heard their native songs. He read Gibbon on the Roman Empire, Hallam on the history of literature, Bacon's *Organon*, Plato, Longinus *On the Sublime*, Lucretius, Fénelon, Scott, Byron.[14]

Early in his first year at Greencastle, while he was still preparing his inaugural address and searching for proof of the superiority of Christianity, he decided impulsively to study Arabic, and asked Uncle Matthew, who was in Cincinnati, to see if he could secure a grammar and lexicon. They could be had in Philadelphia, was the answer; but the grammar, lexicon, and a copy of the Scriptures would cost fifty to a hundred dollars. The price ought not to deter him from the purchase, Uncle Matthew thought, if he had the health and leisure to study a new language. Health and leisure he might have; but of money he had little. He had to abandon the project.[15]

If he could not study Arabic, he would write a book. What would Uncle Matthew think of a preacher's manual, a text on proper pulpit conduct, as well as the management of the society and the circuit?

Uncle Matthew did not think much of it. He doubted that any work on such a subject would be popular enough to defray the expense of printing. He feared, moreover, that neither Professor Simpson nor anyone else would have the courage to tell the truth. Would he not be tempted to "avoid enforcing unpopular truths," to overlook wrong thinking and bad practices in the pulpit, "especially if held or done by men of great influence?" It would be much better if the nephew's health permitted taking on such extra burdens, to write an answer to Mr. Annan, the Presbyterian, with whom he had quarreled at Pittsburgh, and who had since put his bitter diatribes against Methodism into a book. The Methodists at least would wish such a work success.[16]

As far as Uncle Matthew could see, attending to the business of the college was burden enough, and the "incessant labor" involved in attempting other projects would wear the young man down. A protest that Wesley had done much more brought down the rebuke: "Wesley's example proves nothing in your case; he was raised for a special purpose, to reform Protestantism . . . And for this purpose he was held up by a power far above human." [17]

None the less, young Matthew, not yet freed from youth's cycles of ambition and failure, introspection and self-scourging, planned projects which he could not complete, and rigid schedules to which he could not adhere. "Rose at four o'clock," he noted in his journal, and, on successive mornings: "Rose at 5 minutes after 4." "Rose 5 minutes before 5— By some means I am prone to become irregular in my habits." [18]

Charles Elliott, as much interested as Uncle Matthew in President Simpson, and still his benefactor and the instrument of Providence, undertook to induce Wesleyan University in Connecticut to confer the honorary Doctor of Divinity degree on his young protégé. Although much pleased with the prospect, Simpson was impatient with the long delay which ensued, and then, in turn, a little vain when he was finally notified that the degree had been bestowed. In the meantime, Professor Charles Anthon, author of an able and popular Latin prosody, dedicated the volume to him— an honor which Simpson was negligent in acknowledging. Uncle Matthew chided him: "A doctorate is a fine thing, but I should set a higher value on Mr. Anthons dedication of the Latin Prosody, for that implies that he considers you at least a judge of that work. But D. D. is as empty as an acorn shell and often conferred on those that know but little about Theology." [19]

On the whole, these early years in Indiana were rich and rewarding. Sometimes Matthew Simpson seemed to forget himself, his old feeling of "weakness" and "inability," the morbid, introspective fears of his young manhood. Faced with the increasing success of the college, he dared to "lay large plans for future action . . . to enjoy the idea of mingling with the world, and moulding to some extent the public mind." He even dreamed of success in all his "enterprises." [20]

There was the college itself. Travelers to Greencastle, when they came to the first break in the dense forest, expressed astonishment at the red-brick building rising three stories high. Matthew, too, after his long trips into the countryside, knew the thrill of coming suddenly upon the clearing and seeing the great red wall and white cupola against the green woods and the blue sky; but he knew even better the wild ringing of the bell when some student, learning of his return, called the others to shake his hand and welcome him back to the campus. He knew, also, the slower peal of the bell, calling students to prayer, its imperious tones announcing the beginning of classes, or its gay call to dinner. [21]

He was as well pleased with his home life as with the college. After a year or two in rented houses, he and Ellen built a high-gabled, two-story brick building adjacent to the campus. The students called frequently, visiting preachers stayed with them at commencement time, John and Mary Wheeler were in and out like members of the family. Edward R. Ames, who at the General Conference of 1840 was elected Missionary Secretary for the West, moved his family to Greencastle, and he and "Sister" Ames became frequent callers. Brother Ames, back now and then from travels in the West, brought news and gossip of the church and its officials, and grave talk of politics and the Methodist difficulties with the Presbyterians.

Matthew Simpson liked best the long winter evenings when he sat before the fire with "some musty old volume" in his hand, and his feet on the fender. There was Jimmy, his oldest son, in the light of the flaming fire on the hearth, "earnestly engaged in fathoming the awful mysteries of a-b-ab," and on the floor, all about the room, little Charley, his second son, cutting antics. Ellen would sit, work basket in her lap, rocking to and fro, stitching a garment for one of the children, or knitting a sweater for her husband. Now and then she would interrupt to ask about some household matter or to tease from Matthew some bit of gossip concerning the college or the church. Charley had been born in the first summer at Greencastle; in the next four years Ellen gave birth to two daughters, Anna and Mathilda. Matthew jiggled them on his knee and cooed to them when they were well and happy, pressed their warm, soft bodies to his own when they were hurt and cried for comfort, sat up nights with them when they suffered with the croup, even stayed home from his classes and the office when the croup was serious.[22]

In January of 1842, before the birth of the little girls, tragedy struck swiftly and unexpectedly. Four-year-old Jimmy, active and healthy, was suddenly stricken ill, and died. The great bell of the college tolled out a solemn dirge, and the neighbors gathered to stand or sit quietly, and to mourn with Matthew and Ellen.

Uncle Matthew tried to give comfort with the thought that little James had been "placed beyond the reach of sin or pain and of death among the spirits of just men made perfect,"[23] but the young college president would not be comforted. He could read in his loss only the judgment of God. He had been wrong to dream of success, to believe that he had achieved so much. He was after all "a mere drone in the great human hive." It was wrong for him, possessed of a nature "so defective and impure," to live upon the resources of the church, to talk of things that he knew so little about, to instruct when most of all he needed to be taught.

Ellen, unable to bear the sorrow, went home to Pittsburgh, taking little Charles. Her husband remained at his duties, mourning over his loss, perplexed by the contradictions of God, overwhelmed by loneliness.

He could not get out of his mind the little boy climbing upon his knee, begging for a story; the round, rosy cheeks, the soft voice; and then, in the box at home, the forehead "so smooth and cold," that he and Ellen had kissed before they laid him away.

He could not comprehend his loneliness. It was as though there were not one heart in the universe that beat in unison with his own, as though he stood alone, "like some solitary tree on a little island with the wild waves . . . washing away the evil" from about his roots, or like "a tree struck in mid-summer by the scathing lightning which has torn the bark and turned to yellow paleness the leaves that but yesterday were beautifully green." Granted only the presence of Ellen and Charles, he could perhaps have had brighter thoughts—even of a fairer world, of a "grace which may make it possible even for me to become an heir of a joyful immortality." [24]

IX

"BLUE PUP" AND INDIANA
POLITICS

WHEN Matthew Simpson moved to Indiana in 1839 he was cheered by the financial prospect of Indiana Asbury University. The total subscription of funds stood at $60,000, and the two agents of the college confidently expected another $20,000 by the fall. Construction costs were low, brick for the new building was to be burned on the campus, and a large percentage of the subscriptions could go into a permanent endowment fund. Simpson, unable to collect his salary at Allegheny, or even to sell the few household goods he had left behind, looked upon his new circumstances with relief and satisfaction.[1]

Indiana, feverishly engaged in building canals, railroads, and turnpikes, had suffered less from the staggering Panic of 1837 than most of the nation; but the effect had been postponed, not averted. Legislation authorizing internal improvements, a gigantic pork barrel which promised a railroad, a turnpike, or a canal to nearly every county in Indiana, overtaxed the resources of the state. In August, four months after Simpson's arrival, the board in control of internal improvements had to suspend work on all projects. Depression spread, paralyzing trade and darkening the doors of business. The currency, bolstered by the legislature, held reasonably firm until 1842 but then suddenly depreciated from 40 to 50 per cent. The market was flooded with bank notes, bank scrip, and canal scrip—the last variously called "white dog," "red dog," "blue dog," and "blue pup." [2]

The promising subscription to the university shrank until it was scarcely enough to pay for the building. The "permanent" endowment vanished like a spark from Matthew's electric machine, a spectacular but fleeting phenomenon: subscribers, unable to secure

specie or even bank notes, wrote off their pledges in the worthless
scrip of the Wabash and Erie Canal. Concluding his first year as
president, Simpson had to report a deficit of $449.02; and the in-
debtedness grew by 1842 to $4,610.26. The board had to pay the pro-
fessors in its own scrip.

Professor Larrabee began to look about for another position,
and arrogant young Professor Benjamin Tefft, whom Simpson had
brought from upstate New York and New England to teach Greek,
threatened to resign. The president himself, in a "great pinch" for
money, now and then borrowed from his uncle on a strictly business
basis, promising to pay on demand, with interest. He even ventured
briefly into the merchandise business—hard-shell almonds, plows,
rock candy, and other items which Uncle Matthew sent out from Cincinnati; and, caught up in the feverish excitement of Indiana pro-
motional schemes, he began to speculate a little with his wife's
money in real estate, railroad stock, and short-term loans.[3]

Although the professors suffered from the depression they did
as well as the preachers, or better. In southern Indiana, Isaac Owen,
agent for the university and "the greatest beggar on earth," obtained nearly seven hundred dollars in subscriptions for the college
while the junior preacher on the circuit could collect only $7.50
for the first quarter of his year's salary. The people, Owen reported,
would subscribe for the college when they would do nothing for
the church, and scarcely anything for the preachers.[4]

Acting on this observation, Simpson prepared a plan for raising money, and an address to whip his brethren into action. Apply-
ing the lash where the flesh was still tender, he reminded them that
there had been a time when the Methodists of Indiana had no
college, when, in spite of being the most numerous religious body
in the state, they had no part in the management of the public
institution. Even now, when Asbury enrolled more students than
any other college in Indiana, critics stigmatized it as the "Poor Man's
College," or denounced it as "sectarian." "Ah, brethren, I have
misjudged both your intelligence and piety if such a course will
have any other effect than to awaken pity for your enemies, and to
show them by your acts that you are both able and willing to rally
unitedly around your own university." There were more than 50,000
Methodists in Indiana; if each gave forty cents, there would be
enough at least to buy philosophical equipment and a magnificent

library. Every preacher must become an agent, must request every friend and member to give. Quite aside from the forty cents, they could raise $20,000 if two hundred would give $25, a thousand give $10, and another thousand give $5.[5]

The board, impressed with the need and with Simpson's plan, adopted it in modified form. Each Methodist was asked to contribute a dollar a year for ten years, and, after 1844, each of the two conferences to raise $2,000.[6]

I I

The preachers quickly saw, however, that the key to the success of any fund-raising plan was not the presence of agents in the field, nor their own pleas to members, but the preaching of Matthew Simpson. He was not only a remarkable preacher but, what the college agents were not, a man of learning and an able combatant for the anti-Methodist forces.

The Presbyterian colleges at Wabash and Hanover, as hard put by the depression as was Indiana Asbury, also had agents out seeking support from the people; these men, who were college-educated, did not hesitate to raise doubts about Methodist learning, and to revive Senator Bigger's question as to the ability of the Methodists to conduct a college. The only answer was to let the people listen to Simpson.

The preachers overwhelmed him with invitations to quarterly meetings, camp meetings, dedications, Sabbath-school conventions, debates against Calvinists. They tried to bribe him: one thought his presence would increase donations for the library and philosophical apparatus; another had "three boys on the stocks" ready to launch for Asbury; a third had to have his help against "this Crawfordsville thing." Up in Fort Wayne, the people were mightily stirred and the harvest was ripe, but the Methodist preacher was "unable to gather it": Simpson must come immediately, or the Beechers—Lyman, Henry Ward, and all the rest—who were due soon, "must reap the advantage." [7]

In the fall of 1841, the annual conference petitioned the Indiana Asbury board of trustees to make arrangements for its president to travel in the state during the summer months. The trustees approved, and, in the summer of 1842, he set out on horse-back, riding north through Crawfordsville and Lafayette to South Bend, and on into Michigan. In 1843, traveling by horse and buggy, and frequently attended by circuit riders and Methodist business-men and their "ladies," he toured the southwest section of Indiana. On a circuit of six hundred miles he delivered forty-three sermons and thirty-three lectures on education.[8]

Whatever the effect of his travels upon the university and the people of Indiana, the benefits to himself were incalculable. The Methodists had long believed that the itinerant ministry was ideally suited to the training of preachers and pulpit orators. Traveling from place to place, the circuit rider preached the same sermon over and over, enlarging, polishing, and refining. "It is very seldom," Simpson said to the Yale College students many years later, "that a sermon can be very ably wrought out by the first effort of either speaker or writer." [9] There on the Indiana frontier he began to test the themes which later marked him as the most eloquent voice of Methodism.

Out in the state the people who came to hear him ran the same gamut of emotions that the congregation at Greencastle had experienced on his first Sunday morning in Indiana. Eager to hear the new president, they were shocked and disappointed by his appearance. Tall, stooped, and ungainly, he was dressed not in the broadcloth store clothes worn by E. R. Ames and William M. Daily, but in the homespun blue jeans of the farmer. When he began to speak the effect was heightened by the contrast between his "unpromising appearance" and his "over-powering eloquence." The people listened with an apprehension which soon changed to pleasure and then quickened to exhilaration and occasionally to unrestrained shouting and weeping.

He preached different sermons from different texts, but always with the same theme and in the same manner: over against the hardships of the Christian church, and of Methodism and Methodists in particular, he set the glorious triumph of the church eternal and the life everlasting. He had learned to paint with words—pictures with such sharp detail and vivid color that the people cried out in pain or anguish, in joy or ecstasy. Argument played little part: like the fabled artist, he painted with the blood of life, taking his colors from the stream of human experience. The people, watching him at work and viewing the portraits, were prostrated with joy or grief.

He developed a pattern of eloquence which audiences came to recognize and expect. He began indifferently, but soon was transformed: he appeared to grow in stature, his stooping shoulders straightened, his face lighted up until it became "radiant with thought," his high thin voice deepened into tones of "wonderful pathos," and his eye kindled and flashed.[10]

Men who had sat under his spell were not able, in other circumstances, to divest him of the aura which surrounded him in the pulpit. On his travels about the state laymen and preachers alike extended the hospitality of the "better" homes. Joseph A. Wright, successful lawyer and aspiring politician of Rockville, became his friend. John Evans, young and enterprising Quaker physician from Fountain County, first "turned thought to God" one night in a mill house where President Simpson preached on "Lord, Show Me Thy Glory." Impressed by the speaker's views on education and religion, Evans soon became a Methodist. Thus began a warm friendship which extended over nearly half a century, and a union of interests which was exerted time and again in behalf of Methodism and its institutions.[11]

Lucien Berry, tall and dark, a brilliant preacher famous for a three-day debate with a Universalist preacher, was drawn to Simpson by an intellectual compatibility, a common hunger for knowledge, and a common evangelical zeal. Together they planned and plotted for the welfare of Indiana Asbury and looked forward to the day when the prejudice of the church against preacher training institutions would relax sufficiently to permit Berry to join the college as professor of theology.[12]

Closest among the president's friends, next to Berry, was the impetuous William M. Daily. In sharp contrast to the staid and circumspect Simpson, he was frequently under suspicion in the conference of conduct unbecoming a minister. Once he was censured for "unministerial and unchristian intimacy" with a married woman; namely, "laying your arms around her and kissing her in the absence of company." But he could preach, and he was a man of some learning. Entering the pulpit at sixteen, he had become famous as the "boy preacher"; and he had been admitted to the conference at nineteen. In his youth he had made it a practice to rise early to study; and he had read his books diligently as he traveled on horseback on the circuit. A graduate of Indiana University, he had taught one year at St. Charles College in Missouri. Simpson defended him once, vigorously, when suspicious members of the conference wrongly charged him with infractions of the code. Daily, who was used to fighting his own battles, was overcome with emotion. Simpson had made an impression on his heart which could "never be effaced"—he had found at last the man who "dared to do right," the "loving, generous hearted christian, and Methodist Preacher." [13]

There were other close friends and admirers: the Reverend John Bayless, who advised him on his land speculations; John L. Smith, preacher and agent for the university, who saw a great future for its president; Thomas M. Eddy, junior preacher and future editor of the church, who, knowing and admiring Simpson's power as a preacher, once raised a plank to the window of a church and crawled up it to secure a seat before the doors opened; Father James Havens, who had been on the committee to establish a "conference seminary"; and even Edward R. Ames, Missionary Secretary for the western area and resident of Greencastle, who would be Simpson's chief competitor for the honors of the church.

The people of the state, the Methodists who filled the pews and crowded the benches at camp meeting, learned to admire and love Simpson not only for his oratory but for his commonness. College president though he was, and eloquent speaker, he was one of them in the simplicity of his manners and the coarseness of his clothes. They liked to hear and to tell the story of his dedication of a church in Ohio, where the responsible citizens, anxious to make an impression upon the visiting college president, had arranged for him to be the guest in the home of Thomas Parrott, one of the wealthier residents. Parrott had invited in a number of community leaders to have supper with the eminent visitor that evening.

The stage was late, no one was waiting to meet him. Dr. Simpson walked to Parrott's home, his valise in hand. The oldest daughter answered the bell. Assuming the tall, uncouth stranger before her was one of the local preachers also assigned to the Parrotts, she invited him in and announced that there was a "plain-looking man" in the parlor.

"Prepare him a place at the corner of the table," her father said, "and I will come down and see him."

As the stranger sat eating the food that was brought Parrott approached and said:

"We are expecting Dr. Simpson to arrive from Greencastle to dedicate our church tomorrow, and we have delayed supper for him."

The stranger looked up, with a characteristic twinkle in his eye.

"That," he said, "is the name they call me by at home."

After a moment of embarrassed silence the host called in his other guests, and they all sat down to a pleasant evening.

The next day Parrott accompanied the illustrious if ill-favored guest to the dedication exercises, and fell under the spell of his eloquence. "There is no judging from people's looks," he said, "what they can do or who they are." [14]

III

The denominational jealousy toward the state university, the bitter sectarian rivalries among the church schools, the desperate financial struggle of Indiana Asbury, and Matthew Simpson's growing eminence as preacher and orator—these factors acting and reacting upon one another constituted a polygon of forces which propelled him irresistibly into state politics.

He was extremely sensitive to Presbyterian contempt of Methodist learning and was incurably suspicious of Presbyterian motives. In September, 1839, fire destroyed the main building of the New School Presbyterian college. Unable to raise the money for reconstruction, the Wabash College authorities cast about for a loan and hit upon a happy idea. The sinking fund set up by the state to stabilize the banks, was to go to the support of public education when the banks fully repaid their loans. Why should not a small part of the more than a million dollars in it be loaned to the college? Wabash College promptly applied to the commissioners of the fund and received a loan of $8,000 on which interest was to be paid annually, in advance. When the college defaulted on its interest payments in the financial collapse of 1842, friends rushed to the legislature and obtained the suspension of interest payments until December 31, 1846.[15]

In the meantime, the Presbyterians inflamed Methodist suspicions by what seemed to be an open attempt to gain control of the common schools and the sinking fund. While the legislature of 1842–1843 was in session Henry Ward Beecher, Samuel Merrill, James M. Ray, and others sponsored a convention on education. Beecher was pastor of the Second Presbyterian Church of Indianapolis, and Merrill was the president of the State Bank and the leading member of his church; both were trustees of Wabash College. Ray, also a Presbyterian, was the cashier of the bank. On the day before the convention, Beecher, Merrill, and Ray met secretly in the bank, named themselves the principal officers of the convention, and invited Governor Samuel Bigger, a Presbyterian, to preside over it.

Simpson's friends now began to create a considerable disturbance, and the organizers of the convention thought well to request him to address it. He promptly declined, and the word went forth among the Methodists that he had been publicly insulted.[16]

Bigger, elected governor in 1840, was the member of the state legislature who had spoken so derisively of Methodist educators in 1834. Simpson began to suspect influence and favoritism in high places. Bigger, he reminded his Methodist friends, had said there was "not a Methodist in America with sufficient learning to fill a professor's chair." [17]

Simpson's dissatisfaction spread like an irritating rash among the Methodists; but it was catching among the Whigs, too, and soon reached the governor. Alarmed at the prospect of losing Methodist support in the coming summer's campaign for reelection, Bigger called for help. L. G. Thompson of Fort Wayne, a prominent Methodist physician who was also a Whig, brought Simpson, E. R. Ames, S. C. Cooper (Indiana Asbury agent), to a meeting in the governor's office. Simpson repeated his charges, and Bigger hotly denied having been moved by contempt, or having uttered derogatory remarks about Methodist educators such as had been attributed to him. Scarcely convinced, but unwilling to call the governor a liar, Simpson promised not to repeat the charges. Ames, an ardent Democrat and a skillful politician, looked on with satisfaction while he began to calculate the political power of the "Amen corner" of the Methodist Episcopal Church.[18]

In the spring of 1843 the Whigs, as expected, nominated Bigger for reelection. To oppose him, the Democrats named James Whitcomb, who attended a Methodist church and was a strong supporter of the Methodist cause. It was generally assumed by the Whigs, and conceded by the Democrats, that Methodists and Presbyterians alike were predominantly Whigs. In this campaign, however, the Democrats, noting the tenseness of the denominational struggle, saw an opportunity to break a large segment of the Methodist vote off from the Whig party.

The *State Sentinel*, a Democratic paper published in Indianapolis, opened the campaign with a cleverly conceived rumor that the Whigs were attacking Whitcomb because he was a Methodist. The Lafayette *Advertiser*, also Democratic, added that his being a Methodist ought to be "a recommendation instead of an objection." "What," it exclaimed piously, "has it come to that, that a desperate political press shall urge it as an objection to James Whitcomb . . . that he is a Christian!" [19]

The Whigs, alarmed by the turn of affairs, wheeled out their biggest gun, Noah Noble, former governor and a worshiper in Lucien Berry's Methodist chapel in Indianapolis. Noble and others issued an "Appeal to Methodists" in the Whig *Indiana State Journal*, denying that the Whig press had ever made any such objection to Whitcomb, and calling on the *State Sentinel* and the *Advertiser* to produce their evidence.[20]

The *State Sentinel* answered by taunting the Whigs. Subtly reviving the anti-Methodist charge against Bigger, it opined that "enlightened" Methodists were not "to be insulted to their faces by the highest dignitary in the State, and then do the bidding of men, one of whom, at least, had been refused admission, even on a probationary basis," to the Methodist Church.[21]

President Simpson, on a speaking tour in southeastern Indiana in behalf of his university, found himself embroiled in the political battle. A literalist when the occasion demanded, he adhered strictly to his pledge not to repeat the charges against Governor Bigger. But in his conversation and in his lecture on education he gave the definite impression that Methodists were "competent" to conduct their own educational enterprises, notwithstanding the opinion of persons "high in authority." Some who sat in his audience or heard reports of his speeches thought that his allusions to the governor were plain enough. Ready to magnify their significance, or to read into them what he had not said, they reported to Bigger that the president of Indiana Asbury, ostensibly on the circuit to raise money for his college, was actually on an anti-Whig electioneering expedition.[22]

The flame burned high in Indianapolis and lighted up the far corners of the state. The editor of the *Indiana State Journal* heard from twenty "veritable sources" that Simpson was trying to defeat Bigger. Lucien Berry, an ardent Whig but a more ardent Methodist, reported delightedly that in forty-eight hours there had been scarcely a half-hour in which he had not received a visit or a note from some leading Whig or Democrat, anxious to know the truth about Governor Bigger, Simpson, and the Methodists.[23]

Beecher, Ray, Merrill, and company were incensed by Simpson's politicking. They denounced his electioneering; they discredited the Bigger stories; they denied that Simpson had been affronted at the educational convention; they affirmed that he had been invited early to address it but had refused "in order to create sympathy & make the publick believe he was overlooked." Beecher was goaded into the egregious blunder of castigating "P-r-e-s-i-d-e-n-t S-i-m-p-s-o-n" at the Wabash College commencement exercises for meddling with the educational convention and attempting to thwart its purpose.[24]

A Methodist straightway reported this to the receptive *State Sentinel.* The editor of the Whiggish *Indiana State Journal* hastened to reply; but unhappily he revealed more than the public was supposed to know. Wise Methodists, he said, would regard the attempt to visit the supposed sins of Mr. Beecher upon Governor Bigger as "an insult to their sense." Besides, Mr. Beecher, who of course would not "notice, in the least degree, an anonymous correspondent," had assured the editor that the tale of his castigation of President Simpson was "false in every sense." [25]

Lucien Berry could restrain himself no longer. In a cleverly written anonymous letter he exposed Beecher, Merrill, and Ray, gave further credence to the rumors about the governor, and accused the *Journal* of intrigue. Why did the editor of the *Journal* connect Beecher's insult to President Simpson with the campaign of Governor Bigger? The public knew of no such connection. Was it because the editor knew that Beecher, Merrill, and Ray had met in the bank to elect themselves officers of the convention? Did he mean to insinuate that, because the governor *"happened* to be called to preside, therefore, they *all* conspired to insult Simpson, and Cooper, and Ames, and all of the Church, by forcibly excluding them from any participation?" Furthermore, Berry wrote with sarcasm, he was too well acquainted with Beecher's "character for veracity" to believe he had declared the story "false in every sense." Too many men who had heard Beecher at Crawfordsville were willing to say that the story was "TRUE IN NEARLY EVERY SENSE." [26]

Democrats intrigued with Methodists to get the Beecher speech published. An excited Whig dared the Methodists "to vote against us. . . . if they do, THE WHIG PARTY WILL BLOW THEIR COLLEGE AND CHURCH TO HELL." [27]

Simpson's interest in the campaign was quickened also by the political activities of his friends Joseph Wright and John Evans. Wright, a member of the state legislature and a trustee of Indiana Asbury, was a candidate for the United States Congress. Dr. Evans, having vainly tried to secure Governor Bigger's support for reform measures, particularly in the care of the insane, was directing a Whig revolt against him in Fountain County.

In the mid-August election, with a total of 110,000 votes, Whitcomb won over Bigger by the narrow margin of 2,000. It was the first Democratic victory in a decade. In Fountain County, where Dr. Evans, a Whig, had campaigned against his own party, Whitcomb led his opponent decisively. In the Seventh Congressional district Joseph Wright squeaked through by a majority of three votes.[28]

The *Indiana Whig* charged the Methodists with voting "almost to a man" against Bigger, and the Bloomington *Post* warned the Methodists to "look well to the safety" of their college. An "insulted and exasperated" public would wreak vengeance upon an institution whose "holy head" would go through the country "making political speeches in behalf of so base a hypocrite" as James Whitcomb. The editor of the *State Journal*, perceiving that the Methodists must not be permanently alienated from the Whig party, repudiated the charges of the *Post*. The Locofocos might have kept a few Methodists from voting for Bigger, he wrote, but an analysis of the returns would show that Whitcomb had received 6,000 votes fewer than the electorate had given to Bigger in 1840. The trouble was that the "slumbering mass" of Whigs had stayed at home, not bothering to vote.[29]

That winter, when the legislature convened, the senate committee on education was "pleased" to invite President Simpson to deliver a "public address" on education, and he accepted. In January a Methodist member of the Whig nominating committee proposed Simpson for a place on the Whig Electoral ticket; he declined. When the new governor entered upon his duties he promptly recommended the establishment of a hospital for the insane and named Dr. Evans as the first superintendent; and he appointed Simpson to the board of directors of a proposed school for the deaf and dumb.[30]

In the meantime, Joseph Wright discovered seven other Methodists in Congress and organized a weekly prayer meeting and a class meeting which convened at sunrise on the Sabbath. He pleaded with Simpson to travel through Washington on his trip East next spring and preach at the Methodist chapel there. When Simpson and Berry sought the exercise of his influence with President Tyler for the appointment of Samuel Henderson (who had so warmly "espoused the cause of Methodism *versus* Bigger") to the Indianapolis postmastership, Wright happily complied. In a short time he was able to report that the President had sent Henderson's name to the United States Senate for confirmation.[31] The Methodists were doing well in Indiana politics.

However, the matter which had precipitated the whole struggle, the Wabash College loan from the sinking fund, had not been settled. The grace period extended to December, 1846, and the convening of the legislature after Whitcomb's second gubernatorial campaign. Whitcomb being reelected and political affairs settled, friends of Wabash College in the legislature brought in a bill to write off the college's indebtedness, now grown to $10,600. The college, in lieu of payment of the debt, would surrender bonds (which were worthless) and would give five years' free instruction to some one hundred young men, one from each county, who wished to become common-school teachers.[32]

Berry, in accordance with Methodist practice, had been sent

on to another station, but John Bayless, his successor at Indianapolis, had quite as deep a concern for Methodist interests. Alarmed at the prospect of establishing all over the state one hundred "preparatory departments" for Wabash (an advantage he would give ten years' labor to secure for Asbury), he begged Simpson to come to Indianapolis "without delay." [33]

Simpson and Ames (of whom it was said that he ruled the governor) hurried to the capital to try to defeat the bill. It was soon rumored that, although the legislature had passed the Wabash bill, Governor Whitcomb would veto it. The rumors were correct. The governor vetoed the bill, and there was loud talk about the "influence" which had been brought to bear upon him, and murmurs about the Bigger affair. The Methodists were jubilant, but the "visage of Mr. Beecher" was ghastly.[34]

It was not long before the blood returned to Beecher's face. In rejecting the bill, the wily governor had held his veto until the last moment allotted him by law; it arrived at the legislature at a doubtful hour, and the senate overrode it. The "iniquitous" Wabash College bill became law.[35]

Berry, in his new post at Oxford, Ohio, was furious with the legislature and not a little surprised at the failure of Simpson, Ames, and Bayless to defeat the New School Presbyterians. He could find only one consoling thought in the transaction: The next common-school convention would recommend the appointment of a state superintendent of public instruction, and the legislature, after having "petted and favored" the New School Presbyterians, would not dare deny the superintendency to the Methodists.

He was wrong in the details but right in the results. Five years later when the state of Indiana was ready to name its first superintendent of public instruction, it chose William C. Larrabee, Methodist preacher and professor of mathematics at Indiana Asbury University.

X

"NO SHADING OFF ... FROM

RIGHT TO WRONG"

PRESIDENT SIMPSON'S subtle participation in the Bigger campaign angered the Whig politicians; but it in no way impaired his standing among the Methodist preachers. The Indiana annual conference in the fall of 1843 elected him on the first ballot to head its delegation to the quadrennial general conference of the church in New York City the following May.

The general conference was the supreme legislative and judicial body of the church; it elected bishops, editors, and other officers, served as the final court of appeals in ecclesiastical cases, and enacted the laws by which the denomination was governed. The Indiana annual conference of two hundred preachers was entitled to only eight delegates. Election therefore was a signal honor, the highest in the power of the conference—enhanced in Simpson's case by the fact that he was but thirty-two years old and had lived in Indiana only four years.

He made careful preparation for the trip and the conference. Feeling, in the Wesley tradition, the weight of his responsibility, he solemnly set down in his memorandum book several "projects" to propose to the general conference. All had to do with church polity: fixing the time of annual conferences, giving the bishops power to make interim appointments to the offices of the general conference, and permitting editors and other officers of the church to hold membership in the conference of their choice.[1]

To the details of the trip East, Simpson gave much more attention. He was young, there was a world to see, and he must see it. He carefully laid out his itinerary, jotting down the items which he wished to see: the statehouse at Harrisburg, Pool's farm at Hagerstown, Harpers Ferry. At Washington he would visit Joe

Wright, see the Patent Office, the President's house, examine the census return for possible advantages to Asbury. At Baltimore he would see the Washington Monument and the Eutaw Street church where Bishop Asbury was buried; at Philadelphia, the water works and Girard College.[2]

He held a certificate from Governor James Whitcomb stating that he was a trustee of the state asylum for the education of the deaf and dumb, and requesting officials of other states to permit him to visit their institutions, and to look particularly at the *"internal economy* . . . and upon those *minute practical details."* There were also items to be bought in New York: a watch and key, a shawl, a skirt, print and gingham, alpaca, and gloves, for Ellen; books for himself; and favors for the children.[3]

In the middle of March, six weeks before the conference, Simpson and E. R. Ames, who was also a delegate, set out for New York City. Mrs. Simpson and four-year-old Charles and little Anna traveled with them to Pittsburgh and two young women went along as far as Cincinnati. The weather was crisp, and the roads muddy; but the company were in fine spirits, and the gay and lively conversation was punctuated now and then by the protests and screams of the ladies as the wagon plunged into a deep hole or hit a slippery spot.

On the fourth day out Brother Ames discovered that his carpetbag had come loose from the side of the wagon and dropped along the way. Already delayed by mud and snow and the rough road, they could not lose more time if they were to make their train connection at Columbus, Indiana. Ames came to the rescue. Sending the wagoner back to hunt for the bag, he himself turned teamster. Mounting the saddle horse, which had no saddle and had a back "as sharp as a Nor'wester," he rested his feet on the trace chains, gathered the reins in one hand, and held a large beech stick erect over his shoulder for a whip. When he shouted to the horses they tugged at the traces, and the large red wagon with the white muslin cover began to roll. "All together," wrote Simpson, "not a bad subject for a Cruikshank or a Chapman."

The wagoner recovered the bag and overtook the party at Columbus, and they reached the "cars" with only minutes to spare. They rode the train to Madison, where they took a steamboat up the Ohio to Cincinnati, docking at daybreak on Sunday.

They had three busy days in Cincinnati—visiting Simpson's mother and Uncle Matthew, his sister Hetty and her husband George McCullough, letting the children run and play and stretch their legs from the long ride, going to church on Sunday morning and evening, and hearing their old friend Charles Elliott preach.

On Monday morning Simpson began to pay his bills: $26.25 to George McCullough; interest payments of $22 to his mother and $6.85 to Uncle Matthew for money he had borrowed; $70 to Moore & Co. for books for the university. He and Ellen went shopping, too: silk and laces, edgings, corsets, and side combs for Ellen; shoes and stockings, candy, nuts, and apples for the children.

At the Methodist bookstore he found a number of preachers en route to the conference who, stopping over the Sabbath in Cincinnati, congregated now at the western headquarters to catch up on the news. Around the fire and at the book counters, they boasted of the gains on their circuits and speculated about the candidates for bishop. The Ohio delegates thought that Elliott would run strongly—both Ohio and Kentucky would go for him. There was a little talk about slavery, but no one was greatly concerned.[4]

On Tuesday afternoon Simpson's mother and Uncle Matthew joined the travelers for the trip up the river as far as Wheeling. Although the *Majestic* plowed very creditably ten to twelve miles an hour against the stream, it was a long, slow trip of more than four hundred miles to Pittsburgh, with many stops.

Matthew Simpson rose early at Wheeling to help his mother and Uncle Matthew onto the gangplank, on their way to Cadiz. It was three o'clock in the morning. There on the dark, cold deck he slipped and fell, striking his leg against an iron bar, and bruising and tearing the flesh. When the boat reached Pittsburgh on Friday evening the leg was badly swollen. The doctor ordered him to bed, insisted that he cancel his Sabbath preaching engagements and postpone the continuation of his trip. On Monday, Ames went on without him.

The delay was not altogether unpleasant. In the comfortable home of Ellen's father, he journalized and read, and received a steady stream of old Pittsburgh friends. They begged him to return to the conference. They needed an editor for the Pittsburgh *Christian Advocate*. The recent election of delegates to the general conference had aroused a good deal of dissension, which the editor could not quiet. The former editor, Will Hunter, perhaps could be persuaded to accept the office again, but Matthew Simpson was the man they needed. He was pleased by the suggestion, but demurred. His work in Indiana was not done.

After a week in bed he was able to get around, and to make his final preparations for the trip. Accompanied by little Charles, he went downtown, purchased a penknife and a pencil for himself, a twenty-five-cent hat for Charles, and two volumes for travel reading: Bishop Emory's compact little history of the discipline of the Methodist Church, and the account of an English Methodist preacher's impression of American Methodism and the general conference of 1836.[5] On Sunday he preached at Liberty and Smithfield churches, and noted that the congregations were smaller than they had been in his time. On Monday he left Pittsburgh on the canal boat *Kentucky* for Baltimore and Washington.

He was much impressed by the "grand and magnificent scenery" of the Alleghenies: the summits rising 1,150 feet above Johnstown and 1,400 above Hollidaysburg; the winding valley of the Juniata; the perpendicular strata of limestone which seemed to have been thrown up by some great convulsion, and now and then resembled mighty cathedrals. He had a fright at Hollidaysburg when on a downgrade the brakes failed to hold and the cars rushed down the incline with increasing momentum until they were brought to a stop just short of the canal.

At Baltimore, where he stopped for the Sabbath, he tramped the streets that Bishop Asbury had trod, and visited the Eutaw Street church where the great bishop was buried, musing the while on the humble beginnings and the magnificent achievements of American Methodism.

He stayed a week at Washington, saw Joe Wright, visited the Capitol, the White House, the Patent Office, Mount Vernon, and the shad fishery at Alexandria. He met President Tyler: "a very plain man, affable and courteous, but sufficiently dignified." He was "mortified" at the "exhibition of decay" in the White House furniture. The chairs were covered with linen to hide the ragged seats, and the window curtains were "much the worse for wear."

On the front steps of the Capitol his attention was drawn to a group of statuary, the figures of nude women, commemorating the services and death of Richard Somers, a United States naval hero. He thought the work of art "fine"; but he thought also that "different views might be entertained as to the propriety of presenting the figures in a state of nudity or nearly so." The matter seemed to have been decided by an "ancient taste" which modern sculptors were fond of copying. But of one thing he was certain: "the present State of Society would not allow such exhibitions of the female form as would be necessary to give artists proper models for such statuary." The fact that the Greeks were not so "sensitive" gave modern sculptors "fine opportunities of studying their models." [6]

II

Not until they approached New York did many of the delegates, including Simpson, have any foreboding that tragedy awaited the church. Their talk had been mostly of church politics—the election of bishops and editors. The conference itself, they believed, would be quiet; but there might be an exciting race for bishop, and Ames might be a candidate. Then just before they reached New York came the rumor, spreading like fire in prairie grass, that Bishop Andrew had become the owner of slaves through marriage. Simpson trusted and loved Andrew, the bishop who had ordained him, and who only the previous fall, on a visit to the Indiana Asbury campus, had prophesied a great future for the school. He therefore dismissed the evil word as only a rumor. If the bishop had married a slave-owning lady, he must have made some satisfactory arrangement for the slaves.[7]

The slavery problem had not troubled Simpson greatly since leaving the Pittsburgh conference. The subject was not much agitated in Indiana. Even the Quakers forbade the use of their meetinghouses for antislavery lectures.[8]

Uncle Matthew, it was true, had continued to prod him gently. Down in Cincinnati he had aroused the wrath and "Patriarchal temper" of good Methodists, some of whom lived in Ohio and held slaves in Kentucky. A few leaders of the church, officers of the Western Book Concern, had denounced his opinions as those of "Mobocrats, disorganizers," and "rebels against the laws of the land," which his "sensible" young nephew would certainly condemn.

However keen the conflict in Cincinnati, Uncle Matthew did not choose to involve that sensible young nephew in his own quarrels, and therefore had declined his invitation to visit the Indiana annual conference. Some one might "speak evil" in his presence, and he would feel obliged to defend his principles, even though it "mortified" his nephew. He would, therefore, remain at home.[9]

For half a dozen years the bishops had suppressed the abolitionist movement among the Methodists in New England. They had not succeeded, however, in extinguishing the antislavery fire. Smoldering in the majority of northern conferences, abolitionism broke out in the early 1840's in a score of places and its flames threatened material damage to institutional Methodism. By 1843 between six and eight thousand laymen and about one hundred and fifty ministers, under Orange Scott, had seceded to organize the antislavery Wesleyan Methodist Church.

The whole church was alarmed by this exodus. The bishops relaxed their rule over the annual conferences, permitted members to talk against slavery, and even appointed some abolitionist preachers. Several conferences introduced resolutions to strengthen the general rule of the discipline on slavery. The Indiana conference, presided over by James Andrew, endorsed one of these resolutions by the overwhelming vote of 91 to 11.[10]

The changed attitude of the bishops and the vigorous proposals of the northern conferences, although arousing the suspicions of the South, checked the exodus of the abolitionists. Many of them elected to stay with the "old church." Thomas E. Bond, editor of the New York *Christian Advocate,* pronounced the threats of further secession to be the "harmless puffings of an extinct volcano."[11] With that view Simpson was in complete accord. Somewhat apprehensive about the Andrew rumor, he was still confident that the matter could be adjusted, and that the session would be short and uneventful. So he turned his attention to the more exciting prospect of seeing New York.

Simpson's train reached the Jersey City terminus on April 30, the day before the general conference, and he took the ferry for New York. The exciting metropolis of America had a buzzing population of 300,000. To the passengers looking out from the rail of the ferryboat across the wide expanse of river and bay, the mass of ruddy brickwork soon developed the firm outlines of a great city. Innumerable spires and cupolas, small, trim white wooden steeples rose above the brickwork. Visitors who were acquainted with the city pointed out the wall along the bay at the southern tip of the island, and the green bank of trees behind it. That, they said, was the Battery, and from it reached the great thoroughfare Broadway, eighty feet wide and three miles long.

Carts and carriages, vehicles of all kinds, filled the streets of Manhattan. Drivers shouted to prospective riders, to their horses, and to one another, twisted about in the traffic, shot into this opening or that to secure the most strategic spot, and, once having obtained passengers, maneuvered to get clear.

Simpson hailed a carriage and ordered the driver to take him the short distance to Harper & Brothers. There he went at once to the business office to pay the $81.85 that Indiana Asbury University owed to the firm, and was warmly welcomed. To his surprise, he learned that he was to enjoy the hospitality during the conference of the senior member of the firm: James Harper, who had just been elected mayor of New York on the ticket of the Native American party.[12]

III

The general conference opened on Wednesday May 1. The delegates gathered early that day at the Greene Street Church, eager to talk to old friends. They clustered on the steps that led up abruptly from the sidewalk to the door, leaned against the iron picket fence, or met inside.[13]

It was immediately apparent that the slavery question would not down. Some said that the bishop would resign; others, that he owned no slaves, that they belonged to his wife's children; still others, that the South would not let him resign, that there had even been a caucus the night before, and that the southern delegates had threatened to secede to a man if the bishop resigned or were censured.

Simpson found his way into the auditorium, sat down among his Indiana colleagues, and looked around. The building was long and narrow like a warehouse: at the front was the platform with chairs and tables for the bishops and the secretaries; at the rear, a balcony, to which a considerable number of visitors had been admitted. Already one hundred and fifty delegates were present for the first roll call.

Promptly at nine o'clock the senior bishop, Joshua Soule, called the conference to order. Tall, slender, gray-haired, but muscular and commanding, he was iron-willed—a Westerner by residence but still possessed of the New England austerity of his youth. He read the Scripture, announced the hymn, and called upon George Pickering of New England and William Capers of South Carolina to pray.[14]

The first business of the conference was routine but brisk: the election of secretaries and reporters, the ordering of standing committees, and fixing the hours of the general session, which were set to begin at half past eight and end at one o'clock. On the second day the conference named its committees. Simpson, entitled as chairman of the Indiana delegation to first choice, coveted appointment to the special committee on the episcopacy: if rumor were correct, it should have a lively part in the deliberations. But he was young, this was his first general conference, and the older men of his delegation thought that he, as president of the college, ought to be on the education committee. He yielded graciously if a little unhappily, and Augustus Eddy received the assignment to the committee on the episcopacy.[15]

In the regular order of business, following roll call, the delegates presented resolutions from their respective annual conferences. When on the third day the secretary called for Indiana, Simpson presented a resolution calling for the division of the conference, another praying for a reduction in the price of Methodist books, and a third on German missions, all of which were referred to committees.[16]

The following day, having found his conference legs, he presented his first motion, a question of privilege. Conditions for the conducting of business were not ideal. A few delegates, never able to settle down to the routine of the conference, scurried busily in or out, a few were more or less regularly engaged in whispered conversation. The room was hot, and the doors were open to let in the least stir of air. Over and above the noise of the conference room, the rattle and clatter of passing vehicles and the drumming of hoofs sometimes drowned out the speakers' voices.

Calling for a suspension of the order of the day, Simpson moved that the conference instruct the Book Agents, with permis-

sion from the city authorities, to have the street covered with tan-
bark. After a lively and entertaining discussion on street noises, loud
speaking, and Methodist preachers, the motion prevailed, and Simpson settled back, more an observer than a participant.[17]

The conference was less than a week old when the delegates
had an opportunity to preview the case of Bishop Andrew. F. A.
Harding, a minister of the Baltimore conference who had been suspended because of his refusal to manumit slaves, petitioned the
general conference to reinstate him. He had come into possession
of his slaves by marriage in a manner remarkably parallel to that
which was rumored of the bishop.

The debate on the appeal was highly dramatic and divisive.
Many preachers in the deep South, yielding to state laws which
forbade manumission, continued to hold slaves, men and women
and children, who had come into their possession through marriage or bequest, and the last general conference had guaranteed
them the privileges of the church. In the Baltimore conference,
however, no preacher yet had been allowed to remain in the conference and hold slaves. William A. Smith of Randolph-Macon
College in Virginia defended Harding. Tall, dark, and balding,
with a fine physique and a magnificent voice, he argued that Harding had no control over the slaves, who really belonged to his
wife, that Maryland forbade emancipation, and that the church
at the last general conference in 1840, had approved the admitting
of slaveholders to "all grades of the ministry." [18]

Smith's real problem was to win the border conferences and
the conservative North, which heretofore had allied themselves with
the South against the New England abolitionists. But the Baltimore conference had never had a slaveholding preacher, and the
Harding case threatened to upset the status quo, to enlarge the
slave power. Baltimore resisted, but at the same time disdained any
open alliance with the abolitionists. It took a conservative, "middle
ground" position between the abolitionists who felt that slavery was
a sin under any circumstance and the extremists of the South who
maintained that slavery was a national blessing.

Every southerner could see that the Baltimore doctrine, if
maintained, would shift the balance of power from the South to
the border and to New England. Smith therefore rejected in-
dignantly the definition of "middle ground" conservatives. He

himself and his brethren were the real conservatives of the discipline. All others were abolitionists. Men of the South stood upon the principle that slavery was "a great evil" but "not necessarily a sin." Thoroughly aroused and well practiced in the art that a principle is never so effectively comprehended by an audience as when it is reenforced with loud tones and vigorous action, he spoke with a "voice of thunder" and struck the table violently with his copy of the discipline. The professed conservatism of the Baltimore conference, he said, was not a balance between North and South; rather, it was like one of New York City's two-wheeled cabs: remove the horse, and it would let down on one side. The caricature evoked laughter from the southern men. To the Baltimore conference he must say there was no middle ground between the South and the abolitionists. Where the brethren stood, if not with the "ultra abolitionists," he could not say. There was "no shading off . . . at the margin of guilt, but the bold and abrupt step from right to wrong." [19]

John G. Collins, who presented the case against Harding and for the Baltimore conference, was no match for Smith in appearance and oratory. Smaller, dark, sharp-featured, he was "rapid in his movements and style of speaking"; and his voice soon became hoarse. But he had some of the arts of argument. His rebukes were "withering," and his strong conviction, bluntly expressed, gave him the role of champion and served to solidify the North.[20] Smith, interrupting to call him a "gladiator," well characterized the whole contest. There was conflict, showmanship, verbal thrust and parry, and a sharp division of interested spectators whose partisanship grew intense as the struggle approached its climax.

Collins charged Harding with violation of the discipline—he could have freed his slaves but would not. He denounced him for making himself unavailable to the non-slaveholding circuits of the Baltimore conference; he rebuked him for becoming involved with slavery. "He knew all these things," shouted Collins, lashing out at Harding and striking the bishop as well, "and with his eyes open, he married these slaves!" He would not have the Baltimore conference weighed down with the "dark subject" or besmirched with the "dark stain" which encumbered and disfigured the South.[21]

Smith in turn was furious as he reviewed Collins's argument. "His eyes flashed fire. With flushed cheek and a voice of thunder," he looked at Collins and shouted, "What 'dark subject,' sir, do you know of, connected with my Conference? What 'foul stain' is found upon the pages of its history?" And what did the speaker mean in begging the conference "for God's sake not to drive the Baltimore Conference to take rank with a slaveholding conference"? " *'Take rank!'* . . . What do you mean, sir, by this insinuation? *'Take rank'* with Virginia!" [22]

The conference was reduced to pandemonium. The bishop pounded with his gavel but was unable to quiet the "multitude of voices." Those acknowledged by the chair were scarcely able to speak until Peter Cartwright, rustic from Illinois, gained the floor. Brethren professed that they were keeping "very cool," he said, once more admonishing them to be patient; but if they were "iron instead of flesh and blood," and if they were thrown into water, "they would fiz-z-z a good deal!" [23]

Shortly the confusion was interrupted by the ordering of the yeas and nays. The cleavage wrought by the debaters was sharp and clear. Heretofore at general conferences a large block of northern delegates, recognizing the unity of the church as of first importance, had rallied to the support of the South on the slavery question. But now the line of difference ran along the jagged edge of the border conferences. The vote was 56 for Harding, 117 against him. Only two southerners voted against Harding, only nine delegates from the border conferences voted for him. The split was sharply and clearly geographical.[24]

XI

THE CHURCH DIVIDED

DESPONDENCY hung over the conference. It lingered until the Andrew case was disposed of, breaking now and then to let in some bright new hope, but only to thicken again into deeper gloom. Fearing that disaster would follow the action on Harding, the conference ordered a special committee on pacification and set aside an hour for prayer. The southerners in a closed session resolved to withdraw from the church with Andrew if any measures were taken against him.[1]

The northerners also met together in caucus and named a committee of one from each conference, Matthew Simpson representing Indiana, to deal with Bishop Andrew. The committee met once only, called the venerable Nathan Bangs of New York to the chair and Simpson to the secretary's desk. It then conducted but one item of business, the naming of five of its members to confer with Andrew. The bishop would not receive the committee. He had heard of the caucus. There was no point in talking, he said, when it was known all over the city that his "degradation" was resolved on. The same day the special committee on pacification reported that it was unable to agree on any plan of compromise. And that night Matthew wrote to Ellen: "I think it possible that we shall split." [2]

With the delegates thus busy in special caucuses, sidewalk and parlor deliberations, and the framing of proposals and counterproposals, the conference itself was officially and ominously silent on the Andrew case. While it dawdled over routine business Simpson had but little to do. Standing committees met in the afternoon, when the conference was not in session; but the committee on education, on which he served, scarcely met after the early days of the conference, because its chairman, Dr. Henry Bascom, was so fully occupied by the very important committee on the episcopacy of

123

which he was also a member. Twice the presiding bishop called on Simpson to open the session with Scripture reading and prayer.

On such afternoons as he was not busy, Simpson saw the wonders of the city: the Astor House, an enormous pile of granite facing City Hall Park; the City Hall, a handsome edifice in white marble with an entrance flight of white marble steps, a first floor of Ionic and the whole surmounted by a lofty cupola from which the fire watcher had a view of the entire city; the great fountain with water gushing thirty feet into the air and falling in a large cloud of cooling spray; the shops along Broadway and the business center where he purchased Irish linen, the watch and key, and a dozen smaller items for Ellen; the handsome new Customhouse, done in white marble like a Greek temple of the Doric order; the even more imposing blue granite temple of the Merchants' Exchange; and at the very end of Wall Street, competing with the shrines of Mammon, old Trinity, its spire rising 300 feet heavenward. He viewed with particular interest the old John Street Church, where American Methodism had begun less than a hundred years earlier in a structure built to resemble a house and so to deceive the local defenders of the state-supported church. He visited the museums and was especially interested in the new eccaleobion, that ingenious invention which would hatch eggs without the assistance of a hen. He took the ferry across to Brooklyn. Mayor Harper drove him into the country, past the great reservoir of Eighty-sixth Street, some thirty-five acres of water brought into the city nearly forty miles from the Croton River. On Broadway he looked with amazement at the fashionable people, at the close of a hot afternoon, promenading up and down from the Battery to the Park, the men in the newest cuts and the women in fashions direct from Paris.[3] In response to Ellen's teasing letter he protested, however, that his acquaintance with "the ladies of the city" was "small." Of those he had met, some were "handsome," some "ugly," many "very amiable and accomplished"; but all in all, " 'I wad'na gie my ain wife for ony wife I see.' " [4]

As the conference approached the end of its third week, and the caucuses and informal negotiations proved unproductive, John Collins of Baltimore brought the issue to the floor by calling for the facts in the Andrew case. The bishop admitted that he was in truth the legal owner of two slaves, both of whom had been bequeathed to him some years past. The one had refused exportation to Liberia, the other was only a child, not old enough to be placed on his own responsibility. Only a few months before the conference, he, a widower, had taken a second wife who had a number of slaves. Because it was not possible to emancipate them in Georgia and he was "unwilling to become their owner," he had secured them to his wife by a deed of trust, and therefore had "no legal responsibility in the premises." [5]

The debate which followed centered chiefly on the issue of expediency. The preachers were deeply moved as they argued. They wept over the old church, expressed their pride in its achievement, their indebtedness to it, vowed affection for one another, and affirmed their intention to preserve it if possible.

Stephen Olin, president of Wesleyan University, represented the northern view in a conciliatory and moving speech. He was a sick man, and his brethren knew that he ought not make the effort to speak. His great frame shook with emotion, and tears coursed down his cheeks. A New Englander by birth, he had taught in the South as a youth and had lived in the home of Bishop Andrew. He had talked with the bishop only the night before; and he felt that if they could adopt some measure which would not censure Andrew, and yet would meet the needs of the North, they might avoid the rock on which the church seemed likely to split. [6]

Others of the North were less conciliatory. Seymour Coleman of the Troy conference avowed his opposition to abolitionism but bluntly warned: "Give us a slaveholding Bishop, and the whole North will be gunpowder, and there are those who will apply the match; it will make abolitionists of hundreds of the preachers and thousands of the people." [7]

William Winans, "tall, thin, weatherworn" circuit rider of the old frontier in Mississippi, asked: Was it expedient to cut off, as they would by their action, thirteen hundred preachers and four hundred and fifty thousand members "against whom lies no allegation of having departed from the principles of your book of Discipline"? In asking this of his brethren in the North he would not leave out of consideration "the spiritual welfare of thousands of those poor oppressed people for whose interests and welfare you profess so much solicitation—the bleeding slave himself." Already the abolition excitement had hedged in the poor Negro, and "shut the mouth of the minister." Would the North by its vote "throw the blackness and darkness of death over him"? [8]

The South was most aroused over the incongruity of the northern position—the North sought to depose Andrew without a trial and yet admitted that he was "pure and spotless" and in "every way qualified for the Christian ministry." Asked the young George Pierce, a firebrand of Georgia, "Are they heaping garlands upon the victim before they have bound him for the sacrifice?" [9]

The North, hard put to meet this argument, answered through Leonidas L. Hamline of Ohio who insisted that the question of first importance was, "Has the General Conference constitutional authority to pass this resolution?" [10] The "genius" of the Methodist Church, he argued, was "strict amenability in Church officers, subordinate and superior." The presiding elder, the itinerant minister, the exhorter and the unordained local preacher, the class leader, all were subject to removal by the bishop, without cause save that they were "unpopular" and ineffective with the people. There was reason for such administrative policy. It promoted religion. It bound the church "in a strong and almost indissoluble unity." All Methodism knew and understood these words. How often had the preachers defended the administrative system on this very point against assaults from without the denomination and revolt from within. A bishop, Hamline said, was a minister no higher in the orders of the church than any elder, distinguished only by the fact that he had been elected to an administrative office. The general conference was the supreme legislative, judicial, and executive body of the church and had the power to expel a bishop for "improper conduct if it seem necessary."

The argument dragged on for more than a week. On three days there were afternoon sessions to allow extra time for the debate. Simpson was deeply moved by Olin's plea for the unity of the church and was impressed with the ability of young Pierce from Georgia; but he was thoroughly convinced by the inexorable logic of Hamline. From that point on the debates were over, so far as he was concerned. The conference had jurisdiction over Andrew; it ought to act for the good of the church, and the bishop, who was an itinerant, need only move to a free state and liberate his slaves. He

did not see any merit in the expediency argument of the southerners: they threatened grave consequences in order to get their way,
but he did not believe that they would act to divide the church.[11]

He found most of the argument tedious. Old men, long in the
service of the church, wept over the good old days. They talked end-
lessly—the conference having suspended the fifteen-minute rule on
debate—pronounced encomiums to the past, and recited in detail
the exploits of their youth. He squirmed uncomfortably in his place
in the hot auditorium, exhausted by the tension, the heat, and the
long speeches. A month more, he wrote home, "would destroy my
health." [12]

Only once did he participate briefly in the debate. A north-
erner who followed Hamline, much impressed by the argument and
convinced that division was inevitable, began to discuss the conditions of separation. Simpson immediately called him to order. There
need be no division of the church, the resolution before the house
had nothing to do with division, he said, and the speaker was out
of order in discussing it.[13]

Bishop Soule, in the chair, wryly observed that the speaker was
"not more out of order than others had been." [14]

Simpson appealed to the assembly from the decision of the chair.
Soule asked him to present his point of order in writing. The debate
was suspended while the young man strode down the aisle to write
out and present his statement. The bishop with practiced skill then
ruled that the point of order, as restated in writing, was such that he
must rule favorably upon it. The speaker might resume, but he
must confine his argument to expediency.[15]

It was rumored that the representatives of the two factions had
devised a compromise resolution, milder in form, which would be
satisfactory to both parties; but support collapsed before the resolution could be introduced. There was nothing to do but vote on the
suspension of Andrew. The conference sat in deep and oppressive
silence as the secretary called the roll. The division, as in the Harding case, was sharply sectional. Of the affirmative votes, only one was
from the South, and that was cast by a New Yorker temporarily stationed in Texas. Only seventeen northern delegates, all but two of
them from border conferences, allied themselves with the South.
The vote stood 110 for the resolution to suspend Andrew, 68 opposed.[16]

II

Once the northern delegates had taken the decisive step against Bishop Andrew, they were overcome by a spirit of conciliation. Although they declined to take the initiative in dividing the church, a number of them let it be known that they would not oppose such division if the South could not bear the action against Andrew.

Simpson, not at all pleased with such talk, drafted a statement calling for the postponement of action; but before he could introduce his resolution a special committee reported favorably on a plan of separation.[17]

Charles Elliott thought division necessary because the church had become too large and unwieldy. L. L. Hamline, who was a member of the special committee, believed the plan was constitutional and fraternal: if the brethren found that they must go, they could go peaceably, and not "as an arm torn out of the body, leaving the point of junction all gory and ghastly." [18] In vain Dr. Thomas E. Bond, editor of the New York *Christian Advocate,* argued that the plan was unconstitutional and warned that it would result in bitter warfare along the border. The delegates adopted the plan overwhelmingly, with only eighteen dissenting votes.[19]

The unity was short-lived. The South, in a summary which raked over and exposed the still live coals of the Andrew controversy, entered a long and solemn protest against the majority action against the bishop. The North, on motion of Matthew Simpson, immediately named a committee to reply to the protest. An excited southerner denounced the reply as "an insult to the whole South." Great disaster would result from its publication, and he would "not be surprised at its leading to a civil war, so utterly did it deny the rights and trample upon the feelings of all the slaveholding states." [20]

Immediately upon adjournment of the general conference, the southern delegates convened in a rump session and called upon their several conferences to send representatives to Louisville, Kentucky, on May 1, 1845, to consider the question of dividing the church.

The northern delegates had not believed that the South would act so precipitately. As Peter Cartwright put it, they had seen the lightning and heard the thunder before; and therefore they had not been unduly alarmed by the threats of the southern delegates. Before they left New York they had begun to regret their approval of the plan of separation.

As they returned to their homes they found their fellow ministers and the people aggrieved and shocked at the thought of the split in the church. Methodism had weathered many another storm and had come through with colors flying and hull undamaged. There was no institution like it in all Protestantism. Youngest of the major American churches, it had more than a million members in 1844— which was considerably above the combined membership of the Presbyterians, the Congregationalists, and the Episcopalians. Methodism was the religious sensation of the century. Its growth was a source of pride to the members, especially to the preachers. More than 400,000 members lived south of the Mason-Dixon line. To permit them to withdraw was to rend the church in two, to destroy its strength and its glory. The prospect was too grim to endure.

Why, the preachers of Indiana wanted to know, did Simpson and the other delegates favor a plan of separation? Why didn't they postpone action for another four years? Was there still some way of avoiding the catastrophe? [21]

In this new climate of opinion, the returning delegates found their regrets over the plan of separation quickly ripening to censure of the South. Overlooking the South's argument that the necessity for division existed "even now," they remembered only the assurance that the southern conferences could not act in less than a year or eighteen months. That, thought the North, would allow time for southern tempers to cool. The plan of separation had clearly stated that the general conference approved the withdrawal of the South, if the action against Andrew made division necessary. Why, then, had the southern delegates, without demonstrating necessity, met in New York immediately after the general conference to issue a call for the Louisville convention? To Simpson the answer was clear. The men of the South had acted hastily and not in good faith. Without consulting their people, they had "acted on the premises," and so had violated the spirit and intent of the measure adopted by the general conference. [22]

The ensuing strife between the sections centered on the issue of separation, not of slavery. The North, having no desire to drive Baltimore and the border conferences to the South, appealed to the discipline and tradition of the church. Even if the South should withdraw, the position of the "Old Church" would remain unchanged. Had it not always denounced the evil of slavery? And yet, had it not left the institution alone when state laws protected it? It was the South, with its acquisition of a slaveholding bishop, that had changed, not the "Old Church."

However, the argument was two-edged, and the church editors used it not only to soothe the border but to placate New England. Proud of the stand the conference had taken against slavery, the editors held up the Andrew case to repudiate the taunts of William Lloyd Garrison and the abolitionists. The people at home who had censured the delegates for the plan of separation quite as heartily praised them for their deposition of Andrew. Even in southern Indiana, where there had been little sympathy with abolitionists, the annual conference in the fall of 1844 voted overwhelming approval to their delegates for deposing Andrew.[23]

Simpson, tortured by the thought of the division of his beloved Zion, and quick to blame those whom he believed responsible, moved steadily forward in his antislavery views, and became increasingly perceptive to the antislavery opinions of others. In the spring of 1845, attracted to the Louisville convention of the southern conferences, he traveled leisurely through southwestern Indiana to Cincinnati, and thence down the Ohio to Louisville. Everywhere men were talking about the southern convention and the determination of the South to split the church. Everywhere he found the antislavery feeling "deepening and widening." Even the men who had migrated from Virginia and Kentucky, and who a year before had bitterly condemned the abolitionists, were now speaking up against slavery "in the most decided manner." Destruction of the old church had become associated in men's minds with slavery. Aggrieved by the one, they blamed the other as the cause of the approaching disaster. So, twelve months had produced "a wonderful revolution" in public opinion. He had no doubt that in two or three years the "line of *feeling*" between the North and the South would be "deep and broad." [24]

At Louisville, Simpson and several of his Indiana colleagues made their way to the Fourth Street Methodist Episcopal Church, where the convention was held. They found seats in the gallery where they could look down at the delegates, on the main floor. William Winans was there, tough old circuit rider from Mississippi; the fiery young George Pierce from Georgia and his father, Dr. Lovick Pierce; influential William Capers of South Carolina; ponderous William A. Smith of Virginia; and the judicious Robert Paine of Tennessee, chairman of the general conference committee which had brought in the plan of separation.

The delegates proceeded at once to the business of dividing the church. It was impossible to maintain unity, said Winans, without "the ruin of Southern Methodism." "Agitation" was the watchword of the North, and they had even consecrated religion to their evil purpose. The South could outspeak the North in the general conference, but could not outvote it. The only way to stop the agitation was by separation, and he would favor disunion even if it brought political disunion—"for with me principle outweighs expediency." [25]

Simpson was most impressed and angered by the outburst of George Pierce: Reconciliation was hopeless and impossible because the North would make no concessions, he said. He charged, not without warrant, that the abolitionists were ignorant of the Bible, and that they appealed not to the Holy Scriptures for "the justice of their cause but to the writings of Jefferson." The northern Methodists had become radical—they had introduced pews, organs, fiddles into their churches; they stood up to pray, they no longer used bread and water in their love feasts, and their exhortations sounded like Fourth of July toasts. In ten years "there would not be a vestige of the peculiarities of Methodism among them." [26]

While the delegates of the deep South thus railed at the North, they were careful to appease the border, for they had no intention of losing the Kentucky conference. They therefore shouted down the suggestion of a Mississippian that they alter the discipline to protect the institution of slavery. They would stand by the constitution of the "old church" without change. And they would keep the door open for fraternal relations and even for reunion when, as young Pierce said, the North "are convinced of their sins."

When the resolution to form a new church was put 94 delegates voted aye, only 3, all from Kentucky, voted nay. [27]

Simpson had no doubt that the whole South would go *en masse* to the new church. Division was inevitable, and slavery was the cause. And it would be the cause, ultimately, of "severing the Union as well as the Church." His pessimism deepened with the passage of time. Six months after the convention he saw the South "rushing towards ruin." The spirit of slavery was "so tyrannical and ungovernable" that it would respect no regulations. He foresaw the rapid deterioration of the relations between the two bodies of Methodism. The South could not be expected to obey the plan of separation. Even worse, he saw slavery so blasting the hopes of political unity that only foreign war or Providence could save the Union. And then the annexation of Texas and probably California, and possibly even Cuba would strengthen and perpetuate slavery. He desired no communion with the southern church that would in any way identify the North with "their views of slavery." [28]

Only one thing saved him from radicalism. All along the border the jurisdiction of the Methodist Episcopal Church extended into slave territory. The plan of separation provided that the border conferences and societies should choose whether to adhere to the North or the South; but, once the line was drawn, neither branch of the church was to invade the territory of the other. The Baltimore conference, which was still allied with the old church, was wholly in slave territory, and its boundaries and those of the Philadelphia, Pittsburgh, and Ohio conferences cut deeply into Maryland and Virginia from the Eastern Shore to Wheeling. Who could best serve Methodism in these border regions? The old church, with its avowed antislavery views, or the new southern church with its increasingly proslavery bias? Simpson had no doubt that his own church ought to maintain its hold on the border. Furthermore, there seemed to be little doubt that the South, made fanatically aggressive by slavery, would, as William Hunter said, violate the plan of separation, and thus open up even more territory to the northern church. But the border societies could not endure any ultraism, and therefore the church ought not to agitate the question. Already Baltimore was worrying lest it be driven out of the church by the antislavery agitation and a slaveholding ministry be forced on it.[29]

The formation of the southern general conference had not solved the slavery problem for the Methodist Episcopal Church.

XII

"SON OF MAN, PROPHESY"

WHILE President Simpson was thus concerned with the problems of the church, affairs at Indiana Asbury University were in good order. The student body, 177 in 1844, gave promise of exceeding 200 in the fall of 1846. The youngest college in the State, Indiana Asbury stood in enrollment "proudly at the head of all of the Institutions." [1]

In 1842 Simpson had appointed John Wheeler, his friend and protégé, and a member of the first graduating class, to the chair of Latin languages and literature; and a year later he had strengthened the faculty by naming Benjamin Tefft, two years younger than himself, professor of Greek and Hebrew. Tefft, reserved and polished in dress and manner, was unrestrained to the point of boastfulness in his admiration of Methodism. He was a graduate of Wesleyan University in Connecticut, the strongest of the Methodist colleges, and had served in New England and New York as pastor and teacher. Wheeler, Tefft, William Larrabee, and Charles Downey—also a graduate of Wesleyan and the tutor in natural sciences—constituted a respectable faculty. [2]

By the fall of 1845 the board of trustees was planning the establishment of a law school in Indianapolis, and John Wheeler was beginning to think about a department of normal training at Greencastle. Some friends of the university were insisting upon departments of agriculture and medicine. Indiana Asbury was on the way to becoming a real university.

Financial conditions were much improved, too, after the adoption of the new scholarship plan in 1844, and the appointment of Isaac Owen as agent. An unlettered young itinerant of Simpson's age, Owen eagerly sought the assistance of the professors at Indiana Asbury, and even learned to read a little from his Greek New Testament. As agent for the university he exhibited a boyish enthusiasm and a remarkable ability to raise funds. Reporting to Simpson about his success in the field during the summer of 1846, he begged him to keep his report a secret. He hoped to collect a good deal more before conference, and he wanted to see how the treasurer would look, "counting a thousand or two thousand dollars all at wonce." In two years Owen sold the greater portion of $84,000 worth of scholarships and raised funds to endow a chair for Simpson and some of his faculty.[3]

Once in 1845, when the financial pinch was severe, Simpson was tempted to resign. Woodward College, a new institution in Cincinnati, had elected him to its presidency. The advantages of the new school were considerable. Woodward, the officials assured him, was the best endowed and, "in all human judgment," "the most permanent institution of learning in the West." Many times Simpson himself had complained to others that the Methodists were not properly represented in nonsectarian institutions. Woodward officials used his own protest as leverage to move him. He ought to accept the position as an "honor and obligation" to Methodism.[4] He need not sever his connection with the ministry, for he could at the same time pastor a Methodist chapel in Cincinnati and preside over the destinies of Woodward. There were the further advantages that Cincinnati was not only the cultural and commercial center of the West, but the very heart of western Methodism. The *Western Christian Advocate* and the *Ladies' Repository,* Methodist journals, were published there, along with a considerable number of books and tracts put out by the Western Book Concern of the church.

In Cincinnati on business, Simpson looked into the matter and wrote to John Wheeler at Greencastle suggesting that he quietly give out the news to the rest of the faculty and determine what they would think of his leaving Indiana Asbury.

The reaction of the faculty was immediate and decided. Wheeler answered that they would consider his resignation as "one of the greatest misfortunes that can happen to us an Institution": They knew no man "North, South, East or West that they would be willing to see president"; Larrabee and Tefft would begin immediately to look for other jobs—they had suffered long enough from unpaid salaries, and were unwilling to face the collapse of the endowment plan, which they believed would follow his resignation.[5]

For a month Simpson dallied. Word got out to the students, and they added their protest to that of the faculty but named Tefft as their choice to succeed him. Heartened by the response of students and faculty, Simpson turned down the Woodward offer and went back to Indiana Asbury. However, John Wheeler had observed enough in that month of uncertainty to know that the day was not far distant when both the demands of the church and Simpson's own inclination would impel him into "a wider field of operation." [6]

Simpson had, in fact, never been more popular in Indiana than in the months following the general conference of 1844. Although all the delegates from that state had held together on the critical issues before the conference, and none had taken part in the debates on Andrew, he was the one who had demanded on the conference floor that the majority reply formally to the written protest of the South. Likewise, he had objected in writing to a discussion of the division of the church and had been sustained by the reluctant Bishop Soule. His strong opposition to the tactics of the South since his return home had further enhanced his standing.

Edward R. Ames was his only rival for honors among Methodists. Five years older, Ames was a robust-looking man who stood six feet tall and weighed 200 pounds. His hair was black; his head, large; his cheeks, full and florid; his eyes, small and light blue. He was commanding and yet conciliatory in manner, with the reputation of a diplomat and a politician. The councils of the church listened to him and knew that he was in the inner Democratic circle which advised Governor Whitcomb and Congressman Joe Wright. He had served two years as agent for the Preachers' Aid Society before Simpson came to Indiana, had been secretary of the Indiana annual conference in 1839 and 1840, a delegate to the general conference in 1840, one of three general secretaries of the Missionary Society from 1840 to 1844, and a leading candidate for bishop in 1844.

Simpson soon began to rival Ames's popularity. Both were able preachers, but Simpson was more eloquent and more profound. The 1841 annual conference elected him secretary in the absence of Ames, who had been elected by earlier conferences; and succeeding annual conferences kept him in that office. Both men were delegates to the 1844 general conference, Simpson being head of the delegation, and Ames third on the list. Ames lost a little prestige at the general conference when he was shunted aside in the race for the episcopacy; and in the sectional strife his fellow Methodists, the majority of whom were Whigs, suspected him as a Democrat of being soft on the question of slavery and the division of the church.

The relations between the two men were for the most part warm and friendly. Ames was a strong supporter of Indiana Asbury and was delighted, when enrollment increased, to see "the tide of popular favor setting toward Greencastle with such strength." As a presiding elder he got behind the endowment and scholarship plans, determined that his district should do its share. He visited the president often, and urged the Simpson family to come to his new home for a month's visit. They loved to talk politics as well as church, and when Polk was elected Ames chided Simpson about the defeat of the Whigs: Hard times would be over, once Polk got into office; until then, he hoped the president would bear with patience the financial disappointments he must experience under the Whig administration. Once, after being urged by Bishop Hamline to go to China as one of two missionaries, he wrote impulsively to Simpson, "I will say explicitly if you will be one of the men I will be the other." [7]

There were also strained relations between them, induced in part by the ardor of their followers, and in part by their unspoken awareness that they were rivals for the favors of Indiana Methodism. In 1846 their differences ignited and burst into flame.

The churchmen of Scotland had issued a call to Evangelical Christians all over the world to meet at Liverpool for a consideration of their joint interests. Early in 1846 friends of Simpson at Greencastle began a movement to name him a delegate to the Liverpool convention. Other Indiana circuits and stations took up the cry and passed resolutions requesting him to go.[8]

After two months of discussion and agitation, Simpson called his trustees and his board of visitors together. In explaining the opportunity not only to represent Methodism but to purchase books and apparatus long needed by the university, he alluded to the offer from Woodward College and his reluctance in turning it down.

With two exceptions the trustees and visitors were unanimous in the recommendation that Simpson attend the convention. The two were Allen Wiley and Ames. Ames, who had also been mentioned as a possible delegate, was cynical about the allusion to Woodward College and intimated that Simpson was trying to produce a demonstration of esteem. Lucien Berry, who was passionately determined that Simpson should make the trip, felt from Ames's manner that he looked upon the Woodward affair as a ruse. He seemed to be saying of Simpson: "He cannot leave. There is no danger. It is all for effect." [9]

However, the trustees and visitors appointed a committee to raise funds. The committee hastily directed a circular to the Methodists of the state: If each district in the two conferences would raise about forty dollars, the five or six hundred dollars necessary to meet the delegate's expenses would be supplied.[10]

Thus assured of support, Simpson began immediately to plan his itinerary and to study the countries he hoped to visit. He would go first to Liverpool for the convention in August and then travel through the Mediterranean to Egypt, Palestine, Greece, and thence up the Danube into central Europe. He would be absent ten months. He wrote to Stephen Olin, president of Wesleyan University and a delegate elect, to ask if he might join him as a traveling companion. Olin had visited Europe and the eastern Mediterranean countries some years before and had written a popular account of his journey.[11]

The opposition of Ames and Wiley, however, did not cease. Wiley refused to raise funds in his district, and Ames was outspoken in his disapproval. Earlier in the year Ames's support of Professor Tefft for the editorship of the Ladies' Repository in Cincinnati had drawn a sharp reproof from Simpson for deliberately weakening the staff of Indiana Asbury. Ames now turned the argument on Simpson. The college could ill afford to get along without any one of its staff members, and Tefft was leaving. How could it also dispense with its president for a full year? Even more important, the success of the endowment plan was dependent upon him. In his absence the people would not contribute. Furthermore, the university was too hard pressed financially to attempt the raising of funds to send a delegate to Europe.[12]

Simpson's close friends Lucien Berry and William Daily were outraged by the conduct and arguments of Ames and Wiley. Berry thought the reasons they assigned for opposing the trip "absolutely unendurable." After all of the sacrifices of personal interests Simpson had made for years together for the university, to be told that the preachers would not continue the collection of funds was "actually insufferable." [13] Daily was sure that either Ames or Wiley would have gone quickly enough. So far as he could see, their action was only an expression of their littleness. Afraid that he might be the next victim of the turn of their wheel, he begged Simpson to keep his confidence. He had already suffered at the hands of both, and he thought he had cause to "dread the ire of some." [14]

Other friends, however, saw the force of the argument. Simpson announced therefore that he must decline the kind offer of his friends to send him to Liverpool. He was keenly disappointed; but, as Ames shrewdly anticipated, he suffered no loss of prestige.

That summer, after the long exercises of commencement day, Simpson and John L. Smith, one of the college agents, went for a long walk through the fields. Stopping at the edge of the woods, they sat down in the shade of a large tree. Smith was a fiery preacher of the president's own age, self-educated, who had had little sympathy with colleges and seminaries until he fell under the spell of Simpson's discourse on education and straightway became a disciple. There were two giants in Indiana Methodism whom he greatly admired: Matthew Simpson and Edward R. Ames. He thought Ames was on the way to becoming the greatest statesman in the church and could have risen to the top in politics and government; but, of the two, he favored Simpson.

That afternoon, Smith and Simpson indulged in a good deal of "free talk," reviewing the events of commencement and the deliberations of the board of trustees.

In an impish mood, Smith broke a long silence by saying, "The spirit of prophecy has come upon me."

Simpson replied in kind, "Son of man, prophesy."

"Two years hence, you will be a member of the general conference which is to meet in Pittsburgh."

Simpson demurred, expressing doubt that Indiana Methodists generally were well pleased with the general conference delegates of 1844 who had approved the division of the church.

Brushing his objections aside, Smith continued. "In 1852 you will lead the delegation of the Indiana conference; and at that conference from two to four bishops will be elected, and Matthew Simpson will be one of that number." [15]

XIII

WAR ON THE BORDER

As a prophet John L. Smith had read well the crystal ball. In the fall of 1847 the Indiana conference named Matthew Simpson to head its delegation to the Pittsburgh general conference— the only one of the eight men who had represented Indiana in 1844 to be elected again. Revulsion against the plan for dividing the church had swept the northern Methodists. Indiana, determined to send no one to Pittsburgh unless he was "unwavering" in his opposition to the division of the church, rejected even the popular E. R. Ames. Simpson's friend Lucien Berry was elected, but not William Daily, who like Ames was a Democrat and a temporizer; in addition, he was still regarded by some as an impertinent young upstart. The Indiana pattern prevailed throughout the church. Of the more than 150 delegates sent to Pittsburgh only 30 had voted at New York for the plan of separation.[1]

The years between the general conferences had been bitter with conflict. There was misunderstanding over the line of separation. Most of the warfare, however, was at the local level. The membership of many border societies was almost evenly divided between northern and southern sympathizers, and the adherents of one party or the other sometimes seized the property. At Parkersburg, (West) Virginia, a station seventy-five miles within the bounds of the Ohio conference and therefore, according to the northern interpretation, not a border society, the southerners ran the northern preacher out of town and took over the property. Likewise, in Cincinnati, at the very heart of western Methodism, Bishop Joshua Soule of the southern church organized two chapels—one named for himself, the other for Bishop Andrew. On the other hand, a small band of northern sympathizers in St. Louis refused to leave the "old church," organized their own society, and called upon the North for recognition.

In preparation for the conference Simpson reviewed and discussed these events with Berry, Daily, and other associates. He deplored the state of affairs but saw no easy remedy. He doubted that it would do any good to declare the plan of separation null and void. No declaration could make it null: the work was done for weal or woe. They must look to the future, but how and where to find the remedy he did not know.[2]

He was determined to propose a compromise. Let the church recognize the *de facto* division, and then in the spirit of Christian brotherhood submit the question of the property to legal arbitrators, each segment of the church agreeing to abide by the recommendation. Daily was enthusiastic about the idea. It ought to pacify all claimants, North and South.[3]

I I

When the general conference convened on May 1 Simpson was ready with a general plan of action. At the opening session he called for a committee on the state of the church, composed of two members from each of the annual conferences, to be charged with consulting "privately on the business of Church difficulties." [4] If the jurisdictional conflict could be channeled through a committee, it might prove much less explosive when it reached the floor of the conference.

The committee was quickly authorized. It met on the afternoon of the first day and made George Peck, editor of the *Methodist Quarterly Review,* its chairman and Matthew Simpson its secretary. Peck requested the members to state briefly the attitudes of their respective conferences toward the plan of separation. They were overwhelmingly in favor of repudiating the plan. The westerners had been incensed by the conduct of Bishop Soule. New England and Providence surprised Simpson by their calmness. Where Illinois and Ohio treated every suggestion of compromise with contempt, New England was willing to retain the line where possible. Baltimore was distraught, believing that if the line were given up it would lose the whole slaveholding territory to the southern church. The Philadelphia men said the same.[5]

Having canvassed its members, the committee began a systematic collection of data. Day by day it received complaints against the plan, and charges of southern aggression. Elliott and others presented petitions from Kentucky, Missouri, Arkansas, and western Virginia, signed by 3,000 persons who had been forced out of the Methodist Episcopal Church against their wishes. The bishops reported innumerable "violations" of the plan—preachers whom the southern bishops had "deliberately" sent across the line. In an effort to winnow out every grievance, the committee threshed over again all the famous cases: the Soule and Andrew chapels in Cincinnati; Parkersburg, Virginia; the plea of the beleaguered antislavery group in St. Louis. It reviewed again the history of the plan of separation; it repeated the charges of the northern press that the southern delegates at New York had not acted in good faith, that they had preached not peace but rebellion, that they had acted without determining any need for division.[6]

Simpson had gone into the committee hearings able to name many grievances against the South; but they assumed no clearly rational pattern. Now as he listened to the reports of grievances and studied the violations of the plan he perceived the great design. He was like a child on a hillside at night, searching the stars for the Big Dipper—finding at first only the pointers, moving from them to the North Star and back, and fixing his eyes at last upon the flickering stars of the bowl and the broken handle until at last the whole cluster took shape and meaning. So, he isolated the more significant facts and noted how they clustered and revolved about secession and slavery. There was the troublesome line, with the southern aggression above it for the obvious purpose of extending the boundaries of the proslavery church (had he not remarked before how aggressive was the spirit of slavery?). There were the two publishing houses, New York and Cincinnati, based upon the legitimate claims of the southern preachers, but desired as well for their value in promoting the proslavery institution. There was the problem of fraternal relations between the two churches, important in establishing legal separation. There was the new and inviting missionary territory on the Pacific coast, an opportunity for the further aggrandizement of the southern church. And there was the matter of local church property: deeds poorly drawn, churches seized, rightful owners driven out or denied any share in the chapels and parsonages to which they had contributed. Viewing these facts, Matthew Simpson felt the spirit of compromise drain out of him. He was ready and willing not merely to accept the repudiation of the South but to advocate it.[7]

The issues came in quick succession. Dr. Lovick Pierce of Georgia asked to be recognized as a fraternal delegate from the Methodist Episcopal Church, South. Although it was a common practice among Methodist bodies to recognize such delegates the conference refused to receive him and thus, implicitly, to recognize the southern church. It was not "proper," said Matthew Simpson from the floor, "to enter into fraternal relations with the Methodist Episcopal Church, South," when there were "serious questions and difficulties existing between the two bodies." Pierce, denied recognition as a fraternal delegate, refused to attend the conference as a visitor. Assuming the role of a champion, he threw down a challenge: his was the final communication from the Methodist Episcopal Church, South. "She can never renew the offer of fraternal relations between the two great bodies of Wesleyan Methodists in the United States." [8]

Simpson himself took the lead in calling for the organization of a mission conference in California and New Mexico to embrace the territory seized from Mexico. There were smiles and laughter, and even a shout or two of derision, when he introduced the measure; but, dead in earnest, he quickly checked the laughter and brushed away the smiles. He did not offer the resolution in order that it "become a matter of amusement." The territory was large, people were pouring in by thousands, and the Methodist Episcopal Church ought to make some provision to occupy it. "Our people are going there," he said, "and our ministers will soon be on the ground, and it will be in the power of our people to occupy it." George Gary, who had been three years in Oregon, made the matter more explicit. Describing the wonders of the Willamette valley, he warned his brethren that some ministers of the Methodist Episcopal Church, South, had recently entered Oregon with a company of three to five thousand emigrants.[9] The delegates quickly altered the resolution so that the new conference embraced Oregon and California, and passed it without dissent, although some regarded it as premature.

Simpson was also deeply concerned about deeds to property. Men and women along the border, and even in the South, had contributed liberally from their frugal means to the erection of a chapel for worship or a parsonage for the minister, only to see them seized by the proslavery element, which in some instances was in the minor-

ity. The crux of the problem was in defective titles, deeds made out
often to local trustees, rather than to the church, or not made out at
all. He proposed, therefore, that responsible officials of the church
ascertain the provisions of the various states and have deeds drawn
that should then be printed in quantity by the book concern and
distributed to presiding elders and through them to the local
churches. His resolution, laid over for later action,[10] was never acted
upon. However, he did not forget it. The sense of injustice, the
grievance over property stolen, he believed, from the members of the
old church, pricked and irritated him like a festering thorn. Some
day he would manage to pluck it out.

Altogether, Simpson made a deep impression on the conference.
He rarely engaged in debate or parliamentary tactics, but when he
took the floor he spoke impressively and pertinently on key questions. It was known that he was chairman of the subcommittee
charged with phrasing the committee's recommendation on the plan
of separation. Easterners, who had scarcely noticed him in 1844, now
not only recognized him as a leader but discovered that he was a
"very popular preacher in the west." [11] His Indiana friend William
Daily, in Baltimore to attend the Democratic National Convention,
heard that he was "the leading spirit of the General Conference."
The people there, Daily wrote, approved of his plan of arbitration of
the book concern claim (which they undoubtedly heard of, greatly
embellished, from Daily himself), and if he could carry the plan
through he would "immortalize" his name.[12] W. C. Larrabee, in Indiana, heard that he was to be elected bishop. "Is it true?" he asked.[13]

Abel Stevens, the young editor of *Zion's Herald* at Boston, was
especially attracted to Simpson. He thought his depressed and contracted forehead "very unhandsomely obscured by shaggy locks." He
observed that Simpson was tall and stooped, that his eyes were small
and keen, and that his cheekbones were prominent with "a sort of
Indian breadth" which gave a triangular outline to his face. And yet
the Indianan was already known as a great preacher marked by
strength of thought. Moreover, he was the author of conference resolutions on the plan of separation. Certainly this man's appearance
was "altogether 'dumbfumbling.' " [14]

The resolutions on the plan of separation constituted the most
important business of the conference. The temper of the delegates
was for repudiation; but simple repudiation would fix the blame

for separation on the North and not on the South. Simpson saw the point. A repudiation that fixed the blame on the South would at least strengthen his church's claim to certain properties and to southern members who sympathized with the North—in short, would assert the church's right to extend its boundaries.

The portion of the report which declared the plan of separation null and void had been amended several times in the committee on the state of the church, and therefore came to the conference floor poorly written and ambiguous. "Prolix and confused," Norval Wilson of Baltimore said of it.[15] The delegates agreed, and proceeded to offer a number of substitutes, one of which was a simple statement of nullification of the plan. Simpson, alarmed at the prospect that his carefully worked-out statement of reasons for declaring the plan null and void would be tabled, with loss of the advantage of fixing culpability on the South, offered another substitute. For support he called on Daniel Curry, a preacher of his own age from the New York conference. Curry had already spoken in favor of the third resolution on the right of trial. Tall, with a rugged form and somber face, he had a square jaw and thin firm lips well suited to the utterance of caustic phrases and positive opinions.[16]

Simpson's substitute declared that the plan of separation was intended to meet a necessity which might arise, that it was dependent upon a three-fourths vote of the annual conferences, and upon the observance of a boundary line; that the South had not waited for the necessity to be demonstrated but had acted "in the premises"; that the annual conferences had refused to concur as required; and, finally, that the South had violated the boundary line. Therefore the Methodist Episcopal Church had no obligation to observe the plan, and it was null and void.[17]

He argued the merits of his resolution and moved to lay the simple null-and-void declaration on the table. The conference concurred, 83 to 36, approved the previous question, and proceeded at once to adopt, seriatim, the Simpson-Curry resolution.[18] The most important action of the conference was then concluded. To the Church, South, the Simpson resolutions were a declaration of war; to Simpson and the Methodist Episcopal Church they constituted a philosophy of action, a platform for the long struggle with the southern body which lay ahead.

On the book concern Simpson was much more conciliatory. He thought that the property should be divided, but that the conference should act through its agents. He and Curry, once more acting together, moved to authorize the agents of the church to arbitrate, if legal counsel advised them that they had the constitutional authority to do so. If not, the bishops were to refer the issue to the annual conferences.

But even in this compromise measure the rights of the South, as stated in the resolution, were placed on moral and not on legal grounds. The South perceived the point and felt that it was being patronized—perhaps, even worse, that the entire action was an empty gesture "to propitiate common scorn and public indignation," a delaying tactic to make it possible for the North to steal the property of the South by indirection.[19] Bishop Soule immediately called a meeting at Louisville of the southern bishops and commissioners to determine a course of action.[20]

III

Simpson's active leadership in the conference, his youthfulness, his modesty, and his homely and friendly manner, together with the strong support he could expect from the Indiana and Pittsburgh conferences, made him a likely candidate for one of the church appointments. Of these there were but few: two book agents—one stationed at New York, the other at Cincinnati—and two assistant agents; a missionary secretary; editors of a half-dozen papers, two quarterly reviews, and the Sunday-school and tract publications.

A caucus of the western delegates on May 21 put Simpson down as assistant editor of the New York *Christian Advocate and Journal,* the church's leading weekly paper.[21] William Daily at the Democratic convention in Baltimore heard the rumor that he was wanted for the editorship of the New York journal, and thought that the *Western Christian Advocate* at Cincinnati would be much better.[22]

Simpson had gone to the conference not unaware of the possibility that he would be urged to take some other position. His old friend William Hunter had already begged him to return to Pittsburgh to edit the *Advocate,* and he was ready to welcome some sort of change. As John Wheeler had seen, he was troubled in spirit and determined to leave Indiana Asbury. The business of the English conference still rankled in his breast, with Ames's insinuation that he could not leave, that his bringing of the invitation to Woodward had been a ruse, a play for favorable response from the people.[23] He had declined somewhat reluctantly to consider the presidency of Dickinson College.[24] But while he desired to go he hesitated to take any initiative. As in his younger days, the great decisions of his life must rest upon Providence and not upon ambition. He could admit no personal consideration, save one—health. In an age when good health was so transient a possession, that one consideration would suffice, both for himself and for his friends.

In the summer before, he had suffered a severe attack of typhoid fever, following chills and fever. His Indiana doctor told him plainly that he was working too hard, and that he must change his manner of living. At Pittsburgh he again consulted physicians, old friends, who were even more emphatic. It would be good, they said, for him to return to the Pittsburgh area where he had had good health. Thus advised, he toyed with the idea of resigning from Indiana Asbury and of returning to the itinerancy in the Pittsburgh conference.[25]

Now he kept his own counsel until the results of the caucus of the western delegates, proposing him as assistant editor at New York, forced the issue. His Indiana brethren gathered eagerly, wanting to know what he would do. Recounting to them the advice of his physicians, he admitted that if Providence gave him the position he would feel obliged to accept it. Only to John L. Smith and one or two other close friends did he explain, afterward, that there were other reasons.[26] The Indiana delegation would have none of his going East. He must remain in the West. If he must leave Asbury they would make him editor of the *Western Christian Advocate*.

For Simpson that introduced another problem—his old friend and guardian angel, Charles Elliott, was editor of the Cincinnati paper and had been renominated at the western caucus. He demurred at the suggestion of displacing the older man. He would be pleased, he said, to be Dr. Elliott's assistant. It was only a polite gesture, for the conference had refused to allow an assistant editor at either New York or Cincinnati.

The ways of Providence and of Methodism were inexorable. Simpson was nominated by an Indiana colleague and elected on the first ballot with 80 votes to his friend's 57. Elliott was then placed in competition with William Hunter, the other lad whom he had helped to bring up at Pittsburgh, for the editorship of the Pittsburgh *Christian Advocate,* and again he lost, 70 to 66. Remorseful, Simpson begged the old man to remain at Cincinnati on full salary until the end of the summer term at Asbury.[27]

XIV

CINCINNATI EDITOR

COUNTRY-BRED though he was, Matthew Simpson loved Cincinnati, the "Queen City of the West." The bustle of activity, the streets filled with carriages, the hurried gait of the pedestrians, the columns of black smoke, the pounding of steam engines, the long row of river boats swaying at the wharf, all spoke of enterprise and progress. He yielded easily to the throbbing rhythm. Rising early, he bolted his breakfast and strode down the street, sometimes with little Charlie clutching at his hand and trotting to keep up. Even so early, the stores were open, and the merchants had their displays—from trinkets and jewelry to stoves and furniture—on the sidewalk for quick sales. At the Methodist Book Concern the presses were already rolling. He was proud of the Book Concern. The third largest printing establishment in Cincinnati, it ran four cylinder and power presses, employed twenty hands in the plant alone, published three weekly papers, a monthly magazine, hundreds of books and tracts. Its capital stock was valued at some $200,000.[1]

Reporting the last week in July, Simpson found his desk piled high with "exchanges," but singularly free of original articles. He clipped freely from other religious and secular newspapers, filled up the columns of the first issue, and begged his readers to send in "short articles written in a plain hand." He had nothing for next week's paper, he stated, but obituary notices.[2]

The *Western Christian Advocate,* with 12,000 subscribers and 50,000 readers, was a powerful organ of the Methodist Church. Some thought it more influential than the entire board of bishops. Simpson had already reflected at length on his responsibilities and his policy. For four years Charles Elliott had blown so steadily upon the fires of sectional dissension that all western Methodism was lighted up by the flames. Bishop Morris, whom Simpson consulted, thought everyone

was tired of these "controversial products." He had been bitterly criticized in the correspondence columns of the *Advocate* for his disregard of the "loyal" Methodists in St. Louis, and he believed that an
editor should be conciliatory, explaining and defending truth—but
"let it be the truth in love, free from anything offensive in manner."
Simpson agreed. He would not enter the lists with the South. Nor
would he take up the controversies Dr. Elliott had been carrying on
with two Cincinnati religious editors. His would be a term of no controversy. He would avoid all personalities and rigidly exclude all
subtle allusions and criticisms.[3]

The primary purpose of the religious press as he saw it was
"to assist the pulpit in the diffusion of religious truth." He heartily
approved of the "usages," "institutions," and "enterprises" of the
Methodist Episcopal Church, and he proposed to state clearly and
forcibly the Methodist doctrines so as to "bring the truth to operate
practically upon the conscience and life of the individual." He would
try to remember, however, that denominations differed only in name
and organization, and that Christians of whatever church could be
one in Christ Jesus, "one in spirit—one in benevolent effort." [4]

He ran articles and editorials on camp meetings, revivals, exposi-
tion of prophecy, the locality of heaven. He wrote long articles, filled
with general historical and geographical facts on missions to Germany, France, Italy, China, New Mexico. He warmly espoused the
cause of California missions, writing at length on the great possibili-
ties in that new empire and expressing the fear that the southern
church would occupy the field if his own did not move with more
vigor and aggressiveness.

He kept a memorandum book, jotting down topics which might
be of interest—parks in Cincinnati, Miami College, discovery of
iodine, World's Industrial Fair, Sunday-school singing, the poor in
winter, church architecture, religious politics, asylums for the insane.
He fussed at the writers of obituaries. It was not the purpose of the
paper to eulogize the dead but to edify the living. Such phrases as
"weeping friends," or "mourning relatives" should be omitted.
Readers would not, like one good friend, cancel their subscriptions
because an obituary notice was reduced in length if they realized that
fifteen or twenty notices might quote the same verse from a hymn or
contain the same eulogistic phrases.[5]

He ran a summary of national news, published political speeches (including one by his Indiana friend Joe Wright), gave market reports. He ran articles on discovery and travel, on geology, on Fourier and Fourierism, on politeness, on the cure of hiccups. He lauded cities which sponsored fairs with their exhibitions of improved implements, and he praised Professor William Larrabee for his lecture on progress before the Cincinnati Young Men's Mercantile Library Association. He urged every town to "get up a course of lectures for the winter," and thus displace "unworthy amusements." "Society," he wrote, "will use either their *heels* or their *heads*." [6]

He discoursed on the events of the first half of the century: the overthrow of Napoleon; the rise of Austria; the stirrings of the German and Italian peoples; the expulsion of Spain from South and Central America; the quadrupling of American territorial holdings and the consequent extension of "civil freedom"; the advances in the arts and crafts, in science, commerce and industry; the diffusion of learning through schools and colleges; the interpretation of hieroglyphics and their "testimony to the truth of Biblical declarations"; the establishment of foreign missions, and the translation of the Bible into two hundred languages. In all these he found evidence of progress and the mighty workings of Providence.[7]

The book concern agents, both of whom were members of the Ohio conference, made some difficulty in Simpson's efforts to improve the *Advocate*. On the basis of cost, they opposed the use of blocks and cuts, and the paying of correspondents: the paper had done very well in the past without these luxuries. But they had other reasons for their resistance. The Ohio delegation had been opposed to Simpson's election. And now it was apparent that he traveled too much—to Indiana for dedications, to conference sessions, to Indiana and Ohio churches as special preacher. He did not write enough. Most of his editorials were short, and frequently he dispensed with a leader and filled his column with short editorial notes. Dr. Elliott, staying at his desk, had managed to fill his columns without benefit of cuts or correspondents.[8]

But Simpson stood his ground. On the last day of the Pittsburgh general conference he had secured a resolution authorizing the New York and Cincinnati papers to employ correspondents. Daniel Curry of the New York East conference reported that the New York paper had a budget of $900 for assistance to the editor, and he agreed that the weeklies must be "progressive." "If the Western shall be cooped in the strait jacket limits proposed by your Agents," he wrote, "its circulation will necessarily be greatly circumscribed." [9]

Simpson appealed to the book committee (elected quadrennially by the general conference to supervise the publications of the Western Book Concern) and received approval of the expenditures, over the opposition of the agents. He hired correspondents in Washington and Philadelphia, New York (his friend Curry), and Paris. He began to use cuts—representing public buildings, colleges, churches, ordinarily with a woman in the foreground, her full skirts sweeping the street and her parasol delicately raised, or a carriage drawn by a spirited horse, his neck arched, his forefoot in mid-air at the beginning of the downward stroke.[10]

II

Simpson's policy of "no controversy" kept him out of the long and invective-laden exchanges with fellow editors; but he had scarcely settled into the editorial chair when his eye fell upon a letter from a Protestant Episcopal minister to his own church paper, complaining that "the Church" could not advance in the West because of the influence of preachers who were "very generally men of no education, no talent, and very little good manners." Simpson taunted him. Why did not the western people appreciate these " 'sons of the church,' " who, without doubt, were "men of *education,* of *talent,* and of *very good manners*"? Ought not such men to "shine like stars amidst the darkness of surrounding space"? Or could it be that the man's letter really savored strongly of "disappointed expectations"? Could it be that the ministers of the West compared so favorably with the sons of "the Church" that these could not win the support of the people and were left "the sole admirers of their own *education, talents,* and *good manners*"? [11]

The condescension of the Calvinists was much more bitter to the Methodist taste. The Protestant Episcopal Church, after all, was small and was the mother church of Methodism. But the Calvinists were an aggressive lot, railing against Methodist doctrines as well as Methodist manners. Simpson ignored Dr. Rice and the *Presbyterian of the West* for some months; but he took notice when Rice, chafing at the phenomenal increase in membership among the Methodists, accused them of receiving sinners into the church. The subsequent quarrel ranged from biblical to theological to personal grounds. Rice cited the Scriptures, the Methodist discipline, appealed to logic, and censured Simpson for his tart replies: "Such a spirit savors much more of the world, than of the gospel." Simpson hoped that Rice would "keep cool," for he himself was "in perfect good humor, notwithstanding the partial excommunication . . . leveled at our head." He was not greatly troubled by the Presbyterian's wrath, however, for he had learned to disregard such bulls, "whether they emanate from Rome or from Geneva." As for the point of controversy, he thought the Methodist practice of taking in seekers not so different from the Presbyterian practice of admitting "penitent sinners." [12]

He then brought the controversy to a close. He could not, he wrote, attribute to all his Presbyterian friends the feelings which actuated Dr. Rice. Thousands, he believed, would regret with him the controversial spirit which marred the peace that ought to exist between true Christians. "So many are the evils which now press upon the Christian Church that it cannot well spare time and strength for controversy among its own members. In this city Sabbath-breaking, profanity, intemperance, and licentiousness are fearfully on the increase." Dr. Rice ought to see the "array of vice," rather than to account it "small dust in the balance" when weighed against the "evils of Methodism." [13]

If Nathan Rice was irritating, the activities of the American Home Missionary Society, the American Tract Society, and the American Sunday School Union—all with offices in Cincinnati, and all dominated by the New School Presbyterians and the Congregationalists—were exasperating. The American Home Missionary Society helped to support nearly 500 missionaries in western states and territories, and boasted of an enrollment of 83,500 pupils in Sunday schools; the American Tract Society had 268 colporteurs on the highways and trails, visiting 350,000 families a year and distributing half a million books. The support of these missionary enterprises came largely from established and wealthy congregations in the East, and the money flowed readily when agents and missionaries exposed the evil plottings of the Pope and his emissaries to take over the whole western region for Catholicism. On these grounds the more ecumenically minded Calvinists, among them Dr. Albert Barnes, whom Simpson admired, were able to advance the cause of peace and unity among the Protestants. However, missionaries hard pressed for funds found that portrayal of hardships of the West, of the pitiful condition of these benighted people, also brought results. The temptation to exaggerate was considerable. The missionaries recounted the terrible conditions in the West, where families lived "three, five, and ten miles from each other, as a general thing," and were served only by "ignorant circuit-riders." [14]

When Albert Barnes, in an address praising the Presbyterians and Congregationalists for their home missionary work in the West, characterized the preachers of other churches (Baptist and Methodist) as purveyors of superstition not unlike Buddhist priests, Simpson replied with asperity.

Drawing for the moment on the kinship of the Episcopalians and the Methodists, he boasted of the growth of Methodism in America, and asked, sarcastically, "Is America, then, sinking toward barbarism?" What did Dr. Barnes mean by the Christian Union which he pretended to espouse? That he would welcome Episcopalians and Methodists to the Platform, saying, "Come and sit down by our light, and be improved by our refinement"? Did he mean by his platform of Christian union that there was "one side for the educated, the other for the uneducated; and Mr. Barnes to decide the fact of education by Church membership"? [15]

III

True to his admonition to the Presbyterian editor, Simpson was a keeper of the people's morals. He protested that the parading of the streets by a German military company, with an address by the chaplain, was a "curious way of sanctifying the Sabbath." He condemned the Christians who thronged the theater to hear Jenny Lind and expended huge sums ($15,000 to $20,000 per night) for "mere amusement" while "thousands are perishing for lack of the bread of life." [16] He praised John B. Gough for his "eloquent" lectures on temperance, and he urged legislation to curb and punish the liquor dealers. When a measure to permit state licensing of liquor dealers was put before the voters of Ohio in 1851, he campaigned vigorously and successfully against it, despite a protest from some Methodists (whom he called "timid" or "constitutionally conservative") that he was "meddling" in politics. Arguing that the contest was against "profanity, Sabbath-breaking, rioting, and licentiousness," and in behalf of "the sobriety of your sons" and "the safety and happiness of your daughters," he urged the church people to organize every county and every district, and to call upon every voter.[17]

No event agitated him more than the public exhibition of the "Greek Slave," a statue by the famous sculptor Hiram Powers, formerly of Cincinnati. One of the most famous works of art shown in America during the decade, it presented a young woman "wholly divested of clothing." [18]

Much more sophisticated than he had been in 1844, Simpson did not register the shock of a simple moralist. He raised the moral question, but argued it from the tenets of art itself, the "lessons" of history, and the "practical" results. "Our emotions," he wrote, "are implanted for the purpose of leading to action"; excited emotion that does not lead to action "tends to impair the mental economy. We learn to sympathize without making exertions to relieve." The slaves in America were not white, like the slave portrayed, and he doubted that many persons would be led by it "to sympathize with and make efforts for the amelioration of the condition of the suffering African race." More than that—the compassion, it was said, was aroused by the chain on the slave's arm, and the consequent realization that her exposure was forced. But he doubted the effect of this "fiction." "Take off that chain—present no fiction of its being a helpless slave, and what remains but a licentious exhibition?"

He argued then from history, pointing out the decline of Grecian purity and the shame of Praxiteles, who selected the model for his statue of the naked Venus from among the most beautiful women in the *"abandoned* classes." He cited Aristotle, Seneca, Pliny, Propertius, and the early Christians. He argued from contemporary life. If a superior artist were permitted to exhibit such a statue, so would an inferior, "and soon we may have rude imitations of the nude female figure exhibited to the youth in every village in our land." Licentiousness, he said, was an increasing problem.

Our eastern cities are growing in impurity and so is the great west . . . Our coffee-houses contain licentious paintings; and some of our book-stores are guilty of trafficking in the most corrupt literature. Model artists, or naked women, representing the Greek Slave and other pieces of statuary, are traveling from city to city, and from town to town, exhibiting themselves for money; and, strange to say, they draw large audiences even among the ladies!

At the risk of giving offense, he must say that an exhibition like that of the Greek Slave "prepares the way for the model artists; and they for that house which leads to the chambers of death, and to the gates of hell." And he pleaded, "Christian reader, would Christ, or his apostles, have patronized such an exhibition?"

I V

Simpson's most extended editorial controversy was in the political field, and with the secular press, over the Compromise of 1850. The compromise was an attempt to settle, at least temporarily, the complex political problem which resulted from the acquisition of territory after the war with Mexico. California brought the issue to a head in December, 1849, when it sought admission to the Union with a free constitution.

In the next month Henry Clay introduced a series of resolutions which, modified in the course of heated and acrimonious debate, Congress finally enacted into law in September, 1850. Among other matters, the compromise included the admission of California as a free state and the enactment of a new drastic fugitive slave law. Simpson recognized the seriousness of the problem early in March and expressed the opinion that the current session of Congress would "yet rank among the most important ever held." California, he believed, should come in as a free state. The proposal to give up a part of the territory received from Mexico to slavery was "a compromise against which every feeling of humanity, and every principle of republicanism, strongly revolts." [19]

In succeeding weeks he arraigned the Senate for permitting Henry Stuart Foote of Mississippi to threaten Thomas Hart Benton in its chamber with a drawn pistol, unreprimanded; he charged that men of the North, in using their votes to mix the California bill with the dispute over the New Mexico and Texas boundary, had "bowed the knee to the dark spirit of slavery"; he warned that—if he "read aright the will of the people"—a "terrible and political retribution" awaited these senators.[20]

Such excursions into the political field, he realized, needed explanation and justification. The Methodist press traditionally held itself above politics; its province was spiritual affairs. In all the months of the dramatic battle over the Compromise measures, the chief organ of the Methodist Episcopal Church, the New York *Christian Advocate and Journal*, contained only one short article noticing it—a description of Webster's Seventh of March speech, which pleased the editor because the great orator declared that he could see no necessity for the separation of the Methodist Episcopal Church.[21]

The longer the battle in Washington continued, and the more Simpson talked, wrote, and thought about it, the angrier he became. On May 1 he tossed restraint aside and strongly impugned the motives of the politicians. "Why all these flaming speeches at Washington? Is there any danger of disunion?" So far as he could see there was "not the slightest indication of it." It was simply this: wishing to introduce slavery into New Mexico, the South felt the need of more stringent laws for the recovery of fugitive slaves. Such laws could not be passed without northern votes. How might these votes be obtained? By bargain, by the trading of office and emoluments for votes. But how then should the politicians escape "the indignation and curses of the North"?

> Only by the South getting up the cry of disunion. Then when they get the country excited, these Northern champions magnanimously step forward to save the Union . . . Among themselves they laugh at the scheme, but they expect to gull the "dear people." Nay, these very men will claim the honor and gratitude of the North for their efforts to save the Union . . .

Did he hear an objection from "a sensitive politician who dreads free speech"? Is not the *Advocate* "a religious paper—how dare you discuss political questions?" Yes, it was "a religious paper," and that was the reason it dared pursue an independent course. "We are not sold to the Whigs or Democrats or Free-soil men. . . . We stand upon higher ground. We are Christians—we are Christian freemen —and this question deeply affects us." He did not stand upon an abolitionist platform, however. He objected to the extension of slavery, but he was alarmed also at the increased proscription of the Methodist Episcopal Church. Northern churches were excluded, in a large measure, from slaveholding territory. Some Methodist ministers had been mobbed, some compelled to escape for their lives, "simply for preaching the gospel among slaveholders." Slaveholders had driven one of his brethren, sent into the southwest by the bishop, out of the Indian Territory. Let New Mexico be opened to slavery, and it would be closed to the churches of the North.

Aspiring politicians had warned him "to let these objects alone." To such threats he could only reply, "Gentlemen of the political school, you may muzzle the political press if you can, *but the religious press shall be free, and for its support we shall throw ourselves upon the country.*" [22]

The reaction to his editorial course, and particularly to his article "The Union," was highly favorable. Methodists of the West liked a man who would fight. Senator Benton commended him for his stand on California, and Senator Salmon P. Chase wrote pompously, "I do not choose to resist the inclination which impels me to offer to you my sincere thanks for your manly, and more than manly, your Christian article on the late scene [Foote and Benton] in the Senate." John L. Smith was ecstatic: "Your Editorial on the 'Union' has given me heart-felt joy. O how glad I am to see a man at the head of our church organ who has the *nerve* to dare to do right." William Daily, who felt that Simpson was a "little *too ultra*," none the less admired the editorial: It made *"everything tingle*. Politicians hear of it, enquire for it, read it, and some commend, and a few condemn. But, believe me, it is the most popular editorial you have written . . . It has *ginger* in it. You talk like a man." [23]

Simpson continued the attack during the summer. He was particularly aroused by the Fugitive Slave Law, which, he felt, encouraged southern kidnapers of free Negroes and bribed judges by paying them a higher fee for delivering a Negro to a southern claimant than for freeing him.

He would not object to a law which would enforce the provisions of the Constitution. If the enactments were made "in a fair spirit," if they would "secure the free against the kidnapper, while they arrest the fugitive, we have no word to offer in opposition." But he warned Congress of a higher law, dwelling in the bosoms of Christian people, which would render unfair laws "comparatively nugatory." [24]

His attack on the Fugitive Slave bill received the same "universal approbation" which had greeted his editorial on the Union. The Indiana conference gave him a rising vote of confidence. On the Indiana Asbury University campus D. W. Voorhees and others condemned the editorial before the students and tried to secure a censure. Lucien W. Berry, who was now president, replied to the arguments, and the students supported Simpson by a vote of 100 to 4.[25]

William J. Brown, editor of the Indiana *State Sentinel* and congressman from Indiana, was alarmed at the criticism of his own conduct implied in Simpson's editorials and in the vote of the Indiana conference. Although a Democrat, he had supported the Whig-sponsored Compromise measures; and because of his alleged Free Soil sympathies he had lost the Speaker's chair. He had no intention now of permitting a Methodist editor to belittle him over the Fugitive Slave Law before his own constituents.

Dr. Simpson's editorial, he wrote, "was no doubt a hasty and unguarded production, written without due reflection, but prompted by pure and honest motives, but with mistaken views of the law"; and the Indiana conference, likewise, was "hasty" in its endorsement. We admire Dr. Simpson, he continued, "for his talents, we respect him for his piety. But when he leaves the pure and limpid stream of divinity, to sail his bark on the turbid and boisterous ocean of politics, he must look out, or he will have frequent collisions with more experienced navigators." He did not doubt Dr. Simpson's "fidelity" to the Constitution. He was fully aware of (and not a little concerned by) the "wide circulation" and "controlling influence" of the *Western Christian Advocate*. He would suggest to the editor and to the ministers of his church, and of other churches, and to "all editors of religious newspapers" that it would be "better for them to inculcate the principles of 'peace on earth, and good-will to all men,' rather than to influence the public mind to resist and disregard a constitutional law." [26]

Simpson replied with spirit. He did not understand "how being a divine renders us unfit to judge of these measures." He would leave matters of bank, subtreasury, protection, revenue, and election of candidates to politicians. "But great questions of right and equity are as much in the province of the divine as of the politician. They belong to God's law, and this must be the study of the theologian." He was no lawyer, but he had read law books. He cited Blackstone, "If any human law shall allow or require us to commit crime, we are bound to transgress that human law," and Noyes, "The inferior must

give place to the superior; men's laws to God's laws." He quoted
from Vattel, Coke, Littleton, Hobart, to show the supremacy of a
higher law, and finally from John McLean, Associate Justice of the
United States Supreme Court and a Methodist: "Statutes against
fundamental morality are void." If these great jurists taught the
doctrine of the higher law, he went on, "we cannot help it." And if a
law is to be obeyed not as law "merely," but "because it is right,"
then surely law must be subject to examination "even by the divine."
Was not the Bible the "great charter of human freedom"? Could a
politician by enacting laws close the lips of the theologian? "We
wholly demur to this assumption of the exclusive right of the politicians to discuss moral topics. As long as our lips shall have utterance, or our fingers move a pen, we shall fearlessly speak and write
what our judgment and our conscience approve." [27]

The *Advocate* containing this editorial was passed from hand
to hand in the hotels of Indianapolis, where it created "quite a flut-
tering among the 'smaller fry' politicians" and led to "a tremendous
fumbling over of the law books." Lucien Berry, delighted, wrote
mockingly: "We talk of commencing suit against you forthwith for
murdering Bill Brown. He is dead with law—dead by the hand of a
divine." [28]

The *Indiana State Journal* (Whig), pleased with the opportunity
to join in the thwacking of Bill Brown, praised Simpson for his
"very able" writing and reprinted his editorial on the Fugitive Slave
Law. It accused Brown of quoting the Washington correspondent of
the *Advocate* to show that Simpson favored compromise—"a very
cunning trick." Hugely enjoying Brown's discomfiture, it taunted
him for undertaking to read the Methodist conference a lecture on
"Christian duty." "The propriety of such a lecture from *such* a Christian, will not be questioned." [29]

A friend reported that Bill Brown's "barking" had been followed by "the yelpings of most of the little editors in Indiana." There
was a strong inclination to brand Simpson an abolitionist—one
Congressman and many others had openly done so since September.
During the congressional canvass that was about to open Simpson
and his paper would be the subject of stump oratory all over the
state if the controversy continued; and "you may rest assured that
however decorously such fellows as Bill Brown may affect to treat

you in their newspapers, they will not scruple to say anything in their speeches." Simpson would be "calumniated" and the whole Methodist Church drawn into the "whirlpool of politics." [30]

Brown himself soon reentered the fray, protesting that Simpson's article on the higher law had been "copied everywhere by the political press. . . . We might fill our columns with their comments." Wary, lest he alienate Methodist voters, he praised the *Advocate* for its theology but averred that many Methodists disagreed with its editor in politics and could not be "swerved in their opinions by his views, however much they may respect and love him as a Divine." In heretofore dealing "tenderly" with the editor he had assumed that Simpson as a minister of God was better informed in his own calling than in law or politics. But "we were mistaken. . . . He understands politics like a book, and quotes law equal to S. P. Chase Esq." Once more reviewing the arguments, he accused Simpson of "special pleading" and of being the "unintentional instrument" of the abolitionists. He closed with a patronizing gesture: "We have now done with Dr. Simpson, and dismiss him with the best and warmest feelings of our heart, in the language of the Saviour: 'May the Grace of God abide with you, now and forever more, amen.' " [31]

Simpson was much amused by Brown's "Scripture," to which he replied, despite warnings from friends that a continuance of the controversy into the forthcoming elections might injure the church: "We fully reciprocate these kind feelings and would ask, as a special favor, of Mr. Brown, that he would tell us where we may find those beautiful words which he quotes from our Savior. We strongly suspect that they must be in the same chapter with the text reported to have been quoted by a member of the Illinois Legislature some years since. He said that his heart had often been cheered by that beautiful text, 'Blessed be they who expect nothing, for they shall never be disappointed.' " [32]

That summer the voters of Indiana retired an unwilling Congressman Brown from public office.

The controversy was of significance to Simpson not only as editor but as churchman and orator. His concept of Christian responsibility had broadened from evangelism and the doctrine of Christian influence, which he had preached to his students, to the belief that the Christian must do battle for what was right, and that *right* was inextricably bound up with public affairs.

V

During his editorship Simpson remained a member of the Indiana conference and continued to act as its secretary. He attended a large number of public services within its bounds and dedicated many churches. He also preached frequently in Cincinnati, spoke at temperance meetings, appeared on lecture series, and gave commencement talks. Altogether, he did nearly as much preaching as he would have done in a pastorate. His popularity in Indiana was not at all diminished. In 1851, for the third successive time, he was elected to head the Indiana delegation to a general conference—this one at Boston. There were only four dissenting votes: one, his own; one, that of a very good friend who knew he would be elected anyway; and two whom he "never knew or sought to know." [33]

John L. Smith's belief that Simpson would make a good bishop had gained currency. Several friends had whispered to him their intention to elect him to the episcopacy at the first opportunity; but there were obstacles, one being Edward R. Ames's ambition for the office. Never yet had two bishops been elected from the same annual conference; and there was no reason to assume that it would happen now. All through the quadrennium he and Ames had maintained friendly relations. Unsuccessfully (and perhaps with mixed motives) he sought the appointment of Ames to a missionary secretaryship when a vacancy occurred; and he won Ames's gratitude by favoring him to direct the educational work of the church in California. Ames as presiding elder, in a characteristically friendly and humorous vein, charged Simpson to be present to assist in the quarterly meeting at Indianapolis; and he relayed political news, predicted correctly that Whitcomb would be Senator, and that Joseph Wright or some one else "friendly to Methodists" would be elected governor.[34]

But there were also difficulties between the two. In 1848 Ames was elected to succeed Simpson as president of Indiana Asbury University, in a spirited contest with several ambitious candidates. Therefore, when Ames after brief deliberation declined the office, stating that the North Indiana conference had opposed him, and that his real call was to preach ("First apostles, then teachers"), some of Simpson's friends suspected that the whole matter had been simply a bid for popularity. At conference Ames spoke angrily from the floor,

attacking Simpson by indirection. "One man," he said, had been entirely responsible for the protest of the North Indiana conference;
and the implication to the assembly was plain. "You can be no longer
in doubt," Lucien Berry wrote, "that all of Ames Friendships are
sinister." Why did he "strike such a blow at that one man . . . *He
considers you in his way to a certain office.*" [35]

Much more serious was the possibility that the political controversy with Congressman Brown would alienate delegates from the
border conferences. Some of the Missouri Methodists did protest
against the editorial course of the *Advocate*. Simpson's friends, aware
that a candidate for the episcopacy must, like an aspirant to the
Presidency of the United States, be "available" to somewhat antago-
nistic interests, warned him to be cautious. He rejected the warning.
He did steer clear of the bitter sectional conflict (which also might
have alienated the men of the border), with one brief exception.
When Judge Nelson of the United States Circuit Court in New York
handed down a decision on the Book Concern property case favoring the South he dissented sharply. The case rested on "necessity,"
he wrote, and the South had failed to demonstrate any "necessity"
for division. The South therefore was schismatic, the old church
continued unimpaired, and the property of the book concerns belonged legally to the Methodist Episcopal Church. [36]

A much more serious obstacle to his election was his relation to
the Ohio conference. Living in Cincinnati, he had chosen to keep
his membership in Indiana. Ohioans, who had opposed his election
in the first place, were jealous. They thought he showed favoritism to
his own conference through the *Advocate;* and the agents, displeased by his frequent excursions into Indiana, charged him with
"neglect" of his duties. [37]

In the last year he had become involved in a local quarrel. The
general Methodist practice, as advised by the discipline, was that
seats should be "free"; but a few churches, particularly in New England, rented or sold pews. When a new, aristocratic church in western, democratic Cincinnati adopted this practice the Methodist
brethren were outraged. Simpson attended the dedication, noting in
his journal, "The Ohio preachers strongly oppose it and Bro Raper
is censored for consenting to preach the dedication sermon." For
himself, he only prayed that "every movement result in additional
glory to the blessed Redeemer." His Ohio brethren, displeased with

his "liberalism," demanded that he hold aloof from the dispute over pews. He consented, generally, but permitted selected representatives from both sides of the controversy to carry on an extended argument in the *Advocate*. By an ironical turn of events (arising out of his policy of excluding all but selected arguments on the subject from his paper), he soon had both Ohio and New England opposed to him: Ohio because he was too friendly toward pewed churches; New England because he published "false representations" against pewed churches! [38]

Just before the general conference it was rumored in Indiana that Simpson had bargained to recommend William Daily for the editorship of the *Advocate* in the event of his own election to the episcopacy.[39] After his departure for Boston the Book Committee, at the instance of the agents, reviewed his editorial course and questioned his clerks, one of whom then wrote to him that, although the committee was displeased, it would take no action.[40]

So Matthew Simpson, editor, proceeded to Boston, not at all sure what honors awaited him. He apparently thought well of his prospects, for he had packed his household goods and shipped them to Pittsburgh two months before. His purpose, he wrote in a manner reminiscent of 1848, was to return to the active ministry in the Pittsburgh conference.[41]

XV

AND SOME, BISHOPS

WHATEVER honors were to befall Matthew Simpson, his wife determined to share. Leaving Master Charles and his three sisters with their grandmother Verner in Pittsburgh, she went with him to Boston. They were still young in 1852, he not quite forty-one, and she but thirty-four. Matthew, with his scraggly hair, his low forehead and small triangular face, his tall frame, long arms and stooping shoulders, was uncouth even in his black broadcloth suit. Ellen by contrast was regal: tall, slender, elegant in ruffled silk and jewels. Much more fashionably dressed than some people expected the wife of a Methodist preacher to be, she made a striking figure in a Methodist gathering.[1] They found an apartment in a hotel not far from the seat of the conference, where they could entertain friends and have meals in private when they chose, and then turned their attention to business, Matthew taking his place among the delegates and Ellen finding a seat in the gallery.

After 1844 and 1848, the general conference of 1852 was unusually quiet. The North generally and New England particularly were still agitated over the Fugitive Slave Law. *Uncle Tom's Cabin*, published only a month earlier, had already sold 20,000 copies. Boston was astir over the "story of the age," but the delegates to the general conference showed no disposition to debate slavery.[2] No general conference had ever arraigned Congress or otherwise intervened in "political" affairs; and there seemed to be no reason for breaking the precedent now. Not even Matthew Simpson, who had criticized Congress so severely for the compromise measures of 1850, considered pursuing the question here.

Most of the business was routine. Some excitement arose over pewed churches and over the boundary lines of the border conferences; but the all-absorbing question was the election of bishops.

Elijah Hedding, senior bishop, twenty-eight years on the episcopal bench, had died in April, three weeks before the conference. Of the remaining bishops, L. L. Hamline had let it be known that he would resign because of ill health, and Beverly Waugh, now sixty-three, was scarcely able to perform his duties. Only Thomas Morris and Edmund Janes were equal to their responsibilities. The church had declined in membership after the division of 1844 but was again showing a rapid rate of increase. There were nearly three-quarters of a million members, administered to by some five thousand "traveling" preachers. The bishops must preside over thirty-nine annual conferences and appoint the traveling preachers to their posts. Clearly the conference must elect new bishops—three and possibly four.

Simpson, keenly aware of his own prospects, refused to enter the lists. He stood precisely where he had stood twenty years before, when he had declined to preach a trial sermon as a condition of being admitted to the Pittsburgh conference. He believed simply that men were appointed of God to perform the offices of the church. Some were ordained to be apostles; some, prophets; some, teachers—and some, bishops. He would not exert himself in his own behalf, but he would obey Providence.[3]

Several friends felt no such reticence. Lucien Berry, William M. Daily, John L. Smith, eager instruments of Providence, circulated among the delegates, urging the election of Simpson. Daily, one of the secretaries of the general conference, sat on the platform and soon became known to all the delegates. Aggressive, friendly, voluble, and persuasive, he swept from one group to another, taking the opposition by storm. Berry was less aggressive but perhaps more effective. He inspired confidence, and men came to ask his advice on the western candidates.[4]

As the time for the election of bishops drew near, the tension increased. The conference voted to elect four men to the high office. Party lines yielded largely to sections, with candidates from New England, the middle states, and the West. Each section advanced its favorite son, but each needed supporting votes from other sections. In the West a spirited contest developed among Simpson and Ames of Indiana and Edward Thomson, president of Ohio Wesleyan University. Ames was the best known, but some delegates thought that he had lost his opportunity when he failed of election in 1844. Thomson was strongly supported by the Ohio conferences; but opponents circulated reports that he was "sickly, somewhat hard of hearing, inexperienced in the itinerancy, and necessary to the college" —all true, he wrote to his wife.[5]

From the opening of the conference Simpson was regarded favorably. It was said against him that he had been too short a time in the active ministry. Border delegates, fearing that his views were too antislavery, sent a committee to question him. He refused to commit himself, referring simply to his "course as editor." The Baltimore men were not satisfied with his response and lined up behind Thomson.[6]

Simpson's stand on the pew question was even more hazardous. Ohio was solidly opposed because he was too friendly to pewed churches. New England suspected that he was unfriendly. In the debate on a proposal to solicit funds from the church at large for a house of worship in Washington, he further alienated New England. He said the Methodists ought to have a church where senators and congressmen and other public officials could worship: he had talked with some of these men and had learned that they could not even find the Methodist meeting place. He did not demand a "grand church"; but he hoped that it would be as fine as the Boston edifice in which they were gathered, save "these bonds." And he pointed "playfully" at the doors to the pews. Father Edward Taylor of Boston was angered by the allusion, and "complained bitterly" of his western prejudice. Abel Stevens, editor of *Zion's Herald* and a friend, suggested to Simpson that the phrase be omitted from the report; but he refused.[7]

He had several other opportunities to create a favorable impression. His address on Sabbath schools, emphasizing the impact of religious instruction on civilization, was "fervid and appropriate." Stevens apologized to the readers of the *Daily Zion's Herald* for having to abridge a speech from which not a "syllable" should have been omitted. In an address on California missions Simpson achieved some of the eloquence that had met with such favor in the West. Leading off with "railroad speed and power," he swept the audience with his "sustained and connected train of thought." His body swayed slightly as he spoke, marking out the rhythm of his speech. The effect was hypnotic. Stevens thought the speech "powerful"; but he felt constrained to say little about the speaker, who, "unfortunately," was "one of 'the noble army' of candidates for the Episcopacy."

The committee on local arrangements, however, seemed to think more highly of Edward Thomson's prospects, for it placed him in the Bromfield Street pulpit on the Sunday morning before the election.[8]

The balloting was set for Tuesday May 25. By Monday morning Berry was confident that Simpson could win by a bare majority—if the delegates pledged to support him would hold steady. But two Indianans were wavering—nothing that they could do would elect Simpson, they feared. The problem was the Ames-Simpson rivalry. No conference could expect two of its members to be named bishop, and for Indiana to support two candidates was to risk splitting the vote in the East and the middle states between them and thus defeat both. The Ohio delegation saw the point, and in an effort to elect Thomson, decided to go for Ames and thus eliminate Simpson. Berry held firm, however: Indiana must support both its candidates. At the last moment he convinced Benjamin Tefft, former faculty member at Indiana Asbury and friend of both Simpson and Thomson, that the former was the better candidate; and Tefft swung a number of his colleagues in western New York into line. On Tuesday morning some twenty delegates, already pledged to Simpson, sought Berry's judgment on the respective merits of Thomson and Ames. He quickly "set them right": Ames, of course, was the better man.[9]

That morning the bishop ordered the bar of the conference cleared, and prayed for divine guidance in the balloting. The tellers, passing through the aisles, distributed slips of paper upon which each delegate was to write the names of his four candidates for the episcopacy. The tellers then collected the ballots and read them, one by one, while the secretaries tabulated the results. With 173 delegates voting 87 votes were necessary to elect. Long before the final ballot was counted, Simpson could foretell the result. Levi Scott of Philadelphia, candidate of the middle states, received 113 votes; Simpson, 110; Osman G. Baker of New England, 90; and Edward R. Ames, 89. Four men had been elected on the first ballot: two from Indiana. Thomson stood fifth. The Ohio delegation, in supporting Ames, had insured his election and the defeat of its own candidate.[10]

That afternoon at the hotel, Bishop elect and Mrs. Simpson had tea for several "select" friends. As his former colleagues eagerly expressed their congratulations he suddenly remarked:

"This day have the words of the prophet been fulfilled."

"Who is the prophet?" someone called out.

"None other than Brother John L. Smith." Then Simpson told them of the walk through the Indiana fields six years earlier, of the long talk under a tree, of his taunt, "Son of man, prophesy," and of Smith's prediction that he would be elected bishop in 1852.[11]

But that night, reviewing in his journal the election and the basis for the opposition to him, he wrote:

> . . . the vote I received was wholly unexpected, and deeply impressed me with the kind feelings of my brethren. May I have the wisdom and grace to fit me for the high responsibilities which may devolve upon me, and especially may I be led to a more thorough consecration to God and his cause.

He felt that the election was "wholly Providential," because he had taken no part in the canvass for votes. The next morning, standing between "Brother" Hudson, who had been his senior minister at Pittsburgh twenty years before, and "Father" Havens, grizzled and muscular itinerant from Indiana, he was ordained to the episcopacy. On the Sabbath he was invited to preach at the Bromfield Street Church.[12]

II

The office of bishop was the highest in the Methodist Episcopal Church. Great and sometimes eloquent men had graced it: Francis Asbury, the foremost itinerant and traveler of the long road; William McKendree and Robert Roberts, circuit riders of the old West; and Elijah Hedding and Joshua Soule, strong-willed leaders of the slavery battle. The field of the bishop was as extensive as the church itself, for the general conference, proud of the itinerant character of the ministry and of the episcopacy, had steadfastly refused to adopt the diocese plan, or to make any territorial restriction. A bishop supervised the work of only four or five annual conferences at one time; but from year to year his supervision was shifted from one group of conferences to another. Presumably, as time passed, each bishop would thus exercise his authority over the whole territory of the church. His chief responsibilities were presiding at the annual conferences and appointing pastors to circuits or stations—which was arduous indeed, for conferences averaged 100 to 125 ministers each, every one of whom must be assigned to a church or circuit. The changes were numerous, for the rule of the church limited the stay of any minister at one charge to two years.

To a man of Simpson's eloquence the office of bishop offered an extraordinary opportunity to exercise his talents: it gave him prestige of office, a wide audience, and his speaking engagements were frequently special occasions—anniversaries of the church, ordinations, dedications, and conventions. In fact, however, the office was so circumscribed that in public affairs and social issues, and even in denominational polity, a bishop tended to be neutral. He was a moderator, presiding over meetings, who had no part in debate or discussion. "Dr. Simpson ought never to have been elected," wrote Abel Stevens, journalist and historian of the church, adding that so powerful a preacher, with his vigor and his outspokenness on public affairs, should not have his talents "neutralized forever." [13] Simpson would long remember those words and reflect upon them.

The last afternoon and evening in Boston, he met with the other bishops to discuss plans for conferences and to copy a number of important episcopal decisions into his notebook. He contended briefly for the privilege of being the first to visit California, but yielded to Ames. En route to Pittsburgh he paused in New York to breakfast with Mayor Harper and to purchase supplies from the Methodist Book Room—journals, parchments, portfolio, all to be shipped to the seat of his first conference. At Pittsburgh he had but Saturday and Monday to settle his family in a boarding place, and to take care of his personal business. On Sunday, visiting the Smithfield and Liberty Street churches where he had served as a young minister, he addressed two Sabbath schools, assisted in administering the Lord's supper in the afternoon, and preached to a "large congregation" at night.[14] He had already begun to experience something of the tempo and duties of the office of bishop.

His first conference was set for Morgantown, (West) Virginia, some two days' travel from his home at Pittsburgh. On the way he passed through Uniontown, the village to which he had come a quarter of a century before, eager to begin his studies at Madison College, having walked from Cadiz, Ohio, with his books and his clothes on his back and eleven dollars in his pocket. The contrasting circumstances did not escape him. "Uniontown to me has some pleas-

ant reminiscences," he wrote to Ellen. "Nearly twenty-four years ago
I entered it one afternoon, as a poor student. . . . I could not afford
a stage passage, nor could I well afford to pay for regular meals, and
hence I got but one meal a day, and lived on cakes for the other two
till I reached the town. . . . Change after change has since occurred,
until this evening I entered it again by the same road on which I
travelled then." [15]

The brethren at Morgantown received him kindly, and he was
able to assign the preachers to their charges with "comparatively
little trouble," although he sat with his cabinet of presiding elders
until ten o'clock at night, and once until after midnight. He presided at the business sessions of the conference, he spoke at the Sunday-school and missionary anniversaries, preached twice, and, with
appropriate charges, ordained the deacons and elders.[16]

Appointments soon proved to be his most harassing problem.
Old friends and new acquaintances, ministers and laymen brought
pressure upon him. One layman insisted on having Brother Babcock
"because revivals have always followed him." A minister, hearing
early in the conference that a man who was both a Mason and a
poor preacher was to be appointed his presiding elder, protested that
such an arrangement would "seriously militate against the interests
of work and church." Over in Ohio a brother rather ingenuously
urged that the bishop make him a presiding elder because his wife's
rich relatives from the East expected to visit them the next summer
and he wanted them to find him in an "influential position in the
church." Another layman complained of his preacher's lack of spiritual qualities:

He wares verry nice whiskers and they ware not nice without going
to the Barbers and haveing them blacked he also favours checker playing as
strengthning the mind he favors nick nicks start off in a boat four or five
mile along with a mixed crowd not one of his own members along and spend
the day and to ten Oclock at night & speaks of being out in the grass the
same as the Mericle performed by our savour where he fed the five thousand
with the loavs & fishes there being mutch grass there.[17]

Because every preacher had to be moved at the end of a two-
year period, the whole problem was singularly trying. Simpson welcomed information and carefully prepared in advance for the decisions he would have to make. He secured maps of the conferences

and of each district and circuit, with records of the church property, size of house, and drawing of the property; he made out forms with spaces to show the number of years a man had served a given charge, and what charges he had served, and he made an effort to call cabinet sessions in advance of the regular conference. He soon discovered that oratory was his greatest asset, even in the unhappy responsibility of making appointments. Men loved him not only for his "spiritual" preaching—his "unction" and "power," and his personal goodness and kindness—but for his vivid portrayals of the triumphs of Methodism. Once caught in his spell, the preachers were more disposed to accept their appointments. He had not been in the episcopal office many years before it was generally said that there was no better loved man in all Methodism.[18]

Other duties of the conferences, he found nearly as onerous as appointments. Church trials—one being of a minister who held slaves—prolonged each of his first conferences. He presided day after day, sometimes "stealing" a few minutes from the discussion to write to his wife, sometimes listening to the long debates and then complaining to his diary: "Did but little work. Had a night session . . . closed Conf. before 10 o'clock. Had some headache." [19]

The details and problems of travel always interested, sometimes irritated him, and occupied a large place in his life and his journals. Trains, when he could get them, were often late, forcing him to sit in a tavern or station without sleep; on one such occasion he felt fortunate in crawling into a bed of straw on the floor. He traveled sometimes on horseback, sometimes by boat or stage, occasionally by a hack or "mud wagon." Once, en route to a western conference with six other preachers, weighing the wagon down so that there was no play in the springs, he jolted the whole of a cold and snowy day over slightly frozen roads. He preferred the trains, although it sometimes "seemed rather tedious to stop between thirty and forty times at towns and where no towns were but spots where some trade could be found or a Post Office existed." He was delighted with the "very fast" travel one winter's afternoon in western Pennsylvania when the train went thirty-one miles in one hour, including "the time spent slowly in passing through Bayardstown & up grade." [20]

He was pleased, also, when he could get a "fair dinner of home poached eggs, potatoes & biscuit," but not a little irritated when he felt he was overcharged, as at West Point, where he paid $2.50 for "supper, lodging & breakfast—the highest bill I ever had, and yet the most ordinary fare." At Harrisburg he became very nearly angry when the landlord, calling him to his train just after he had "fairly started" on his dinner, charged the full half-dollar. "I suppose," he said, tartly, "if we had been allowed to get through supper it would have been a dollar." [21]

In due time, and with characteristic good intention, he outlined for himself in "Thoughts for health and comfort," a set of rules to be followed: retire always as early as ten; get enough sleep, but try to rise at six o'clock; if possible get regular hours for meals; avoid night traveling; use salt sponge bath every morning, "be firm to *talk less*." There were conveniences, also, which he felt he must have: a trunk arranged with hatbox, a case for parchments, writing materials, traveling case, umbrella for traveling and another for home, and a round-top desk.[22]

One rule was inflexible, so much a part of his routine and belief that he did not feel it necessary to list it among his "thoughts." He would not travel on Sunday. The observance of this custom led, in the second year of his episcopacy, to an incident which delighted his Methodist brethren.

He reached Lancaster, Pennsylvania, on his way to Philadelphia, after midnight on Saturday. A fellow minister and his wife kept on, but since the train would not reach the city until six or seven o'clock in the morning, Simpson got off. ("How ministers," he wrote to his wife, "can reconcile Sabbath travelling with a sense of duty I cannot tell.") The next morning he set out to find the Methodist church and fell into the company of a member, who learned that he was a preacher and introduced him as such to the pastor. The latter, without realizing that he was a bishop, invited him to preach and introduced him to the congregation simply as "Brother Simpson from Pittsburgh." The visitor enjoyed "peculiar liberty," the congregation was considerably stirred, and the pastor, astonished by the eloquence, suddenly perceived that the man in the pulpit was the bishop. At the conclusion of the sermon he seized his hand and called to the congregation that the man to whom they had listened was Bishop Simpson! To his wife, Simpson laconically reported, "Whether they thought any more of the sermon for the name I cannot tell." [23]

He sent home short notes of his activities, now and then a bit of gossip, an exciting incident, or a fashion note—as when in New York he first saw hoop skirts: "Oh dear, what skirts are hanging at the windows and doors of the Ladies dressing and trimming stores— filled with whalebone hoops and looking about the size of very large barrels. It is very hard for them when dressed to get in & out of the omnibus or cars." [24]

Ordinarily his letters ended with somber preachments. "Be careful of your health," he wrote to Ellen. "Be cheerful. Look aloft. The stars display their beauty to us only when we look at them; and if we look down at the earth our hearts are never charmed." [25]

Constantly away from home, he was often harassed by household needs: credit drafts for Ellen; painters who ought not be paid until the job was done and the quality of their work inspected; the care of his property and investments, including the still troublesome brewery, of which Ellen had by this time inherited a share. The brewery was a particularly distressing problem, for the other heirs, although apparently not wishing to operate the plant themselves, desired to rent the kiln. Times were so out of joint that they had "to regard their income more watchfully"; and they had been "kind" to the Simpsons. "Still," the bishop wrote, "I would much sooner pay them the rent" which they would lose "and then let the building stand idle, than to aid in the spread of vice either directly or indirectly." [26]

III

The greatest demands upon Simpson's time were for sermons, addresses, and lectures. He became widely recognized as the most effective preacher on the episcopal board. In order to assure the success of the General Missionary Demonstration in New York City in the fall of 1853, all the bishops were urged to attend. Who should be selected as speaker? One bishop was too old, another too feeble in voice, and yet another too well acquainted in the city to attract attention. Of the remaining bishops, wrote a member of the committee on arrangements two (one of whom was Ames) were hardly known in New York; but "Bishop Simpson, during his visit here last spring became widely known, and left our city to the regret of many who long again to hear his voice. I think, dear sir, I can truly say . . . 'thou art the man.' " [27]

However demanding of time and energy, the speaking engagements were a source of pleasure and satisfaction. It pleased Simpson to think that he was setting "an example of earnestness in the Christian ministry" both in manner and in quantity.[28]

In the fall of 1852 he studied "very busily" preparing a lecture on the "preternatural." There had been much stir about spiritualism and table rappings, and people were both curious and fearful. The first American mediums to hear the mysterious knockings from the "spirit world" were the Fox sisters, Margaret and Kate, daughters of a humble Methodist farmer in western New York. About the same time mesmerism and the somnambulic trance had come to general attention. A number of journals on spiritualism and animal magnetism sprang into existence, and one of the best was edited by La Roy Sunderland, a former Methodist preacher and editor who, in the thirties, had published one of Simpson's early writings. Among the Methodists intrigued by these strange manifestations of "supernatural" forces, was one of Simpson's former students.[29]

Prompted to look into this subject both by his concern for Methodism and by his own curiosity, Simpson soon came to regard the movement with contempt. By this modern delusion, he said, "telegraphic communications with heaven and hell . . . were now made about as cheaply and as quickly as with Boston or New York." They might be accounted for by ventriloquism, by collusion, by natural causes not yet explained. The duty of thinking men and women was to explain them "and not act like the Brahmin who broke the microscope because it showed him what he did not wish to see."

He could not look with favor upon belief in the preternatural, for, upon the whole, the tendency of such belief was to

retard the progress of science, and knowledge, because it checked inquiry. . . . Eclipses had once been considered as indicative of Divine displeasure. So, too, comets had once been regarded as ominous of woe, and the Pope, in view of this, had once actually made one of these heavenly wanderers the subject of an excommunicating bull!

True religion differed from the mysticism which saw phantoms and apparitions, in that it revealed the spiritual world, and gave light for earthly toil. There were just two modes of communication with the spirit world. "One was, by *spiritual communion;* the other was, by *material or physical signs*. The latter must be rejected." If the existence of the spiritual were assumed, a man could ascertain its laws only by patient inquiry, and he could "at best but form an imperfect idea of futurity." [30]

The lecture was filled with "capital hits" at the " 'spiritual' follies of the day" and with illustration and allusions to science. It was enthusiastically received at Pittsburgh and Philadelphia. The Pittsburgh *Christian Advocate* called for its publication; the Young Men's Mercantile Library Association and the Mechanics' Institute persuaded Simpson to appear on their lecture series; and other organizations besieged him with requests.[31]

He had made no dramatic entrance into the discussion of public affairs—of secular matters; yet his public lecture was a departure from the course of one who was supposed to be forever neutralized by his election to the episcopal office, and it set the pattern by which he was to sustain himself on the lecture platform for twenty-five years.

I V

Simpson was not satisfied with his personal relationship to the church and to God. "May I have wisdom and grace to fit me for the high responsibilities which may devolve upon me, and especially may I be led to a more thorough consecration to God and his cause," he wrote in his journal on the day of his election to the episcopacy. In the succeeding weeks he was much too busy with conferences to keep up his diary or give an account of his "religious experience." His first real leisure came during an inspection trip into western Virginia, where he was detained by high water. The churches were small; the congregations, discouraged and apathetic. "Much depressed," he sought to analyze his condition. In some respects he labored "sufficiently." Indeed, he felt sometimes that the combined "physical efforts" and "mental excitement" in his work were unendurable. Yet the good which resulted from his pulpit labors was little, compared with what he might expect if he were in "the full spirit" of his mission. What his heart greatly needed was "a deeper work of grace." "Something not yet possessed" was requisite to make him victorious over all his "infirmities and temptations." "I need to be *created anew* in Christ Jesus." [32]

New Year's Day found him first prostrate with penitence and then strengthened by new and pious resolutions. Awakened at two in the morning by the striking of a clock, he knelt by his bedside to ask for "wisdom and grace." Weary with his work, he doubted that he would live through another year; yet he was thankful that Death had not yet been "commissioned" to cut him down. He would aim at a higher life than ever before; he would seek to cultivate and guard his physical powers, he would better redeem his time—converse less with friends, "especially on topics other than the Church and its institutions and personal holiness." That morning he rose at six, and after his bath, having read *"three* chapters in the beginning of the Old Testament and *two* in the New," he purposed "a regular reading after this general method."

He was once again facing the problem of his youth. Behind his physical weariness and the mental anxiety of the new responsibilities was the high doctrine of his church: Christian perfection or entire sanctification. Among the early Methodist teachings none was more carefully nourished or faithfully championed by some leaders than this. In theological language the doctrine, or "experience," was "a state of grace implying purity of heart or a heart cleansed from sin by the blood of Christ." It was a crisis experience, subsequent to and not unlike conversion. Christian perfection, John Wesley had written, "implies that no wrong temper, none contrary to love remains in the soul; and that all the thoughts, words, and actions are governed by pure love." Simpson knew that his heart was not "cleansed from all iniquity," that he did not have the "full consecration which devoted every moment to the divine service." [33]

These matters he wrote into his journal. Not often did he confess them to others; but in the spring, after his trip into Virginia, he talked over his religious state with Mrs. Phoebe Palmer, distributor of tracts and one of the earliest female class leaders in New York City, who was noted for her promotion of "holiness." She was surprised and much concerned to learn that Bishop Simpson did not have the "experience." In fact, using the language and the tactic which her group found most effective, she expressed the belief that his lack was not the experience, but the "witness"; and she wrote: "I hope you will not longer permit the tempter to hinder you from laying hold upon the promise . . . from the persuasion that you may not have set yourself apart wholly, for the Lord knows the sincerity of your intention." Other bishops were persuaded and preached the doctrine. Perhaps it was of significance to Methodism that the most eloquent of the bishops never discovered the satisfying spiritual condition of which she wrote. The following New Year's Day he was again "covenanting that, if spared, the New Year should be one of greater devotion to God." [34]

XVI

TO CALIFORNIA AND OREGON

THE episcopal plan of visitation for 1853 called upon Simpson to make the long journey to California and Oregon; and in December of that year he began the trip, sailing from New York via Panama.[1]

He had made up his mind to write an account of his journey for publication. Travel books were much in vogue. What could be more exciting than an account of travels to the fabulous Pacific Coast? In preparation, he read extensively in history and geography of the region he was to visit; and on board the ship he was alert to every incident that might please the fancy of his Methodist readers.

There were six in his party, including Brother Nelson Reasoner, a young preacher who was transferring to the Pacific Coast; two young women who expected "to fulfil matrimonial engagements"; and two wives who were rejoining their husbands in California. Among the other passengers were several gentlemen from California who "were reputed to have amassed large sums of money," and William Kip, missionary bishop of California in the Protestant Episcopal Church, en route with his wife and son to his new diocese.[2]

As they set sail Bishop Simpson stood on the deck watching, impressed by the "forests of masts" and the "receding mansions and steeples of the commercial emporium of the world."

That night, when he retired early, with a slight dizziness and thoughts of seasickness, the ship was still in sight of land. But when he arose the next morning he saw only the ocean's "vast expanse with its ceaseless undulations. The heavens came down as if to greet and encircle the watery plains. The fleecy clouds now veiled and now enriched the glories of the sky. The blushing tints of the east grew brighter and brighter until the golden rays of the sun sparkled upon the waters."

They entered the Gulf Stream the second night. Simpson awakened to note the change in the temperature and the increased motion of the ship. With a mind habituated to the drawing of morals, he began to reflect upon domestic scenes. As an infant he had been rocked in a cradle or carried in loving arms which lulled him to sleep. "Why not think of this ship as a cradle rocked by the winds and waves of the Almighty!" Knowing that "the arms of the ever-lasting love" were around and beneath him, and that God's will was best for "time or eternity," he accommodated himself to the motion of the vessel and soon was lost in sleep. Most of the passengers, how-ever, looked "very languid" in the morning, and several were not at the breakfast table. Nor would he intimate, the bishop slyly ob-served, "that it was christian philosophy that saved me from sea-sickness."

He reflected on the discovery of the Gulf Stream, the theories and facts concerning it, and the effects which it produced. He thought the seaweed (*Fucus natans,* he classified it in a momentary revival of his old interest in botany) accurately as well as quaintly described by Columbus as "similar to small branches of pine covered with pistachio nuts." He recorded the temperature of the water and noted that observations showed the latitude 25° 53′ N. and the longi-tude 73° from London. He was not pleased to think that American mariners still recorded their longitude from London, when "our metropolis answers equally well." Americans consulted British charts, which they considered the most reliable, and made all calcula-tions in accordance with the plan of English navigators. He was willing to concede that "we owe much to British science—we rever-ence the names of her philosophers and statesmen"; but he believed America was "destined to surpass" all other nations in "commercial greatness" and its mariners ought to conform their notes to the meridian of their own metropolis.

From this little essay in patriotism, he returned to reflections on Columbus, particularly to suggestions that Commander Pinzon had persuaded him to change his course to southwesterly. Had he not done so, he would have sailed directly to Florida, and the North American continent might have been opened to Catholic settle-ment. But "the wisdom of God ordered it otherwise."

Flying fish at last drew him away from his digression. They "seemed to throw themselves from the water by a rapid stroke of the tail, and skimming near the water, as they touched it, another stroke of the tail raised them again, thus resembling the flight of a bird." He could never ascertain "whether they fled from some pursuing enemy, or whether they were rejoicing in their power of rising above their watery home."

In the late afternoon of Christmas Day they saw the blue mountains of Jamaica; they rounded the point about sunset, sailed along the southern coast, and anchored off Port Royal. They would make their way up the channel to Kingston the next morning.

The passengers had several hours to observe life in Jamaica. Simpson set out with Brother Reasoner and was delighted with the tropical vegetation, "so green and luxurious even in mid-winter." He noted the scene at the wharf: women carrying baskets of coal on their heads; little boys diving for dimes and darting about in the water "like some amphibious animals"; loafers lounging on the docks; and in the background the coconut palm "tall and slender with a single issue of leaves at its summit . . . spreading like an umbrella."

On one of the principal streets they found a "crowd of colored women and boys offering for sale every species of fruit growing on the island." They pushed through "with almost as much difficulty as through a crowd of New York hackmen," heading for the Methodists' Coke Chapel. The church was wide and capacious with galleries on three sides, well finished pews and an organ of "respectable size." The main part of the floor—in strange contrast to American churches —was filled with movable benches that had no backs. The pulpit, "shaped somewhat after the tub fashion" and approached by spiral steps, looked "as though the architect designed to get the preacher as near heaven as possible." By asking questions of the pastor "in true Yankee style," Simpson secured details concerning the number of churches, the pastors, the financial condition, and the relation of church to state.

Brother Reasoner had enough of exploration and went back to the ship; but Simpson with an unquenchable curiosity made his way down to the station and took the "cars" to Spanish Town, the capital of the island. It disappointed him. In spite of a good location and an abundance of tropical shrubbery, the residences lacked architectural beauty; the rich and the poor, with their contrasting homes, lived in close proximity; and there was no indication of recent building. He saw the government square and questioned the sentinels on guard—who, in their red uniforms, were "as black as ever night frowned upon"—about local history and government. He learned, with amazement, that there were some six hundred soldiers stationed in the place. Why, he did not know, for "the poor people had scarcely spirit enough to live." He visited the Catholic Cathedral and the·Wesleyan chapel, and inquired into the beginnings of Methodism.

As he returned to the cars he was joined by an Englishman who, upon learning that Simpson was one of five or six hundred passengers on the steamer, expressed his surprise that "so many people could be kept in *h'order*."

Simpson, piqued by the obvious thrust, inquired why so many soldiers were on duty in Spanish Town, adding that people in the United States were "not troubled with soldiers parading our streets on guard."

" 'Ah,' said the Englishman, 'yours is an 'orrible government—it is only mob law.' "

Simpson pressed the argument, but the Englishman only repeated his original indictment. He had been in New York, and it was governed by the mob, and was wholly unsafe; and "the Irish rule Philadelphia, and keep it in a state of siege."

The bishop retorted that many native-born American citizens had lived in the country from their youth up without being aware of any serious danger. He had "no time to dispute," and so he *"merely remarked,"* in a burst of epideictic oratory, that his country everywhere showed signs of prosperity, that the population was increasing, the cities growing, the borders enlarging, and that they had never been more prosperous and happy.

The Englishman, with "the marks of decay and dilapidation" visible around him, was silent for a moment. Then, "giving a sigh, he replied with great emphasis" that he knew that "financially" Americans were successful, but " 'every Englishman had a perfect *h'aversion* to the form of government—there was no *h'order* in it.' "

Catching the train back to Kingston, Simpson hired a hack and drove about the streets collecting items of interest for his book. Back on the steamer, he sat down to reflect upon the life on the island, and particularly the conditions which had followed the emancipation of the slaves.

Bishop Kip also had gone ashore, and had observed the indolence and degradation of the free blacks and made inquiries about them. "Lazy, shiftless, and diseased," he concluded. "Even coaling the steamer is done by women." " 'Once,' " a gentleman had said to him, " 'you did not see an untidy negro in the streets. Now, look at them!' " [3]

Simpson agreed that "so much indolence, degradation, filth, and vice are seldom seen," but questioned the conclusion that the American slaves were "far superior to the free colored people of Jamaica." The women's coaling of the ship was not a result of freedom but had been a practice in the time of slavery; and it remained the practice in some islands where slavery continued to exist. Nor could the prevalence of vice be attributed to emancipation. Jamaica was "suffering the result of her former wickedness." He searched his history books and found evidence of licentiousness and concubinage among the ruling classes, and the low state of morals among the blacks before emancipation. He noted the restraining influence of religion upon the majority of the blacks, the growing strength of the Baptists and the Wesleyans. He reflected on the depression and its benefits to the blacks, a great number of whom were securing their own little farms; he pointed out with sanguine hope the tendency of the blacks to regard themselves as superior to the mulattoes, and the consequent pride of caste which was expressing itself through acquisition of property, business enterprise, and education of children. To the stranger, the appearances were unfavorable; but "full investigation will lead any reflecting mind to approve of the emancipation of the negroes in Jamaica."

II

Three days from Kingston the steamer came to Aspinwall (Colón), the Atlantic terminal of the Panama railroad. The passengers disembarked the next morning and traveled by train and boat halfway across the Isthmus to Cruces, where Simpson had reserved rooms from New York; but travelers from the Pacific had arrived first, and the hotel had no sleeping places of any sort. He hurried to the other hotel and arrived just in time to secure for the ladies the last room—a garret on the third floor—and for himself and Brother Reasoner two cots in the gentlemen's commons. That night he lay in the commons where there were nearly a hundred and fifty cots and beds, many of them occupied by men "highly excited with drink." They sang and shouted and cursed and laughed at the jests of the "lewd women" in an adjacent room, separated from them only by a thin partition. In the barroom beneath, men who could get no cots "were drinking, swearing, and carousing, and making night more hideous by their revelry." Even in the native huts there was alternate singing and hallooing, long after midnight.

Simpson was up at four o'clock, trying to get the breakfast for which he had paid. As soon as it was sufficiently light, he looked for mules—seven of them, including one for luggage and four with side saddles for the ladies. Months ago in New York he had bought the first transit tickets for the trip, entitling him to first choice of mules —indeed, he had even received "sundry lessons" on "the qualities of mules and how to make our selection." He found the New York directions somehow not applicable to the "miserable specimens" available and first rights proved to be vested entirely in the man who was first able to seize a mule.

After much haggling they secured their mounts, and the party, in light clothes and palm-leaf hats, equipped with long-pointed spurs and whips, started on the muddy trail. Two of the women, lacking side saddles, were mounted "after the fashion of men." Now and then on the flat, spurring and whipping their mules into a gallop, members of the party would shout out gayly, like the natives, "mucha mula." "Our friends," thought the bishop, "would scarcely have recognized us."

The trip over the mountains was hazardous at times. On either side the hills "rose abruptly; the bottom of the pass was so narrow that the slender legs of the mule had scarcely room for motion." The ascents and descents were steep, and the holes worn by the mules resembled flights of stairs. It was impossible to pass another train in narrow gorges, and then the muleteers would utter shrill cries warning of their approach. Such places were well suited to robbery, and the rumor spread that a specie train had recently been seized and six persons murdered. Brother Reasoner borrowed a revolver from a Californian but had no occasion to use it.

The hot, humid climate, the difficulties of the trail, and the slow gait of the mules, made the twenty-four-mile trip exceedingly tiring. Now and then the party stopped at a stream to bathe hands, arms, and temples. At five o'clock in the afternoon, nearly exhausted, they came out on a hillside and looked down on the twin towers of the Cathedral of Panama.

It was New Year's Eve. After supper the bishop and Brother Reasoner passed an hour with the ladies "in religious conversation," and then "bowed together in grateful prayer . . . trying to be thankful for the mercies of the past and covenanting that, if spared, the new year should be one of greater devotion to God."

The bishop, suffering from fever, called for his bed; but, despite his earlier payment, only a broken cot remained in a room where twenty men were already sleeping. He lay on the cot until it gave way, and then rolled over on the floor and rested fitfully. His head ached, his mouth and lips were dry and thirsty. Noting the "feverish throb" in his pulse, he thought with dread of the "Isthmus fever" but tried to "believe that all was right, and that arms of love were around and beneath me." Then the fever grew milder, the current of air less annoying, and he sank into a "calm and peaceful slumber."

The following day he was still weak and feverish; and, unable to find his trunk, he could not dress until after the church hour. Passengers were allowed to board the ship at one o'clock, but were given notice that it would not sail until six; so, although his fever was increasing, he took "a short walk about the town." He rested little during the first night on the Pacific. Possessed of the adventurer's love of seeing, he rose between three and four and walked out on deck to look at a part of the sky he had never seen before. The Southern Cross "shone in full brilliancy," and the North Star was but seven degrees above the horizon. "All the stars beamed with that soft planetary lustre which is peculiar to tropical climes. The sea was full of phosphorescence."

Some days out of Panama, the *Golden Gate* broke her shaft and had to lie to until it could be repaired. Meanwhile food and water were rationed, and uneasiness prevailed among the passengers. At last the repairs were completed, and the ship proceeded to San Diego. On the way out of that harbor late in the afternoon, she grounded, and wind and tide prevented her freeing herself. Another vessel answered the captain's signal for aid but failed to dislodge her. As they waited for high tide the wind rose, and the other ship made for shore. "The storm raged fiercely; the cordage creaked; the sail . . . was torn into shreds; the shrouds cracked like whip-cords. . . .

The waves rose high, dashing furiously against the vessel, and every now and then breaking even over the top of the cabin. The foremast was cracked . . . and the cabin-work around the mainmast began to crack and give way." When midnight approached the ship leaned to the "larboard" and Simpson stood for three hours with many of the other passengers on the "starboard guard." There seemed to be "but little hope of the ship's outriding the storm." Some of the "wildest men" went to Simpson "to converse on religious subjects," and he proposed to Bishop Kip "the propriety of prayer." The ship's physician objected "lest it should increase the terror of the passengers." About one o'clock the storm began to subside, and shortly after daybreak the passengers were able to go ashore.

Simpson and his party with others transferred to a smaller ship, the *Goliad,* for the rest of the trip to San Francisco.

III

From his landing in San Francisco to the opening of the conference some three weeks later at Sacramento, Simpson preached almost daily—on Sundays, two or three times. He traveled by stage, horseback or muleback to the towns on the mother lode, all still feverish with the gold rush. He visited the diggings and went afoot among the hills; he ran into old acquaintances: one was working in a groggery; another, making $1,000 a month as a doctor; several, digging gold. The distance between appointments, which he always covered in a day, was often thirty or forty miles; once it was seventy. He encountered snow, and rain, and mud; and in climbing Mokelumne Butte, near Stockton, he fell and tore the skin from his knuckles, "and worse still the knee of my trousers." Yet, with all the strenuous living, his health remained good.

He was delighted with California, and his brethren urged him to make his residence there. "I confess," he wrote to his wife, "were you and the children with me, I think I could spend a few years very pleasantly, in trying to lay the foundations of the Church on the Pacific coast. . . . But I think I almost see you throw down the letter and say, 'Catch me going to California!' Well, then, pick it up again, and I will drop that subject." He complained about her failure to write. He had been in California three weeks, making the rounds of the churches, dedicating several meetinghouses, preaching before the legislature at Benicia, and returning to Sacramento, and had been away from home two months—and still no letter. Had he no one *"who loves to write letters to me"?* [4]

After completing his official business in California, he was scheduled to conduct the Oregon conference which was to convene on March 16. However, steamers to Portland were uncertain, and he began to fear that he would not arrive in time for any of it. At last he was able to arrange passage on a steamer due in Portland on Wednesday, the evening before the conference.

But Belknap Settlement, the small community between Corvallis and Eugene where the conference was to meet, was a hundred miles (four days' journey) south of Portland. He hoped, by travelling long days and all night Saturday, if necessary, through the "wild, woody country," to reach his brethren by Sabbath morning. He took a small steamer from Oregon City up the Willamette River, but was delayed first when at darkness they tied up to wait for the moon to rise, and again about ten miles from Salem when the boat caught on a sand bar. They finally freed the boat about nine o'clock the next morning, but were not on their way until eleven. At Salem, with the journey scarcely half over, he and the friend who had joined him at Portland hired the driver of a light spring wagon with a small team to take them "very rapidly" to Corvallis for forty dollars. In a short distance the traces broke, the wagon bed spread and let down one end of the seat. The friend then sat on his baggage and the bishop on the seat, "one end of it elevated, the other on the floor."

Along the Willamette River he caught brief glimpses of the snow peaks of the Cascades—Mount Hood and Mount Jefferson. He was pleased by the winding Willamette, the low plains green with wheat in mid-March, the wooded hills, and snow-covered Marys Peak in the Coast Range. They were still far from Corvallis when the driver lost his way. "After winding to several points of the compass," they drew up at a farmhouse, and made a new bargain for transportation.

At ten o'clock Saturday night, after supper and a little rest, they started on their way again. The bishop lay down in the back of the wagon on some oats, and thus rode "through sloughs and mud" until two in the morning, when he reached Corvallis—still some fifteen or twenty miles from the conference. The Methodist brother who was to have accompanied him, despairing of his coming, had turned out the horses and gone on. Simpson slept until sunrise, then secured a horse, and was in the saddle a little after eight o'clock, riding rapidly in the company of two "pioneers," to Belknap Settlement. At the settlement, thinking he had reached his destination, he dismissed his guides. The meeting place was yet five miles distant! He rode on, carrying his satchel, and at last came in sight of a log schoolhouse with horses and wagons tied around it.

In the meantime, members of the conference were anxiously awaiting his arrival. On Wednesday the preachers had started coming in, from Puget Sound to the California border. "Their ware Jiants in the Oregon Conference in Those days," Ketturah Belknap wrote a half-century later. "After a years seperation and hard toil they greet each other with great warmth and fervor after which their first inquiry is concerning the Bishop Has he been heard from, or, has he yet arrived, where can he be . . . is it Posible he has *been lost at Sea.*" [5]

The conference opened on Thursday morning, but no word had been received. "With sad hearts," Mrs. Belknap wrote, "the Breathren Elect the Rev. T H Pearne who is a Presiding Elder to act as Presiding oficer until the Bishop shall arrive if he comes at all." He did not come Thursday, or Friday, or Saturday. Nor had he arrived by Sunday morning. Suppose he should come during the sermon? Would anybody recognize him?

The Sabbath-day religious exercise proceeded and Pearne had reached the "peroration" of his sermon when he saw a man "wearing a linen duster and bearing a gripsack" enter and seat himself just inside the door. Pearne ceased to preach and, amid "breathless silence" said: "If the stranger who just came in is Bishop Simpson, he will please advance to the front." [6]

The stranger, badly bespattered with mud, walked slowly up the aisle, to the accompaniment of shouts and hallelujahs from all sides. "I was their," said Mrs. Belknap, "and surely the sene was beyond discription." Order was finally restored, "for all would Honor the Bishop and wait on his words." [7]

He delivered an exhortation, telling of his efforts to come to them and of the storm in which his ship had almost been wrecked. His feelings at the time of the greatest peril, he said, were expressed in the hymn of Henry Kirke White:

> Once on the raging Seas I rode
> The storm was loud, the night was dark . . .

The company again broke out into shouts and hallelujahs. As soon as order could be restored he promised to preach at two o'clock. Then he was driven to the Belknap home, and lay down and slept until dinner was ready.

That afternoon the bishop, mindful of the trials and tribulations of an itinerant minister, preached on Paul. Transporting his listeners to a time long past, he re-created one by one the persecutions which Paul had suffered—thrice beaten with rods, once stoned, and five times given forty stripes save one. Every preacher in the congregation had endured his own share of want and deprivation and was able to project himself into the struggles of the great apostle, suffering with him, but conquering too, and at last shouting in triumph with the bishop who straightened himself to his full height, drew his coat about him, and uttered the words of Paul: "But none of these things move me."

"Who shall describe the indescribable or speak the unutterable" one enthusiastic hearer said of the sermon: "Its imagery was celestial, its pathos divine, its power omnipotent. It was more than Bishop Simpson's own; it was God's and Christ's." Mrs. Belknap too enjoyed it, for when the bishop came to portray heaven, "he Just Soared A way up and took the Congregation with him." However, with shrewd insight, she observed that the sermon was "more for the Preachers than the comen People." [8]

Two days later, having concluded his conference, the bishop returned down the Willamette to Portland. After a short but perilous trip by steamer and canoe up the Columbia to The Dalles and back, he sailed for San Francisco and thence home. On the newly completed Panama railroad he crossed the Isthmus in a few hours. Early in June, he was once more with his family in Pittsburgh.

XVII

THE OLD ORDER CHANGETH

BISHOP SIMPSON returned from the Pacific coast to find his reputation as an orator greatly enhanced by the reports of his success. In California he had walked "with the tread of a giant." The preachers and people at the conference in Sacramento thought that he had preached "the king of sermons—the very greatest and best to which they had ever listened." It had been "permeated by that peculiar fire which sanctified genius alone can kindle." Indianans read the report and nodded their heads. "It could not be otherwise" with the man who had moved among them leaving such an impression of "devotedness and eloquence." [1]

Where he had been regarded as effective and popular, he now became known as an orator of power, and the press began to publish extravagant accounts of his eloquence. He combined emotion and reason; he was, oddly enough, both "abundant in knowledge" and "rich in speech." When fully fired he was "unsurpassed in the majesty, weight, and richness of his truth." Like the mesmerist, he had the strange power of seeming to transfigure himself into a medium—but he was the "strong and gifted medium of an idea," and the truth which he thus preached was "the pure metal unalloyed, unadulterated, and perfectly solid." [2]

In appearance, too, the bishop had become more imposing. He had gained in weight without becoming corpulent, and so had lost something of the angular, the loose and shuffling features of his earlier years. He had not yet become "handsome," wrote one of his journalist friends, tauntingly, "and we presume he never will"; but he had developed into "what might be denominated a fine looking man." His slightly graying hair softened the asperity of his features. Under the emotion of speech his eye might kindle in a moment "all aglow," and the emotion would leap from speaker to audience with the tingling of an electric spark. The people heaped adulation upon him, but he maintained a "singularly gentle air" which was yet "impressive with sweet dignity." [3]

In his first quadrennium in the episcopacy, Simpson had struck out a new pattern. All his predecessors in the office of bishop had yielded to the routine of conference business; not one was remembered for eloquence, although an extraordinary sermon had brought about William McKendree's election in 1816, and Robert R. Roberts had been known in the West for his power in the pulpit. Simpson was the first who turned to the lecture platform with a message of enlightenment to the people: none before him had accepted the duty to teach as well as to preach.

Greatly pleased with their preaching bishop, delegates to the general conference of 1856 began to talk about sending him to England and Ireland as a fraternal delegate. Who could better represent American Methodism?

Simpson knew his power and sensed his responsibility. He welcomed opportunities to preach, that he might set an example for the young men in the ministry. He wondered if he ought not take time at each of the annual conferences for a special series of lectures to the younger preachers. Could he not meet them, say, at six o'clock in the morning before the regular breakfast hour and talk to them on homiletics and practical theology? In the winter, when he was free from conference duties, he went on lecture tours—out into Ohio and Indiana, east to Philadelphia and New York City to answer calls for his old lecture on the Preternatural and for his new one, "The Influence of the Bible on Language." [4]

The old order was changing, and Methodism must change with it. An educated people demanded an educated ministry. The founding of a theological school at Evanston, Illinois, in 1856 met Simpson's hearty approval. He defended the venture on the basis that, although American Methodists had always demonstrated an antipathy for theological seminaries—manufactories for preachers—the church "had always carefully exacted study of her ministers." [5]

Peter Cartwright, muscular itinerant from Illinois, never very friendly to Simpson, took vigorous exception to the new emphasis on theological training. Holding a low opinion of the "extorted concessions from these velvet-mouthed and downy D.D.'s" who spoke "in rapturous and exalted strains" of the old pioneer preachers and yet demanded an improved and educated ministry, he thought that they really felt the circuit riders owed their success to the ignorance of the people! [6]

But the bishop was adamant. He thought it "the destiny of man upon earth" to learn "all that can be learned of nature." There yet slumbered "unreached truths of a scientific and economical nature, which only await the evoking power of expanded intellect." This expansion was conditioned upon "the more general and equal enlightenment of nations." Then "like the galvanic battery, when the number of plates is increased, the quantity of electricity remaining the same, the intensity is heightened." [7]

Simpson was not satisfied with an educated ministry. Since his election as bishop he had become increasingly aware that "the great social changes" demanded other changes in Methodism. The followers of John Wesley had been humble, but they had also been virtuous and enterprising. They had done well in the world. John McLean, associate justice in the United States Supreme Court and an aspirant in 1856 for the Republican nomination for the Presidency, was a Methodist. So were Joseph W. Wright, governor of Indiana, and the four Harper brothers, proprietors of the largest publishing house in America. Simpson's former student, James Harlan, had been elected United States Senator from Iowa in 1855, and William M. Daily, former chaplain to the United States House of Representatives, was now president of Indiana University. Dr. John Evans of Indiana had joined the staff of Rush Medical College in Chicago. In that rapidly growing metropolis of the West, he had learned to conduct real estate and railroad operations with a great deal of success. A devoted Methodist as well as a successful businessman and brilliant physician, he helped to establish Northwestern University and Garrett Biblical Institute; and the city of Evanston was named for him.

Everywhere, at the insistence of the local ministers and congregations, Simpson was entertained in the "best" homes. Thus he came to know Mark and Oliver Hoyt, New York leather merchants who lived in Stamford, Connecticut, and Daniel Ross, a New York banker. In Philadelphia he was the guest of Colonel A. W. Cummings, editor of the *Evening Bulletin,* in a beautiful mansion near Girard College.[8] Simpson himself, although always pinched for money, was doing well for a Methodist preacher. As bishop he received a salary of $3,500, and expenses. Although he never demanded a fee for his lectures, he often received payments of $25 to $100. Mrs. Simpson owned property in Pittsburgh including a warehouse which yielded an annual income of $500, lots in Jeffersonville, Indiana, valued at $7,000, and with her husband had other investments in Indiana, in Chicago, and, under Harlan's supervision, in Iowa.[9]

With an increasing number of "respectable" people assuming leadership in the church, ought it not to undergo some changes? Simpson pondered the question. Take architecture, for instance. The typical Methodist church was an unadorned meeting house, more like a warehouse than like a temple or a cathedral. And yet might it not be said that a church was "a house of God's glory," that it was erected "for the honor of his great name," and was, therefore, "partly monumental"? On the frontier of civilization a log cabin might show forth the glory of God as fully as a large edifice in a great city; but when men built houses for themselves "lined with cedar" ought not the house of God to be equal to the "grandest edifices of men"? Such a house would be a "source of great social refinement," "the keystone of the arch of literature, of science, and of art," an inspiration of noble undertakings—orphanages, homes for the aged and the infirm —the dwelling place of God, the ark of salvation.[10]

Methodism ought to have such churches, Simpson believed. With his encouragement Pittsburgh led the way and completed in 1855 Christ Church, the first Gothic structure in America built by Methodists.[11] Other cities followed, and he answered many demands for help in raising funds and in dedicating the new edifices.

If the churches were architecturally more beautiful, and if in some instances—as at Christ Church—the seatings were formal pews, might not the use of liturgy be justified? Simpson thought so, and believed that in time some of the churches would adopt a more formal ritual of worship. Could not liturgy be justified by the example of John Wesley? Were not his rules for the Methodist societies based upon the assumption that they would remain within the Church of England? Would he not, otherwise, have set forth rules governing liturgy? As a beginning, it might be a good idea to publish a new edition of John Wesley's prayer book.[12]

No less important was lay participation in church management. The preachers and bishops constituted the sole governing body, setting forth the doctrines, the disciplinary rules, and even naming the preachers for the local congregations. The church had split over lay participation in 1828, when the Methodist Protestant Church was founded. At the 1852 general conference Simpson had been named chairman of a committee to consider lay representation in the conference, and its report, although unfavorable, left the door open for future action: it was then "inexpedient" to admit laymen. But as he had traveled about in his official duties, enlarging his acquaintance among laymen as well as with clergymen, Simpson had come to look with increasing favor upon taking laymen into the councils of the church; and in 1856 he was confident that it was only a matter of time until the general conference would make the change.[13]

Surely the old order was giving way to the new.

II

In one particular, Simpson was against change: the old discipline of the church was good enough for handling the problem of slavery, in spite of the anxiety and alarm felt all over the country with the passage of the Kansas-Nebraska Act in 1854 and the beginning of the bloody strife in Kansas. One of his students at Indiana Asbury, a border preacher, had died from maltreatment by a mob, and another Methodist preacher had been tarred and feathered in Missouri. Simpson himself, in 1855, was forced to move his conference to St. Louis, because citizens of Independence, Missouri, refused to provide entertainment for the delegates and warned that the presence of antislavery preachers might "lead to results and acts to be regretted." [14]

To Simpson, the times called for moderation. He believed that the church was as thoroughly antislavery in its policies as conditions would permit. It forbade slaveholding among its active ministers, and slave trading by its lay members; and it permitted slaveholding among the latter only when their state laws forbade emancipation.

Many Methodists of the North, however, took a different stand. Alarmed by the situation in Kansas, taunted by Garrison, Theodore Parker, and others for holding a proslavery attitude, and embarrassed by the fact that there were slaveholder members in the church, they began to prepare for decisive action at the 1856 general conference. Some church papers carried on a campaign, not only for antislavery action but for withdrawal of the church from the border.

Feelings still ran high when the conference assembled at Indianapolis in May. The regular address of the bishops, read to the conference by the mild-mannered Bishop Janes, pointed out the importance of the church's work in slave territory and declared that "the existence of these conferences and churches does not tend to extend or perpetuate slavery." Moreover, the bishops doubted that the general conference had the authority to change the constitutional rule on slavery without prior action by the annual conferences.[15]

The address was "very severely criticized by the ultra party and strongly denounced." Simpson, writing to his wife, was concerned over the possibility of a split in the church, though he hoped for the best. He had no doubt, however, that the editors and other officers elected by the conference would be "anti-slavery men of strong type." The peace of the church for the next four years could not be guaranteed.[16]

Some of the antislavery brethren remembered Simpson's vigorous attack on the Fugitive Slave Law in 1850 and came to him for "counsel and support" in amending the discipline. He thought the proposed action unconstitutional, and told them so. "I suppose I have pretty deeply offended them," he wrote, sorry for having had to take so firm a position, for it was these same brethren who had said they were going to send him to England. Now he thought they would not support him. Ellen, at least, would be pleased, for then he would have more time to be at home.[17]

However reluctant to antagonize his friends, Simpson was thoroughly opposed to the constitutional change advocated by the antislavery delegates and sought to defeat it. Bishops were not permitted to participate in open floor debate, but he prepared the argument in collaboration with Abel Stevens and others. Stevens, a New Englander, had once been strongly antislavery; but since moving to New York in 1852 to edit the church's newly launched *National Magazine* he had imbibed much of the spirit of moderation and tolerance toward the border.

As brilliant in declamation as in writing, Stevens swept the conference before him, scattering the abolitionists. His argument was historical: the church from the early days, although strongly antislavery in sentiment, had permitted slaveholding; in short, it had always been both an antislavery and a slaveholding church, and to make it otherwise without approval of the annual conferences would change the basis of membership, and would therefore be unconstitutional.[18] In lieu of the drastic change proposed by the anti-slavery forces, he was prepared to introduce a mild, declaratory resolution which Simpson had drafted with the hope that it would gain the support of both factions, stating simply that the church was opposed in spirit to "slaveholding for mercenary purposes" and that it was the duty of the pastors of the churches to apply the general rule.[19]

In the parliamentary skirmishes which followed the debates the whole antislavery matter was put off, and Stevens had no occasion to introduce Simpson's resolution. The conference, suddenly grown conservative, turned out the radical editor of one of the church papers and elected Stevens to the most important editorial post in the church—that of the New York *Christian Advocate and Journal.*

And it named Matthew Simpson as one of two fraternal delegates to the Wesleyan conference in England. He was to attend the British and Irish conferences of 1857, to go as a delegate to the Evangelical Alliance meeting at Berlin, and to oversee Methodist interests in Germany and the Scandinavian countries.

XVIII

ENGLAND, THE CONTINENT, AND THE HOLY LAND

WITH a dream at last come true, Matthew Simpson carefully planned his travel abroad. He arranged his episcopal duties and his affairs at home to permit extending his itinerary from the scheduled conferences to eastern Europe and the Holy Land. He contracted to supply travel letters to the *Pittsburgh* and the *Western Christian Advocate;* through his New York banker friend, Daniel Ross, he established a credit of £500 with a Liverpool banking house; and he put in a supply of guide and travel books and an ample volume for his own note-taking and journalizing.[1] With his seventeen-year-old son Charles, he sailed from New York in the middle of May, 1857.

Ellen Simpson went with them to New York and to the dock to see them off. Father and son stood at the rail, waving until they could no longer identify her and the group of friends. That last white handkerchief he saw waved: was it Ellen's? Matthew fancied so. If all went well it would be nearly a year before he again set foot on American soil and joined the family at Pittsburgh, a year away from Ellen and the children. He wrote good-humoredly: "I waved, and Charles waved, and we all waved. But when . . . we quit waving our pocket-handkerchiefs . . . we kept waving away, sometimes a great deal more than we wished. At least Charles thought so." [2]

After a routine passage to Liverpool the bishop was immediately caught up in a whirl of conferences, special preaching engagements, and sight-seeing. In July he was to attend the Irish Wesleyan conference at Cork and the English Wesleyan conference at Liverpool; but first he made a hurried visit to his church's missionary projects in northern Germany and Norway.

En route, he indulged his passion for sight-seeing. At Antwerp he visited the Cathedral of Notre Dame and viewed in awe and admiration the paintings by Rubens; at Aix la Chapelle he saw the throne and the tomb of Charlemagne, and watched with mild astonishment as a priest exhibited a hair from the head of John the Baptist, a tooth of St. Stephen, pieces of the true cross, and a cloth that had "wiped the sweat and blood from the face of the Saviour." He looked intently on the face of the priest "to see whether he could possibly seem to believe these stories." In Copenhagen he visited the old round tower where Tycho Brahe had watched the heavens, and up whose stairway Peter the Great is said to have driven with a coach and four; he went by railroad and steamer north to the 61st parallel, beyond the reach of night, for it was the time of the summer solstice.[3]

Back in the British Isles, the bishop preached at London, Liverpool, Belfast, Dublin, and Limerick, and crowded his free time with side trips to points of interest. He and Charles visited the Lakes of Killarney, saw the famous stone at Blarney Castle, the Round Tower at Antrim ("the most perfect in Ireland"), and the pleasant grounds of Antrim Castle. It was late afternoon when, with Dr. McClintock, they reached the Giant's Causeway; but they spent two hours "inspecting the wonders." Returning to town too late to find a room, they ate a hearty supper and went to sleep on the floor of the sitting room. The next morning they "took another run to the Causeway in the rain." In England, Simpson was particularly interested in the places made sacred to Methodists by the activities of John Wesley. He went to Epworth and stood on the site of Wesley's birthplace; he sought out the tombstone of the first Samuel Wesley, where his son John had preached in the open air to the crowd; he went to Leeds and searched out the spot where John Wesley had first asked for volunteers to carry the gospel to America. In London he climbed the steps to the pulpit in City Road Chapel where Wesley himself had stood.[4]

At the Liverpool conference the bishop not only gave fraternal greetings from the American church but defended its policy on slavery (the English papers, prompted by the southern Methodists and northern Abolitionists, had openly accused him of proslaveryism). It was a tense situation, thought an American friend in the audience, heightened by the "proverbial English reserve." The bishop's argument was a hard one, put pointedly to his English brethren.

The action of the Methodist Episcopal Church in refusing to accept a slaveholding episcopacy had resulted in the withdrawal of nearly half a million members. "By that one act of resisting the progress of the spirit of slavery among us we lost," he said, "more members than you ever had in the Methodist body in Great Britain." Most of his remarks were much more felicitous, and the argument on slavery was thrust down in the middle of the speech, at a point where he had long since gained the favor of the audience. He had spoken but a few minutes when there was a murmur of "Hear, hear!" all over the house, and in a short while the English reserve, the "well-nigh paralyzing" chill, melted and the thaw became a flood as the audience stamped and shouted its approval. Even a southern Methodist who regarded the address as a "flaming speech" of "bitterness against the South," thought the bishop one of the most "eloquent and powerful" speakers he had ever heard.[5]

I I

From England, Bishop Simpson went to Germany to oversee the Methodist Mission Conference and to attend, as delegate, a convention of the Evangelical Alliance. Sponsored chiefly by churches of Europe, the convention was attended also by representatives from England and the United States. The majority of the delegates were German Protestants, and the deliberations were carried on primarily in German. On the agenda were papers to be read, addresses to be given, discussions to be conducted. W. F. Warren, young Methodist preacher in Germany and correspondent for the *Christian Advocate and Journal,* was not very hopeful of the achievements of the Alliance. Among other topics, he said, the delegates were to discuss religious liberty. However, they would be invited to affirm the principle on "religious, as distinct from political, grounds." The Prussian government would admit of no free discussion. In fact, the convention was given over to a rather vigorous discussion of theological points of likeness—of the unity of faith notwithstanding the differences in creeds. But once the assembly convened, young Warren forgot the business of the conference in his concern for the effect of Methodist speakers upon the gathering.[6]

Two American Methodists had prominent places on the program: Bishop Simpson and his old friend Joseph A. Wright, now the American Minister to Prussia. Wright had already won a certain renown among the diplomatic corps by his dramatic refusal to serve wine at an important dinner engagement. As a believer in democracy he protested to his home government against the "miserable humbug of dress in foreign courts" and "all kinds of flummery" required of an American diplomat before he could see the head of a principality whose territory, frequently, was not "larger than a hoosier's corn-field." None the less, he was popular with the Prussian Court; and there can be little doubt that the bishop owed his own prominent place on the Alliance program to the influence of his friend, the Minister to Prussia.[7]

The court preacher, Dr. Krummacher, opened the convention with an address which Warren felt "hardly worthy of him," for it was only a garbled lecture that he had delivered before; but Simpson's colleague John McClintock thought it "exceedingly well-conceived," especially in the reference to Methodism as "the angel flying through the heaven, summoning the dead churches to a new Christian life." Wright made the first response to the welcome in a brief address with such "great force and earnestness of voice and manner" that the audience was "fairly taken by surprise." Simpson followed immediately with a few remarks on the object of the convention, the "sublime spectacle to the world" of Christians being one in Christ Jesus. Yet it was not a union of creeds, nor of organization, but rather of "heart and Christian activity." It was like the little streams that rose among the hills, some flowing faster, some slower: "they might, indeed, singly quench the thirst of the passing traveller, but only by union could they bear the treasures of commerce, and so bring the ends of the earth together." Or the union might be compared to that of the several sovereignties of Germany and the United States, each securing to its subjects "freedom of thought and action, while the confederation gave strength and power to the whole." Dr. Baird, an American Presbyterian, Sir Culling Eardley, president of the British branch of the Alliance, and "one or two other English brethren" followed Simpson. Warren reported with some pride, that he had overheard a Congregationalist express preference for Bishop Simpson, because his remarks had "some substance." [8]

On the Sabbath, Simpson was invited to preach in the Garrison Church at Berlin. Never before had an evangelical minister from England or America been invited to a pulpit of the established church in Prussia. The Methodists, as spiritual descendants of the despised Moravians of Herrnhut, were justifiably proud of the honor to their bishop. McClintock thought the event not the least of the wonders of his European trip. Some Lutherans, however, were affronted by the spectacle of these foreigners, American schismatics, exulting in "voluble tongue" as if they had wrung from the Germans the admission, "Your Lutheran church is also nothing but a sect." [9]

The building, which was under the direct control of the king, was large, impressive, and aristocratic. Six doors led from the street to as many different sections of the church. Each person, "from the king and his ministers down to the forlornest *Dienst-matchen*," was expected to find his or her place according to political and social status. Simpson, as he approached the pulpit, was impressed by the contrast: the grandeur and the aristocracy of the edifice, the humble and democratic genesis of the speaker. But he had "a fine English & American congregation," and so, he reported to Ellen, "I talked just as I usually do in plain Methodist style." [10]

He chose for his discourse the theme on which he had spoken at the opening of the convention: Christian unity. It was a sermon which he had often preached from the Methodist pulpit, and which he would preach many times more. Some men see chiefly that which is different in the ideals and beliefs of men: Simpson saw that which was alike. He searched for the common denominators of mankind; and, finding a basic humanity, he found also a strong hope.

The doctrine of unity was not an easy one to preach to Methodists or to any other religious denomination of that day. Not the least of the admirers of Methodism was Simpson himself; but with the Methodist disdain for doctrine he had no blind attachment to the lesser items in its creed. In speaking on Christian unity, therefore, he combined action and thought, the energetic promotion of Methodism and the appreciation of truth beyond the denominational horizon. His sermon pointed the way toward Methodist participation in the ecumenical movement, and contained the seeds of a tolerant religious humanism.

He saw the principle of unity as undergirding all life—the same law for "the tides which rise upon our seas, the particles of dust which float in our atmosphere, the vapors which surround our earth." And yet he recognized that there was endless variety. If men could view so simple an object as an orange only partially, how could they be expected to see alike on religious matters? They would not perceive oneness in all the details of a creed, nor could they agree upon the forms and practices of worship. There were some principles "around which the light of heaven shines so clearly that we all see them alike. There is the unity of the Divine character; there is, to some extent, the depravity of the human heart; the necessity of man's becoming vastly improved; a consciousness of human weakness; the relation of man to God."

But the unity of which Christ spoke (Simpson's text was "And the glory which thou gavest me I have given them; that they may be one, even as we are one") arose from the "glory" which God had given him. What was this glory? It was not his divinity, for he did not receive that; nor was it his suffering, for that he could not give to another. What, then, was it? "Was it not the glory of benevolent effort, the glory of . . . wiping away the tear, the comforting of the sorrowful, the making the lame to leap, the blind to see, the deaf to hear . . ." Was not the legacy of the church "to do good, to make the world happier, to teach, to bless, and to improve this earth"? [11]

McClintock, with the Methodist critic's concern for the feelings of an audience, thought the sermon "masterly, both in the structure and the filling up." He noted in the congregation that "many an eye was dimmed with tears." An Englishman felt the impact of the statement of principle and the sudden spurt of illuminating illustration and said to him: "Ah, sir, that was preaching; what a backbone of hard stout thinking was behind all that tenderness and unction." [12]

III

When the Berlin convention adjourned on September 17, Simpson had already written to Ellen that he could be home in October, but that "if life, health, and circumstances should permit," he would be pleased to visit the East. Now that his official business was over, how much he would enjoy "one hour's real romp with the children," and how he would love to look into Ellen's "bright eyes and cheerful face." But how many years had he dreamed of a journey to the Holy Land? and how often since early childhood had he yearned for those gardens where in imagination he saw blooming the rose of

Sharon and the lily of the valley? Ought he not deny himself the pleasure of a quick return to his family? [13]

At the last moment a kind Providence intervened in his behalf. Three young men volunteered to go with him: W. F. Warren, the fellow Methodist whom he had met first on his arrival for the convention; a Lutheran minister from Pennsylvania; and Ambassador Wright's son. Placing Charles in a German home and school at Hameln with the admonition to "play the man," he turned his eyes to the East.[14]

From Berlin he went to Leipzig, to Weimar, to Halle. He sought out the places made famous by Luther and Melanchthon, traveled all night on a stage to Eisleben to see the house where Luther was born; he stood in the square in Wittenberg where Luther burned the papal bull, saw the table at which he wrote, the gown he wore, the beads he counted, the wall hit by the inkstand he aimed at "his Satanic majesty." Castles, paintings, ornaments "almost without number," he saw. At Dresden he bribed the guards to admit him to a gallery of paintings in the royal palace. At the sight of the money, he said, "the guards thought it a pity that travellers should be prevented from the privelege [sic] of examination, and passed us in." [15]

He went to the village of Herrnhut, reflecting the while upon the humble Moravians and their profound influence on Wesley. He stopped a day at Prague and was so stirred by "thoughts of the martyrs of old Bohemia, the preaching of Huss and Jerome, the bloody contest" that he could scarcely sleep that night.[16]

When he took the steamer from Vienna down the Danube he felt for the first time that his face was really turned to the lands of the East. He stopped over the Sabbath at Pest, visited a number of churches, followed the Archduke Albert and his retinue into the Cathedral for mass—a Sabbath service conducted, to his surprise, "without one word of sermon or instruction." He talked with friends of Kossuth who regarded him highly as a man, scholar, and orator, but had no confidence in his ability as a leader.[17]

After six days the party reached the Black Sea, and proceeded to Constantinople and Smyrna. The idle fancy struck the bishop of growing a beard, and in due time he made a picture, sitting on deck, with his low, soft white hat secured to his buttonhole by a ribbon, and his book in his lap—his beard white on his chin, brown on his cheeks, and sandy on his upper lip. What would Ellen say! He could see her curl her lip, or draw down her eyebrows and flash her eyes with indignation. Well, he would find a barber before he reached civilization again. In the meantime he had a notion to have a daguerreotype taken, just to preserve for her his "Oriental antiquity." [18]

On the passage through the Aegean the bishop, excited by the Trojan shore, Chios' rocky isle, and, more than all, Patmos, could scarcely take time from the deck for food or sleep. Great was his amusement when a Scotch professor ventured a question in Latin to a Greek priest and mistook the answer, "Nescio" ("I do not know"), for the name of an island.[19]

En route from Crete to Beirut he became very ill. He thought at first that he had malaria, but his fever did not rise. He was too weak to walk; but there were outbreakings of the plague in the East, and he feared a panic would follow if he were taken off the boat on a stretcher. His young traveling companions therefore dressed him and, placing his arms about their shoulders, carried him upright between them. Sick as he was, he turned his eyes to the coast, where he could see the "bold mountains of Lebanon." On shore, one of his companions summoned a physician, a missionary of the American Board who applied anodynes, leeches, mustard plasters, blisters, and poultices.

After three days between life and death, the bishop began to mend. He sat up and insisted that his companions ride inland to Damascus without him. The day was November 3, the twenty-second anniversary of his marriage. He thought of the tall, awkward young man and the young woman who had stood trembling beside him in the parlor in Penn Street, Pittsburgh, as they exchanged their vows, and he sent across the Atlantic "greetings of unchanged, undying affection" to the woman who was "not now quite so roseate, but more thoughtful, and even more worthy to be beloved." "How strange to whisper affection from Asia to America." [20]

That night he had the best rest he had had in a week. In another day he felt well enough to walk about and to tease Ellen a little: Mrs. Ford, the wife of the missionary, had brought him some jelly, very good; he thought that he would call on her. Might he? [21]

Although he was scarcely strong enough to leave Beirut when his companions returned from Damascus, he insisted on continuing with them. He started off early in the morning with Warren and rode at a slow walk, leaving the luggage to the others' care. Almost too weak to sit in the saddle, he none the less took note of the rocky hillside, the prickly pear along the way, the treelike hedges, and the black guard who talked French.

Constantly battling the recurring illness, he traveled the length and breadth of Palestine, much moved by the "sublime associations." He stood on the plains of Hebron and drank from the fountain where the servants of Abraham had watered the flocks. He saw Nazareth, the Sea of Galilee, Bethlehem, Jerusalem, the Mount of Olives, and the Garden of Gethsemane with the old olive trees, knotted and gnarled, "perhaps some of the very trees beneath which the Savior prayed and sweat great drops of blood." He visited every spot in the Holy Land which, according to the scriptural account, "was trodden by the Savior's feet," save Caesarea and Philippi.[22]

Ellen, very much worried, expressed her concern about the dangerous Arabs. "Dismiss all fears," he reassured her. "There is no danger whatever. Think not of me as among strangers. Three young men are with me. And then I find friends everywhere. At the Hotel here they speak English." When she reported that she had been reading about Palestine and thought of making the trip herself, he was amused: "It would be an utter impossibility for you to travel in the Holy Land, unless carried in a kind of chair by men as some are. When you take a horse and ride up and down the various paths on the side of Coal Hill at Pittsburgh you might form some idea of travelling in Judea."[23]

He went to Egypt late in December and visited the catacombs, wondered over the ruins of old Memphis, saw the petrified forest, and climbed the highest of the pyramids—a "hard task." He sailed from Alexandria to Athens and thence to Naples. In Greece he was delighted with Mounts Parnassus and Helicon, which "raise their snow-capped summits towards the clear blue skies." As in Palestine, everything reminded him of the past. "Achilles carries my luggage; Ulysses rows the boat; Demetrius acts as pilot; Themistocles waits to carry a passenger in an old rickety wagon; and Hercules carries, if not *the* club . . . a good stout cudgel to ward off the furious dogs."[24]

All the time he was quite unfit for travel. Now and then he stopped over an extra day for rest; at Sidon, when he was too ill to ride his horse any further he engaged a boatman to row him to Haifa. Twice, doubting that he would live until morning, he gave Warren farewell messages for his family and friends. Several times he considered going home at once; but then he regained enough strength to travel, and hoped to improve in health as he continued the tour.[25]

Meanwhile, his wife, worried over his long illness and extended absence from home, wrote with some complaint about his taking the Eastern trip. He *"lived to himself,"* she said, without any real thought for the happiness of his wife and family. For these thoughts, he replied, he could not chide her, nor would he complain, but he could not feel "other than . . . sad." He thought he had her full concurrence or he would never have made the trip. And Providence seemed in so many ways to open the way for him. As for his family, strange as it might seem to her, the happiness of his wife and children was ever before him. For what else should he live? Next to God and his church, no other interest so impelled him onward.[26]

He had not yet told her, however, about the purpose of his travels in the East: his intent to write a book. Uncle Matthew knew or surmised, and admonished him to look at things as though he happened upon them: "Having no previous knowledge of their existence the Idea will in that way be more original than if looked at with the memory occupied with other mens descriptions." He should go to places where others had not gone; then his descriptions would be "read with the interest which novelty gives." [27]

IV

As Bishop Simpson neared the end of his travels in the East, he awaited with anxiety the receipt of his spring conference appointments. He still had much to see, time was short, and his illness made it necessary to travel slowly and rest frequently. If the first appointment was in New England or New York, and late in the spring, he would still have time to complete his tour and fulfill his conference duties on the way home to Pittsburgh. When the schedule came he was greatly disappointed to find that his colleagues had assigned him to the Arkansas conference, in late March, and that he would have to hurry home. He had visited Arkansas only three years before, and could not see why he should go again. Suspecting Ames, he complained to his wife and his friend Alexander Cummings of Philadelphia, but cautioned her against "unpleasant feelings" in her heart, or "unkind words of any concerned": The plan *"must* be all right . . . For even if it were designed for evil, God can overrule it for good." Ellen none the less accosted Ames with a good deal of spirit, and Colonel Cummings, through a friend, passed the complaint on to Bishop Janes. The bishops hastily explained that they had assigned Arkansas to Simpson because that conference least needed a presiding bishop: Simpson could supervise the work without visiting the territory. He was determined, however, to hurry home to meet his official responsibilities.[28]

At Naples in mid-January he was again prostrated by illness and had to rest for a week. He still chafed under the arrangement for conferences which did not allow him time "to lie by with sickness" and then to complete his route. Already in Italy, he would pass within eight hours of Rome but must give it up.[29]

By the time he reached Paris his health had improved. He stopped to purchase books, maps, and plates. In London, early in February, he devoted a few days to the same purpose, concentrating on Methodist materials. In explaining his delay, and his excursions to places of interest in England, he revealed to Ellen his intention to write the book: "After spending so much money and so much time I wish . . . to get some return from it." His desires were confidential, for he did not "wish the one half of the plans . . . to be guessed at by anybody." Charles was again with him and in good health.[30]

He was ill again in London, confined to his bed on the order of his physician, who said he must rest, for his liver and right lung were "in great danger."[31]

Late in February he at last reached Pittsburgh; but he was still too ill to attend the Arkansas conference, or to perform his other official duties, or to write his book.

XIX

FOR GOD AND COUNTRY

THE days and months of 1858 dragged on for the Simpson family. The bishop's illness was a recurring one. With Ellen hovering over him, he slowly gained strength, only to be prostrated again. In July he was able to attend the meeting of the board of bishops in New York, but six weeks later he was once more at the point of death.

For weeks Matthew Simpson was unable to leave his upstairs room. Quietness hung over the place: Ellen shushed the children, and Mary, the chambermaid, tiptoed about her household duties. Friends and neighbors brought delicacies to tempt the bishop's appetite: Dr. Dickson, a pheasant; Dr. Wright's wife, two dressed squirrels; Mrs. Kidd, a bowl of tapioca; Mr. Knox, a tumbler of blackberry jam. Mr. Heazelton sent fifty pounds of buckwheat flour; Colonel Cummings and other friends in Philadelphia sent a tidy sum of money; the Hoyt brothers of New York, a thousand dollars to help him with his extra expenses. Mrs. Bradley of Pittsburgh presented him with a photograph of Mr. Bradley.[1]

Bishop Ames visited him in the fall and, shocked by the pale, gaunt figure stretched out on the bed, scribbled to Bishop Janes: "I fear Bp Simpson will never again mingle with us in labor." Uncle Matthew fretted lest his nephew's friends, crowding in by day and sitting with him by night, kill him with kindness: How could they be "so blind and so injudicious"? [2]

Late in the fall Bishop Simpson began to mend, and his physician allowed him to sit up. Calling for his journal, he began making entries, to pass the time. He itemized the gifts brought in by friends; he made long lists of "winter provisions to be attended to," marking the items off in categories in usual pulpit style. He must have meats —beef, and a barrel for salting; pork, cask for salting; lard; venison;

fish—mackerel, herring, cod, salmon, sardines; flour—buckwheat, cornmeal, unbolted.[3]

When he was stronger he made an effort to put his travel notes in shape, and for that purpose read extensively in the books he had brought from England. The Methodist Publishing House wanted a narrative in two volumes to be sold at one dollar each, and Harper & Brothers reminded him that he would "meet with no difficulty in finding a publisher so long as your old friends of Franklin Square can command the use of a printing press." He wrote at length of his travels in central Europe but borrowed heavily from the guide books and histories, with only an occasional refreshing experience of his own. The project bogged down, perhaps as much from its own weight as from the fact that the business of the church began to make demands upon him.[4]

Late in January, 1859, he was well enough to get out on the street. Mrs. Bradley called in her carriage and took him and Mrs. Simpson to see a friend. They had "a pleasant ride, dined and returned without injury"—his first carriage ride since September. Soon his physician was saying that he might take up his official duties— the preaching omitted.[5]

He went reluctantly from his home and family to the first of his spring conferences. The long absence in Europe, the protracted and serious, almost fatal illness, his frequent thoughts of death, had rendered him emotionally tender. He tried to comfort Ellen with admonitions to "look upward," to remember that "life at best is short, its scenes will soon pass away, eternity will be our home— our *only* home." He assured her of his wish to be with his family, so far as duty permitted. However, God could take care of his loved ones in his absence. Sometimes he asked himself: " 'What if God had removed me altogether when I was sick? What then for my loved ones?' " [6]

He listed his engagements for Ellen—by July he was able to preach again, "out of doors, without much injury"; he picked up bits of gossip and reported them. Sometimes he teased her. What about the new bonnet? Had she bought it, and did it please her? And were the ribbons "greenish-blue," or "bluish-green?" And was it the new "coal-scuttle" pattern or the old "kiss-me-quick" shape? He preferred the latter.[7]

Now nearing his fiftieth birthday, he thought of himself as

growing old and wrote often in a tender, even sentimental, and reminiscent mood. "How blest is it that hearts once joined may be united forever." Other things might change—their bodies grow old, their eyes weak, their limbs infirm—but the heart would remain ever young. And why should they not love more truly and strongly as they grew older? Their playmates and schoolmates had, one by one, passed on or parted from them; but they still had each other and their children to love. They had started down the river of life together, and together they would sail on until they should reach the great ocean, or one of them drop from the other to perish in the waters. But why should he moralize? Were his heart silent, other hearts would beat on. A few hearts would bleed, a few eyes would weep, and then all would be as though he had never been.[8]

I I

All through his long illness one problem had worried Simpson considerably: should he change his episcopal residence from Pittsburgh? Baltimore wanted him. So did eastern Pennsylvania, and Chicago. The problem was a complex one involving his interest in theological training for ministers, his concern over slavery in the church, his close friendship with Dr. John Evans of Chicago, his desire to live in the East, and the increasing strain upon his private finances involved in his role as bishop.

Chicago made the strongest appeal. Dr. Evans was anxious to secure close support from Simpson for the new Garrett Biblical Institute. If the bishop moved to Chicago or Evanston, he could devote time between conferences to the theological school and, what was more important, could lend it his name. Furthermore, his presence on the faculty would assure the institution of success. Simpson thought well of the idea, and Evans offered the further inducement of an episcopal residence, to be built and presented by friends of the church.

An exciting interval in the negotiating occurred when Bishop Ames decided to move to Chicago. Simpson's friends wanted none of this "financial speculator," whom they regarded as sympathetic to slavery. They needed a "pious man—& one devoted *to God* & to the building up the Church of God and saving souls." When a committee confronted Ames with the argument that they must have

Simpson's help for the newly organized Garrett Institute, he "cordially assented" to the arrangement.

Late in 1859 the Simpson family moved to Illinois and settled in
the village of Evanston. The move was an important one, for down
in Springfield was a man whom he would come to know, and the
association would have a considerable influence upon Matthew Simpson's place in the history of his country and his church.[9]

III

The northwest winds blew cold in Evanston that winter, and the
snow swept down the village streets swirling about the trunks of the
old oak trees and drifting high in the yards of the villagers. Along-
side Garrett Biblical Institute the muddy waters congealed in the
ditch, mockingly called the Rubicon, and the blue waters along Lake
Michigan's edge gave way to ice and snow. How often that winter
did the bishop draw his great coat tightly about him as he hurried
from his home on Hinman Avenue to the railroad cars, bound for
Chicago and wherever episcopal duties led him.

And yet the winds scarcely blew so cold as the events that lashed
at his spirit. Thoughts of what lay in store for his church chilled
him to the marrow. May 1, 1860, the general conference would
gather. That quadrennial meeting, once the seat of optimism and
self-approbation, had become a convocation of dissension and threatened schism. There had been no peace in the church since the advent of abolitionism. Only for a brief interval had the agitation
ceased, after the withdrawal of Andrew and his southern cohorts in
1844. Simpson himself, through Abel Stevens, had helped to quiet
the unrest at the 1856 general conference.

But much had happened since 1856, catastrophic events that
lightly swept aside appeals for unity and revealed the deep cleavage
between North and South: Dred Scott, Negro, free, they said, in
Illinois, enslaved again in Missouri, and now his name a coal on
the lips of every dedicated Isaiah of the North; the Missouri Compromise, negated by Dred Scott, pronounced null and void in fact by
the Supreme Court; firebrands of the South spreading the inflamma-
tory doctrines of John Calhoun, and a tall gaunt man on the prairies
solemnly warning the new Republican party and the nation, in the
words of Jesus, "A house divided against itself cannot stand"; John

Brown and the blood coursing thick and red at Pottawatomie and Osawatomie; and John Brown storming the arsenal at Harpers Ferry, seizing citizens as hostages, barricading himself in the engine-house, captured at last by the United States marines, tried in the Virginia courts, hung by the neck until dead. But John Brown's body went marching on, a signal of frenzied alarm to the South and a shibboleth and a battle cry to the North. They debated John Brown that winter in Evanston, at the Methodist college, from two o'clock in the afternoon until seven-thirty: "Resolved, That the Harper's Ferry crisis is calculated to create a separation between North and South." [10]

The growing tension in the nation was fully reflected in Methodism. Methodist papers, North and South, screamed at each other, and conferences, preachers, bishops rebuked their erring brethren above or below the Mason-Dixon line. A mob broke up the northern conference in Bonham, Texas; and citizens of Dallas, in public meeting assembled, condemned northern preachers as " 'wolves in sheep's clothing,' who with Bible in hand and evil in their hearts" went forth preaching "the most dangerous and insurrectionary doctrines." Now and then a northern preacher in a border state or in southern territory was pulled from his pulpit, ridden on a rail, threatened with tar and feathers, or locked out of his chapel. Ardent churchmen of the Southwest threatened to take the life of Anthony Bewley if he did not stay out of Arkansas and Texas; and a Virginia legislator introduced a bill to exclude all "nonresident, incendiary preachers" from the state.[11]

Simpson, exasperated by the tactics of the South, was much more concerned by the troubles within his own church. His people, united in their bitter struggle with the Church, South, were divided among themselves: New England against Baltimore, northern conferences against the border, "progressives" against "conservatives." How long had New England been proud of the antislavery rule of the discipline, proud of the courage of 1844 that had accepted division in preference to slaveholding by a bishop! Simpson himself had made the boast in England in 1857. But the pride crumbled under the bludgeoning facts of slavery. Theodore Parker, he who had battered down the door of a jail to free a Negro, knew how to use such facts —one buttressed by another—to demolish the fiction of antislavery Methodism. William Lloyd Garrison used them, too, not to batter, but to lash and scourge the Methodists with charges of proslaveryism, with charges that they harbored proslavery members, that they were unable to muster sufficient strength to alter the ambiguous general rule of the discipline.[12]

Where did Parker and Garrison get their evidence? Why, from among the Methodists themselves: the Reverend J. D. Long of Philadelphia charging that his own conference sheltered as many as 1,000 slaveholders, that a wealthy Methodist of Cambridge, Maryland, a licensed local preacher, had advertised a reward of $300 for the capture and return of two runaway slaves; Hiram Mattison of Black River Conference reprinting a Methodist advertisement that called for the return of "fourteen head" of runaway slaves, seven of them children under eight years of age; a Methodist, rebuking Bishops Simpson and Janes for appearing on the platform and participating in dedicatory services with the slaveholding Bishop George Pierce of Georgia. The southern church joined the chorus of condemnation. Would Bishop Simpson deny, asked the Richmond *Christian Advocate,* that there were *"many* slaveholders and slave-workers among the private members, and official members, and ministers of the Northern division of the M. E. Church"? Nor was the South embarrassed by apparent inconsistency in labeling New England proslavery and the border abolitionist. The paradox was easily explained: the North was hypocritical. It preached dangerous abolitionist doctrines, but in its mad desire for power and bigness it practiced slavery.[13]

Lashed by Garrison, taunted by the South, and scourged by conscience, the radical Methodists of the North, the "progressives," redoubled their efforts to strengthen the church's rule on slavery. The border caught between two fires—called abolitionist by the South, proslavery by the North—renewed its threats to secede and form a new church.

Simpson was engulfed by the struggle but not a party to it. Although he was a "progressive" by nature and "the most able man on the Methodist bench of Bishops," a correspondent of Theodore Tilton's *Independent* explained that he was held "in check" by his episcopal office. No bishop had ever been "seen in any Church anti-slavery meeting or convention even as a spectator, much less as a participant." Some of Simpson's friends knew that he had proposed rewriting the chapter on slavery to include a "Golden Rule" declaration; but no one had drawn his name into the public controversy.[14]

His position was moderate and cautious, one of watchful wait-ing. Despising slavery—perhaps as much for the dissension and strife it brought into the church as for what it did to bind men's souls—he dared not strike at it lest he destroy the unity of northern Method-ism. He believed that his first task was to preserve the church. In due course, the states along the border would abolish slavery of their own accord. Was it not wise in the meantime, while bearing witness to the evil, to avoid action which would drive border Method-ists into the proslavery southern church?

The bishops opened the general conference of 1860 with an attempt to pour oil on troubled waters. The presence of the border conferences in the church "does not tend to extend or perpetuate Slavery," they said, reiterating the statement of 1856.[15] But the anti-slavery forces, greatly in the majority and dominating the commit-tees, grimly went about the business of altering the discipline. With-out the two-thirds majority requisite for a constitutional change to exclude slaveholding members, they easily carried a "new chap-ter," a "golden rule declaration" against slavery, similar to that which Simpson had recommended in 1856.[16]

What might have been acceptable to both parties in 1856 now appeased the North but inflamed the border. The general confer-ence had scarcely adjourned when the radical majority in Baltimore began to make good their threats of secession. In conventions, church meetings, and private conversation, laymen and ministers alike de-nounced the new chapter. A friend wrote to Simpson that there were only two parties in the Baltimore conference: those who called for secession, and those who sought to repeal the chapter in a con-stitutional manner.[17]

For months the battle raged, with Simpson directing the strategy. John Lanahan, one of his ablest lieutenants, had already written to the Baltimore *Sun* (from the general conference) that he believed the new chapter "a more mild and temperate expression of doctrine than could have been hoped for." Encouraged by Simpson, he now conducted an intensive and sometimes ruthless campaign among the preachers. He argued that the new chapter was mild, he pleaded with them to remain loyal to the church of their fathers, he searched the record to find flaws in the character of leading secessionists, as-suring Simpson that he would reveal all, in the event of a crisis.

Taking a leaf from Cicero, he saw a Catiline in every pulpit where the preacher was not avowedly for the new chapter; he accused leading men of a conspiracy, not simply to form a new church as they asserted, but to collaborate with the southern bishops in taking the conference over bodily to the Church, South.[18]

Simpson's efforts quickly showed results. A presiding elder reported that he had succeeded in blocking the extra session of the Baltimore conference which some had demanded, and, although he could not prevent the call of a laymen's convention, he had induced all the churches of his district to send conservatives. A timid preacher in Baltimore, unwilling to speak out on the subject, confided to the bishop that he would not leave the church; and although Thomas Sewall, eloquent defender of the border at the general conference, wavered, he at last stayed with the North. Members of the Laymen's and Ministers' Union, attempting to exercise a conservative influence, established a new paper in New York, the *Methodist,* and circulated it freely on the border. Much more ably edited than the official papers of the church, the *Methodist* decried the aggressiveness of the antislavery forces, and pleaded with the border to remain with the old church.[19]

Political developments—the dramatic secession of the southern states, and the inability of statesmen to effect a compromise—intensified the struggle. John Lanahan, bold and crafty in his operations and intensely loyal both to the church and to the government, seized upon patriotism and love of Methodism as double leverage to keep the preachers in the church. At the same time, the Baltimore conference ministers who resided in Virginia, and constituted nearly two-thirds of the membership of the conference, found in the political affairs new motives for ecclesiastical separation.

Meanwhile the conflict with the Church, South, grew in bitterness and violence. Bishop Pierce, throwing restraint to the winds, declared that southern Methodism was free to go anywhere: "She knows no North, or South, or East, or West." His brethren, however, continued to resist the presence of northern preachers in the South, not only with words but with tar, feathers, and rails. In Missouri a preacher, treated rather roughly, mobbed twice, ridden on a rail, annoyed the crowd by singing "with animation,"

> Children of the Heavenly King,
> As we journey let us sing.

But he agreed to leave town. Anthony Bewley, itinerant preacher with whom Simpson had traveled to Texas in 1855, accused of conspiracy, was pursued when he fled into Missouri, taken back to Texas, and hanged by the mob.[20]

Inevitably, the cherished doctrine of the "separation" of church and state, as interpreted by the Methodists, broke down. In North and South alike ecclesiastical interests were too intimately bound up with those of the civil powers to admit of such separation. In fulfillment of the prophecy George Pierce had made at Louisville in 1845, nearly every Methodist conference in the North established its committee "on the State of the Country," which then made demands on the state or federal government. Long before the election of 1860, the North Carolina *Christian Advocate* warned that, if Lincoln were named President, "a dissolution of the Union, within twelve months, is inevitable." Five days before South Carolina seceded from the Union, the Methodist conference of that state declared itself in favor of the action. Alabama, Virginia, Georgia quickly fell into line. The northern Methodist press, equally quick to denounce the secession of the southern states, demanded "the prompt execution of the national law." The "inevitable conflict," stated the *Northwestern Christian Advocate* of Chicago, will be "short, sharp, and bloody" but "necessary," because it is a "greater calamity to permit the spirit of mobocracy to remain rampant." [21]

The Baltimore conference, at its spring session in March, 1861, angrily voted itself "separate and independent" from the Methodist Episcopal Church. Forty-one members abstained from the vote; the presiding bishop refused to recognize the action as official; and the great majority of the Maryland preachers and members remained in the "old church." But more than 100 ministers and nearly 12,000 laymen, most of whom lived in Virginia, withdrew from the conference.[22]

It was scarcely a month until Sumter.

I V

War was still a month off, but the lower South had already seceded: South Carolina in December, Alabama, Mississippi, and Florida in early January, followed in quick succession by Georgia, Louisiana, and Texas. The southern leaders had gathered at Montgomery, deliberated for five weeks, brought forth a new constitution and elected a provisional President. While Abraham Lincoln journeyed from Springfield to Washington, making commonplace remarks to the curious crowds along the way, President elect Jefferson Davis, en route to Montgomery, hurried from one ovation to another. Lincoln pledged in his inaugural address on March 4 that there would be no invasion, no bloodshed, no civil war, unless the South itself proved the aggressor; none the less he warned his southern countrymen that he was sworn to "preserve, protect, and defend" the federal government. That same afternoon in Montgomery, in the presence of a "large concourse of spectators on Capitol Hill," Letitia Tyler, granddaughter of the venerable ex-President, John Tyler, her heart "throbbing with patriotic emotion," released the new Confederate flag—the Stars and Bars—to the staff and the breeze.[23]

North Carolina, Virginia, Tennessee, and Arkansas still clung to the Union and the faint hope that disaster might somehow be averted. A segment of the northern press continued to plead for moderation. But there had been outbursts of patriotism in the North as well as the South, little flames of hysteria that needed only to be blown upon to envelope the whole nation in a holocaust: the *Star of the West* fired upon in Charleston harbor; a Palmetto flag torn from the staff of old Fort Kearney in Nebraska Territory, and the Stars and Stripes run up in its place; Washington's birthday celebrated in every northern city; citizens of Massachusetts "exalted" by Governor Andrew's presentation to the legislature of two Revolutionary muskets bequeathed by Theodore Parker; "The Star-Spangled Banner" or "Hail, Columbia" sung at public concerts; and everywhere, North and South, flag-raising a signal for the outburst of patriotic feeling. How men's hearts throbbed as they watched the folded bunting drop from its own weight, pull at the cord, yield to the stiff breeze, and swell and ripple as it rose to the top of the staff. Cannons roared, and men shouted themselves hoarse. Northern sentiment was rapidly fashioning itself into a holy crusade.[24]

Then Sumter, long awaited, more than half expected; yet it finally came as an electric shock, a surcharge that instantly polarized North and South. For weeks the newspapers had been filled with speculation about the fort: the necessity for abandoning it; assurances that it could be defended; Major Anderson's need of provisions; the opinion of General Scott; the opinion of Senator Douglas; the deliberations of the cabinet; the unexpected appearance in Charleston of the President's personal emissary; rumors of activity in the navy yard; word that transports bearing provisions were en route; the call in Washington and the mustering in of the Voluntary Militia. In Charleston "fearful excitement" prevailed. Business was suspended, General Beauregard ordered out 5,000 more troops, and South Carolina's new floating battery lifted anchor and moved from the harbor to a point near Fort Sumter. "It is plain," stated the Montgomery, Alabama, *Telegraph*, "that a gigantic war is about to be inaugurated." [25]

At half past four in the morning of April 12, the batteries along the shore began their bombardment, and Sumter returned the fire. The New York *Tribune* reported in hopeful headlines: "MAJOR ANDERSON STRONGER THAN SUPPOSED. SEVERAL REBELS WOUNDED." But before the day was over the walls of the fort were crumbling, two of its guns were silenced, and the supply of ammunition was running out. For forty hours the bloodless bombardment continued, and then Anderson surrendered. Beauregard permitted him to salute the flag and withdraw his men to a Union transport.

That was Saturday night. On Monday morning Lincoln called for 75,000 troops. Already 20,000 had tendered their services in Boston alone. Governor Morton of Indiana pledged 30,000; New York offered to lend the government a million dollars, and Pennsylvania appropriated half a million to buy munitions. On Wednesday the first detachment of troops from Minnesota passed through Chicago en route to Washington. Ten thousand people were at the station to greet them. The war had begun.[26]

V

The first official expression of the Methodist Episcopal Church on the war came from the New York East conference, which was in session when Sumter fell. "While we love peace and are the ministers of Peace," said the members in a series of resolutions compounded of piety and patriotism, "yet we hold it to be the sacred duty of all men to love their country and to cherish freedom, and especially in times of peril to offer our civil rulers our aid and sympathy." [27]

Within a month every Methodist journal in the North had asserted that the war was a religious duty. The bishops too, for once, took an unequivocal stand upon a public question. Secession was "rebellion without any plausible excuse," said Thomas A. Morris, the senior bishop. E. R. Ames, in a rousing address to the ministers of Genesee conference said that, were it his duty to join the Union army and fight the rebels, he should shoot very fast, he would "fire into them most benevolently." [28]

Simpson, in central New York when war broke out, rushed to Washington as soon as official business permitted. He had met Abraham Lincoln earlier in the year at the Illinois capital, where he and John Evans had gone in behalf of a bill to recharter Northwestern University. On the morning of February 11, he was one of the company at the Chenery House to wish Lincoln well, and a little while later in the cold drizzly morning he stood with the throng of citizens at the depot to hear the words of the Farewell Address.[29]

Now he called on the President at the White House. Lincoln received him cordially. The cabinet was to meet that morning, and several members dropped in, including Seward. In the course of general talk about the war and its conduct Simpson expressed the opinion that 75,000 was but a beginning of the number of men needed. Seward wondered, acidly, how a clergyman could judge of these matters. Another present defended Simpson: as a traveling bishop he had an opportunity that few persons possessed to test the temper of the people, North and South. As the time for the cabinet meeting approached, the bishop bowed out; but he was to come again.[30]

He was back in Evanston for the last Sunday of the month. For the second consecutive Sabbath the quiet of the little town was broken by the whistles and the thundering of railroad trains. The thoughts of the people were more on the war than on the "God of battles" whom they tried to worship. Fresh from Washington, the bishop was an awesome figure as he strode down Hinman Avenue to the little white chapel on Church Street, his son Verner clutching at his hand and trotting to keep up. There was a grimness about his face as he knelt to lead the congregation in prayer—such an assault on heaven for the triumph of the Union arms and the overthrow of human bondage as few among those present had ever thought to hear from human lips. "The very air seemed surcharged with the thunder and lightning of God's wrath against secession and slavery." [31]

That afternoon Bishop Simpson spoke in Chicago at the Wigwam, which had been constructed for the Republican convention of 1860, and six thousand people crowded into the great hall to hear him. He developed first a religious theme, showing that God reigns over a world of order, that God's government is one of wisdom, righteousness, goodness, and power, and that God's hand is in history, directing the affairs of His people and destroying whom He chooses. But the nation had sinned. Raised up of God to be "a pattern of piety" and "to bear the truth abroad through the nations of the world," it had not given of its wealth for the dissemination of the gospel. There were dark spots upon the nation's escutcheon, among them the great national sin itself which thwarted God's justice and the very purpose for which He had raised up the nation. He believed that God would not permit the government to be destroyed. It would survive the baptism of blood, cast away its sin, and stand once more, united, pure, and eloquent, a source of hope to the struggling peoples of Europe. But if God had laid the foundation of this government it was man's duty to protect it. Therefore "the man who goes to the war, goes in the order of God, goes to uphold order, goes to uphold the government, 'ordained of God,' goes for the right." [32]

Simpson was in Washington again in July shortly after the disaster at Bull Run, a "messenger of God" self-commissioned to assure Simon Cameron, the Secretary of War, that God was "with our country." The defeat of the Union forces, the wild disorder of the retreat, the shame of the North followed by anger and grim determination, only deepened his conviction. Did not God chasten His own before he redeemed them? [33]

All that summer, raising funds for church missions, and that fall and winter and spring at his conferences, he preached God, church, and country. At Rockport and South Bend, Indiana, at Rockland, Maine, at Washington, to the Eighth Illinois Cavalry regiment, at St. Louis, in Michigan, Wisconsin, Illinois, he traced the hand of Providence in the affairs of the nation. His calm sure voice rose at moments to the frenzy of the zealot.

He was like a medium, his tall, angular figure tense, his face transparent and glowing with an all but supernatural light, his voice a high, lyrical, hypnotic chant. Men and women sat or stood silent and breathless, giving way now and then to tears or to applause.

The peroration of his first war address at Chicago had brushed aside the curtain which hides the future to reveal the great white throne of God, the clouds dispersed, the darkness rolled away, the peoples of all nations, all realms, purified at last, shouting: "Alleluia! The Lord God Omnipotent reigneth!" But as the high hopes of an early end to the war were ended by defeat at Bull Run and Wilson's Creek, by inconsequential victories, by the paralysis of the Union armies, and as tensions increased and people sought release for their emotions, he developed a new peroration. He pictured his travels abroad, his illness, his sense of remoteness and alienation, and then the sheer joy that came to him when he beheld the flag of his country, the Stars and Stripes, rippling from the top of a tall mast. Surely some angel's hand had "cut those stars and that patch of blue out of the fair field of heaven" and sent them on "their mission of benevolence to us and to the nation. Flag of my country, ever wave; be not one star erased." Yet there was a higher symbol than the flag: the cross. "The cross first, our country next. Let us, by its benign influences, cultivate love to our enemies while we love our country and our God." [34]

XX

LINCOLN AND METHODIST POLITICS

ON slavery and the war Simpson was torn in sentiment, his mind divided into factions, one set against the other. He loathed slavery, and his outbursts of patriotic oratory cursed it as the great sin of the Republic, the blot on the national honor. Early in the war he had told President Lincoln that emancipation was necessary; and to friends he had expressed approval of Frémont's order freeing the slaves in Missouri.[1]

His private opinions did not bear public expression. He was silent on emancipation for much the same reason that Lincoln was. The war was for the preservation of the Union, the President had declared in revoking Frémont's order and stolidly resisting the demands of the Radicals for emancipation. To win the war, he must hold the border states in line; and if he could best maintain their support—and so preserve the Union—by refraining from interference with slavery, then he would let it alone. Simpson felt a like responsibility for preserving the unity of the church, large segments of which lay within slave territory. The bishops had never been abolitionist in sentiment, nor had they presumed to direct the affairs of state. The "new chapter" had sown dissension all along the border; thousands of members had withdrawn, and other withdrawals seemed imminent. What then could he gain for the church by preaching emancipation? He was not ready to join the Radicals, either in church or in government.

Emancipation came, none the less—pressed upon Lincoln by events and by the politics of the Radical Republicans. However commonplace in language and ambiguous in intent, the proclamation was a great document, clothed in essential humanity—an event which would grow in stature and dignity and sentiment with the years. Men would clamor that they or their friends had had a part in it: that they had thought of it first, had urged it upon the President, had suggested this phrase or that. Nor would the Methodists be the least of the claimants. Was not Bishop Simpson a friend of Lincoln? Had he not visited him often in the White House? Had he not reported with his own lips that he had been one of the first to urge upon Mr. Lincoln the necessity of emancipation?

The bishop would have been amused by the picture his friends conjured up for posterity: Matthew Simpson, prophet, a modern Nathan, confronting Abraham Lincoln, the David of his people, with a bony finger and crying, "Thou Art the Man—Emancipate, or I go to tell the people"; and Lincoln, able to fend for himself against Horace Greeley, Ben Wade, Thad Stevens, and the Radicals on Capitol Hill, abashed before the man of God, kneeling, joining the company in praying twice around, rising with tears in his eyes, pledging "I will do it," and then, a few days later, issuing the immortal Emancipation Proclamation.[2]

Unhappily for the myth makers, events rendered the tale implausible. Under the plan of episcopal visitation the bishop was to travel to California and Oregon in the summer of 1861. Mrs. Simpson was indignant over the arrangement. He had not yet fully regained his strength after the long illness of 1858–1859, and he was scarcely fit for so exhausting a journey. She was even more concerned over the dangers of travel: Indians if he went overland, Jefferson Davis and his privateers if he went by steamer.[3]

Urged by his wife and his friends in Evanston and Chicago, Simpson wrote to each of his episcopal colleagues, outlining the possible dangers and seeking their advice. Ames, taciturn, and reviving perhaps some of the old antagonism he had felt for his Indiana competitor, was blunt and scornful: The work on the Pacific required attention; the dangers of the ocean voyage were not greatly increased by the war; nor would he himself be fearful, because of hostile Indians, of making the overland journey. However, his "opinion of duty would be the same even if the danger were certain, and imminent." As he understood it, one ordained to the episcopal office accepted "the toils, and danger . . . as well as the honors and emoluments." He knew no instance in the history of their church in which a bishop had "refused to perform his official work through fear of personal danger." Yet he did not feel free to give advice, "for this thing of courage, or cowardice, is owing, perhaps, in part to physical organization"; and he hardly knew "how to sympathize with weak nerves." [4]

The other bishops were more charitable. Baker, Janes, and Scott thought Simpson ought not to go, although Scott confessed that had he been designated he might have been "imprudent enough to go despite the danger." Ames in the meantime satisfied himself after some investigation of the overland route that it was safe, and forwarded the conclusion to his hesitant colleague.[5]

Ames's spleen gave Simpson but one possible course: to go to California. Reserving passage from New York to Panama, he left Chicago on June 17, 1861. By this time friends had begun to fight his battle in good earnest. Unable to appeal on the basis of danger, they pleaded for his services in behalf of missions; the fund was exhausted, the cause was suffering, and Simpson above all others was best able to solicit contributions. The Missionary Board met in New York, attended to the appeal, and resolved that Simpson, "if consistent with his convictions of duty," should omit the visit in 1861 to California and Oregon and devote himself to raising funds for missions. All the bishops save Ames concurred. On this intervention of "Providence," Simpson agreed to a postponement of the California trip.[6]

When the plan of episcopal visitation for 1862 was drawn up, Simpson was accordingly scheduled to meet the Oregon and California conferences in August and September. Allowing extra time for supervision of the work, he sailed from New York early in June. He was in California in mid-July when Lincoln, returning from a funeral with Secretaries Seward and Welles, declared that he was going to issue a proclamation of emancipation. When the President discussed the matter with his cabinet a week later, Simpson was on the high seas, bound from San Francisco to Portland. In the days that followed, the bishop was busy preaching, lecturing, laying cornerstones, and dedicating new buildings. He returned to San Francisco by river steamer and stage, and left by stage for Chicago on September 16. He reached his home in Evanston on October 15, three weeks after Lincoln issued the proclamation.[7]

I I

If Simpson's primary purpose in seeing the President was not to demand emancipation, what was it? He himself explained it simply as "matters of the Church"; and, indeed, it was. John Lanahan said the bishop was much concerned about the treatment of Methodists by the government, by Lincoln and the dispensers of patronage.[8]

His was not an unusual pursuit. However calamitous the war, it did not command the President's undivided attention; the extent of the disaster was hidden by the future, and men's hopes for an early peace were not yet shattered. In the meantime each man of influence must think the affairs of the nation best provided for if he himself had some hand in the distribution of patronage. The Republican victory at the polls had been the triumph of a party, and the spoils must be divided by political means. Lincoln made the most thoroughgoing sweep of personnel that had been made by any President; and in filling the vacancies he took pains to consult "every one who had a right to be heard." [9]

Not least among the aspirants were the Methodists. Exceptionally conscious of their numerical strength and the growing prestige derived from their property holdings and educational ventures, and from the prominent positions held by a few of their laymen, they sought what seemed to them a fair proportion of the political spoils. Simpson was pressed by office seekers: one desired the superintendency of Indian affairs for the Northwest; one, a commission to the Sandwich Islands; one, a connection in the German consulate for his son who was studying abroad; one, the governorship of a territory; and numbers sought clerkships at Washington or chaplaincies in the army or navy. Even John Lanahan, irascible preacher at Alexandria, confessed: "If Lincoln should *want* a Methodist for a respectable place—which is not likely—and would appoint me 'Navy Agent for the D.C.' I would not *decline*." [10]

From the outset the Methodists fared rather poorly. Simpson was thoroughly displeased when Minister Joseph Wright was "summarily ejected" from Berlin and no comparable post was found for another Methodist. John Lanahan charged that the "treatment of our people by this Administration is an open, standing insult to the

Church." If he could get the other preachers of the region to join him he "would let Mr. Lincoln know it *in no measured terms.*" In one way or another they succeeded in making the President aware of their demands. It was whispered about that he would give "very great weight" to "the cordial & hearty recommendations of our church authorities." Late in July of 1861, Henry C. Whitney overheard the President reading a letter of introduction to Secretary Chase which he had just written for an elderly gentleman who was waiting. The letter stated that "the bearer's recommendations were satisfactory and the fact that he was urged by the Methodists should be in his favor, as they were 'complaining some of us.' " [11]

Simpson, extremely sensitive to the charge which the Church, South, and the secular press were quick to make, that he was dabbling in politics, was cautious. So far as possible he made his recommendations through James Harlan, senator from Iowa and a long-time friend; Harlan in turn called upon the bishop to strengthen his own hand, as in the case of Jesse Bowen of Iowa City. Harlan wanted a letter from the bishop in Bowen's behalf. "We recommended his appointment to Bogato [*sic*]," the senator explained, a place which probably had been filled, "but a letter mentioning that place—*dated back,* so as not to seem rediculous would answer my purpose, and I doubt not be of great service to Gen. Bowen." [12]

Whatever his sensitivity, the bishop did not hesitate to confront the President himself with the claims of the Methodists when he had the opportunity. Such an occasion arose in the fall of 1861, and Secretary of War Simon Cameron presented him to the President. Briefly and pointedly, he contrasted the unfavorable attitude toward appointments from among the numerically strong Methodists as compared with members of smaller denominations.

To Simpson's astonishment Lincoln, through Cameron, promptly invited him to name the minister to Honduras! Nonplused and cautious, Simpson protested that he had "no wish to make appointments to office": he had simply been objecting to "unjust distinctions between Churches." He took the opportunity, however, to rebuke the President once more for ejecting Joseph Wright from Berlin without finding a comparable post for any other Methodist. Had Lincoln "proffered an appointment of the same grade"—thus "restoring us in this respect to the position we held under the last administration" —he would have suggested his friend Colonel Alexander Cummings of Philadelphia, who had been "overlooked by this administration." There was at hand, however, an opportunity for the President to exhibit his good will. Cameron had promised the chaplaincy at West Point to Dr. John McClintock "because of his peculiar fitness." He would so confer it unless the President refused authority. It was clearly a "test point, which would indicate whether or not Lincoln was fairly disposed towards the Methodists." The President evidently failed in the test, for McClintock did not get the appointment.[13]

In the meantime, Simpson—and Bishop Ames, who collaborated with him—made some effort to cultivate members of the cabinet. They were on particularly friendly terms with Edwin M. Stanton, Cameron's successor in the War Department, and Salmon P. Chase, the Secretary of the Treasury.

Simpson was most favorably disposed toward Stanton. Despite an irascible temper and political double dealing, the Secretary of War was earnestly religious at the verbal level. He frequently consulted with the leaders of the church, felt no embarrassment in asking them to pray, "habitually invoked divine favor in behalf of his generals and their armies," and had "the firmest conviction" that the Lord directed the Union forces. Apparently he had known Simpson since the early 1830's, when he had gone to Cadiz, Ohio, from his native Steubenville to practice law. One of his first official acts as Secretary of War, in January, 1862, and his first friendly gesture toward Methodism, was to appoint Bishop Ames a commissioner, along with Hamilton Fish, to visit Federal prisoners at Richmond. He yielded to Methodist demands for chaplaincies, named Simpson's son to a commission, and requested the bishop himself early in 1863 to serve as chairman of a commission to visit Fortress Monroe, New Bern, Port Royal, and New Orleans "to examine the condition of the colored people and make suggestions." Simpson, sensitive to the hallowed tradition and spiritual sanctity of his office, "declined any such position." [14]

Simpson had known Chase in Cincinnati—had won his praise for editorials on the Fugitive Slave Law. He now saw an opportunity to forge a closer alliance between the statesman and the church. Was not the unparalleled success of the English Wesleyans in their missionary enterprises largely due to the practice of associating "public men" with their meetings, either as speakers or as presiding officers?

Would it not be wise to invite Chase to preside over missionary rallies of the church and to make an address if "compatible with his feelings"? Chase, a religious man and an inordinately ambitious politician, well aware of the Methodists' numerical strength, accepted the invitation with alacrity.[15]

Quite willing to take Methodist claims into account, Chase balked when Senator Harlan urged his old friend Jesse Bowen for an auditorship or a chief clerkship: both positions required specialized training which Bowen did not have. But he had in mind a Mr. Walker who, "if not a member is a regular attendant in the same Church and should become a member." Would Ames and Simpson concur in recommending him? And would they accept his appointment "as evidence of the appreciation justly due to the body whom you represent"? [16]

Simpson had "but little acquaintance with Mr. W." As for church membership, he knew nothing of his "predilections" nor "how his sympathies may lead him." However, with the resignation of the present officer the Methodists had lost "the *only man* which the Administration has seen fit to appoint to the head of a bureau." Of course he knew of the difficulty in making changes, and of the pressure of applicants; and he assured the secretary that he believed in his friendship and his "determination to do what is right. May God direct you in all things." John Lanahan, in the meantime, confirmed the bishop's suspicion that Walker "was not even an attendant at any of the Methodist churches." [17]

The first political triumph of moment was the appointment early in 1862 of John Evans as governor of Colorado Territory. Simpson had recommended him for Nebraska Territory; but Lincoln, passing him by, had offered him first Washington and then Colorado. Evans, the Indiana physician and, later, Chicago operator in real estate and promoter of railroads, was an able appointee. His selection was a coup for the Methodists, and he and Simpson planned together how best to use it. Calling upon their Indiana friend J. L. Smith—who had been an agent for Indiana Asbury University, they offered him a proposition: the bishop would appoint him superintendent of missions in the Colorado country, and Dr. Evans would name him Secretary of State for the territory. Evans assured him that there would be "no difficulty in having the work of the Secretary's office done by a deputy, so as not to hinder the evangelistic services of the superintendent of missions." Smith was already serving in the dual capacity of collector of internal revenue for the government and presiding elder in the Methodist church. Considering these advantages and the fact that his wife disapproved of the move to the frontier, he declined the offer.[18]

Simpson was considerably less successful with Postmaster General Montgomery Blair than with Chase or Stanton. In 1863, with John Lanahan and other friends, he called to complain of the "proscription" of Methodists in the Post Office Department "because of their religion." He had already talked with the President and had his word that Blair had reported a number of Methodist appointees in his department. Now the bishop asked for a roll of department employees, with an indication as to which of them were Methodists. Blair refused, saying that such an inquiry would make an improper religious test for officeholders. There followed an exchange of plain and pointed, even sharp words. Blair delivered himself of a "long and . . . excited denunciation of ministers," concluding with the remark that he thought himself quite unbiased, that he had servants in his kitchen who were Methodists, and that he did not object to them because of their religion.

Simpson immediately took offense and stalked from the office. The comparison was a reproach to the church. Methodists were "fit for the kitchen but not for Office in Washington." [19]

The incident, closed for the moment, arose to haunt Blair for the rest of his life. Maryland was a Methodist stronghold, and had been since the beginning of the denomination. When he sought election to the United States Senate the choleric John Lanahan spread the story that he had insulted Bishop Simpson in Washington. In vain Blair approached the bishop and Harlan and others, seeking a disclaimer. With the opposition of the Methodists and the onus of having been a Union Democrat, he was never again elected to public office.[20]

Notwithstanding Simpson's growing influence with the government, his friends continued to complain bitterly about the discrimination against Methodists. Agitation had brought few appointments. The governorship of "an inconsiderable Territory, and a few consuls" was no essential change in the "proscriptive Policy" of the administration. Every Presbyterian and Episcopal private seemed to be provided with "some other position than that of carrying a Gun," whereas the Methodists who, some estimated rather generously, furnished "more than fifty per cent of the entire Army," did the fighting and had not one single prominent officer.[21]

One of Simpson's dissatisfied friends, the Reverend J. H. Whallon, resorted to a frontal attack. Openly declaring to Chase and Welles, "As a people we are ignored," he let them know that he expressed Simpson's opinion. It was galling to realize that although the Methodists did "a large share of the voting and fighting" they were "not known in the Government in any department." From Chase and Welles he went to General Joseph Lane, former governor of Oregon Territory, and a friend of Simpson from Indiana days. Lane agreed to discuss the matter with the President but asked for a letter from the bishop. The time had come for action, Whallon wrote to Simpson. The President would listen to the Methodists now, "and I know you are the Orricle of our people with him Speak He wants to be Prest again he cannot well do without us." Incidentally, he would be pleased to have the bishop's "earnest support" for the governorship of a territory which he thought would be created.[22]

As the elections of 1864 approached, Simpson and his associates began to plot the means of enforcing upon the government appropriate honors for Methodism. The least which should be expected was a place in the cabinet. The Methodist best qualified for such a position, and the one most available, was Senator James Harlan of Iowa. A graduate of Indiana Asbury during Simpson's administration, a lawyer, a former preacher and college president, he had had a phenomenally successful career in Iowa politics culminating in election to the United States Senate in 1854 and reelection in 1860. As a senator he had largely supported the President's conservative policies, in opposition to Ben Wade and the Radicals. By 1864 it was "quite generally recognized" that he had some measure of influence with Lincoln.[23]

Simpson decided to concentrate upon this one office, to the exclusion of all others. As his friend James Mitchell wrote, it will "take all the power we can muster to force our member" on the government. In consequence, the bishop refused to lend his influence to other office seekers, in the fall of 1864, even to Joseph Wright who wanted a judgeship. By mid-December, Governor John Evans of Colorado Territory, calling on the President in company with others, found, "The matter of Senator Harlan looks well." [24]

III

Political preferment was only one of the matters that took Simpson to the War office and the White House. As the Union forces gained control in Missouri, Kentucky, Tennessee, and Louisiana, the churches in general, and the Methodists especially, began to reflect upon their responsibilities and opportunities in the conquered areas. Many of the southern preachers had fled from their pulpits before the Union armies, leaving their congregations without regular preaching.

For two decades the leaders of northern Methodism had reproached themselves for permitting the division of their beloved Zion; and recently they had suffered reproach from others, including Methodists, for failing to tear the church apart once again over the slavery issue. Only through the war had they found relief—and, as if to purge themselves of their transgression, they entered into it with the fierceness of zealots. Equating God and patriotism, sin and rebellion, they sought to put down the forces which they believed had fostered disunion in church and state alike.

In 1863 the bishops at their regular fall meeting planned to have the southern territory then within the Federal lines "explored," with a view to making temporary arrangements "for the supply of the spiritual needs of the forsaken people." "Providentially," and largely through the preaching of Simpson in 1861, there was a surplus of nearly half a million dollars in the treasury of the Missionary society. As a beginning the board appropriated the modest sum of $35,000 for carrying on the work.[25]

Simpson, charged with the supervision of the territory in East Tennessee, immediately requested a report on conditions in Nashville from a chaplain who had followed the Union armies into that city. The chaplain reported that most of the pastors had deserted their flocks. The churches were empty or occupied by the army, and the Methodist Church, South, was "disorganized beyond the hope of recovery." He believed it possible to "regain" the churches "if the matter could be properly presented to the government authorities." It would be easy "to show to our government that the M. E. Church South as a body was thoroughly disloyal, and more, that every cent of her property belongs to us." On the latter issue Simpson had no doubt. Had he not written the legislation of 1848 repudiating the plan of separation? And had he not bitterly criticized the Supreme Court for awarding the property to the Church, South? [26]

At that moment Bishop Ames hit upon a scheme to enlist the support of the War Department. Apparently the idea was suggested to him by Brigadier General John P. Hawkins of the Union forces, stationed in Louisiana. Hawkins, who had heard of Ames's success in land speculation (it was a proverb in Indiana that "a scheme in which the Bishop has a hand is sure to succeed"), proposed that he encourage northern farmers to colonize the abandoned plantations. By using Negro help they would soon be able to make the small farms "better gold mines than California ever saw." The *tour de force* of Hawkins's letter, however, was his observation that many of the Negroes, destitute for help, were Methodists and ought, therefore, to have the protection of the church.[27]

Ames hurried to Washington to consult Stanton, notifying Simpson of his intention. The secretary of war, always ready to oblige the church in its combinations with the government against the common enemy, issued an order which directed the generals commanding the Departments of the Missouri, the Tennessee, and the Gulf "to place at the disposal of Rev. Bishop Ames all houses of worship belonging to the Methodist Episcopal Church, South, in which a loyal minister, who has been appointed by a loyal Bishop of said church, does not now officiate." In December he issued a similar order to three other departments, instructing commanders to turn over church property to Bishops Simpson, James, and Baker.[28]

Ames set out for western Tennessee and Louisiana almost at once, and reported in a short time that he had "appropriated, under the order of the War Department," and supplied nine churches "formerly belonging" to the Methodist Episcopal Church, South. The *Methodist*, in New York City, remarked that the occupation was to be temporary, and that the question of possession or ownership would not be raised until civil rule was once more established. However, it continued hopefully: "The Methodist Episcopal Church, South, is shivered to atoms. It is doubtful if its General Conference will ever meet again." Therefore the people of the South, as they returned to their homes after the defeat of their armies, should be "gathered into loyal churches." Some spokesman for the northern Methodists made the unfortunate remark that the policy should be to "disintegrate and absorb" the southern church.[29]

Meanwhile, "Parson" William G. Brownlow, in the self-appointed role of John the Baptist, began to make preparations for the advent of Bishop Simpson in East Tennessee. Pouring his vitriol into the columns of his Knoxville *Whig and Rebel Ventilator,* he heartily approved the action of the Federal armies in seizing the churches of Knoxville and using them as hospitals. They "would be used for better purposes if turned into *grog shops,* selling mean corn whiskey for rebel money, than to be used to preach and pray such treason, blasphemy and blackguardism, as have disgraced their walls and pulpits for the last three years." [30]

On January 15, 1864, Simpson arrived in Nashville "to look after Methodism" in that "benighted region," and to see what he could do "toward reorganizing and reestablishing its institution." The "desolation of war" was "everywhere apparent," a retribution to the seceding states for "their crime." He found everywhere a "deep prejudice against the North," and nothing of the warm welcome for himself and his enterprise that Parson Brownlow had prophesied.

Conducting his business with dispatch, he placed M. J. Cramer in charge of the work at Nashville, authorized Chaplain Calvin Holman, at Chattanooga, to confer with generals of the Army "as to Churches that may be occupied under the direction of orders from the War Department and to receive and use the same in my name," and commissioned the chaplains to receive members and ministers "that may be truly loyal." [31]

Back at home, he received reports of the success of his agents. Cramer, in the face of vigorous opposition from the southern church, secured an order from General Grant giving him possession of McKendree Chapel and the German Methodist church at Nashville, and instructions to the army to make any necessary repairs. Holman had difficulty getting the army out of the building at Chattanooga; he held services anyway, but had only thirty in attendance, "mostly blacks." The first chaplain of the Union Army at Murfreesboro at once secured an order from General George Thomas for the possession of the Methodist chapel. When the southern preacher protested, the general, with no eye for fine distinctions, replied that the chaplain was a Methodist, and that if the "Rebel Methodists" could not worship with him "they could go without worship." At Knoxville the chaplain found the Methodists in East Tennessee "extremely anxious for our religious services," but "particularly sensitive to outside interference." The troublesome southern preachers were spreading the incendiary rumor that the War Department was helping the northern Methodists to "establish a Religion by the Sword and at the point of the Bayonet." Parson Brownlow, unmoved by the opposition of the southern preachers, urged Simpson to return for an official conference in the summer, and began to beat the drums for a union of East Tennessee Methodists with the Methodist Episcopal Church. Fully two-thirds of the membership of the region, he said, "are loyal." "Only the *Preachers* showed themselves to be traitors," and even a fair proportion of them were loyal.[32]

Simpson was jubilant over the prospect of an enlarged Methodism, a church whose banner should fly from Canada to the Gulf, from the Atlantic to the Pacific. There is "a vast field opening, which we must enter or be derelict in Christian Duty," he told the Missionary Society of the church at its anniversary meeting. There were hundreds and thousands of "white refugees" who had been left "utterly destitute," and the church must "sustain ministers of the sanctuary among them till they are able to do it themselves." Of that "other class" which had been "so strangely and wonderfully made free," he thought "God has thrown on our Church a tremendous responsibility." His stirring peroration, mingling the emotions of patriotism and religion, recounted the war maneuvers at Lookout Mountain. The result "was in doubt until the clouds dispersed, when the Stars and Stripes were seen flying on the top of the mountain." The outcome of the war, too, was uncertain; but the mists "would soon be dispelled, and we should see the flag of the Union floating over the whole South. What a work will there be to carry the Gospel to them; they have it not. Once back in the Union we will tell them that the door of the old Church is wide enough to let them all in, and we will all be happy together." [33]

Lincoln, in the meantime, remained quite unaware of the order which his secretary of war had issued, and of the ambitious enterprise of the Methodists. He had countermanded an order of the provost-marshal of St. Louis giving control of a southern church to the northern Presbyterians; and a month after the issuance of Stanton's order to Ames he denied that he had ever interfered "as to who shall or shall not preach in any church." Nor had he knowingly tolerated similar interference by anyone else under his authority. Confronted with Stanton's order in behalf of Ames, he addressed an acid note to the secretary of war. Stanton immediately issued a second order exempting Missouri from the provisions of the first. His only intention, he explained to Lincoln, was to provide "a means of rallying the Methodist people in favor of the Union, in localities where the rebellion had disorganized and scattered them." [34]

The incident was well designed to alienate the Methodists from Lincoln and to move them in the direction of sympathy with the Radical Republicans. By 1864 the church had little reason to remain in the conservative camp. Slavery, outlawed by the quadrennial general conference meeting that year in Philadelphia, was already a dead issue. The church was united in its deep-felt enmity toward the South; even the border, embittered by long years of conflict, supported the bishops in their aggressions.

Hiding behind the ambiguity of the President's order and his own free construction of the rights of the Methodist Episcopal Church, Simpson continued to occupy the territory his agents had taken over in East Tennessee. Ames likewise stubbornly held onto the properties he had seized in Memphis and New Orleans, even when the President, thoroughly exasperated with the "most extraordinary" situation, for a second time ordered him to surrender the chapel at Memphis. [35]

The conflict between the bishops and the President was, however, far from open warfare. Still playing for Lincoln's favor, the general conference of 1864 passed a series of resolutions and detailed a committee under the chairmanship of Bishop Ames to present them to Lincoln in person. The resolutions, affirming the duty of Christian ministers and citizens to do all in their power "to sustain the Government," and asserting the loyalty and devotion of the church "to the best interests of the country," pledged remembrance of the President and his chief officers in "never-ceasing prayer," called upon the government to prosecute the war "until this wicked rebellion be subdued," and demanded the outlawing of slavery by constitutional amendment. [36]

One member of the committee, anticipating the political advantage of a formal reply from the President, notified his secretary, John Nicolay, that the delegation would call, and obtained an interview in which, without informing the others, he presented in advance a copy of the resolutions. When Ames and his party entered the White House the next morning they were ushered in to the President and introduced by the secretary of state, William H. Seward.

A member of the committee read the address and formally presented a copy of it. The President, much to the committee's surprise, reached into his desk for a paper and remarked good-humoredly that, having seen the address, he had prepared his reply.

Lincoln was acutely aware of the very real service which Simpson and Ames, and the Methodist church, had rendered, not only in engendering an intense patriotism but in keeping thousands of border citizens in the Union. He had no intention, however, of committing himself on the property question, nor of alienating the other northern churches. His reply was astutely ambiguous.

"Nobly sustained as the government has been by all the churches," he said, "I would utter nothing which might, in the least, appear invidious against any." He thought the Methodist Episcopal Church, "by its greater numbers, the most important of all. . . . It is no fault in others that the Methodist Church sends more soldiers to the field, more nurses to the hospital, and more prayers to Heaven than any. God Bless the Methodist Church—bless all the churches—and blessed be God, who, in this our great trial, giveth us the churches."

While the committee waited for the secretary to make a copy of the President's statement, Ames turned the subject to the rights of the Methodist church in southern territory. The President skillfully evaded a direct answer.

Thwarted in their desire to gain some advantage in the property question, the members of the committee were none the less generally pleased with the result of their mission. As they took their leave, one of them said, "Mr. President, we all hope the country will rest in Abraham's bosom for the next four years." Lincoln joined in the laughter, and the interview closed.[37]

XXI

YANKEE PURITAN

FOR the most part Matthew Simpson was cautious and a little uncomfortable in the presence of Lincoln and official Washington, whether he sought political preferment for his friends or bounties for his church. His province was eloquence, not politics, and even in his oratory he eschewed that which was openly political. But speak he must. The cause of the Union possessed and overwhelmed him. The mingled emotions—his hatred of slavery, his frustration from the long years of struggle with the southern church, his intense love of country and church, quickened to deep passion by the alternate anxieties and exaltations, the fluctuating griefs and joys of war—all boiled within him and overflowed in a torrent of words.

He believed with the conviction of a zealot in the operations of Providence—that God was "working out some great wise purposes in all the movements of men, and in all the combinations of evil men." His was a romantic faith born of the phenomenal advance in technology and of the incredible sweep of civilization across the American continent. He saw Providence in every detail, from the "strange combinations of circumstances preceding and connected" with the discovery of the western world, to the great cataclysm of war itself which must come even to God's chosen people when they would not seek His ends peaceably.[1]

For the first two years of the war he spoke chiefly to the Methodists, at their conferences, missionary rallies, and special conventions.

Early in 1863, at the first anniversary of the Christian Commission at Philadelphia, he carried his message of optimism beyond the confines of his church. The Commission, organized shortly after the beginning of the war under the sponsorship of the Young Men's Christian Association, promoted the "spiritual good" of the soldiers and sent its agents among the sick and wounded to distribute food, clothing, Bibles, and good cheer. The Academy of Music auditorium, the largest in Philadelphia, was crowded for the celebration. For an hour, interrupted by frequent applause, he poured out his praise of the nation and his faith in the future.[2]

He was immediately besieged by requests from other communities for aid in their public meetings in support of the Commission. The demands of his own church were so heavy, and his residence at Evanston so far removed from the centers of population, that he often had to decline. It was regrettable, wrote George H. Stuart, chairman of the Commission, that the bishop had not "the power of being in more places than one at the same time" so that he might arouse "by his fervid eloquence the multitude of Christian patriots." [3]

For months the remoteness of Evanston from the affairs of church and country had weighed heavily upon him. He spoke frequently and traveled much. Train connections were poor, travel conditions difficult, Evanston inaccessible from Chicago. He was not well—largely, he felt, because the lake air disagreed with his lungs. His brethren in several cities of the East besought him to make his home among them. It was rumored that he would move to Washington. He looked seriously at a house in Baltimore, but at last chose Philadelphia, where the laymen purchased a house and presented it to him. In midsummer, 1863, he moved his family to the East and plunged immediately into the affairs of the church and community.[4]

His new residence made it possible for him to be more often in Washington. He preached frequently at the Methodist charges in the Capital and numbered among his auditors many political leaders, including Chase, Stanton, Harlan, and the President himself.

He was called upon repeatedly for his "War Address." Variously called "Our National Conflict," "State of Country," "Future of the Country," and "The Providence of God As Seen in Our War," it achieved widespread and enthusiastic favor. It "swept like a whirlwind over the hearts of the hearers. Men clenched their hands, shouted, stamped, stood on their feet, and were left at the end in a tumult of patriotic excitement." In Philadelphia standing where he had stood to celebrate the Christian Commission, he was repeatedly interrupted by "bursts of enthusiastic applause." At Chillicothe, Ohio, the audience grew wild with excitement. "Ladies threw away their fans and handkerchiefs; men threw their hats in the air, stood erect, and mounted the seats." The Rochester *Democrat*, after the presentation in that city, stated that nothing could exceed the "fervor and animation" of the bishop. Was it wise, the editor queried, "to employ such men in presiding in Annual Conferences"? "Ought they not to travel . . . at large . . . to address the public mind upon those great questions which concern so vitally the Church and the nation?" A college president, not a Methodist, thought, "The Government should employ that man to visit all the principal cities in the loyal States." Secretary Stanton praised him as "one of the most eloquent, learned, and patriotic men of our country and age." No one, he wrote in introducing the bishop to General Sheridan, had done "so much to encourage and strengthen loyal and patriotic sentiments and to sustain the army by appeals to the benevolence of the people." [5]

At Washington, President Lincoln, Secretary Stanton, and a number of members of Congress heard him in a presentation which the *National Intelligencer* thought "worthy of the name and fame of the distinguished divine and orator." He caused considerable merriment, in which the President "heartily participated," when in praising the self-made character of the leaders of the nation he remarked that "some may have heard that even a rail-splitter may become president." At the conclusion Lincoln warmly congratulated him for the manner in which he had marked out the progress of the country, adding shrewdly, "But, Bishop, you did not 'strike 'Ile.' " Simpson promised not to overlook thereafter the newly discovered oil interests.[6]

In the summer of 1864, shortly after the close of the general conference, Lincoln made a singular request: that the bishop, substituting for him, officially open the Sanitary Fair at Philadelphia. Simpson, at West Point attending the annual examinations as a member of the Board of Visitors when the request came, hurried home to prepare his address. "As the bishop's eloquence is well known," stated the Philadelphia *Press,* "the President will no doubt be well represented." [7]

The occasion was an important one: the raising of funds for the United States Sanitary Commission, which was charged with supervising the medical and sanitary facilities of the army camps, and not infrequently supplying the men with clothes and food. The fair, initiated by the City of New York, had proved to be the most successful enterprise for the raising of money: New York had made a million dollars for the Commission, and Philadelphia expected to do as well.

Made up of sixteen buildings, promenades, ponds, playgrounds, the Philadelphia fair extended over a two-mile area. The main building was sixty-four feet wide, five hundred feet long, and had an arch of fifty feet. There was an art gallery, a display of horticultural wonders, of military curiosities, and many other attractions. A speakers' platform stood near the main building. As the crowds gathered for the formal opening the cannons roared out a salute, there were exercises of prayer, the transfer of the buildings and their contents from the Executive Committee to the people, and orations by Mayor Alexander Henry, Governor William Cannon of Delaware, and Governor Andrew Curtin of Pennsylvania, and Bishop Simpson.

The bishop adapted his remarks to the occasion, but his theme was unchanged: he preached the providence of God in the affairs of the nation. He drew applause as he paid tribute to the absent President, and again as he denounced the leaders of the South, and "long-continued and deafening applause" as he soared briefly in oratorical praise of the Union soldier and the flag he served. He contemplated the woes of the war, the "multiplied thousands of husbands, and brothers, and sons . . . lying among the sick and wounded"; but he found solace and hope in a recital of the resources of the country. He praised the noble spirit of much giving, the devotion of "families of narrow means—the laboring man, the working-woman." He praised the city of Philadelphia; he praised the women upon whom the success of the fair and the Sanitary Commission was chiefly dependent. In a series of sharply etched pictures, crowded together with the dramatic movement of a cinema, he mingled together pathos and humor, swept his great audience alternately from "tremendous cheers" to the quick silence of pathos, and back again to "cheers and laughter," and finally he brought them to a "tremendous outburst of applause" as he called by name and praised the heroes of the war: Sherman, "a Northern man with Southern proclivities"; Howard, who, "one-armed, is still within himself a host"; Butler, "the terror of the Confederacy"; Pennsylvania's Hancock and her "*Meade* of honor"; and added to all of these, the "giant West, from the shores of her broad Mississippi, sends a Grant of unconditional victory!"

He closed by dedicating the treasures of the fair in the name of the people and for the benefit of the wounded soldiers and sailors. "May God, in his infinite mercy, restore them to health and to their friends and to their country!" The audience shouted: "Amen! Amen!" [8]

I I

The summer and early fall of 1864 were filled with uncertainty and even gloom for the North and for Lincoln and his sympathizers. In July the southern general, Jubal A. Early, in a bold raid advanced within sight of Washington; in the bloody Peninsula campaign Lee was successfully holding off Grant from Richmond. Greenbacks fell to their lowest point; Horace Greeley and others sought to achieve peace through negotiation; the Radicals in Congress, attempting to displace Lincoln, sponsored an abortive Chase-for-President boom; and Lincoln himself wrote out and sealed into an envelope a prediction of his own defeat. As the elections drew near there were signs of victory for Lincoln and the North: Atlanta fell to Sherman, the peace negotiations came to naught, and the Radicals, finding it expedient to support the President, abandoned Chase. [9]

Simpson spoke twice that fall on the war theme: in Pittsburgh in mid-October, when he aroused the audience to pandemonium; and at New York on November 3, five days before the election. Mark Hoyt and the Methodist laymen of New York had high hopes for the address in that city. The *Tribune, Times, Evening Post,* and *Herald,* all promised full reports. To speak in New York five days before the election with newspaper coverage was to speak to the whole nation. Five thousand war-weary people crowded into the Academy of Music to hear the bishop. [10]

His address, well suited to dispel doubt and despair, was in the epic mode,—if chauvinism may be described as epic—a narrative of the greatness of the American nation which rose to the brazen, climactic theme, "God cannot afford to do without America." It was, thought the London *Saturday Review,* the very essence of Yankee Puritanism, characterized by the "fearless Puritan handling of religious names," and the Puritan preempting of God. [11]

At the outset the bishop announced his intention to "stand far above all party dialect," declaring his belief in the Providence of God and his conviction that "the old ship will yet ride among the breakers, and by and by, in spite of all dangers, shall be safely moored in the haven of peace and prosperity." The audience responded with "great applause," and the emotional tone of the address was set.[12]

He could see four possible results of the conflict: first, the nation might fall prey to some foreign power; secondly, it might be divided; thirdly, it might remain united, but with its institutions overthrown and those of the South established; and fourthly, "having passed through this fiery ordeal," it would come out "purer, stronger and more glorious and more useful than ever before." The audience applauded, and renewed its applause a moment later when he said he believed it "the design of Providence" to secure the last alternative.

He recited the stories of the ancient nations, Phoenicia, Greece, Rome, all of which had endured more than a century; he told of the adventures of Columbus in the discovery of the long-hidden continent—how the prows of his ships were pointed to the West Indies, and the great land area reserved for the English and the settlers in search of a place to worship God. Would God have allowed other great countries to endure so long and this one "to go down in ruins in so short a period," unless it had "disobeyed His laws more than any other nation"? And was not this country discovered and settled in a manner to suggest that "God had intended this nation to work out greater destinies than any other nation"?

He then assembled the evidences of national greatness. For one thing, the nation had severed church and state. Again, it was an "asylum for all the nations of the earth." Its education was superior to that of any other nation, for not only had it taught the masses, but it had taken the mothers of the coming generation and fitted them to educate "a grand race of sovereigns." It had opened the way for all to rise to highest offices: "The humblest cabin-boy may lead our armies, and the poor hostler may sit in the Senate. Who has not heard of Henry Clay the mill boy of the slashes [applause] and Jackson the child of poor Irish parents [applause] and some may have heard that even a rail-splitter may become President." Every few sentences the audience applauded, and at the reference to Lincoln it broke forth in "tremendous applause and cheers."

The second and third propositions—that the nation might be divided into two confederacies, and that the South might prevail—he ridiculed. But he could find a series of Providences which assured him that God would bring out of the conflict a nation "purer, grander, and more glorious than ever before." He saw the hand of Providence in the invention of new plows, drilling machines, reapers, all designed to husband labor; he saw Providence in the building of the railroads so that the West was able in the hour of crisis to send its produce to the eastern cities; he saw Providence in the simple matter of the sewing machine, in the discovery of the electric telegraph, in the starving of the poor in England at the time when they sympathized with the rebellion; he saw Providence in the sending of food by the North to England in "beautiful fulfillment of the Scriptures," "If thine enemy hunger, feed him." He cited the providential migration from England, twenty years before, of a young engineer "with strange notions in his head about running vessels with hot air engines, and about iron-clad monitors," and he told with some detail the story of the providential acquisition of California and the discovery of gold and silver.

He paid tribute to the heroes of the war, calling their names one by one, citing in short epigrammatic phrases the deeds of each. "I used to pray," he said, "for a General Jackson and heard others praying for the same. I heard them often say, Oh for a man with independent purpose such as Old Hickory was when he fought the battle of New Orleans . . . But I have ceased to say so. The prayer has been *Granted*." The audience responded with "tremendous cheering."

He praised the advances made against slavery, paid brief tribute to the Negroes for the part they had played in the conflict, suggested that they be given a state of their own, perhaps on the border between Mexico and Texas, and then concluded with a dramatic peroration, an apostrophe to the flag.

Taking up a "war-torn, shot-riddled flag" which was greeted with "tremendous cheers," he advanced a step toward the audience and said:

Your 55th Regiment carried this flag; it has been at Newbern, and at South Mountain and Antietam. The blood of our brave boys is upon it, the bullets of Rebels have gone through and through it, but yet it is the same old flag.

The audience, high-keyed and ready for emotional outburst, could take no more. Beating their hands in enthusiastic applause, they rose to their feet to give three "rousing cheers" for the flag. The noise of the explosion subsided and Simpson continued:

Our fathers followed that flag; we expect our children and our children's children will follow it; there is nothing on earth like it for beauty!

Again there was cheering, "long and loud." As the crowd quieted Simpson moved to his climax. His tall frame towering above the people, his shoulders erect, his face aglow with feeling, his tenor voice throbbing with emotion, his mist-filled eyes gazing into the future, he exclaimed:

Long may those stars shine! Just now there are clouds upon it and mists gathering around it but the stars are coming out and others are joining them, and they grow brighter, and so may they shine until the last star falls in the heavens, and the great angel swears that time shall be no longer!

The crowd took over, and the meeting broke up with great cheering and hurrahing and waving of hats and handkerchiefs.

Only the New York *Tribune* carried more than a brief report of the address, and that appeared on November 7, the day before the election, too late to speak to the nation. In the meantime, Sherman was on his way from Atlanta to the sea, and the reelection of the President seemed certain.

III

Simpson was in Washington in January to deliver the War Address, and again in March to attend the inauguration exercises. Things looked well for the Methodists: Harlan was to be in the cabinet as secretary of the interior, Evans continued as governor of Colorado Territory, Simpson had been invited to preach in the Capital on the Sabbath after inauguration, and Lincoln received him cordially at the White House.[13]

Saturday March 4 was overcast and gloomy with occasional rain, hardly fit for the inaugural ceremonies. The crowd, milling about in the muddy streets, grew silent as Lincoln stepped forward to read the Second Inaugural: "With malice toward none, with charity for all, with firmness in the right as God gives us to see the right . . ." He then took his place, the Vice President elect, Andrew Johnson, beside him, to receive the oath of office. At that moment the clouds broke and the sun shone brightly, lighting the scene up "with dazzling splendor." The court dress of the diplomatic corps sparkled with diamond light, and the golden rays glittered from the sabers and bayonets of the soldiers.[14]

The following morning the hall of the House of Representatives was filled to capacity for the sermon of Bishop Simpson. In the audience were President and Mrs. Lincoln, Chief Justice Chase, Secretaries Seward and Stanton, Speaker Schuyler Colfax, and the Honorable Simon Cameron. The bishop spoke of the doctrines of the cross— the brotherhood of man, the equality of races, universal liberty, and a community of interests. War, he said, had once been the rule of all nations; but it had become the exception, an outlaw among all peoples. And even this war among brothers, the most terrible of all wars, was about to end. He could not but think "when yesterday the sun burst brightly upon the chief magistrate of the nation, just as he stepped forward to take the oath of the highest office in the land, that so the sun of peace would suddenly, and without noise or warning, burst upon the nation and dispel the clouds of war."

Although it was Sunday morning, and a sermon, "the people clapped their hands, stamped their feet, and waved their handkerchiefs" in approval of the hope he had expressed. Mr. Lincoln himself pounded vigorously on the floor with his cane, and the tears coursed down his bronzed cheeks.[15]

XXII

HIGH PRIEST OF THE RADICAL REPUBLICANS

THE good omen, the benediction of the eternal sun, was short-lived, clouded over in a moment by the arrogant depravity of man. There were five weeks of hope: Grant advancing on Petersburg and Richmond; Sherman consolidating his position and holding Johnston at bay in North Carolina; Jefferson Davis fleeing from Richmond; and Abraham Lincoln walking the streets of the Confederate capital, unmolested.

On the afternoon of April 9, Lee surrendered to Grant at Appomattox. At dawn cannons roared the announcement in Washington, government departments declared a holiday, and the crowds, delirious with victory, swarmed into the streets cheering and singing. That day the President sat for a photograph, his sad face yielding to a scarcely perceptible smile.

On April 11 he spoke to the people, a great throng on the White House lawn, eager for the victory celebration. He addressed them, not in rousing periods that called for antiphonal hurrahs, but in close-reasoned argument, a defense of his own mild and generous policy for reconstruction of the states of the South. On April 14, Good Friday, he met the cabinet, and again discussed the terms of reconstruction. That night he went to Ford's Theatre.[1]

The play had reached the third act when a shot rang out, and a man, balancing a moment on the rail of the President's box, jumped to the stage, paused to shout, some said, "Sic semper tyrannis" (Ever thus to tyrants), and hurried off the stage, dragging a foot which he had injured in the leap. And then from the President's box, following the shot like a delayed echo, came a woman's scream, pitched high with anguish.[2]

Matthew Simpson read the story in the black-bordered columns of the newspaper: how the frenzied crowd swarmed into the aisles, wrenched seats from their moorings, clambered onto the stage, poured into the streets; how the soldiers arrived, cleared a passage-way, and bore the unconscious President across the street into the humble house of a tailor. Even the early press reports gave no hope. The President was "just alive at 3 a.m.," said a dispatch from the War Department. At six o'clock his pulse was failing, at 7:22 he breathed his last. Phineas Gurley, kneeling at his bedside, prayed for the comfort of his country and his family.[3]

The cabinet wired, inviting Simpson to take charge of the funeral services. He hurried to Washington, called upon Mrs. Lincoln, prayed with her, heard from her a recital of the events of the President's last day and the story of his view of two reflections of his own face in the mirror—one of the living man, the other of the dead.[4]

At the White House services the bishop offered the opening prayer: invoked God's grace "to bow in submission to Thy holy will," begged consolation for the widow, guidance for the sons, wisdom for the successor to the late lamented President; and pledged that "by every possible means" the citizens of the North should give themselves to their country's service "until every vestige of this re-bellion shall have been wiped out, and until slavery, its cause, shall be forever eradicated . . . 'Thy will be done in earth as it is in heaven.' "[5]

From Washington, Simpson hurried to his conference at New York, and to further reflection on the career of the President, for he had been asked to deliver the funeral oration at Springfield.

The slow procession; the black-draped train, bearing the body of Abraham Lincoln made its way to Springfield, sixteen hundred miles over the triumphant route he had traveled in 1861. It was a pageant of mourning: every city hung with crape, flags at half-mast; Baltimore grief-stricken; three hundred thousand people crowding the streets of Philadelphia, nearly a million in New York; throngs in Albany, Buffalo, Cleveland, Columbus, Indianapolis, Chicago; public rites in major cities—silent, weeping crowds filing past the open coffin, a score of funeral addresses, dirges, the reading of the Second In-augural, Protestant, Catholic, Jew uniting in solemn obsequies. At the villages and the country crossroads, too, the people gathered, grim-visaged and bareheaded, to see the train go by. Thirteen days from Washington to Springfield.[6]

At noon on May 4 the coffin was taken from the place where it had stood in the Illinois capitol at Springfield, and the procession— governors, senators, congressmen, state and municipal authorities, clergymen, and military men—moved to the burial ground. A little to the left of the vault, at the foot of a knoll, was a platform for the band and the choir; beyond that, the speakers' stand; and sweeping back over the hillside, the thousands of listeners. There was the chanting of a dirge, the reading of Scripture, prayer, a hymn, the reading of the Second Inaugural, the chanting of another dirge. Then the bishop rose to speak.[7]

He recalled for the people Lincoln's farewell remarks at Springfield—the tall man eloquent, on the rear platform of the train, speaking simply and humbly to his neighbors of his pain in parting, of the great responsibilities which had fallen upon him, of his desire for their prayers, of his hope that all would be well.

The people's grief was understandable, said the bishop, for "Mr. Lincoln was no ordinary man." Providence had had a hand in his early life, through the physical toil which gave him an iron frame for his herculean labors, and even more important, through his "identification with the heart of the great people, understanding their feeling, because he was one of them, and connected with them in their movements and life."

His greatness rested on the mental characteristics of "a quick and ready perception of facts," "a memory unusually tenacious and retentive," "a logical turn of mind, which followed sternly and unwaveringly every link in the chain of thought." And who among men in reading his messages had failed to perceive "the directness and simplicity of his style," which had "so powerfully influenced the destiny of this nation," and which should "for ages to come influence the destiny of humanity"?

It was not, however, chiefly through his mental faculties that he gained such control over mankind. "His moral power gave him preeminence." He called able counselors. "He summoned able generals into the field, but . . . the great act of the mighty chieftain, on which his fame shall rest long after his frame shall molder away is that of giving freedom to a race."

Simpson praised the words of the Second Inaugural—"With malice toward none"—but even as he repeated the words of mercy he charged the people to go on to their "painful duty." To the deluded masses he would extend the "arms of forgiveness." But every man who, as a senator or a representative, had aided in the rebellion, must be "brought to speedy and to certain punishment," and every southern military leader, educated at public expense, must be "doomed to a traitor's death." Men might attempt to compromise and to restore these "traitors and murderers" to society again. But the American people would "rise in their majesty and sweep all such compromises and compromisers away."

From this vengeful mood, he returned quickly to words of praise for his country and its flag, and a final tribute to the late President:

Chieftain, farewell! The nation mourns thee. Mothers shall teach thy name to their lisping children. The youth of our land shall emulate thy virtues. Statesmen shall study thy record, and from it learn the lessons of wisdom. . . . We crown thee as our martyr, and humanity enthrones thee as her triumphant son. Hero, Martyr, Friend, farewell.[8]

The Chicago *Tribune* thought the address "a critical and wonderfully accurate analysis of the late President's character" and "one of the most masterly efforts ever delivered by this eloquent speaker." [9]

II

In March, 1865, Matthew Simpson, sitting in the House of Representatives to observe the inauguration ceremonies, had been outraged. Andrew Johnson, the Vice President elect, was obviously intoxicated. That night, jabbing his pen into his diary, Simpson characterized him with trenchant brevity: "Heard Mr. Johnson—drunk." [10] But the death of Abraham Lincoln brought him up short. How could he reckon with this event, how could he explain the sudden elevation of Johnson, if he did not find the hand of Providence in it?

A week after the assassination he had determined his answer. Speaking to the New York conference, he praised President Lincoln's goodness and mercy. His death was sad and heartbreaking, but in the end great good would come of it. "God does all things well." Mr.

Johnson in some respects was not the equal of Mr. Lincoln; yet he was "probably his superior in the determination to crush every vestige of rebellion, and punish the leaders."

The conference of ministers approved the remark with "great applause," and the bishop continued. "He was driven from his home in Tennessee, his property destroyed, his family made refugees, his son-in-law fell in the battle of Nashville—he has in himself the strongest cause to hate the rebellion." [11]

Some two weeks later Bishop Simpson with four other ministers journeyed to the White House to pledge the "hearty support" of the "loyal Methodist public" of Philadelphia. The President received them "handsomely" and responded by "referring to his antecedents for assurances of what may be expected in the future," especially in regard to "the punishment of treason as a crime of the highest magnitude."

Mr. Johnson also seemed friendly and *right* on the Methodist property question. Several months earlier, as governor of Tennessee, he had said to Bishop Davis W. Clark, "Tennessee will tolerate no two sects of the same denomination, one founded upon slavery and treason, and the other loyal." Johnson had thought so well of his remark that he had repeated it.[12]

Nor was the new President disposed to disregard Methodist claims in the matter of James Harlan. Lincoln had designated Harlan as his Secretary of Interior, but out of consideration to the retiring secretary, had delayed the appointment until a few weeks after the inauguration. Johnson inducted Harlan into the office without hesitation.

Matters did not go so well, however, with Simpson's old friend Governor Evans of Colorado Territory. Months before the assassination Evans had been censured in Congress for the unseemly conduct of Colonel John M. Chivington, United States Marshal for Colorado. Chivington, a militant Methodist preacher who had declined a chaplaincy during the war because he wanted a "fighting commission," had directed a surprise attack against a band of Indians encamped peacefully on a government reservation at Sand Creek, Colorado. His men, angered by Indian raids on white settlers, slaughtered the Indian women and children and warriors, indiscriminately. The nation was horrified by the massacre. Evans, in Washington at the time, explained satisfactorily to Lincoln that he was in no way responsible; but a committee of Congress, investigating the incident, and urged on by Evans's political opponents, recommended his removal as governor late in May, 1865. Harlan, who had defended him in the Senate, now hurried to Seward and secured from him a pledge that he would not act until Evans had an opportunity to speak for himself.[13]

It soon became apparent that Evans would be removed without a hearing. Considerably worried, Simpson made the trip to Washington three times to talk with the President but was unable to get an interview. When Harlan told him that Seward was the man to see he went to Cape May, New Jersey, where the secretary was vacationing. Seward was "personally satisfied" with Evans, but not at all disposed to provoke the Congress into an unnecessary attack on the administration. On the other hand, he had no desire to alienate the Methodists. He would, therefore, allow the bishop to name Evans's successor. Appeased, Simpson promptly suggested A. W. Cummings, the Philadelphia publisher. Seward approved, and late that summer the President accepted the resignation of John Evans and named Cummings to succeed him. Simpson was disturbed, however. He had learned that Johnson was not Mr. Lincoln. He did not "seem to have a heart." [14]

In the meantime, trouble had developed over the Methodist holdings in the South. Simpson, along with the Radicals in Congress and much of the northern press, had expected the new President to be severe in his reconstruction policy. Johnson's first militant utterings had confirmed their expectations; but he soon tempered his policy to conform largely to the one which Lincoln had promulgated: amnesty for all who would take the oath of allegiance; an early end to military occupation; speedy return of the states under rewritten constitutions—the rights of citizens, including the enfranchisement of the Negroes, to be determined by the individual states.[15]

In Nashville, Tennessee, Samuel D. Baldwin of the Church, South, looked on Johnson's moderate policies and rejoiced. For some months he had attempted to regain the property seized by the Methodist Episcopal Church. When the northern preacher in charge denied his claims Baldwin applied to Simpson, who likewise refused to yield possession to the chapel. Now, armed with the President's amnesty order, which restored the rights to property as well as to citizenship, Baldwin called on Simpson's preacher at McKendree

Chapel. The preacher replied somewhat testily, first, that Johnson's policy did not revoke the order of Mr. Stanton; secondly, that he would not give up the property without a "special order" from the President; and thirdly, that he would not give it up "even *with it*." [16]

Baldwin reported the incident directly to the President. But he was not satisfied to rest his case on the impertinent remarks of a northern preacher. Knowing Andy Johnson well—and how he had stumped East Tennessee in opposition to a consolidated federal government—he taunted him with *"other questions"*:

1st. Are great consolidated national churches desirable in a *free* government?

2nd. Do not great hierachies tend to great national despotisms as did the national church of Rome?

3rd. Is the reunion of the two great methodist hierachies of America desirable . . . as a duality will they not neutralize any despotic tendancies . . .[17]

The questions cut into Andy Johnson's temper like a rasp. Angrily, he sent for Simpson. Confronting him with the issue, he demanded that he give up the Nashville chapel. The bishop demurred, the two argued the case at length, and the interview ended inconclusively. The matter dragged on for two months until August 12, when Seward telegraphed to Simpson that Johnson wanted to see him. They had a "long talk." Johnson was insistent, and Simpson, not yet an ally of the Radical Republicans, yielded the point. He wired instructions to the preacher in charge at Nashville to turn the building over to Baldwin.

The decision was a great blow to Simpson's preacher. His trustees were "much disheartened." They would have preferred putting the President "to the necessity of ejecting us by Federal forces." Through Simpson's order they had lost "the benefit of sympathy that an ejectment would create for us North and which would aid us much in securing funds to build." [18]

Simpson's astute lieutenant in Maryland, John Lanahan, saw in Johnson's action a precedent which the "old church" might follow in recovering property in Virginia. In 1861, in consequence of the action on slavery at the general conference of 1860, a large number of churches in Virginia and Maryland had withdrawn from the Methodist Episcopal Church and formed an independent organization. It was now rumored that they were negotiating with the Church, South, and that they would unite with that body at its general conference of 1866. Could not Johnson's Nashville order be used to regain these properties for the Methodist Episcopal Church? [19]

Bishop Ames had no doubt about it. Johnson, having restored property to the Church, South, was "shut up to the necessity of granting what we propose to ask." If he should refuse "we shall have a good case to take before the country—which will be worth more to us both in money, and influence than ten fold the value of the property involved." He demanded that Bishops Janes and Simpson meet him in Washington: "Do not fail for it is a grave matter." Janes demurred: "Getting possession of churches by military authority has a great deal of odium attached to it." Simpson was also reluctant; but in the end both agreed to meet Ames in Washington. [20]

The three bishops, accordingly, prepared a plan of action and went to see the President on January 17, 1866. Simpson talked with him first, explaining the Nashville matter "satisfactorily," and then his two colleagues joined him. They had "a very pleasant interview" with Johnson. He "seemed very fair as to church property" and "requested" them to see Secretary Stanton. They, having already drafted an order which they wanted the adjutant general's office to issue, hurried to Stanton and secured his approval. [21]

The order provided that church edifices and parsonages in Virginia were to be occupied by the church which had jurisdiction prior to 1861. Such occupancy was not to be construed as giving legal title—a matter which must be determined by the civil courts.

The order seemed innocent enough, and Johnson approved it the next day in an interview with Ames. The adjutant general issued the statement from his office almost immediately. Johnson, Ames reported, said "if there is any thing wrong in it we must stand by him—for he did just as we advised." "The President is fully aware of its import," Ames said, "and issued it after mature consideration hence its moral value to us as a Church." [22]

It was soon evident that Johnson did not understand the "full import." "Laus Deo," wrote Ames to Simpson. "I find there are 210 Churches and 32 parsonages." It was a figure he had neglected to mention to Johnson. The news was too good to keep. Long before he was able to seize the property, Ames boasted of his conquest. A committee of "rebel" Methodists immediately called on the President, who "entertained them very kindly, to the exclusion of other important business." Johnson denied that he had issued any such order as that of which Ames boasted.[23] A few months later the "rebel" preachers, unimpeded by Ames, voted to adhere to the Church, South, taking most of their 210 churches and 32 parsonages with them.

III

Quite aside from the effort to enlist the aid of the government in the seizure of southern property, the Methodist Episcopal Church had been moving on the South from many fronts. The general conference of 1864 authorized the bishops to organize annual conferences in southern territory and to make the necessary appointment of preachers; and it created the Church Extension Society, which was to aid in the purchase and construction of buildings. In 1866 the church set aside $400,000 for the work in the South.[24]

The policy of the church was not, as the South charged, simply a systematized and malicious scheme to "disintegrate and absorb" the southern church, albeit some northern preachers and church papers were thoroughly committed to disintegration and absorption. The program was compounded, rather, of two elements: Methodist evangelical zeal—the simple and time-honored Methodist technique of opening up a new territory by sending in the most aggressive preachers available—and the utilization of such political tactics as might be improvised to meet the immediate situation. The evangelical task was complicated by the fact that the chief opponents in the field were not Baptists, nor Presbyterians, nor Universalists, nor any others whose doctrines and "usages" could be assailed, but fellow Methodists who could be attacked only for "disloyalty" and pro-slaveryism. Slavery had been ended by the war, and so "disloyalty" proved to be the better issue. The passions of war were transferred from the military to the ecclesiastical front.[25]

The campaign was vigorous and aggressive, and not too concerned with the finer points of southern rights or Christian charity. The press of the Church, South, complained that every Methodist chaplain in the Union Army was a self-constituted missionary. Finding a deserted congregation, he proceeded to take charge, saying to the people that "it was all the same," that slavery was done away with, and "now the churches would unite." In a few places the people went over *en masse*. When the people resisted, the missionary resorted to argument or stratagem. He pleaded that they return to the "old church," or the "Mother church," or the "loyal Methodist Church."

The stratagem sometimes amounted to seizing property by what the southern press called "legal sham." Northern preachers turned up claims against church property, which they were then able to buy at a heavy discount. The South was not a little angered to read the happy report of a corresponding secretary of the Church Extension Society that he had been able to secure, for $250, two small churches valued at $1,000. In Charleston, South Carolina—in an operation which the New York *Christian Advocate and Journal* described as "delicate and difficult," and as exceeding even the "most sanguine hopes"—the official board was induced to pass resolutions requesting the commander of the military post to turn the property over to the missionary of the Methodist Episcopal Church. In due time, a representative of the southern church "made a pilgrimage" to Philadelphia, persuaded that his "old acquaintance" Bishop Simpson would interfere and restore the property. He got "neither redress nor sympathy." [26]

By the time of the general conference of 1868, the work was so successful that Bishop Simpson, in reading the Episcopal address, was able to report that he and his colleagues had organized eight new conferences in southern territory, with a total of 373 traveling preachers (besides a large number of local preachers), and a membership of more than 90,000. One hundred of the traveling preachers and 40,000 of the members (constituting almost the entire accession of whites) were from Tennessee.[27]

Simpson as an executive removed from the field of conflict, and as an orator attuned to the emotional values of particular cases, was much less concerned with means and techniques than with needs and results. He did not doubt for a moment that the Methodist Episcopal Church must be planted firmly in southern territory. Nor had he forgotten his own part, in 1848, in the repudiation of the plan of separation. So far as he was concerned, the property in the South really belonged to the "old church," despite the adverse decision of the Supreme Court.

As an orator speaking to northern audiences on conditions in the South, he recounted the exciting scenes of warfare, and described the destitution of the white population and the bewildering plight of the Negroes. He discussed the shift of population from plantation to village, and the consequent need and opportunity to build churches. Sure of the spiritual "superiority" of his own church, and confident "that the denomination that builds the first Church secures the largest portion of the population and the greatest influence," he favored an aggressive program. He heard the complaints from the South and recognized that some of the northern preachers were "imprudent"; but he thought that most of the accusations were by "evil men" for "political" purposes.[28]

He was particularly proud of the schools planted by his church among the Negroes. He was deeply moved by the zeal with which the young people among them were seeking an education, and even some of the old ones were buying spectacles and asking for primers. Sometimes, he said, "you will see these colored men and women, from sixty to seventy years of age, trying to learn their letters, spelling the name of Jesus, and rejoicing that they are beginning to read the word of God." He had been stirred, too, in conferences where he had heard colored preachers tell of their troubles and testify to their victory, their tears rolling down their cheeks "as they spoke of their gratitude to God, for having permitted them to see a conference, and to become members of it." [29]

Simpson was no reformer. He differed with his colleague Bishop Kingsley, who favored the intermingling of black and white ministers in the southern conferences, and with Gilbert Haven, editor of *Zion's Herald* (elected bishop in 1872), who had radical ideas of equality and miscegenation. During the war he had been elected a member of the Freedmen's Relief Association; but he had also been named a vice president of the Pennsylvania Colonization Society, within the month. Stanton urged him to take over the organization of the Freedmen's Bureau under the direction of the War Department, but he declined. Such an office was out of keeping with his understanding of his "ecclesiastical obligations." In 1865 he was elected president of the National Freedmen's Association (American Freedmen's Aid Commission), a position which he resigned some six months later "owing to the pressure of his other duties." Undoubtedly, he was also motivated by the fact that the Methodists, dissatisfied with the part they had in distributing the funds of the commission, were about to organize their own Freedmen's Aid Society.[30]

On the Negro question, he was essentially conservative, and motivated largely by his belief in evangelism, missions, and the historic call of the Methodist church "to spread scriptural holiness over the earth." In his famous War Address at the Academy of Music in New York in the fall of 1864, he had brought grief to one of his Methodist admirers when he advocated that the Negroes be sent to Africa "to evangelize that continent," or that they be colonized in Texas where they would constitute "a barrier between ourselves & Maximillian." He felt that the church had made a mistake when it first went into the South by giving too much attention to the colored people—the ministers "misconceived" their mission, and so alienated a large part of the white population. He favored separate conferences because, he said, the opportunities for leadership increased the effectiveness of the colored ministers. And when the New York *Independent* took him to task for promoting segregation, "a greater sin" than slavery itself, he testily replied that, notwithstanding its "anathemas," his church would do all in its power "for the downtrodden and the oppressed." [31]

Events, however, weighed more heavily than arguments. Despite his essential conservatism, Simpson soon moved from right to left; the forces which brought about his alienation from Johnson acted also to increase his sympathy toward the Radical Republicans.

Johnson, taking advantage of a long recess of Congress, had instituted a moderate policy for the restoration of the southern states. The Radicals were outraged. Reconstruction had been all too easy. Rebels still unpunished, "white-washed" traitors cleansed by the simple process of subscribing to the oath, had taken over the southern governments. Once admitted to Congress, the "traitors" could ally themselves with the moderates and dictate the policies of the nation itself. On the other hand, a coalition of the Radicals with the poor whites and the Negroes of the South would be powerful enough to control the federal government for years to come.

The ensuing attack of the Radicals on the President was one of the bitterest in American history. They had two powerful propaganda weapons: the charge that the President had violated the rights of Congress, and the indictment of the reconstructed southern governments for debasing the rights and liberties of the Negro. The first, they used to down the objections of the Moderates in Congress; the second, to appeal to the humanitarianism of the northern public. Power politics and the cause of downtrodden humanity proved to be invincible allies. Under the skillful but ruthless leadership of Thad Stevens and with the support of the public the Radicals forced their reluctant colleagues into line and seized control of the government.

Simpson was ready enough to sympathize with the Radicals. In his ejection from the Nashville chapel and the removal of John Evans, he had already suffered humiliation from Andrew Johnson. But his associations with two members of the cabinet, Stanton and Harlan, moved him much more precipitantly into the Radical camp. His friendship with Stanton had deepened appreciably during the war. On more than one occasion in Stanton's private office at the War Department, the doughty, bewhiskered secretary, discoursing on the problems of the war, had said, "Now, Bishop, pray." And Simpson had prayed.[32]

He was much more intimate with Harlan. He could not forget the warm relationship of schoolboy and master. Through the years he had watched the success of his pupil with pleasure and admiration. Once when they had differed sharply over Harlan's status in the church, Simpson as bishop had ruled against him; but they quickly closed the breach. It was to Simpson that Harlan turned to share his sorrow over the death of his little daughter. Time bound them together in common causes and common griefs.[33]

Harlan's success had been a boon to the church, particularly his appointment to the department of Interior. One of his first acts was to name the Reverend D. N. Cooley of Dubuque as Commissioner of Indian Affairs. He made other changes, too—rather slowly, the bishop thought; but both had hope for the future.[34] His peremptory dismissal of Walt Whitman—he would not have the author of the "obscene" *Leaves of Grass* on his payroll—brought a storm of protest and made him the prototype for Brother Balaam in Mark Twain's *The Gilded Age*.

The ousted office holders complained bitterly against him, and by mid-August of his first year had aroused the New York *Herald* to an attack on the administration of the Interior Department. Harlan, meanwhile, had quickly cooled toward the President and his reconstruction policy. He and Stanton alike were equivocal—unwilling to take exception to Johnson's policies when they were discussed in cabinet meetings, but ready enough to lend secret encouragement to the Radicals.[35]

Late in 1865 Harlan, unhappy with the duties of his department and out of sympathy with Johnson, began to maneuver for reelection to the Senate and turned to Simpson for help. A word from the bishop to two Methodist preachers active in Iowa politics might well assure his nomination for the long term. He sought other support, however, with the result, an opponent said, that there was much lobbying in his behalf, both by men connected with his department and by Methodist preachers "without number or piety." After a bitter intraparty struggle he was nominated at the Republican party caucus in January, 1866, and elected by the legislature. Since his term in the Senate would not begin until March, 1867, he held on to his cabinet post determined to prevent the President, as long as possible, from using the patronage of the department to fight the Radicals. Johnson, embarrassed by his presence, thought it "indecent for him to remain," but hesitated to force him out because he did not wish "to excite the hostility of the powerful Methodist Church." As the tension increased, Harlan finally resigned in midsummer, 1866.[36]

Simpson was having trouble with Johnson at the same time, and his own move toward Radicalism was coincident with Harlan's. By the time the secretary was out of the cabinet Simpson, having moved far toward the Radical Republican camp, was preaching that "God designs to do away with every vestige of slavery." Before the "rebellious States" could be received back into the Union "protection of the rights of humanity must be secured." And, as for the conflict between the two sections, "the statesmen of the North are able to cope with those of the South, and are in the majority, so there is no ground for fear." [37]

IV

In the summer and early fall of 1866 Johnson took the stump in an effort to win support in the congressional elections. His famous "swing around the circle" began as a triumphal procession and ended a humiliating spectacle. Effective campaigner that he was, skilled in the rough-and-tumble tactics of East Tennessee, he was unable to resist the crowds and replied in kind to Radical-inspired taunts. His performance, at best undignified for a President of the United States, was characterized by the Radical press as a drunken orgy.

At the polls that fall the Radicals won an overwhelming victory. Intoxicated with power, they moved in for the kill. They seized control of the Electoral College, abridged the President's power as commander in chief of the armies, ignored his constitutional right to call or refuse to call Congress into session. They even brought his cabinet under control by declaring, in the tenure of office act, that removal of cabinet members without consent of the Senate was a "high misdemeanor."

The ground was set for the removal of the President himself by impeachment. A year went by before Johnson gave the Radicals an occasion to move against him. Then, convinced of the unconstitutionality of the tenure of office act and exasperated by Stanton's perfidy, he discharged him. Stanton refused to surrender his office, barricading himself in the War Department. Congress moved at once to impeach the President.

James Harlan, erstwhile cabinet member, and now in the Senate, was openly for impeachment. He was well supported by the Methodist press, which was aggrieved not only by the President's obstruction of "justice" and his "boldly setting at defiance the laws of the land," but by his "moral corruption," which had "ever made him a disgrace to the nation." [38]

Bishop Simpson was deeply stirred. Accompanied by his wife, he rushed to Washington where he listened to several speeches in Congress, talked with "many members," dined with the Harlans, called on General Grant, and went to see Secretary Stanton in the War Office. The Secretary was in "fine spirits," and they had a "very long religious talk . . . with prayer." Mr. Stanton wanted to know whether or not "the God-fearing portion of the people" endorsed his course of action. If they did not, what then ought he to do? Simpson assured him that the "loyal and Christian masses" approved his conduct and "hoped he would never surrender." Stanton, much pleased, requested the bishop to pray, "the hour being 2 o'clock in the morning." [39]

Simpson, in frequent consultation with Harlan, worried over the course the Senate would take in the impeachment proceedings.

When the trial opened in March the Radicals regarded twenty Republican senators as doubtful. By May 1 the number had been reduced to eleven, among whom was Waitman T. Willey of West Virginia, Simpson's Methodist layman friend of many years. Active in the cause of temperance and Methodist affairs, he had had a prominent role in the Methodist centenary celebration of 1866.

As the impeachment trial neared its climax, it was whispered that Harlan and Simpson had conspired to bring the pressure of the church on the recalcitrant Willey. In Chicago the Methodist quadrennial general conference was in session. On May 13, three days before the first vote on the articles of impeachment, a motion was introduced which, by implication, condemned the President as a "wicked person" and called for his removal. A second resolution would have the conference set aside an hour to pray for the President's conviction. An aged brother objected: "My understanding is that impeachment is a judicial proceeding, and that Senators are acting under an oath. Are we here to pray to the Almighty that they may violate their oaths?" Both motions failed.[40]

A Baltimore paper alleged that Senator Harlan, in a desperate effort to win Willey's allegiance, wired to Simpson, "I fear Bro. Willey is lost." Simpson is supposed to have replied: "Tell Bro. Willey he has a soul to save—pray with Bro. Willey." Harlan promptly denied the report. The St. Louis *Christian Advocate* of the Church, South, thought Harlan protested too much. Why was he so quick to issue a denial? Because he "well knew that every one who knew anything of the Bishop, would believe that such dispatches passed." [41]

In the meantime, there had been two more unsuccessful attempts to enforce action endorsing impeachment upon the Methodist conference in Chicago. Simpson, in an extraordinary departure from precedent, then took the floor and read a series of resolutions for the consideration of that body. He set forth several grievances: the fear that without the "rightful decision" the "religious privileges" of his church would be endangered in the South, and the "painful rumors" that "efforts are being made to influence Senators improperly." Since, he argued, "the evidence and pleadings in the case have been fully spread before the people, so that all may form an enlightened opinion," the conference should, therefore, resolve to appoint an hour of prayer to invoke God "to save our senators from error." The resolution was adopted without dissent. It had been "aimed at Senator Willey of West Virginia," the *Nation* remarked, "rather than at the Throne of Grace." The conference paper, the *Daily Christian Advocate,* apparently agreed with the *Nation.* The vote, it boasted, would "be heard in Washington"; it would "reach the penetralia of hesitating Senators, and establish them in the faith." [42]

Chief Justice Chase, who was presiding over the trial, was indignant. "Think of legislatures, political conventions, even religious bodies, undertaking to instruct Senators how to vote, guilty or not guilty." But the Radicals moved on to triumph over Willey, who was already under some pressure from his constituents. With the weight of the Methodist church behind them, and the pressure of the public, they "badgered and disciplined" him until early in the morning of the vote. He at last was said to have capitulated, to have agreed to vote guilty on the eleventh article. The decision of Senator Willey, wrote Secretary Gideon Welles in his diary, "was quite a disappointment to the President." It was to be explained, he thought, by the fact that "Bishop Simpson, the high-priest of the Methodists and a sectarian politician of great shrewdness and ability, had brought his clerical and church influence to bear upon Willey through Harlan, the Methodist elder and organ in the Senate." [43]

The Radicals immediately recognized the value of Simpson's service to their cause. The committee on arrangements for the Republican National Convention offered him the use of their auditorium on Sunday May 24, "for a public discourse at any hour you may think proper." "And I beg to add," the representative of the committee said, "that the citizens of Chicago will be most happy to listen to a discourse from you." [44]

The bishop sought no political prestige for himself. His ventures into politics were so closely related to the welfare of the Methodist Church that he scarcely thought of himself as a shrewd "sectarian politician." He declined the invitation, but did consent, as an office befitting a clergyman, to open the Republican Convention with prayer. His efforts were modest, untainted by political tirade. Offering praise for spiritual and temporal gifts, he sought help in the deliberations of the assembled group—that they might be "peaceful and harmonious." Only the final benediction and petition, coming from the lips of the great and influential bishop, gave comfort to the Republican campaign committee:

> We bless Thee that freedom has diffused its healthful influences all over the land, and that the States so lately in rebellion are being reconstructed in the line of peace and prosperity. Hasten the work so gloriously commenced; may there be nothing that shall mar its progress. And oh, hasten the moment when all parts of our land shall be firmly and intimately and fraternally united . . .[45]

It was not long before the non-Methodist religious press was circulating the rumor that the bishop was to be Secretary of State in Grant's cabinet.[46]

V

The Methodist Episcopal Church, South, fighting for its very existence, and angry over the aggressive action of the northern brethren, was quick to charge that the Methodist Episcopal Church was an arm of the Republican party. Among people who had always heard preached the doctrine of the separation of church and state, and who were now unwilling victims of the Radical reconstruction policy, it was an effective propaganda weapon, one that helped to hold the Church, South, together.

Certainly the evidence was everywhere apparent. The success of the northern church in the South among the whites was largely in those areas where military and civilian personnel of the North demanded services of a "loyal" church. The members were largely Republicans; they were carpetbaggers, employees of the Freedmen's Bureau, and teachers sent out by the Freedmen's Aid Society of the church, and as such, they were strong supporters of Radical reconstruction. Governor Fletcher of Missouri remarked, "It is as necessary to maintain these Methodist Churches as it is to keep possession of the forts and arsenals." [47]

When, at the general conference of 1868, Simpson recounted the success of his church in the South, the New York *Tribune* exulted. The progress of the Methodist Church, said the *Tribune,* had "a *political* no less than an ecclesiastical significance. *There are probably not a dozen voters in all the conferences named, who will vote the Democratic ticket."* The rapid growth of the Methodist Episcopal Church in the South "must be hailed as one of the most promising proofs of all real reconstruction." Said the editor of the St. Louis *Christian Advocate,* commenting on the *Tribune* story: "Brother Greeley and Brother Stanton know very well what Brother Simpson and Brother Ames are about." [48]

Simpson, in the South on official business of his church, felt the impact of southern bitterness. Invited to preach in the Central Presbyterian Church in Atlanta, he was afterward notified that, "in consequence of his prominent position and influence at the North in favor of the Union during the war, the extended courtesy must be withdrawn." At Canton, Mississippi, he delivered an address of "beauty and great power," and preached also to the conference. But, said the reporter, "so great was the prejudice against our Church that only two or three white persons were present." Simpson himself found the impression "general" that "but for the troops in the South we could not safely hold worship at any place." [49]

VI

In view of the bitter reaction of the Church, South, to the program of the Methodist Episcopal Church, it seems incredible that any of the responsible leaders of the latter should have anticipated reunion. Some of them, indeed, looked forward to a Pax Romana, a policy of "disintegration and absorption," of reunion by admitting the once recalcitrant but now repentant southerners back into the "old church." [50]

The northern bishops made the first overture toward reunion in the summer of 1865. Rejoicing at the overthrow of the rebellion and slavery, and declaring that the "cause" which had separated the church had "passed away," they extended "a cordial welcome to all ministers and members of whatever branch of Methodism, who will unite with us on the basis of our loyal and anti-slavery Discipline." They also resolved, however, to "occupy, so far as practicable," those fields in the southern states "which may be opened to us, and which give promise of success." [51]

The southern bishops, in a "Pastoral letter," replied caustically: "While some talk of reunion of the two churches, we forewarn you of a systematic attempt, already inaugurated . . . to disturb, and if

possible, disintegrate, and then absorb our membership individually." [52]

The Methodist press, North and South alike, bereft of the issues
of slavery and war, eagerly laid hold of their new point of difference.
They argued the property question, the tactics of the missionaries,
the relevance of such "political" tests of membership as "loyalty" to
the government, and antislaveryism, the status of the episcopacy;
they revived the debates of 1844 and 1848 and disputed at length
the points in the history of the separation; they proclaimed their
own pious intentions and impugned the motives of their brother
Methodists.

The men of the South, having perhaps the greater cause to
suspect and complain, more often dipped their pens in acid as they
wrote. They pointed scornfully to the "conduct of certain Northern
Methodist bishops and preachers" in seizing churches; they accused
the North of endeavoring, "by misrepresentation, to fix on us the
invidious character of secessionists and schismatics"; they protested
against the "political harangues" which passed for sermons in
northern pulpits, and against the "dangerous" attempts of the
northern bishops to dominate the government—through the control of elections and the appointment of their friends. "Is there not
a purpose," asked Bishop Enoch Marvin, "to swell the church census
and gain prestige, so as to control the government?" They heaped
their censure especially upon Ames and Simpson. In reunion, said the
St. Louis *Christian Advocate,* Bishops Morris, Janes, "and perhaps
Scott" might be "acceptable" to the South. But "what Southern Conference could ever become so lost to all sense of self-respect, and to
all feelings of Christian dignity and true manliness, as to sit under
the presidency of Matthew Simpson or E. R. Ames . . ." [53]

The northern bishops, in 1869, again took the initiative in the
discussion of reunion, when Janes and Simpson, delegated by their
colleagues, journeyed to St. Louis to confer with the southern bishops
who were then in executive session. The northern men were received "with respect" and treated "courteously"; but the consultation
on reunion was limited to an exchange of written statements. Reviewing the issues of separation, fraternity, and the northern invasion, the
bishops of the Church, South, pointed out, "Heart divisions must be
cured before corporate division can be healed." They offered, how-

ever, to appoint a commission to deal with the grievances of both churches.[54]

The incident brought a renewed outburst of acrimony in the press. The St. Louis *Christian Advocate,* speaking of the "surprising overture from the North," thought Simpson "an unfortunate adjunct of the notable commission." It did not believe that Bishop Janes was "dishonest and tricky"; but, "as to Mr. Simpson, he is *capable de tout* in the Bishoping and political way." Bishop Enoch Marvin thought the "proposition for reunion" had come "at an inopportune moment"—just when the policy to "disintegrate and absorb" had failed. "The change of policy and tone are too sudden," he said. "Those warm words smoke with a suspicious odor . . . Time ought to have been given for fumigation, to clear away the effluvium of the so-recently dead 'policy.' " [55]

Simpson was never again active in the movement for reunion. The cause advanced, however, despite the obstacles of bitterness, open warfare, and the needs of the press. Fraternal relations were established, largely on the basis of the southern demands, and a commission was set up with power to adjudicate property claims, out of court.

Reunion was yet three-quarters of a century away, but the essential factor of Methodism, the experience of religion (supported by common usages, a common tradition, and a common symbolic name), like yeast, began to leaven the whole. Even in 1865 the southern bishops had testified "with pleasure" to the "nobler conduct and sentiments of many brethren among them"; and the caustic editor of the St. Louis *Christian Advocate* in the same year confessed that there were "thousands upon thousands of good and true Christian men and women among them." Responsible leaders of the North, in increasing numbers, came to deprecate their church's aggressive policy in the South, and to call for an equitable settlement of grievances.[56]

Even Matthew Simpson, refused the pulpit of the South in the first years after the war, felt the change. From the first he had been invited into the homes of the laymen of the "better class," and had found the former leaders of the Confederacy, especially the military men, cordial in their business relations. By 1869, when he was in Texas on official business, matters had so far improved that he was invited to preach to a congregation of the Methodist Church, South. Later in that year, in the Holston conference of East Tennessee, where the Methodist battle had raged most fiercely, about twenty preachers of the southern church were present to hear him preach at Jonesville. They fell under the spell of his eloquence, and "the tears of many of them flowed freely" under his "master strokes of power." They went away "feeling that Bishop Simpson is a Christian minister, and a very different man from what they supposed." The time would come when even a southern editor, aware of Simpson's war and reconstruction record, would praise him for his eloquence and claim him, along with Wesley and Asbury, for all of Methodism! [57]

XXIII

THE VICTORY OF FAITH

MATTHEW SIMPSON did not wear well the cloak of the politician. A little embarrassed by his own occasional forays into practical politics, he rationalized his conduct as being in the interest of the church. Whenever possible he worked through Harlan. To importuning office seekers he now and then denied that he had any political influence.

His fellow Methodists agreed in the belief that he was above politics. They were quick to recognize that Ames was a politician, "a strong man . . . never noted for meekness in his public life," and they were ready to boast that he "guided the political and military spirit" of the war. They knew that Simpson's temper could flare up like a lighted match, but they more often thought of him for his kindness and gentleness, his humility, and even his "Christ-like-ness." [1] They knew that he was frequently in Washington, and that the doors of great men were open to him. They believed that his influence was great, but they knew also that there were times when he was reluctant to use it for political bargaining. So the rumor grew and persisted that he was an adviser, a counselor to men in high places, a man of God who occasionally brought his spiritual insight to bear upon affairs of state.

His preaching and his politics operated reciprocally to enhance his prestige in both areas. If his name was one to conjure with in Washington, it was because the politicians knew his popularity and strength in the church. At the same time, the whispered rumors of his influence at Washington increased his power in the pulpit and the church.

His war address and his Lincoln oration had won great acclaim. But his fellow Methodists, proud as they were of his patriotic zeal, were somewhat scornful of those who praised his public address without having heard him preach.[2] His great triumphs in the pulpit came in the years immediately before and shortly after the close of the war.

Traditionally, the successful Methodist preacher was expected to "put on the rousements." If he could include emotional excitement he had "power—legitimate and glorious power." It was in this sense of the word that Simpson was popular: he was "powerful."

As a preacher, Simpson departed widely from the tradition of the Methodist pulpit. His importance and appeal lay not only in his dramatic qualities but in his message. He believed it was his duty to counteract fanaticism and to preach the truth not only of the Bible, but of all knowledge. "Science," he said, "is nothing more than catching a glimpse of some of the thoughts of God." [3] His underlying theme—the providence of God in the affairs of men—he adapted from Wesley. But by and large the preaching of Wesley's followers was evangelistic—the call of the sinner to repentance. When it was not evangelistic it was didactic. The bishops, especially, were given to instruction on the doctrines and economy of the church, homilies on stewardship, the importance of class meetings, Christian perfection. Simpson's preaching was neither evangelistic nor didactic. It was epideictic. He called men not so much to repentance as to praise.

In his doctrine of providence he was not a Calvinist. He did not teach the stern and ancient dogmas of depravity and election but the more humanistic, if more delusive, doctrine of human progress—under the providence of God. His hypothesis was simple, but his insights were shrewd. His ideas were a product both of the optimism of the day and of his own excursions into learning. Most of his brethren had the faith to believe what he preached, but few had the knowledge or the eloquence to duplicate his efforts.

He believed first of all in design, the doctrine popularized by William Paley and known to all nineteenth century Protestantism. There was "one God supreme," as revealed not only by the Bible but by the voice of science. "We may take the contents of the earth, the materials of all the strata of rocks," said Simpson, "and though we may make our excavations in Asia, America, Europe, or Africa, we shall find the same conformation, the union of the particles under the same laws—evincing that the mind that planted the western hemisphere must have laid the foundations of the eastern." Or one might take the wing of the smallest insect, "which has breath for but a day, and that wing, when inspected under the microscope, shows a wonderful network of filaments, of vessels and cords, arrangements to fit it for the purpose for which God designed it." [4]

He believed also, as he had preached in the War Address, that God was manifest in history. The strange succession of events, the rise and fall of nations, the pride and degradation of man, these were understandable only in the light of God's purposes.

He did not go along with Wesley, however, in believing that God would interfere with the laws of nature for the benefit of his followers. He sought his explanations of unusual happenings, not by rejecting what he knew of science, but by adapting his theology to the findings of science. If a man ride under a falling mountain, he asked, shall God stay the law of gravitation and save him? If he go to sea in a broken vessel, shall God reach out His hand and save him, while the others perish? No, that was not his understanding of the workings of providence. Nor did he believe that men were pawns in the hands of God, some designated from the beginning of time to be saved, others to be damned.

God, he believed, was *Mind*. How else explain the universe? The "laws" of nature were but a recognition of an existing order, not a statement of causality. If then God was *Mind*, was it not logical that He should operate through the mind or the soul of men? Even among men ultimate power resided chiefly in thought. A strong arm might break in pieces the flinty rock—yet what gave the arm its power but thought? "And in the clash of armies, it is the thought of the general which has led to victory." [5]

A Christian, then, ought to see that his thoughts were God's thoughts. Here again the bishop did not leap to the commonplace assumption that the Bible contained the whole truth. To him all thought was ultimately God's thought. But how then could a Christian give himself up to the providence of God? In the first place, he must make every effort to understand and utilize the laws of God's universe. "If we have the opportunity to learn," he said, "it is our duty to learn. . . . If he has given us minds capable of research; if he has given us leisure and facilities for research, then it is his will that we should understand this world in which we dwell." "There is not," he said, "a current of air that can drive the sails of the ships on the seas of this globe but God hath made it possible for man to understand its laws." [6]

Again, if a man were in the providence of God, he would utilize his learning and his wealth to spread the gospel and to do good. "The purposes of God are all in harmony with the happiness of man." The whole design of revelation was "to produce universal good-will, to fill the hearts of men with the love of God, and with love to each other, to banish strife, discord, jealousy, hatred, and war from the face of this earth." "Where was there a man," he asked, "who ever sought to alleviate suffering as Christ did? He went about always doing good." The social gospel had not yet wrought its effect upon the American conscience, and the bishop had few tools to recommend or techniques to offer; but he pleaded his point again and again. "Here is a reform society, a society to care for the poor, for drunkards and lunatics, for the disabled, for the aged—that is doing Christ's work; but the work is done through Christian men and women. They are carrying out Christ's plans. And it is because Christ lived that these agencies live and flourish." [7]

But was there not a particular way, some special means by which the Christian could lay hold upon the mind of God and know his will? Yes, he believed that a man could know the mind of God and could be aided by an Unseen Power. But even then, he must seek no special privilege; he must walk the avenues open to all mankind. He must cultivate the habit of thinking about God and of contemplating the truth as revealed in the Bible. "I may pass through the garden of a friend," he said, and

observe that there are walks tastefully laid out; that there is beautiful shrubbery on either hand; that there are flowers which may delight. But the friend may ask: "Did you notice that charming variety of pink? Did you notice that passion-flower, or that lily from Southern lands?" I had seen all the flowers as I passed, but I had not paused to look particularly at any one; I step back again, and before that flower I pause until I examine its petals, see the form of its leaves, and dwell on all its charms, and it becomes imprinted on my heart—'a thing of beauty,' which shall be a 'joy forever.' I *saw* it before; I have *looked* at it now.[8]

The power of God, thus cultivated, would yield joy and beauty, prompt men to greater learning, to utilization of resources, to acts of benevolence, and give them, individually, a stability of character.

Just as a man, when swimming in some swollen river, fixes his eye on the opposite bank and gains steadiness, so the "gaze upon the unseen enables one to hold on his course amid the attractions and the allurements of life." [9]

At times, however, the workings of providence were inexplicable. A man of wealth and goodness might suddenly be stripped of his possessions, a pious mother left a widow without means of support, Christian parents bereaved by the loss of a child, a little one "into whose eyes we looked with love." In an age when the mortality rate was high, the bishop had himself known the agony death brings to a young parent. He had but one comfort to offer: one must think of "the invisible, the eternal, the angelic, the spiritual," then he could "soar away from these earthly scenes":

> See the poor widow whose children are crying for bread. The winter's storm rages about her; the fuel is exhausted in her fire. Whither shall she turn? The charity of the world seems cold; but if she can look up and believe that a house is prepared for her, that all are hers, that she is a child of God and an heir of Glory, she can wipe away her tears, and point her children to the spirit-land; and she can be happy even in the midst of suffering, because she knows that earth has no sorrows that heaven cannot cure.[10]

A later generation would condemn him for such escapist doctrine, but the people who then sat in the pews had no thought of Marx's now famous cynicism, "Religion is the opiate of the people." If they were drugged by the preacher's doctrine, they felt not numbness nor sleepy unconcern with world affairs, but the wild ecstasy of release, the delirium of vision and mirage. In a society little concerned with social responsibility, the people found his portrayal of the *invisible* a catharsis, a release for their pent-up emotions, an escape from the hard realities of their lives.

I I

Of Bishop Simpson's sermons, the one attended with the most extravagant response was "the Victory of Faith." The theme was the familiar one of the courage to be derived from the knowledge of Providence. Faith was "the view of the distant that steadies against the whirl of the present." To the educator faith was "not teaching the number and forms of letters, or the marks upon a book," but "the companionship of the great and good and wise in distant lands and distant ages." It was the widening of the circle of thoughts until a man grew "greater and stronger." Faith, for the statesman, was seeing "the tops of far-off thoughts which common men never saw"; for the Christian, it was "a peace that cheers and strengthens," a victory over sin and the "dominion of passions," a joyous triumph over death and the grave.[11]

These thoughts he embellished with illustrations of a sailor boy "sent, in a storm, up the mast . . . amidst the swinging cordage," a student sitting "in the corner of a hearth while the pine knots are blazing" but in his thoughts "crossing the Granicus with Alexander . . . climbing the Alps with Napoleon . . . driving into the depths of Russia with Charles XIII." He related the struggle of Leverrier, whose friends said to him, "Why prison yourself in your study? Come where beauty smiles and wit sparkles." But he "was deaf to their solicitations." He spent his hours looking "away out into the heavens where he had seen some planetary disturbance"; he pursued investigations, resolved formulas. At last he was able to say, "There is a new world and I have found it." "He had faith in the distant; in the immutability of the laws of science; and for that faith he rejected the pleasures of a moment."

Frances E. Willard heard him preach the sermon at the Des Plaines Camp Meeting in Illinois, at the outbreak of the Civil War, and wrote: "I have heard great preachers, Beecher, Talmage, Spurgeon in England, Père Hyacynthe in France, but, to my thought, no flight was ever so steady, so sustained, so lofty, as that of Bishop Simpson on that memorable day." [12]

Eight thousand people were present on that occasion. Two of the number, arriving too late to find seats in the huge auditorium, retreated to the ministers' board tent, which was just to the rear of the speaker's stand. There, although they could not see, they could listen through the cracks between the boards. When Simpson announced his text one of the two, a professor at Garrett Biblical Institute, "threw himself back on the couch in disappointment and vexation." He had heard the sermon before and now had come to the camp "to listen to a twice-told tale." But the bishop had spoken only a few sentences when the professor "rose to a sitting posture; a moment later he sprang to his feet, and stood, tense and strained in his eagerness to catch every word through the screen of boards." He stood thus for an hour and a half, braced against the bunk, "tears often trickling down his cheeks unregarded . . . occasionally catching his breath in the intense excitement." [13]

In New England the bishop preached the same sermon on Sunday morning at an annual conference over which he was presiding. The large church was crowded, and many were compelled to stand. A "love-feast," preceding the sermon, gave many an opportunity to "testify," so that the "mental condition of most of the vast audience was . . . that of eager expectancy and deep spiritual preparation." [14]

When he began to speak he had, as men so often noted, "the languid and exhausted look of a hard-worked man." His voice was thin, nasal, high-pitched, almost feeble. As he gradually worked himself into his subject, as the feeling mounted and he became increasingly aware of the audience reaction, "his quavering tenor voice grew penetrating, resonant, sympathetic, and impassioned"; his stooping shoulders became erect, his gesture was no longer restrained, his dull eyes kindled into a blaze, and "his thoughts seemed to play over his face like a luminously radiating atmosphere." [15]

His climax, an allegorical reply to the objection of some people that religion was outmoded, was the very substance, in narrative form, of his belief in the oneness of science and religion. The genius of infidelity came near and offered him her hand. He took it cheerfully. She led him through the earth, showed him its blooming flowers, called them by name, took him through the forests, showed him the gigantic trees, roamed with him through the animal kingdom, pointed out the "exquisite adaptations of every part of nature." He learned it all with joy from her lips. She passed through society, explained its customs, its history, taught him its languages, and he learned them, eagerly. She dug into the earth and revealed the rocks "in their order of superposition," what the fossils taught of old catastrophes and of wonderful ages. She mounted with him into the heavens, opened up to him the solar system "so harmoniously and beautifully arranged," carried him beyond that system to numberless other systems whose suns were but the fixed stars he had seen. He went with her to the nebulae and looked at the vast worlds that composed them, "away to the fleecy cloud where light just trembles on the verge of shade; away to the suburbs of the universe."

But when he had reached the last star and had sat down he still panted for more. He looked into the face of his guide and asked, "Is this all?" "Is this not enough?" she replied. "Are there not beauties of earth and beauties of heaven enough to satisfy the longing soul? Is there not wisdom and power and skill so manifold, so conspicuous everywhere as to occupy the thought and fill the heart?"

Perhaps. Yet still, somehow, he felt a great void.

Then the genius of Christianity came to his side. She, too, took him by the hand, and he went with her "through the same earth, past the same rocks and forests and hills." She taught him the same languages, took him through the same domain of the sciences, and added one more, "the science of salvation." She taught him the languages of the earth, and to them added another, "the language of heaven." She mounted with him to the skies, and he drank in light from the same sun, hurried past the same fixed stars, resolved the same nebulae, and out again to the last star where his former guide had left him.

He gazed into the face of the genius of Christianity and asked, "Is this all?" "Is this all!" she exclaimed. "This is but the portico; it is but the threshold; it is the entrance to the Father's house." And she put the glass of faith into his hand, and he looked through it, and "away beyond the stars, away beyond the multiplied systems," he saw the great center, the throne of God. And as he looked he saw that there was "One upon the throne; he is my brother; and I look again, and my name is written on his hands; and I cry out with ecstasy:

> " 'Before the throne my surety stands,
>   My name is written on his hands.' "

The effect was "electric." "Hundreds shouted, clapped their hands; some rose to their feet; strong men and women wept and laughed at once . . . It was preaching to a full orchestra with the Hallelujah Chorus." [16]

XXIV

"BISHOPS AS PARTISANS"

As a bishop, Matthew Simpson traveled much. Everywhere the people sent him to the homes of the "better class" laymen. After the rigors of travel he found it agreeable to accept the comfort of a good home, and the convenience of a carriage—when the alternative was to walk. He was a brilliant conversationalist, much sought after as a guest. Urbane and friendly, he recounted anecdotes of his travel with sparkling wit and flashing eye.[1]

Thus, Matthew Simpson was thrown into frequent association with the more prominent laymen of his church. What he saw pleased him. There was John Evans, whom he had known for years. Successful businessman, prominent in politics, Evans was also a sincere and devout churchman liberal with his money, a founder of colleges, a supporter of missions. And by the standards of his day he was rigorously honest in business dealings, even to the payment of debts—when his honor was at stake—that others had made in his name. There was Daniel Ross, gentle but shrewd, who, having made his fortune in San Francisco in the first years of the gold rush, had returned to New York to become president of the Tenth National Bank. A member of the Seventeenth Street Church (Hedding Church) and a leader in local affairs, he was a vice president of the denomination's missionary society. "I never expect to be a very bright light," he said once at prayer meeting, "but I hope to be a steady one." [2] Even Daniel Drew, wizened little Wall Street trader, said to have made a million dollars in a single "operation," wept at class meetings, was a local preacher, contributed liberally to missionary causes, and, before the seventies were over, would give an estate and pledge his fortune to found a theological seminary. James Harlan, Joseph A. Wright, Waitman Willey, Mark and Oliver Hoyt, Orrington Lunt, Washington DePauw—these and their kind contributed generously to the support of the colleges, and made possible the magnificent Gothic structures which Simpson had urged upon the church ever since he entered the episcopacy.

Not only the church, but Simpson himself received their favors. Daniel Ross and others had raised a thousand dollars for him when he was ill in Pittsburgh, and a year later Oliver Hoyt had sent a like sum. Ross and Harlan and Evans looked after his investments and saw that he made a good return on his land and stocks. The laymen of Philadelphia purchased a house for him, and his friends of New York furnished it.

Never before had the Simpsons lived so well. Their two-storied brick home with its marble-faced fireplaces, ornate furnishings, and book-lined study, was a social center for Philadelphia Methodists. General and Mrs. Grant were entertained there and, a decade later, President and Mrs. Rutherford B. Hayes.

Mrs. Simpson, active in welfare and benevolence, was an elegant hostess. With the children in school she was able to travel now and then with the bishop. On one occasion she brought consternation to a Presbyterian banker's wife who was entertaining them during the conference session. Thinking of the Methodists as plain, illiterate people, the hostess, wishing not to overawe her guests at their first dinner, twisted her hair in a tight knot, took off her rings, wore a "big-flowered tycoon-rep wrapper" and a white apron. She had not yet seen her guest, who had been shown to her room by a servant. At dinnertime Mrs. Simpson swept down the stairs, a tall, stately woman in black silk ruffled to the waist, with expensive laces and jewelry, and her hair done in the latest style. The banker's wife, embarrassed and chagrined, sat silent through the meal while Mrs. Simpson, a splendid talker, "charmed everybody." [3]

But while these honored laymen served Methodism and in turn were cultivated and pampered by the church, a voice in its official councils and representation in its government were denied to them. Methodism was ruled almost exclusively by the preachers.

In a democratic society the government of the Methodists was subject to criticism, and the critics were unsparing. The Baptists, particularly, heaped censure upon them, charging that they were anti-American, antirepublican, papists, victims of "clerical despotism," even taunting them with the words of John Wesley himself: "As long as I live the people shall have no share in choosing either stewards or leaders . . . WE ARE NO REPUBLICANS, AND NEVER INTEND TO BE." [4]

The more Simpson thought upon the excellence of Methodist laymen, the more embarrassed he was by their exclusion from the councils of the church—and the more determined he was that they should be given a voice. In 1860 he persuaded the board of bishops to insert a paragraph on lay representation in their address to the general conference. He wrote the section himself—a fact which the delegates generally knew.[5] "We are of the opinion," said the bishops, "that lay delegation might be introduced in one form into the General Conference with safety, and perhaps advantage, that form being a separate house." [6] After considerable discussion, the conference declared itself ready to sanction the change if the people and the preachers desired it.

II

The bishops began taking the vote at the annual conference in 1861. But the people, caught up in the wild fever of war, were indifferent to ecclesiastical reform. The ministers opposed the change, 3,069 to 1,338, and the people likewise turned it down, 47,885 to 28,884.[7]

At this juncture the movement gained support from another quarter. In 1860 a group of conservative preachers and influential laymen, including Daniel Ross and Oliver Hoyt, had established an independent religious weekly in New York, *The Methodist*. The immediate provocation for founding the journal had been the new chapter on slavery enacted by the general conference; but when the war broke out the *Methodist* abandoned its policy of friendliness toward the South and aligned itself with the official press in support of Lincoln and the war. Thus deprived of an issue, and of a reason for existence, it took up in good earnest the cause of lay representation.

Simpson had been both disappointed and troubled over the outcome of the 1860 vote on lay representation, but he was not at all sure that the support of the new journal helped. Everywhere he went, he found opposition to the *Methodist*—preachers loyal to the official *Advocates* would have nothing to do with this interloper in Methodist journalism or with any movement it sponsored.[8] So notwithstanding the support of the *Methodist*—or perhaps because of it—the cause of lay delegation languished. If it were to succeed it must have support from some leaders of the church. As bishop, Simpson had no right to act—or at least no precedent for action. Bishops were "mediators between contending parties" with the duty "to maintain the existing system in its integrity." [9] No one of them had ever broken the traditional neutrality and unanimity of the episcopal board on any issue before the church. Perhaps Abel Stevens had been right—a man who wished to lead ought not to be bishop.

Simpson made up his mind, none the less, to state his conviction publicly. He was at the apex of his popularity in the church. Constantly in demand for the lecture platform—at fees which considerably augmented his episcopal salary—he had remade the war address into an optimistic commentary on current affairs; he lectured also on Lincoln, on the Holy Land, on the Bible and languages. In American Methodism his name had come to stand next to Asbury. But, for the first time in the history of Methodism, he was about to bring severe criticism and censure upon a bishop.

Prompted by a sudden and severe illness when he was in California in 1862, he expressed his views to the one church paper friendly to lay delegation, the *Northwestern Christian Advocate:* "Though in a minority, my judgment and my sympathies are strongly in favor of lay representation." [10]

The friends of lay delegation immediately took new hope. They planned to hold a big rally in New York City in the spring of 1863 and begged him and Bishop Janes to speak. Janes replied curtly: "I judge it inexpedient for me to identify myself with your proposed convention." Daniel Ross importuned Simpson: "On other subjects you would not hesitate a moment." Although it was not "Methodistical" for a bishop "to enter into a progressive movement," it seemed to him that "we must carry on the thing bravely, or it will fail of success." [11] Simpson accepted the invitation.

The rally was held in March, 1863. Simpson, cautious and conciliatory, praised the laymen for their patience and their "brotherly kindness." He wanted this "state of things to continue," so as "not to destroy a single element of Methodism." In Chicago he had seen workmen elevate buildings by means of hundreds of screws, all of which were turned in perfect harmony. With no disturbance to the occupants, a house might go up an entire story. "So, that is what I

want to see you laymen do. I want to see the whole edifice raised up
without jostling or jarring one single arrangement." [12]

In May he spoke to a larger, more representative convention,
arguing that Wesley's "great movement" had "called lay influence
into exercise in the Church." "Class-leaders were appointed, stewards
were called into action, exhorters were licensed, local preachers were
selected, and there came up out of the ranks of the Church a body of
laymen to spread personal holiness through the Church." Methodist
people taught "to work, to pray, to sing, to exhort, to lead class, to
preach, very naturally should inquire: 'Why should we not also have
something to do in planning in the great arrangements of the
Church?' " The opponents of lay delegation, he thought, were afraid
to trust the people, the very people who had been brought into the
church under their ministrations.[13]

The laymen immediately ordered the printing of 50,000 copies
of the speech.[14]

The opponents of lay delegation quickly picked up the gaunt-
let that Simpson had thrown down; but they observed few of the
other conventions of chivalry. A ministerial pamphleteer in Philadelphia was brutal in his attack. He thought the bishop's contention
that preachers who opposed lay delegation were afraid to "trust the
people" might pass for rhetoric but hardly rose to "the dignity of
sober argument." The bishop's associations had led him astray: he
imagined that he had heard the voice of the people, but he had not.
Unhappily the bishops could not even mingle with the people. They
were "monopolized by a class of persons whose *leisure* and *position*"
gave them "facilities for extending an elegant hospitality." Hence,
the bishops knew "but little of preachers or members beyond those
who sparkle in the galaxy of Methodist aristocracy." The preacher,
through "self-denial and wonderful skill," had built Methodism into
a great church; and now self-seeking laymen, aided by a few of the
clergy, sought to deny him the "fruit of his labor." [15]

As the general conference of 1864 approached, some threatened
to bring Simpson to judgment for his advocacy of a "revolutionary
measure." [16] But it came and passed without incident. The bishops
reiterated the stand they had taken in 1860, and the conference itself
took no action. There was only one small cloud on the horizon,
scarcely the size of a man's hand: the election of Daniel Curry as
editor of the *Christian Advocate and Journal*.

Curry and Simpson had been friends in times past. They had joined hands in 1848 to write the legislation which repealed the plan of separation. Simpson, elected editor of the *Western Christian Advocate* that year, had secured Curry as his New York correspondent. But Curry had grown austere with the years. He felt his responsibilities greatly, and he looked the part. He was tall, with a slender but rugged frame, thin, somber face, and shaggy, overhanging brows. His mouth and chin were narrow but firm as lines made with a carpenter's rule, and his ideas were as set as the thin line of his compressed lips.[17]

In the first year of his editorship Curry had no occasion to express his views on lay representation. In May, 1866, the general conference of the Methodist Episcopal Church, South, declared in favor of the admission of lay representatives. They were fully aware that in "being *first* in a good measure" they had "no mean" advantage over their northern brethren. Theodore Tilton's *Independent*, seizing upon the incident to urge lay representation on the northern Methodists, invoked the name of Simpson, who stood "fully and publicly committed to the reform." [18] The next month Simpson renewed his support of the change at a laymen's convention in Boston.

Curry made a caustic appraisal of this new outbreak of the agitation. He thought the whole movement essentially in favor of a "church aristocracy." The leaders were disdainful of the "mediocre minds of the Church, the common herd"; they were concerned only with " 'our best minds,' and those 'especially in the centers of opinion.' " [19]

A year passed, and in the fall of 1867 Simpson again addressed a convention of laymen, in New York. Bishop Calvin Kingsley, who had been a student under Simpson at Allegheny College, also spoke in support of the reform, and Bishop Baker indicated his favor by his presence. Simpson praised the laymen for their moderate and judicious advocacy of the reform: "When history writes up the record, it will be this: that in the two years that the ministers and laymen were talking over this subject of Lay Representation, the Church added more than two hundred thousand to her communion." Whatever else might be said, it could not be asserted that discussion of the question had injured "either the piety of the Church, or its increase in numbers." [20]

Curry, incensed to the point of misinterpreting Simpson's

remark, charged that "there never was a more palpable sophism" than the bishop's argument "that because the Church has greatly prospered during the pendency of this lay delegation discussion, therefore we are indebted to the healthful influence of that discussion for our prosperity." In a scorching editorial he denounced "Bishops as Partisans." Bishops had never been partisan. Not even in the days of the "righteous cause of antislavery" had any bishop ever been seen "in any Church antislavery meeting or convention even as a spectator, much less as a participant." He thought the office of bishop "one of great dignity and responsibility . . . beset about with very delicate relations." "A word, a gesture, a smile, an intonation, from a bishop" might become "painfully significant, and far reaching in its consequences." He could not do "as a bishop, what he might properly do as a man." [21]

The *Methodist* replied with spirit. It thought the church had "never intended that a preacher, in becoming a bishop, should abdicate his manhood." *Zion's Herald* of Boston quoted Charles Sumner's "God made me a man before the government made me a commissioner" and reminded Curry that even bishops were men before they were bishops. All of the other official Advocates lined up in support of Simpson.[22]

In 1868 the friends of lay delegation obtained an almost unanimous vote that the general conference was ready to admit laymen, if the reform were voted by the people and by the requisite three-fourths of the ministers. The bishops were to lay the matter before the people in June, 1869, and before the ministers at the annual conferences of 1869 and 1870.

In June of 1869, shortly before the vote of the people, the laymen met in convention at Pittsburgh. Simpson, heretofore cautious and conciliatory, laid aside his wraps and stepped into the fight with his arms bared. The church, he said, was the "whole body of believers," and as such had "the right to form its own rules, instead of being governed by a hierarchy." He ridiculed those who feared revolutionary change and cried out, "Let well enough alone." He well remembered when people had considered it as rank heresy to allow a musical instrument in the church. Thirty-five years before, there in Pittsburgh at Liberty Street, the laying down of a carpet in the church "came very near driving away . . . half a dozen families." Was not progress a law of society?

It was said that lay delegation would cost too much. He laughed at the thought. Pittsburgh, for example, would be allowed to send two delegates to the quadrennial conference—at a cost of thirty or forty dollars each, fifty at the most. Double the estimated cost, and the total would be two hundred dollars. With forty thousand members in the Pittsburgh conference that would mean one-half cent per member, every four years. Yet that "half-cent argument" was "used by your doctors of divinity in New York and elsewhere." His audience did not miss the allusion to Curry.

He ridiculed also the argument that "factious, ambitious, rich and ungodly men" might capture the high places of the church. Some such men might get in, he admitted, reminding his audience that Judas was among the twelve. But "If such be the general character of the laity, alas! for the work which ministers have been doing in the last century." [23]

A disappointingly small number of laymen (some 150,000) voted, but they favored the change, two to one. The friends of lay delegation claimed a victory morally obligating the ministers to vote the constitutional amendment.

Curry saw matters differently: The vote of the laymen demonstrated that they were not interested in the question—five-sixths of them had "declined the responsibility of advising" the clergy. As for himself, he was more than ever convinced that the movement was of the clergy and not of the laity, and therefore was inexpedient. "Accordingly, in the fear of God, and upon our fidelity to the Church, we must oppose it, and, if granted the opportunity, vote against it." [24] The ministers were to vote in the fall and spring of 1869 and 1870. Both sides girded their loins for the final battle.

III

In the meantime, two other issues complicated the question of lay delegation: an attack upon the episcopacy itself, and the management of the Book Concern. The episcopacy had been under justifiable criticism since 1863, when Simpson moved from Evanston to Philadelphia and thus deprived the West of his extra-conference services. The following January E. R. Ames shifted his residence from Indianapolis to Baltimore. Only the superannuated senior bishop of the church, Thomas A. Morris, remained in the West.

The *Christian Advocate and Journal* promptly suggested that the church establish episcopal districts.[25]

Curry, elected editor the following year, had little to say about this issue until after his broadside against bishops as partisans. Then he came out openly for episcopal districts with a requirement that bishops move from one district to another every four years. It was generally expected that the church would add two or three men to the episcopal board in 1868—there were only seven effective bishops to serve a million and a quarter members and eighty-five hundred ministers. The Church, South, with scarcely half the membership, had elected five new bishops at its last general conference. Thomas Morris, senior bishop of the northern church, called for an addition of three men to the episcopal board. Curry dissented. The church had all the bishops it needed, under the existing system. The proper work of the episcopacy, he said (without alluding directly to Simpson and the lure of politics and the lecture circuit), was to preside over the annual conferences and to appoint preachers to their stations. If the bishops limited their activities to the business of their office they would certainly not be overworked.[26]

The performance of episcopal duties was an arduous task, despite the strictures of Curry. Each bishop presided over four or five annual conferences in the spring and a like number in the fall. Each conference lasted from four or five days to nearly two weeks. The entire period of official business was brief but intense. Mornings were given over to business; afternoons, to committee meetings, evenings, frequently, to preaching. The bishop met his advisers— the presiding elders of the conference—at whatever hours he could for determining the placement of the two hundred or so preachers, and often these sessions ran well past midnight. Simpson, believing that his power for good lay in the pulpit, often took on the additional assignment of preaching. And in the 1860's, in an effort to help the younger ministers, he introduced a series of morning lectures, scheduled at six o'clock, which were well attended and enthusiastically received.[27]

The exhausting labor, the loss of sleep, the strain of conflict and decision, played havoc with the health of the bishops. In 1870, in the midst of the balloting on lay delegation, Bishop Edward Thomson, who had been elected in 1864, was stricken with pneumonia. Weakened by his exertions at the annual conference of West Virginia, he died before he could leave Wheeling. The church had scarcely recovered from the shock when the word was flashed that Bishop Kingsley had died suddenly from "neuralgic seizure" (apparently heart attack) on a trip to the Orient and the Holy Land, at Beirut.

Remorseful, the church began to reflect upon the advisability of calling a special session of the general conference to elect new bishops. Curry pooh-poohed the idea. The church still had five bishops, "every one of them able to do full work." They could, "without any very distressing overwork, get along with their necessary duties for two years." [28]

That fall, Davis Clark, the third of the bishops elected in 1864, was stricken. He rallied sufficiently to meet two of his spring conferences, with the help of a colleague; but by May, 1871, he was dead. There remained only four effective bishops: Scott, Simpson, and Ames, elected in 1862; and Janes, elected in 1844.

The other issue which complicated the question of lay delegation was much more spectacular. John Lanahan, Simpson's lieutenant in the border struggle of 1860, had been named assistant book agent for New York at the general conference of 1868. Irascible and suspicious, almost paranoiac, he was quick to ferret out enemies of the church. In his new office he had ample reason to be suspicious. The book concern was big business: one of the largest publishing houses in America, with sales in 1867 amounting to over a half-million dollars. He had been in office only a few months when he discovered frauds amounting to several hundred thousand dollars. For ten years the son of the former assistant agent, serving as an unauthorized commissioner, had been making purchases for two of the departments at an annual profit to himself of ten to twenty thousand dollars. Two of the departments had been guilty of other fraudulent practices, including the drawing of money without vouchers, and the reselling of goods. When the senior agent, Thomas Carlton, showed no interest Lanahan immediately suspected him of being a party to the fraud and using the funds of the church to speculate in oil. Silenced by his colleagues, who denied him further access to the books, he broke the story in the columns of the New York *Times* in September, 1869. It was the sensation of the year.[29]

The *Methodist* immediately made capital of the story. Lanahan's revelations proved the need for lay participation in the affairs of the church: Preachers were not businessmen, and they were not competent to oversee a huge operation like the book concern.[30]

Curry in the *Christian Advocate* was scornful: Lanahan had presented no proof; and even if his charges were true they proved no *"defalcation"*—only that purchases had not been made "with proper care and economy." He was "reprehensible" for airing the problems of the church through the public press. As for the *Methodist* and the laymen—if there were any fraud it was committed by laymen, and detected and corrected by preachers. Must the editors of the *Methodist*, in an effort to keep their sheet alive, seek always to find something wrong with the church? "Vulture like, they feast their voracious nostrils on the effluvia of putrid reputation, which, if none exists, they endeavor to produce." [31]

Nearly the whole of the official press raised an outcry against Lanahan, who, charged with misconduct, neglect of official duties, untruthfulness, irascibility, insubordination, want of business qualifications, was suspended from office. The bishops, in the official hearing, made short shrift of the unsupported charges and restored him. Still denied access to the books, and determined now to exonerate himself before the public, Lanahan appealed to the courts. It was un-Methodistical—contrary to the rule of the discipline—for a minister to go to court against his brethren. He was, therefore, again suspended and brought to trial.[32]

IV

In the meantime, in the spring of 1870, the preachers voted on lay delegation. Bishop Janes, sweet-tempered and much loved but timid, had finally come out for the reform. Now that the laymen had expressed their preference for the change he thought the preachers were obligated to vote for it. The bishops, therefore, stood five to four for lay delegation—four to three after the deaths of Thomson and Kingsley.

Simpson hoped for the support of Bishop Ames; but in the fall of 1869 a friend warned him that Ames was "doing more harm than any other twenty men in the church." He was opposed to lay delegation, and was speaking against it at every conference. As the votes came in they confirmed the report. Where Ames presided, lay delegation lost. Simpson was despondent. Unless Ames's opposition could be "modified," he feared lay delegation was lost.[33]

On the other hand, wherever Simpson conducted conferences that fall and spring the reform prospered. Southeast Indiana was 76 for, 4 against; Tennessee, 37 for, 0 against; Philadelphia, 142 for, 18 against; Vermont, 71 for, 14 against; and even New Jersey, under the very thumb of Daniel Curry, 80 for, 52 against. Simpson kept his own tabulations; the *Christian Advocate and Journal,* the *Methodist,* and the other papers ran box scores. As the results came in it was apparent that the vote would be very close.[34]

In mid-April, Curry reported with some confidence that if the trend continued in about the same proportion lay delegation would lose by 200 votes. A month later the race was closer, but he was still confident. Maine, in a preliminary skirmish, had divided almost equally. If that vote could be taken as official, there were but two more conferences—East Maine and the foreign conference, in Germany—with 100 votes between them. To win, the reformers would have to secure 49 votes, not an easy task.[35]

Simpson, presiding at the Maine conference, was "sore and sad" at heart. "We shall be beaten," he confessed to Ellen. "Lay-delegation is probably lost." Still the vote might be close enough for the question to be settled at the German conference. Ames had been scheduled to go to Germany but had gladly yielded to Kingsley, who could stop en route home from the Holy Land. Kingsley's presence would have assured a favorable vote; but with his death, Simpson saw that he himself must make the trip. Janes agreed, and the two plotted quietly to gain the assent of the board of bishops. Ames, who suffered from seasickness, agreed to the arrangement. However, when it became apparent that lay delegation might depend upon the German vote he was very "cross," and Simpson feared that he might yet change his mind and make the trip to Germany.[36]

In the end, the crisis occurred at the Maine conference. As the brethren talked among themselves and with the bishop, they began to look more favorably upon lay delegation. Simpson took heart. The vote would not go so badly against them as he had feared. Day by day the situation improved. When the vote was taken, instead of being against lay delegation, it stood 60 for, 31 against. "And now," Simpson reported to Ellen, "there is no question as to our entire success." A week later East Maine, with Simpson presiding, voted for the reform, 43 to 14. Lay delegation was approved without the German vote.[37]

Curry muttered darkly about "influence": the manner in which the canvass had been conducted gave him "inexpressible sorrow." But Simpson found the reform "quietly accepted" by all save Curry, who could not "conquer his wrath." [38] The battle against the bishops, however, was not over.

In the spring of 1871 John Lanahan came to trial the second time. The book committee, angered by his indiscretion and his disregard of the discipline and the reputation of the church, was disposed to act quickly and with minimum interference from the bishops. Simpson, although he looked on Lanahan's act with "entire disapprobation," had no intention of being dictated to by the committee or of rendering judgment until he heard the evidence. He insisted that the bishops must act concurrently with the committee and demanded that they be permitted to employ a secretary and make a complete transcription of the proceedings. The other bishops concurred. In the end, the majority of the committee voted to remove Lanahan; Janes and Ames, delegated to act for the bishops, divided—Janes for removal, Ames against. Concurrence of both bishops was required for removal, and so Lanahan was left in office.[39]

Curry, protesting vigorously against the action of the bishops, renewed his demand that they be assigned to districts; he went a step further: he proposed that they be elected not for life, but for a four-year term.[40]

Simpson was grimly amused. He rather enjoyed the "hackling," he wrote to Ellen, for "this time my colleagues share it with me." As far as he was concerned, "they may elect me out, just as soon as they please." He fancied they would change their tune by the next general conference, even though it was rumored that Curry was opening a "long campaign." He understood, too, that this was to be "war to the knife." [41]

The rumor was well founded. In midsummer Curry released another broadside. The episcopacy must be limited to districts and to a four-year term, in order to protect it from "possible prostitution in worldly and ambitious purposes." In the past the emoluments of the office had been small, the associations humble, and it had offered little but labor and privation. The salary, still far from extravagant ($4,500 per year), was no longer "contemptibly small," and the "incidental emoluments accruing to a popular bishop" (lecture fees, railroad passes, gifts from opulent laymen) were "sufficient to stimulate the cupidity of any one inclined to be covetous." But there was an even greater danger. The Methodist Church was the largest denomination in America. An "able, worldly, and unscrupulous man," enjoying life tenure as chief officer of so large and strong a body, might use the office "to dictate the policy of the government, and to determine the election of Presidents." Curry confessed, lamely, that the episcopacy was yet "pure beyond a suspicion"—but was it not "wise to guard against what is foreseen to be a possible danger of great magnitude in the not remote future?" [42]

Simpson was not without resources. Enlisting the cooperation of Janes, he began to prompt the annual conferences to give an expression of "attachment to the *Itinerancy* and the *Episcopacy* and to instruct their delegates to oppose any material modification in our system." He had no doubt that this stratagem would "excite" Curry; but he would "strain every nerve anyhow," and so more mischief could scarcely be done. The general conference of 1872 promised to be exciting. [43]

As a matter of fact, the conference was an anticlimax to the roaring battles of the quadrennium. Lay delegates were seated without a ripple. A special committee sustained most of Lanahan's charges of fraud in the book concern, and the conference adopted its report without debate. Far from rebuking the bishops for wasting their energies outside the episcopacy, or hedging them about lest they corrupt the church, the conference elected eight new bishops, trebling the number who were effective. But, in the perverse manner of democratic assemblies, the same conference, having denied Curry his reforms, reelected him editor of the *Christian Advocate and Journal*. The clergyman, as well as the philosopher, had good use for the gadfly.

XXV

EVEN THE EAGLE

ON June 21, 1871, Matthew Simpson, scarcely able to get out of his sickbed, bent over his pocket diary, tightened his fingers about his pen, and wrote in a rapid script: "This day I am 60 years old." It was a day to conjure with. Thomson, Kingsley, Clark, fellow bishops, two of them younger than he, all of them dead within these fifteen months. Three weeks before, he himself had suffered a chill, followed by severe palpitations of the heart and a bilious attack. For two weeks he had been confined to his room, and for several days he had been unable to leave his bed. Now, gripping his pen, he looked to the future: "I am admonished that my day is nearly over— The sun declines—the shadows lengthen. The night cometh What my hand finds to do should be done quickly—earnestly—faithfully." [1]

The future was not so short for him as he feared. Despite his sixty years, his sun was still well above the horizon. In two months he would be back at his duties; and a dozen years of energetic and fruitful service stretched before him.

Still, sixty years was a long vista to look back upon. Year by year his friends and loved ones had dropped along the way. Charles Elliott, Father Haven, Allen Wiley—men who had directed his destiny in the Ohio-Indiana days—were gone. Lucien Berry, whom he had bound to his heart like a brother, had been taken in his prime by erysipelas thirteen years ago. Joe Wright was dead, too, the Honorable Joseph A. Wright, congressman from Indiana, governor, minister to Berlin, removed by Lincoln, restored by Andy Johnson in 1865, but dead at his post in less than two years. The irrepressible William M. Daily, friend of the Indiana days, brilliant and indiscreet, lovable and provoking, disgraced by his fondness for women, and removed from the presidency of Indiana University in

1859, had been worse than dead when a friend of Simpson found him early in the war, drunk in a Washington jail. But Daily was resilient. Fired from one government post, he secured another and was sent to New Orleans after the war. In 1869 Simpson had brought him back into the itinerancy, secured his admission to the Louisiana conference, and named him presiding elder for his district.[2]

Other friends had done well. John Wheeler, Simpson's first graduate at Indiana Asbury, not brilliant but steady and plodding, had made his way up to the presidency of Baldwin University in Ohio. John Evans, denied a political career, had settled down to being Colorado's first citizen and chief entrepreneur, and James Harlan was still in the United States Senate. Of more recent business and political friends, only Daniel L. Ross had been stricken. For him and his Methodist friends, death was a double tragedy. He was only forty-seven years old, and he had died in 1868, too soon to know of the winning campaign for lay delegation.[3]

The last deep personal sorrow to afflict Matthew Simpson had come in 1868 with the death from consumption of his elder son, Charles. He and Ellen had worried over him for months. He had taken him to Louisiana and the southern conferences in 1866, and had sent him to Cuba for six months in the warm sun; but the hacking cough and the persistent fever would not let go. The next summer, with Ellen, he had taken Charles to Minnesota, where the climate was said to be good for persons who suffered from diseases of the lungs. But Charles failed to rally, and died in the following spring, before his twenty-ninth birthday.[4]

Even so, there had been some assuaging of grief. As a child Charles had been devoted to the Sunday school and the church; as a young man he had been indifferent to both. But in August before his death he had gone to the camp meeting at Vineland. There, one afternoon, surrounded by importuning friends, he had dropped to his knees and raised his voice to plead for the assurance he had known in childhood. The aging bishop, with the tears streaming down his transparent face, had knelt by his son to welcome him back to the faith of his fathers. It was a satisfying experience to an old man who had given his life to preaching the glories of the Unseen. Still, now that Charles was dead he was shaken. What was it like, after all, in that Spirit World? How many times had he asked himself the same question about Charles? "Does he see me?" [5]

He had lost his widowed mother too, at the advanced age of eighty-six, shortly before the death of Charles. Uncle Matthew was to live until 1874, before finally giving up, weary with the burden of ninety-eight years.

Matthew Simpson had much to look back on in 1871, much to make a man reminisce; but he was not ready to call himself old. The present was full of demands, and the future still an open road. His son Verner was eighteen, and about to enter Wesleyan University. Verner was something of a problem, too much interested in the girls, a little wild, and lacking in application to studies. The bishop worried about him (this son who was to be forty years a Methodist choir-master), warned him against evil, tobacco-using companions, taught him algebra, reviewed mechanics with him. Nor had the two younger girls, Ida, sixteen, and Libbie, twenty-one, been especially diligent about their school work. He had scolded Libbie once when she admitted that she had not applied herself closely but promised to make up for it. "Do you know, Libbie, we never can *'make up'* what is past . . . No moment will ever come back again. That idea of *'making up'* has ruined many a one. We must treasure the moments as they fly." [6]

His oldest daughter, Mathilda, was soon to be married to a Methodist preacher in Philadelphia; and Anna, his second daughter, was already married to Colonel James Riley Weaver, United States consul at Brindisi. Riley was a great favorite of the bishop's. After studies at Allegheny College and three and one-half years in the Union army, much of it in prison camps, he had taken a degree in theology at Garrett Biblical Institute and had taught at West Virginia College at Morgantown. His marriage to Anna in the Philadelphia home had been a great occasion. President and Mrs. Grant were there, and the President's appointment of the young colonel to Brindisi (at the bishop's urgent solicitation) had been a handsome wedding gift. [7]

Now, in 1871, Mrs. Simpson and the three girls had been abroad for months, visiting Consul Riley Weaver, his wife Anna, and their baby, and traveling about western Europe. The bishop had missed them greatly, had begged for details of their travel and personal life. What did they think? How did they feel? Did they sleep well at night? Did they dream? Did they think of *anybody* across the sea? And what of Mr. Weaver, the consul? Did he put on airs, or was he "Riley" still? And Anna? Did she allow herself to be called Anna? or must she be addressed as *Madonna* Weaver? And what of Ida and Ella, and Libbie? Especially Libbie: did she talk most in her sleep about Johnny or Willie? [8]

He himself had been too busy these months with conferences, dedications, lectures, and anniversaries to be lonely. Now and then when he did get home he had played at "make believe"—that he could "get along right pleasantly" without them. But it was terribly hard to win the game. Even the birds were lonely, though Mrs. Stiles, the housekeeper, said they seemed to know when he came home: the canary was once more lively and the mockingbird, which had been mute, had begun to whistle and sing. "That was a pretty welcome, was it not?" Oh, yes, one thing more: he had had all his clothes washed! And he had shaved nearly every other day, brushed his hair, and made an effort to look "tolerably decent." But one night in his terror he had dreamed that Ellen "had come at him with a brush and bottle." [9]

How thankful he was that God had enabled him to give his family a trip to Europe, that their feet had been in the garden of Gethsemane, and on the Mount of Olives, that they had seen the lofty pyramids, had "walked among the ruins of the Parthenon at Athens, and had tasted the honey of Hymattus"! How times had changed since he was young! He had not even crossed the mountains until he was forty, and here his children were, rambling all over Europe. [10]

In one respect, at least, the opponents of lay delegation had been right: Matthew Simpson no longer knew the ways of the poor, nor walked the paths of the downtrodden. His $4,500 salary as bishop was no mean sum, and he also received traveling expenses, fees for lectures, gifts for special sermons, railroad passes, and a mortgage-free house. Moreover, he and Ellen had begun to realize substantial returns on their investments. Who could have believed that Matthew Simpson, leaving Cadiz, Ohio, for Madison College with $11.25 in his pocket, or the newly elected Bishop Simpson of Pittsburgh, too poor to live in the country because it "would require a carriage," would in time make his purchase and casually jot down in his diary, "Bought Phaeton"? Who could have imagined that the same Matthew Simpson would have a summer cottage (purchased for him, it is true, by friends) at Long Branch—the largest, noisiest, and most garish of the summer watering places frequented by the opulent of Philadelphia and New York. And who could have supposed that, before the end of the 1870's, a Pittsburgh layman would bequeath him $60,000, or that a dozen years later the bishop himself, by careful management, would leave a hundred-thousand-dollar estate to his widow? [11]

Matthew Simpson's day was not over in 1871; the darkness was not gathering so quickly as he allowed himself to suppose. Ellen and the girls, hearing of his illness, hurried home; but he rallied before they arrived, and in September was back at the business of conducting his conferences.

II

The declining years gave Matthew Simpson not only affluence but easy access to men in high places. He counted President Grant among his friends, entertaining him in Philadelphia, visiting him in Washington and Long Branch. He had first met the general in 1864 at Nashville and had found him "not very communicative." But Grant had gone along with the occupation of McKendree Chapel. And a little later, after both of them had gone over to the Radical party, the bishop thought Grant "one of the grandest names in all the land." [12]

Grant also had reason to be cordial, outside political considerations. He was the son of a devout Methodist woman, and his wife was warmly sympathetic to the Methodists. If his relations to God were amicable rather than intimate, he none the less attended the Methodist church when he went, was quite often in the congregation when Simpson preached at Washington or at Long Branch. He served on the board of trustees of the Metropolitan Methodist Church in Washington, gave five hundred dollars to the building fund, made a dramatic, last-minute appearance in his pew for the dedication of the new building, contributed when the hat was passed for Simpson's cottage at Long Branch. In 1871 he named Simpson on the commission to investigate Santo Domingo with a view to annexation. For once, the bishop was tempted to step out of his ecclesiastical role; but he had to decline the appointment because of John Lanahan's trial.[13]

In Grant's cabinet Postmaster-General Creswell, a graduate of Dickinson College, was "the friend of the Methodists" and of Simpson; Vice President Schuyler Colfax and Senator Daniel Webster Voorhees, both Indianans, made capital of their Indiana acquaintance with the bishop.[14]

The succession of Rutherford B. Hayes to the Presidency in 1877 only strengthened Simpson's tie with the White House. Lucy Webb Hayes was a Methodist, a graduate of the Wesleyan Female College in Cincinnati, an active leader in Methodist missionary societies, and a long-time friend of the Simpsons. The gentle Hayes, too meek to be devout, too conventional to rebel, had attended church regularly from his youth up. After his marriage he went with Lucy to the Methodist chapel in Cincinnati, and to the Foundry Methodist Church in Washington. In Philadelphia the President and his wife were now and then guests in the home of the bishop, and in Washington he sent his private carriage to meet the Simpsons at the depot, and Mrs. Hayes entertained them in the White House.[15]

The Methodist press, pleased by the growing prestige of the church, published an occasional note on General Grant's attendance at divine worship, on President Hayes's church activities, or on the courtesy which either of them may have extended to Simpson or other Methodists. The non-Methodist press complained of Methodist influence on Grant and Hayes, or accused Simpson of interfering in political appointments. Certainly there was reason for more than the lifting of eyebrows when Grant, in turning the administration of Indians over to the churches, gave the Methodists the lion's share of the agencies; and there was occasion for complaint, too, when he named John P. Newman—three times chaplain of the Senate, and pastor of the Metropolitan Methodist Church—Inspector of United States Consulates. The post was created, said the hostile press, in order to permit Grant's pastor to make "a tour of the world at public expense." [16]

Simpson's political activity was largely that of aiding friends to secure appointments. The word of his influence was abroad, and friends and strangers without number importuned his help. "Now it is said by those who profess to know that my old friend Bishop Simpson has as much influence with General Grant as any other living man . . ." "Knowing your influence with Genl U. S. Grant, I

make bold to ask you a favor . . ." Even the widow of an Episco-
palian minister, seeking an appointment for her daughter, reported
that officials in Washington had told her "if I could get you to
write to our most excellent President . . . he would grant it with
pleasure to you." A former governor wanted a post in China; the
United States Consul at Belfast wanted an increase in salary and
thought that Simpson might aid him; a preacher-postmaster, deprived of his office because he had "occasionally juggled money
order sums" to repay the thefts of his brother-in-law, wanted the
bishop to intercede with Postmaster-General Creswell, who had
removed him.[17]

Simpson, more cautious than he had been a few years earlier,
avoided written recommendations. He was pretty testy when a
Presbyterian sheet wrongly accused him of influencing the transfer
of a military detail from Western University (Presbyterian) to
Dickinson College (Methodist) and labeled him "the wily Bishop."
Such expressions, he thought, ought to be governed by "good taste
& Christian charity." But he played his politics, none the less. He
wrote warm, congratulatory notes to men newly appointed to high
position; he now and then checked the "weather chart" in Congress
(the members, he noted, "watch how the wind blows"); and he did
battle for special friends. He and Harlan maneuvered the election
of John P. Newman to the chaplaincy of the Senate; he intervened
with Hayes to prevent the removal of the secretary of Arizona Territory; and he helped a good brother to a consulship in Central
America. The last produced results which the President scarcely
anticipated: the establishment of a Christian mission and scholars
who "sing our beautiful hymns set to spanish music." [18]

When it came to his son-in-law, Riley Weaver, the bishop put
aside all reticence. He defended him against criticism, urged his
promotion, denied rumors of his resignation. When he thought
"mischief was brewing" he appealed directly to Hamilton Fish, the
Secretary of State, and sent the Methodist preacher in Washington
to see the President. Grant was reassuring—he thought there was
no danger from Fish, for he knew "how the appointment was
made." [19]

In another matter, Simpson was less successful. He was unable
to save his old friend James Harlan. Harlan's administration of the
Interior Department, particularly of Indian affairs, had resulted in

charges (not established) against his personal integrity. He had alienated some ambitious friends in the Republican party by his seizure of the senatorial nomination in 1866, and he had prompted Methodist politicians to revive the charges brought against him in the church many years before. Defeated for renomination in 1872, he entered the lists again in 1875. But he was opposed, among others, by a fellow Methodist and former congressman, Hiram Price. There was, he realized, only one man in the country who could prevail upon Price to step out of the race, and that was Bishop Simpson. Could the bishop make a trip out West "for other business" and look into the matter? But it was no use. Price would not withdraw. Facing sure defeat, Harlan yielded. Simpson had already suggested to the President that he place the Iowan in his cabinet. Grant, characteristically neither offending his friends nor committing himself, had responded with "expressions of confidence" in Harlan, but had taken no action.[20] Simpson's one major political triumph—the placing of a fellow Methodist in the cabinet—had resulted in the end of a career.

I I I

One thing the war years had given Matthew Simpson was assurance. Whatever the traditions of the church, whatever the strictures of Daniel Curry, he felt a new freedom in speaking out on public policy. He did not always speak with insight, but he spoke. Without being a reformer, he helped to broaden the church's concept of things spiritual, and to prepare the way for social leadership.

His most popular lecture was the War Address, revised and brought up to date as a commentary on the times. He praised the reconstruction program of the Radicals, eulogized Bismarck, criticized the American minister to France for "toadyism" to Napoleon III, advocated compulsory education. Above all, he praised the nation's representative form of government as superior to absolute monarchy or any of the parliamentary systems, because the people were "equally represented no matter how far from our seat of government." The country had safely extended from Portland, Maine, to San Francisco, and there was no reason why it should not reach "from Montreal to Mexico." The growth and influence of the country, he said, had only begun to be realized. With the free immigration policy, and "every avenue of labor . . . thrown open to all classes alike," and with freedom of worship preserved for all, the country would soon have not forty but a hundred million of people. Because all this vast multitude would speak the English language, and came from all nations, "the English tongue would become the diplomatic language of the globe." The mission of the United States, the future of the country, was to teach the world the wisdom of the republican form of government.

A Minneapolis paper thought these ideas "rather fanciful," although "truly eloquent and instructive." The Boston *Post* agreed that the mission of the United States was a "sublime one," and "highly hopeful and encouraging" even if "a little rose-colored." The Boston *Daily Advertiser* was caustic. It thought the bishop had "few equals" as a speaker but preached "a great deal too much *'buncombe.'* " The American people had no great need of instruction in "self-glorification." What they needed was "to be taught wisdom in this time of their peril; to be told of their dangers and duties rather than of their greatness and virtues." [21]

Matthew Simpson was impervious to the criticism. He belonged to the new era, the age of capitalism ushered in by the Civil War. Never in the history of the nation had there been such exploitation of resources, such industrial and commercial enterprise, such amassing of fortunes, such hopes for expansion of political borders. The church, following in the wake of economic and social forces, sought not to stem but to interpret the new economy, to lend to it a moral and ethical suasion and responsibility. So were born in the Gilded Age the gospels of wealth and of imperialism. A man might rightly accumulate great riches if he became the steward of the Lord, a nation might with righteousness enlarge its borders and extend its powers if it protected the people's spiritual heritage of freedom.

It was inevitable in a society which produced such a church and doctrine that Matthew Simpson should be one of its prophets. No critic of men, no Amos shouting, "Thus saith the Lord; For three transgressions of Israel, and for four, I will not turn away the punishment thereof," he was a eulogist of country and church. In a new era he found only new cause for praise.

He was sympathetic with the reform movements, remarkably so for a Methodist bishop of his age. He took the platform for women's rights and for temperance, but not as a leader in the reform. From Indiana Asbury days, when he had urged better educational opportunities for young women, he had been sympathetic with women's rights. In the manner insisted upon by the leaders of the suffrage movement, he always addressed his own wife as Mrs. Ellen H. Simpson. He subscribed to Lucy Stone's *Woman's Journal,* and he was induced to write an introduction to her volume *Woman Man's Equal.* In 1873 he gave a rousing speech before the Pennsylvania Constitutional Convention, urging suffrage for women. He thought society, debauched and corrupt under the direction of men, needed the "purifying will" of women. And he was pleased to note that in Wyoming and Utah, where women had the suffrage, the sun still rose and set: "The men are still men, and women are women still." Moreover, in Utah, twenty-four hours after women received the vote "the gamblers had taken flight." [22]

Delighted with his "brave appeal for justice to the powerless," the suffragists sought his continued support. They must have the "religious element" if they were to triumph. With a stubborn unawareness of the ways of Methodism, Lucy Stone tried to coax him to address the annual meeting of the American Woman Suffrage Association. They would pay expenses, and the report in the Boston papers would introduce his speech "to the public more widely than it had been heretofore, and so it would all the sooner be called for by the lyceums and become a paying lecture." [23] How should Lucy Stone know that it was not becoming for him to lead in reforms? or that Matthew Simpson's energies were already so diverted from episcopal duties that he gave Curry and others ample reason to criticize?

He was equally sympathetic toward the temperance movement. As editor of the *Western Christian Advocate* he had campaigned vigorously against the licensing of taverns and "tippling-places." In Philadelphia he was elected president of a temperance society. He indorsed Frances Willard's W.C.T.U. and once "eulogized the crusade" against alcohol. But he declined to ally himself with the Prohibition party, and he was not given to dramatic protests on public occasions. Once in 1874, in Mexico, he attended a banquet of American citizens where wine was served. Unembarrassed, he responded to his toast in a sprightly speech which the company approved with "Great Applause." A few years later he and Mrs. Simp-

son were guests of Chester A. Arthur at the White House when wine
was served. A non-Methodist religious paper, happy with the opportunity to criticize both the politics and the morals of the sister
denomination, thought that the Methodist brethren ought to be
"scandalized and perplexed." They would be "scandalized at their
bishop for going back on the temperance platform of Christianity,
and perplexed whether to give their influence to Arthur for renomination because of his attention to their bishop, or to withdraw
it from him because he pressed the wine cup to his brother's lips." [24]

Simpson was much more interested in a less spectacular reform:
the gradual transformation of his church. He had been a leader in
the change. He had espoused the improvement in architecture, the
introduction of musical instruments and choirs, lay participation in
the government, learning among the people, seminaries for preachers, cooperation with other denominations, the utilization of the
findings of science, the appropriation of all knowledge as coming
from God. There were a few who criticized his views—a Baptist
minister thought the cross was not sufficiently prominent in his
lectures; but there were many who were proud of him. "You are so
broad, Bishop, in your views," wrote one editor (who was himself
to become a bishop), "so catholic, so full of humanity that we cannot
afford to lose you. Why are not more of our ministers able to see
beyond our own walls?" [25]

He spoke out more boldly in these latter days. Men lived in a
new era, and the young preachers of the church ought to recognize
that fact. Once the "only test of Methodism was a desire to flee from
the wrath to come and a desire to be saved from their sins"; but now
Methodism had come to represent "great freedom of individual
opinion," to stand as "the most liberal form of the Christian
Church." The young minister must study human nature, "and especially the human nature of his locality." Great waves of thought
swept over men. They were "under different influences at different
times." For that reason "a sermon which possessed wonderful power
twenty years ago may have little effect now." So the young men
must study these influences. [26]

One of the waves of thought was the doctrine of evolution. It
was not popular among the churches in 1878 when Simpson, attempting to interpret it, made the headlines of the daily press.
Methodists were almost uniformly unfriendly to Darwin, although

Professor Winchell had not yet been expelled from his teaching post for his mild espousal of the dogma. President James McCosh of Princeton had long since called upon a reluctant church to reconcile evolution and religion, but Henry Ward Beecher, however much he loved to shock his congregation with his unorthodox views, had not yet found the courage to speak up.[27]

Characteristically, Simpson approached the subject by reasserting that God was in the hearts of the people, not in the creeds or the rituals. He neither abandoned the Bible nor defended it; nor did he argue for evolution. He simply appropriated the hypothesis as an illustration of his belief in progress. He found the doctrine "one of great comfort." It was permeating society, taking hold of the minds of the day. Although it might be advanced "sometimes in forms a little strange and strained," he believed it came out of the "word of God." Christianity was getting into scientific thought. "The conviction that there is to be a still more glorious state of being is growing. Christian thought is permeating the world." When he read of the "advancement of man from the animal to the intellectual," from the child to the "developed intellect and spirituality," then he saw "how in God's providence I may develop still more and more, in one eternal universal existence."

Nor was he troubled when the geologists asserted that the world had existed for myriads of ages: "I am willing to admit all of that." The "true spirit of Christianity welcomes all investigation." It was better for humanity "that inquiry should not be repressed." The result, he believed, would be that "Revelation and Nature would be found to be in harmony in the end." [28]

IV

In the fall and winter of 1878–1879, Matthew Simpson delivered the annual Lyman Beecher Lectures on Preaching at Yale College. The several Christian Advocates, the *Methodist,* and Theodore Tilton's *Independent* arranged to print the ten lectures as they were delivered, and the Methodist Book Concern secured the rights to publish them in book form. The lectureship had been filled by such distinguished clergymen as Henry Ward Beecher, Phillips Brooks, and the Englishman R. W. Dale, and the invitation to follow them was a great honor to Bishop Simpson and his church, of which he took notice in his first lecture: "I who am of Western birth and education and a minister in the Methodist Episcopal Church am here to address you, who are chiefly sons of New England, and Congregationalists in creed and Church polity. Verily the world moves!" [29]

He packed his lectures with common sense: the preacher should prepare thoroughly; he should master the Bible, Christian doctrine, church history; he should study the sermons of other men, particularly the masters, but should also keep abreast of the times and study the interests and the vocations of the people to whom he ministered—the skills of the assayer of metals, the cases of the attorney, the diseases and remedies of the physician, the economy and thrift of the housewife.

Training in the techniques of speech was good, so far as it helped the preacher to avoid improper gesture or a wrong use of his voice. It was bad if it produced affectation or display. The real source of eloquence rested in the man, not in his delivery. "People judge not so much of truth in its abstract as in its embodied form." So the minister must be circumspect in conduct. He must avoid stimulants, the use of tobacco, poor management of his money; he must eschew dogmatism and self-conceit, he should stay out of politics, he must have a genuine affection for the masses, he should keep his conversation "pure and instructive." [30]

Above all, he must be a man of conviction. He must feel his divine commission so strongly, he must have so great a compassion for men, that he could at all times be assured of divine assistance. Only then could he move men to tears and repentance, only then could he preach with power and unction. He himself had been present when "whole congregations" rose to their feet and were "freely bathed in tears." He could not explain this power—it was known only by its results. "It is not learning, not rhetoric, nor logic, nor oratory; but it can use these for its one great end." It could "burn and shine in the highest periods of the most eloquent speaker," or it could "thrill in the accents of the unlettered man." It was a magnetic power which kindled in the eye and sparkled from the speaker to the audience and from the audience to the speaker. It was the baptism of fire, the reenacting of Pentecost, the indwelling of God, the highest grace of the Christian pulpit. It was the gift which, above all things else, he coveted for the young preacher.[31]

This ministerial power was also the gift which Matthew Simpson all of his long life had most coveted for himself. How often had he played upon his audience like the director of a great choir, moving from a hushed and dramatic pianissimo to the grand swell of the hallelujah chorus!

Even when he reached an age at which other men gave up eloquence for instruction, he still attempted the grand style. He had so often felt the divine afflatus, so often drunk of the Pierian Spring, that he could not slake his thirst on the prose of didactic homilies. But it was no longer easy for him to reach the heights of eloquence. He took flight on broken wing. "He was often slow, sometimes dull, sometimes a failure." He looked "weary and overworked." Hearers who had "hung upon his ministrations in other days thought they could see some tracing of advancing age." Now and then he laid hold on the old power, his clear eye flashing, his white hair and white face transfigured by emotion.[32]

One such occasion took place in San Francisco in 1878, when he spoke in the Opera House. Henry Ward Beecher, preaching in the same place two Sundays earlier, had created a sensation, on which the San Francisco *Chronicle* commented derisively, "The furor attending the delivery of the Sermon on the Mount was tame in comparison." More than three thousand tickets had been issued, and twice as many people crowded the doors to gain admission. The Methodists, not to be outdone, stormed the Opera House in equal numbers to hear their bishop.[33]

Beecher had been iconoclastic. Christianity was to be measured not by doctrine but by goodness. An infidel or a "Brahmin," if he had the qualities of love, joy, peace, long suffering, gentleness, faith, was "more truly a Christian than many a church member." He attempted no argument, assembled no proofs. His technique was simply to put into juxtaposition a scriptural text, a few unorthodox ideas, and a number of homely, telling illustrations—some humorous, some pathetic.[34]

Simpson, nearly as liberal in his views, made no attempt to shock the audience or to entertain it with ridicule and unexpected sallies. Addressing himself to the question, "Is Christianity a Failure?" he marshaled his evidence and assembled his proofs like a lawyer—not a legalist arguing the petty issues, but a Jeremiah Black, drawing upon the great examples of history to make an eloquent plea.[35]

The San Francisco papers, delighted with the opportunity, indulged freely in comparison. In the outward graces of oratory Beecher was "incomparably the superior"; but for "intellectual depth and grasp" the palm "must be accorded to the Bishop." The tall, lean, thin-faced old man with the shrill, piping voice was extraordinarily moving. As he began to speak his face lighted up, his eyes flashed, and he carried men away on a "sparkling stream of thought" that made them forget his ungainly figure and uncouth gesture. The great audience listened with deep attention, broken only by expressions of approval, sobs and shouts. He was the "old man eloquent." [36]

The last great speech of Simpson's career was in England in 1881, when he was seventy. He had gone to London for the Methodist Ecumenical Conference, a gathering of twenty-eight British and American branches of Wesleyanism. On the 2nd of July, President James A. Garfield had been struck by an assassin's bullet. He had lingered until late September, and then, with all the world hoping for his recovery, had died.

James Russell Lowell, American minister to Great Britain, issued a call for memorial services at Exeter Hall, London, at which some three thousand people were present, mostly Americans. There were several speakers, including Lowell and Simpson. Both the man of letters and the bishop joined freely in the grief of the people, and both yielded to the characteristic overstatement of sorrow. Lowell's address, read from manuscript, was more sustained in beauty of language and more lofty in sentiment. Simpson lacked somewhat in the universal qualities demanded by such an occasion. He dwelt laboriously on the President's faithfulness in attending church and took pains to justify Providence for cutting off the life of the statesman; but many of his ideas were similar to those of Lowell. He handled rather better the tribute to the American democratic system, which, for a fourth time, had survived the loss of a President during his term of office.

Lowell was cheered several times during his remarks—once loudly; but in general his "polished eloquence" was restrained and dignified, with "no oratorical climaxes, and no pitfalls for applause." Simpson, deeply moved himself, and supported by great numbers of American Methodists who were in London for the conference, called out "strong emotions." He had spoken but briefly when the audience burst out with long-sustained applause. And then, in a "few thrilling sentences," in tribute to Queen Victoria, he "set all hearts on fire."

Throughout the recent months, the Queen had demonstrated unusual compassion for Mrs. Garfield; and both speakers singled out and praised her expression of sympathy. Lowell was bookish and aloof, but he excited cheers. Simpson, with an equal economy of words, drew a quick, dramatic picture, and then with sudden solemnity pronounced a benediction. It was not America alone, he said, that mourned the death of her President. "Kings and princes gather round his bier, and the queen of the greatest empire in the world drops a tear of sympathy with his widow, and lays a wreath upon his tomb." There were loud cheers and a burst of applause, and then the bishop continued, "God bless Queen Victoria for her womanly sympathy and her queenly courtesy." The whole audience rose spontaneously, waved their handkerchiefs, and "almost convulsively" gave three cheers for Queen Victoria. When they finally sat down "hundreds of strong men and women burst into tears." It was, said an observer, "one of the most impressive scenes ever witnessed." [37]

V

Returning from England, the bishop took up the routine of official duty, held annual conferences, and answered the calls of the churches for his services. Old friends, especially, were anxious to have him for one more conference. "I hope we may yet meet again ere we go hence," he wrote to an aging colleague who had begged him to return to Indiana. Then in reminiscence he called the roll of those who had gone. "Death has reaped a wonderful harvest," he said, "and his sickle has not lost its sharpness yet. . . . Still while we *live*, let us *live*. We need not be sad or indolent, even if death peeps at us through the window or doorway." [38]

Obedient to his own admonition, the old churchman continued to attend his conferences, conduct the business of the church, and to

"preach the word." Ever sensitive to his audiences, he recorded now
and then "Large congregation," "Very large congregation," "Rainy
day but a good congregation," "Attentive audience and some feeling," "Large congregation—deep feeling." [39]

His last public service was the opening of the People's Church
in Boston, early in the spring of 1884. Pleased to see in conservative
New England a church with free pews—a church for the people—
he attempted to preach with the "old-time power"; but he was too
feeble. His eloquence was more pathetic than rousing. He was none
the less full of confidence in the sure spread of the gospel and the
coming reign of peace. "I think I see the light shining now on the
hilltop. Christ's kingdom is coming, and the song shall arise, 'Hallelujah! the Lord God omnipotent reigneth!' " [40]

The trip to Boston, where the cold of the winter yet lingered,
overtaxed his strength, and a few weeks before the meeting of the
general conference of 1884 at Philadelphia illness overtook him and
confined him to bed. All his old colleagues in the episcopacy and
several who had been elected after him, had preceded him in death;
he was the senior bishop of the church. All Methodism, therefore,
watched anxiously as the conference approached—fearful that he
would be unable to attend it, or that, in attending, his iron will
would demand more than his feeble body could bear. [41]

No one knew until the opening of the conference whether or
not he would be present; but when the bishops entered the hall and
walked onto the platform the tall, spare figure of Matthew Simpson
was at their head. The buzzing of conversation abruptly stopped,
and applause rang through the auditorium. Promptly at nine
o'clock he rose and stepped to the front of the platform. His transparent skin was drawn tightly across his cheekbones, giving his face
"an expression as if chastened by the suffering of the sickness which
so nearly prevented his attendance." In a voice not strong but clear,
he called out, "The Conference will please come to order." [42]

He was not often at the deliberations; but he was able to take
part in the consecration of the newly elected bishops and, much to
the surprise and pleasure of the delegates, made the closing speech
at the last session. Regretting that he had not been able "to mingle
more intimately" with members of the conference, he paid respect
to the only three men who, with himself, had attended either the
conference of 1844 or of 1848. Then with the optimism which had

characterized his entire ministry he praised the delegates who were present. He thought there had never been assembled "a more distinguished, a more able, and a more cultured body of delegates in the Methodist Episcopal Church." There had never been a larger proportion of youthful members. It was exceedingly gratifying, as the shadows gathered about him, "to see young men, truly cultured and devoted to the cause of Christ, able to come forward and take the reins of the Church." Praying God to make them "greater than the fathers," and exhorting them to "go forward from this time" and "do more vigorous work than we have ever done," he pronounced a benediction.[43]

The hearers were frightened by his pallor, his emaciated form, his tremulous voice, but "little thought that the dreaded time was so near." For several days after the conference he seemed to improve. He even planned and prepared to go to a near-by sanitarium and resort; but on the day before his scheduled departure his strength gave way, and his physicians reported to the family that there was "no reasonable ground to hope for any improvement." [44]

For a week, suffering greatly, he struggled with death. The anxious family gathered about him, read to him, prayed, sang hymns. Only now and then did he respond, and then only to echo some bit of scripture or line of hymn they had spoken, or to move his hand in feeble gesture. He lingered until June 18. Had he lived three more days, he would have been seventy-three years upon earth.

"Even the eagle," said the *Western Christian Advocate,* "grows weary at last and must rest." [45]

NOTES

Chapter I

LIFE IN CADIZ

The narrative of Simpson's early life is based largely upon his Autobiography and Journal or Diary (referred to here as Diary), both of which are published in part in the first chapters of George R. Crooks, *The Life of Bishop Matthew Simpson* (New York, 1890).

[1] Crooks, 93, 94. W. H. Hunter, "The Pathfinders of Jefferson County," *Ohio Archeological and Historical Quarterly* (1898), VI, 257. Henry Howe, *Historical Collections of Ohio* (Columbus, 1890), I, 891.

[2] Bishop Matthew Simpson Papers (Library of Congress, Manuscript Division), "Lines Written June 6, 1830," by Matthew Simpson, Jr.

[3] Charles A. Hanna, *Historical Collection of Harrison County in the State of Ohio* (New York, 1900), 109. The elder Matthew Simpson was State Senator 1816–1820, 1822–1828; Associate Judge of the County Court, 1818–1819.

[4] Simpson Papers, "Lines Written June 6, 1830."

[5] The figure of the sun on the tops of distant hills and trees became a favorite of Matthew Simpson the preacher.

[6] *Harrison County Telegraph*, March 13 and July 3, 1824, and other issues.

[7] Crooks, 60–61. "Charles Elliott, D.D.," *National Magazine*, I, 560–562 (Dec. 1852).

[8] Crooks, 59, citing Simpson's Diary, Nov. 5, 1828.

[9] Simpson Papers, Simpson's Expense Acct., 1828.

[10] Simpson to Uncle Matthew, Nov. 30, 1828. All correspondence, unless otherwise noted, is from the Simpson Papers. The direct quotation is adapted from Simpson's letter, as is the conversation with Mr. Fielding. There are a half-dozen constructed dialogues in the early chapters, each one noted. The original language is followed almost precisely, the major change being from third to second person.

Chapter II

AMONG THE LITERATI

[1] Simpson Papers: undated fragment, "Travelling on Railroads," 1828.

[2] Warren Jenkins, *The Ohio Gazeteer* (Columbus, 1841), 96–97.

[3] Simpson Papers, "Travelling on Railroads."

4 *Ibid.*, essays: on electricity, Mar. 10, 1831; "Descriptions of the Motions of the Earth," Apr. 12, 1831; "Optics," May 10, 1831.

5 *Ibid.*, undated essay on falling stars.

6 *Ibid.*, undated Essays on Style, and Reflections on a Pen.

7 *Ibid.*, verses, several untitled, one titled "It Must Be Love," and another "The Courtship of Burd."

8 Autobiography, in Crooks, 24–25.

9 *Ibid.*, 12–13.

10 *Ibid.*, 25–28 (the dialogue is constructed). Harry B. McConnell, *Cadiz Year by Year: Gleanings from the Cadiz Republican Files, 1868–1940* (Cadiz, Ohio, 1940).

11 Autobiography, in Crooks, 26–28.

12 *Ibid.*, 28, 36–45. Harrison County, *Records of the Court of Common Pleas,* March Term, 1830, 25–26; Aug. Term, 1830, 50–51, 87, 105; Oct. Term, 1830, 119–120, 122; Apr. Term, 1831, 141, 157–158; Oct. Term, 1831, 191.

13 Simpson Papers, from an undated notebook.

14 *Ibid.*

Chapter III

CROWS AND METHODIST PREACHERS

1 Diary, 1831–1834, *passim,* in Crooks, 36–45.

2 Autobiography, in Crooks, 50–51. Matthew Simpson, *Lectures on Preaching . . . Yale College* (New York, 1879), 63–64.

3 Autobiography, in Crooks, 48–51, 65–67. Diary, in Crooks, 28–31. Simpson, *Lectures,* 61–64. The three dialogues of Matthew with his uncle, his mother, and Mr. Elliott are constructed.

4 Peter Cartwright, *Autobiography,* edited by W. P. Strickland (Cincinnati, 1859), 330. James G. Leyburn, *Frontier Folkways* (New Haven, 1935), 195.

5 Caleb Atwater, *History of the State of Ohio* (Cincinnati, 1838), 307.

6 Autobiography, in Crooks, 67–71; Diary, 1834, *ibid.,* 94–97, *passim.* The dialogue with the presiding elder is constructed.

Chapter IV

STATIONED AT PITTSBURGH

1 Michael Chevalier, *Society, Manners and Politics in the United States,* transl. from the 3rd Paris ed. (Boston, 1834), 169.

2 *Ibid.*, 168–172. *Western Christian Advocate,* May 16, 1834, letter signed J. P. D. (John Price Durbin).

3 Autobiography, in Crooks, 72–73, 78. Isaac Harris, *Harris' Pittsburgh Business Directory for the Year 1837* (Pittsburgh, 1857), reports that Verner and his partner had the largest brewery in Pittsburgh in 1837. Simpson to Ellen Simpson, Nov. 3, 1857.

4 Autobiography, in Crooks, 73. *Minutes of the Pittsburgh Annual Confer-*

ence, July 27, 1836 (MS in possession of Wallace G. Smeltzer, Librarian of the Pittsburgh Annual Conference).

⁵ Thomas M. Hudson, *The Life and Times of the Rev. Thomas M. Hudson* (Cincinnati, 1871), 142.

⁶ Diary, Aug. 26, 30, Sept. 7, 1834, in Crooks, 98. Simpson, *Lectures on Preaching,* 162–163.

⁷ Diary, Nov. 16, 1834, in Crooks, 98–99, 115, 116, 117.

⁸ Crooks, 91. Constructed dialogue.

⁹ Uncle Matthew to Simpson, Oct. 30, 1834, in Crooks, 103.

¹⁰ "A Word to a Drinker," Simpson Papers.

¹¹ "Time Shall Be No Longer," *ibid.*

¹² Simpson to Uncle Matthew, Nov. 10, 1834.

¹³ Sept. 7, Oct. 4, and Aug. 24, 1834; May 27, 1835.

¹⁴ Diary, Aug. 15, 1834, in Crooks, 116. Joseph Tarkington, *Autobiography* (Cincinnati, 1899), 142.

¹⁵ Charles Elliott to Simpson, Feb. 22, 1834.

¹⁶ Autobiography, in Crooks, 79. Diary, Aug. 30, 1834, in Crooks, 98. Uncle Matthew to Simpson, Aug. 20, 1834, in Crooks, 101.

¹⁷ Uncle Matthew to Simpson, *ibid.*

¹⁸ *Ibid.* Diary, Aug. 30, 1834, in Crooks, 98. Uncle Matthew to Simpson, Aug. 20, 1834; Simpson to Uncle Matthew, Sept. 29, 1834.

¹⁹ Autobiography, in Crooks, 80. Constructed dialogue.

²⁰ Simpson to Uncle Matthew, Sept. 29, 1834.

²¹ *Ibid.*

²² *Ibid.* Uncle Matthew to Simpson, Oct. 3, 1834.

²³ Simpson to Uncle Matthew, Oct. 20, 1834 (construction changed from third to second person). Charles Elliott to Simpson, Aug. 2, 1833.

²⁴ Autobiography, in Crooks, 77–78. Uncle Matthew to Simpson, June 14, 1834.

²⁵ Diary, Aug. 12 and 26, Sept. 1 and 7, 1834, in Crooks, 97–98. Uncle Matthew to Simpson, May 11, 1835, in Crooks, 106. Autobiography, in Crooks, 79. Undated fragment on Pittsburgh Conference History.

²⁶ Pittsburgh *Conference Journal,* Aug. 6, 1835.

²⁷ Autobiography. Miscellaneous fragments, Simpson Papers.

²⁸ Pittsburgh *Conference Journal,* Aug. 23 and 30, 1834.

²⁹ *Ibid.,* Aug. 23, 1834.

³⁰ *Ibid.,* April 9, May 7 and 14, 1834—articles signed "Johannes" and "Fenelon."

Chapter V

SENTIMENTS HAVE NO BLOOD

¹ Uncle Matthew to Simpson, Aug. 6, 1834.

² Simpson to Uncle Matthew, Jan. 28, 1836, in Crooks, 112–113.

³ Uncle Matthew to Simpson, Apr. 28 and July 11, 1835, in Crooks, 105–106, 108.

4 Hunter to Simpson, Nov. 2, 1835; Sarah Patterson to Simpson, July 12, 1835. Autobiography, in Crooks, 77.

5 Simpson to Uncle Matthew, July 9 and 17, 1835.

6 Diary, July 31, 1835, in Crooks, 111.

7 Simpson to Uncle Matthew, Aug. 21, 1835, in Crooks, 111–112.

8 Simpson to Ellen Simpson, Oct. 16, 1870.

9 Uncle Matthew to Simpson, Sept. 28, 1835.

10 *Ibid.*

11 Simpson to Ellen Simpson, Nov. 3, 1857.

12 Diary, Nov. 3, 1835, in Crooks, 115.

13 *Ibid.*

14 Diary, Aug. 27 and Sept. 14, 1835, in Crooks, 113–114, 116. Simpson to Uncle Matthew, Jan. 28, 1836, in Crooks, 113.

15 Simpson to Uncle Matthew, Aug. 14, 1835, and Jan. 28, 1836.

16 Diary, Aug. 12 and Nov. 16, 1834, June 21, Oct. 19, and Nov. 30, 1835, in Crooks, 97, 99, 116.

17 Simpson to Uncle Matthew, Aug. 21, 1835. Diary, Oct. 19, 1835, in Crooks, 115.

18 Diary, Oct. 27, 1835, in Crooks, 115.

19 Uncle Matthew to Simpson, May 11, 1835.

20 Pittsburgh *Conference Journal,* Apr. 14, 21, and 28, May 5 and 12, 1836.

21 Pittsburgh *Christian Herald,* Dec. 16, 1836, as cited by Simpson in Pittsburgh *Conference Journal,* Feb. 16, 1837.

22 "Reply to Annan on Methodism," undated MS, Simpson Papers.

23 *Ibid.*

24 Pittsburgh *Conference Journal,* Mar. 16 and Apr. 20, 1837.

25 Gilbert H. Barnes, *The Antislavery Impulse, 1830–1844* (New York, 1933), 89–90. This is the most incisive study of the relation of evangelical Protestantism to the slavery problem.

26 Uncle Matthew to Simpson, Aug. 21, 1834.

27 *Ibid.,* Oct. 30, 1834.

28 *Ibid.,* Mar. 1, 1835.

29 Charles Elliott, *History of the Great Secession from the Methodist Episcopal Church* (Cincinnati, 1855), cols. 158–160.

30 *The Liberator,* June 11, 1836.

31 Uncle Matthew to Simpson, Feb. 10 and Aug. 13, 1836.

32 Undated fragment, Simpson Papers.

33 La Roy Sunderland to Simpson, June 29, 1836. *Zion's Watchman,* July 6, 1836.

34 John Nelson Norwood, *The Schism in the Methodist Episcopal Church, 1844* (Alfred University Studies, Vol. I, Alfred, N.Y., 1923), 35.

35 Uncle Matthew to Simpson, Jan. 24, 1838.

36 Pittsburgh *Conference Journal,* Nov. 26, 1835, Feb. 15 and 23, 1838. Uncle Matthew to Simpson, Mar. 2 and 17, 1838. I draw this inference from Simpson's and the Methodists' opinions generally rather than from any specific statement by Simpson. See his fragment, "Prospectus for Anti-Cannibal Society," n.d.

[37] La Roy Sunderland to Simpson, June 29, 1836.

[38] Ruter to Simpson, Feb. 13, 1837.

[39] Simpson to Ellen Simpson, Nov. 8, 1836.

[40] *Ibid.*, 1836, probably Nov.

[41] Autobiography, in Crooks, 81-83. "Heads of Self Examination," Jan. 11, 1836, memorandum, a part of which is found in Crooks, 84-85.

[42] Autobiography, in Crooks, 131.

Chapter VI

ALLEGHENY PROFESSOR

[1] Uncle Matthew to Simpson, Feb. 22, 1837.

[2] "Notes on Natural Science" [1837]. Simpson Papers.

[3] Simpson to Ellen Simpson, May 3 and 7, 1837.

[4] Ernest Ashton Smith, *Allegheny: A Century of Education, 1815-1915* (Meadville, Pa., 1916), 38-40. *Crawford Democrat and Meadville Courier*, Oct. 16, 1838.

[5] Charles H. Haskins and William I. Hull, *A History of Higher Education in Pennsylvania* (U.S. Bureau of Education, Circular of Information, No. 4, Whole No. 283, Washington, 1902), 8-9.

[6] Simpson to Ellen Simpson, July 8, 1837.

[7] *Ibid.*, July 31, 1837.

[8] *Ibid.*, Aug. 7, 1837.

[9] Allegheny College, *Annual Catalogue*, 1837, 12, 13.

[10] Tiberius Cavallo, *The Elements of Natural or Experimental Philosophy*, 2nd Amer. ed. (Philadelphia, 1819).

[11] Thomas Keith, *A New Treatise on the Use of the Globes or a Philosophical View of the Earth and Heavens*, 24th Amer. ed. (New York, 1826).

[12] "Diary of Thoughts and Reading, 1838." Keith, 97. Uncle Matthew to Simpson, Feb. 22, 1837.

[13] J. W. Ferree to Simpson, n.d.

[14] Scrapbook [1837-1838] #1. *Index Rerum*, 1837-1838. Notes on Origen's Opera [1837-1838]. "Diary of Thoughts and Reading, 1838."

[15] "Diary of Thoughts and Reading, 1838." *Index Rerum*, 1837-1838.

[16] Diary, Jan. 8 and 17, 1838.

[17] *Minutes of the Board of Trustees*, Allegheny College, Aug. 1, Sept. 20 and 22, 1837, and May 4, 1838. Minute Book of Philo-Franklin Society, Jan. 25, 1839. Both manuscript volumes in the possession of Allegheny College library.

[18] Crooks, 131-132. *Crawford Democrat and Meadville Courier*, June 26, 1838. Henry B. Ridgaway, "Bishop Simpson," *Methodist Review*, LXVII, 27 (Jan., 1885).

[19] Fragment written on part of letter to Ellen Simpson, letter dated Aug. 7, 1837.

[20] Uncle Matthew to Simpson, Mar. 2, 1838.

[21] *Ibid.*, Mar. 19, 1838.

22 *Ibid.*

23 W. Hunter to Simpson, Mar. 10, 1838.

24 Uncle Matthew to Simpson, Nov. 10, 1838.

25 Simpson to Ellen Simpson, Mar. 12, 1838, in Crooks, 133.

26 *Ibid.* Simpson to Ellen Simpson, Mar. 15, 1838. Minutes of the Board of Trustees, June 29, 1837.

27 Simpson to Ellen Simpson, Mar. 12, 15, and 22, 1838.

28 Minutes of the Board of Trustees, Aug. 31, 1838. Charles Elliott to Simpson, Feb. 21, 1837. Allen Wiley to Simpson, Jan. 26, 1838.

29 Mar. 12, 1838.

Chapter VII

THE MIND'S THE MEASURE

1 William Warren Sweet, *Indiana Asbury–DePauw University, 1837–1937* (New York, 1937), 26–29.

2 Simpson to James Stryker, July 3, 1843, in Sweet, 29.

3 Jan. 9, 1835, cited in Sweet, 30.

4 Sweet, 26.

5 Charles N. Sims, *The Life of Thomas M. Eddy, D.D.* (New York, 1879), 90.

6 Crooks, 145–148.

7 Irving Frederick Brown, *Indiana Asbury–DePauw University* (DePauw University Bulletin, 1914), 10.

8 *Ibid.,* 6.

9 Crooks, 147.

10 Uncle Matthew to Simpson, Dec. 27, 1840.

11 Crooks, 155. Constructed dialogue.

12 *Ibid.,* 148. Constructed dialogue.

13 *Ibid.,* 155. Andrew Reed and James Matheson, *A Narrative of the Visit to the American Churches* (London, 1835), I, 498. "Reed's and Matheson's Narrative," *Methodist Magazine and Quarterly Review,* XVIII, 80 (Jan., 1836).

14 Crooks, 149–150, 186–187. "Introduction," by T. A. Goodwin, to Joseph Tarkington, *Autobiography* (Cincinnati, 1899), 12–18. Unidentified MS, Simpson Papers.

15 Uncle Matthew to Simpson, June 19 and Aug. 8, 1840.

16 *Ibid.,* Aug. 8, 1840.

17 Complete address, in Crooks, 474–504.

18 E. R. Ames to Simpson, Sept. 18, 1840.

19 Uncle Matthew to Simpson, Dec. 27, 1840.

20 Hunter to Simpson, Aug. 4, 1841.

21 Goodwin, 20.

Chapter VIII

HOOSIER SCHOOLMASTER

1 Indiana Asbury University, *First Annual Catalogue of the Officers and Students* (Greencastle, Aug., 1839).

2 William Warren Sweet, *Indiana Asbury–DePauw University,* 57. W. C. Larrabee, *Rosabower: Essays and Miscellanies* (Cincinnati, 1855). L. W. Berry to Simpson, July 30, 1844. Berry complained that Larrabee was spending half of his classroom time teaching Locofocoism.

3 Simpson Papers: "Lecture on Anatomy," Jan. 24, 1843; "Lecture on the Cranium," 1843.

4 "Commencement Address," n.d. "Lecture on the Mind, No. 3," Dec. 13, 1842. "Musings on the Valley of the Euphrates, No. 2" n.d. "Errors of Thinking and how to Guard against Them," Dec. 20, 1842. "Lecture on the Mind, No. 4," Dec. 20, 1842. Baccalaureate Sermon, n.d. "To Labor for the Elevation of the Masses: the Duty of the American Scholar," n.d.

5 Inaugural Address, in Crooks, 486–487. Johnson Brigham, *James Harlan* (Iowa City, 1913), 350 n.; Indiana Asbury Univ., *First Annual Catalogue,* 11. Sweet, 93. Simpson to the President & Members of the Platonian Society of I.A.U. [Dec., 1845].

6 A. Eddy to Simpson, May 1, 1841. Isaac Owen to Simpson, June 17, 1846. Brown, *Indiana Asbury–DePauw University,* 12. W. C. Larrabee to Simpson, Mar. 25, 1842.

7 Daily to Simpson, probably 1845. Mills to Simpson, Apr. 20, 1841.

8 Brown, 12, 13.

9 Crooks, 162, 165–166.

10 Brigham, 17. E. G. Meek to Ellen Simpson, Dec. 1, 1841. E. Williams to Simpson, Dec. 3, 1848. Crooks, 165, citing A. G. Porter.

11 J. Mills to Simpson, Oct. 18, 1841. William Glenn to Simpson, Sept. 25, 1841. Allen Wiley to Simpson, Jan. 19, 1842.

12 Wheeler to Simpson, May 17 and 31, 1841, and July 6, 1842. Daniel Yanders to Simpson, May 8, 1841.

13 Crooks, 162, citing John Ray. Brigham, 9–14, 16–41, 50.

14 Simpson Papers, "Thoughts & Reflections Upon Various Subjects," 1842; "Collection of facts, bearing upon improper legislation"; Notes on Gibbon's *History of the Roman Empire,* 1842.

15 Uncle Matthew to Simpson, Feb. 29, 1840.

16 *Ibid.*

17 Uncle Matthew to Simpson, May 25, 1841.

18 Diary, May 11, 12, and 14, 1840.

19 L. L. Hamline to Simpson, May 16, 1841—postscript added by Charles Elliott. Uncle Matthew to Simpson, Oct. 27, 1841.

20 Simpson to Ellen Simpson, May 1, 1842.

21 W. C. Larrabee, *Rosabower,* 5, 128. D. L. Southard, untitled, undated MS, written for Crooks.

22 E. G. Meek to Ellen Simpson, Dec. 1, 1841. Simpson Papers, Diary, Jan. 7, 8, 10, and 11, 1844.

23 Uncle Matthew to Simpson, Jan. 21, 1842.

24 Simpson to Ellen Simpson, Apr. 9, 1871, in Crooks, 453. Penciled fragment, May 1, 1842.

Chapter IX

"BLUE PUP" AND INDIANA POLITICS

1 Allen Wiley to Simpson, May 29, 1839. Brown, *Indiana Asbury–DePauw University*, 21.

2 Logan Esarey, *History of Indiana from Its Exploration to 1850* (Indianapolis, 1915), 369, 380–383, 403–406.

3 Simpson to L. W. Berry, probably Dec. 8 or 9, 1845. Uncle Matthew to Simpson, Oct. 17, 1842. George McCullough to Simpson, Dec. 21, 1841.

4 W. C. Larrabee to Simpson, Apr. 22, 1844.

5 Address to Members of the Conference, quoted in part in Crooks, 158–159.

6 Sweet, *Indiana Asbury–DePauw University*, 56.

7 A. Johnson to Simpson, Aug. 9, 1841. John S. Bayless to Simpson, Mar. 31, 1841. Aaron Wood to Simpson, Apr. 24, 1842. Bayless to Simpson, Jan. 8, 1845.

8 "Journal: Tour Through Indiana, 1842." Simpson to Ellen Simpson, probably June, 1843.

9 Simpson, *Lectures on Preaching* (1879), 158–159.

10 Crooks, 186–199, has several accounts of Simpson's appearance and effectiveness as an Indiana preacher.

11 Edgar Carlisle MacMechen, *Life of Governor Evans, Second Territorial Governor of Colorado* (Denver, 1924), 35–37. J. Wesley Whicker, "Dr. John Evans," *Indiana Magazine of History*, XIX, 233 (Sept., 1923).

12 William C. Smith, *Indiana Miscellany* (Cincinnati, 1867), 251–253. The most valuable letters in the Simpson Papers, for the Indiana period, are those from Berry.

13 William Warren Sweet, *Circuit Rider Days in Indiana* (Indianapolis, 1916), 261, citing *Journal of the Indiana Conference*, Oct. 12, 1841. Matthew Simpson, *Cyclopaedia of Methodism* (Philadelphia, 1878), 978.

14 Crooks, 195–196.

15 Gov. James Whitcomb, Veto Message, Jan. 14, 1847, copy in Simpson Papers.

16 *Indiana State Sentinel*, July 24, 1843, letter signed "Education's Friend." *Ibid.*, Aug. 1, 1843, letter signed "Right of Conscience Man." L. W. Berry to Simpson, July 26, 1843.

17 Simpson to James Stryker, July 3, 1843.

18 S. R. Ball to Simpson, July 5, 1843. Sweet, *Indiana Asbury–DePauw University*, 29.

19 *Indiana State Journal*, June 27, 1843, citing *Indiana State Sentinel*, n.d., and Lafayette *Advertiser*, n.d.

20 Letter signed by Noah Noble and others, *Indiana State Journal*, June 27, 1843.

21 *Indiana State Sentinel*, July 4, 1843.

22 Simpson to James Stryker, July 3, 1843. L. W. Berry to Simpson, July 26, 1843. Ira Grove to Simpson, Sept. 15, 1843.

23 L. W. Berry to Simpson, July 26, 1843.

24 *Ibid.*

25 *Indiana State Journal*, July 28, 1843. *Indiana State Sentinel*, Aug. 1, 1843, letter signed "Right of Conscience Man."

26 *Indiana State Sentinel*, Aug. 1, 1843, letter signed "Right of Conscience Man."

27 *Ibid.*, Aug. 1, 1843, "A Sick Whig."

28 *Ibid.*, Sept. 5, 1843.

29 *Ibid.*, Sept. 12, 1843 (citing *Indiana Whig* and New Albany *Democrat*, n.d., and Aug. 22, 1843 (citing Bloomington *Post*, n.d.). *Indiana State Journal*, Aug. 23, 1843.

30 W. T. S. Cornett to Simpson, Dec. 27, 1843. L. W. Berry to Simpson, Jan. 29, 1844.

31 L. W. Berry to Simpson, Jan. 10, 1844. Joseph A. Wright to Simpson, Feb. 7 and Mar. 23, 1844.

32 James Whitcomb, Veto Message, Jan. 14, 1847.

33 J. S. Bayless to Simpson, Dec. 28, 1846.

34 L. W. Berry to Simpson, Mar. 31, 1847. S. T. Gillet to Simpson, Jan. 14, 1847. A. W. Harrison to Simpson, Jan. 15, 1847.

35 L. W. Berry to Simpson, Mar. 31, 1837.

Chapter X

"NO SHADING OFF . . . FROM RIGHT TO WRONG"

1 Autobiography, Simpson Papers. "Private Memoranda for General Conference," 1843.

2 "Private Memoranda for General Conference," 1843.

3 Phineas D. Gurley to Simpson, Mar. 26, 1844. "Private Memoranda for General Conference," 1843.

4 Journal, Mar. 20, 23, 24, 25, 1844. Autobiography. [Expense Account] Mar. 24, 25, and 26, 1844.

5 Autobiography. Diary, Apr. 1, 1844. Expense Account, Apr. 6 and 9, 1844.

6 Autobiography. Diary, Apr. 15, 1844.

7 Autobiography.

8 George W. Julian, *The Rank of Charles Osborn As an Anti-Slavery Pioneer* (Indiana History Society Publications, Vol. II, No. 6, Indianapolis, 1891), 262.

9 Uncle Matthew to Simpson, June 19, 1840, and Oct. 17, 1842.

10 John Nelson Norwood, *The Schism in the Methodist Episcopal Church*, 149. W. W. Sweet, *Circuit-Rider Days in Indiana* (Indianapolis, 1916), 325.

11 *Christian Advocate and Journal*, Sept. 25, 1844.

12 Autobiography. Expense Account, Apr. 30, 1844.

13 John Fletcher Hurst, *The History of Methodism* (7 vols., New York, 1902), V, 932.

14 *Journal of the General Conference of the Methodist Episcopal Church, 1844* (New York, 1844), 5.

15 Autobiography.

16 *Journal of the General Conference,* 15.

17 *Ibid.,* 17.

18 *The Debates of the General Conference of the M.E. Church, May, 1844, to which is added a review of the proceedings of said conference, by Rev. Luther Lee and Rev. E. Smith* (New York, 1845), 40–41. (Later references to this work will be under the short title, *Debates.*)

19 *Ibid.,* 29, 41, 43.

20 *Ibid.,* 60.

21 *Ibid.,* 53–54.

22 *Ibid.,* 63–64.

23 *Ibid.,* 65.

24 *Journal of the General Conference,* 23–24.

Chapter XI

THE CHURCH DIVIDED

1 George G. Smith, *The Life and Letters of James Osgood Andrew* (Nashville, 1883), 368. Resolutions by the Southern Delegates.

2 *Christian Advocate and Journal,* Sept. 25, 1844, Open Letter from Nathan Bangs to Bishop Andrew. Simpson to Ellen Simpson, May 18, 1844.

3 Autobiography. Expense account, May 2 and 6, 1844.

4 Simpson to Ellen Simpson, May 25, 1844, quoted in Crooks, 232.

5 *Journal of the General Conference of the Methodist Episcopal Church, 1844,* 63–64.

6 *Report of Debates in the General Conference of the Methodist Episcopal Church, held in the city of New-York, 1844, by Robert Athow West, official reporter* (New York, 1844), 100–105.

7 *Debates* (Lee and Smith), 82.

8 *Report of Debates,* 89, 90.

9 *Debates,* 146.

10 *Report of Debates,* 128, 129.

11 Autobiography.

12 Simpson to Ellen Simpson, May 25, 1844.

13 *Debates,* 180.

14 *Ibid.*

15 *Ibid.*

16 *Journal of the General Conference,* 84.

17 Diary, probably May, 1844. Two penciled resolutions.

18 *Debates,* 311.

19 *Ibid.*, 311–312.

20 *Journal of the General Conference*, 113. *Report of Debates*, 237.

21 Elliott, *History of the Great Secession*, cols. 406–408.

22 Autobiography. The several Advocates of the period are filled with expressions of this point of view.

23 Elliott, *ibid.*, cols. 406–408.

24 Simpson to Charles Elliott, Dec. 18, 1845. Diary, May 2, 1845. Autobiography.

25 *Debates*, 401–402.

26 *Ibid.*, 212. Simpson, Diary, May 8, 1845.

27 *Debates*, 442.

28 Simpson to Charles Elliott, Dec. 18, 1845.

29 Hunter to Simpson, Feb. 13, 1846.

Chapter XII

"SON OF MAN, PROPHESY"

1 Indiana Asbury University, *Annual Catalogue, 1844.* Isaac Owen to Simpson, Aug. 31, 1846. Marcus C. Smith to Simpson, May 22, 1844.

2 Joseph Tingley, "Reminiscences of Thirty Years in Asbury," *Asbury Review*, I, 1 (May, 1873). B. F. Tefft, *Methodism Successful, and the Internal Causes of Its Success* (New York, 1860), *passim.* Simpson, *Cyclopaedia of Methodism*, 852.

3 Isaac Owen to Simpson, Aug. 31, 1846. Brown, *Indiana Asbury–DePauw University*, 21.

4 William Johnston to Simpson, Oct. 3, 1845.

5 John Wheeler to Simpson, Sept. 10, 1845.

6 *Ibid.*

7 "Bishop Ames," an unsigned article by Abel Stevens in *National Magazine*, VII, 385–386 (Oct., 1855). E. R. Ames to Simpson, Sept. 14, 1846, Jan. 21, 1845, and June 29, 1847.

8 C. W. Ruter to Simpson, Mar. 9, 1846.

9 L. W. Berry to Simpson, Apr. 15, 1846.

10 Circular dated Mar. 10, 1846, signed by W. H. Good, S. T. Gillet, B. F. Tefft, Committee. Copy in Simpson Papers.

11 Stephen Olin to Simpson, Apr. 2, 1846.

12 William Daily to Simpson, May 11, 1846.

13 L. W. Berry to Simpson, Apr. 15, 1846.

14 Daily to Simpson, May 11, 1846.

15 John L. Smith, *Indiana Methodism* (Valparaiso, Ind., 1892), 205–206.

Chapter XIII

WAR ON THE BORDER

[1] Autobiography. Lucius C. Matlack, *The Antislavery Struggle and Triumph in the Methodist Episcopal Church* (New York, 1881), 178.

[2] Simpson, "Memoranda Relating to General Conference, Feb., 1848."

[3] William M. Daily to Simpson, May 24, 1848.

[4] Pittsburgh *Christian Advocate*, May 10, 1848. Diary, May 1, 1848.

[5] Minutes of the Committee on the State of the Church, Simpson Papers, written in Simpson's hand. Oddly enough, his old friend Charles Elliott asserts in *History of the Great Secession* (col. 635) that Simpson was not on this committee; however, the minutes record his election as secretary, and the report in the Pittsburgh *Christian Advocate*, May 10, 1848, lists him as a member. W. P. Harrison of the Methodist Episcopal Church, South, published *Methodist Union, Threatened in 1844, was formally dissolved in 1848, by the legislation of Dr. (afterward Bishop) Simpson . . .* (Nashville, 1892).

[6] Minutes, etc., Simpson Papers. Pittsburgh *Christian Advocate*, May 31, 1848.

[7] Simpson, "Memoranda Relating to General Conference, Feb., 1848." He was the author of the resolution to declare the Plan of Separation null and void. See below.

[8] Debates reported in *Christian Advocate and Journal*, May 17, 1848.

[9] Pittsburgh *Christian Advocate*, May 17 and 31, 1848—speeches by Simpson and George Gary.

[10] *Ibid.*, May 17, 1848—speech on deeds.

[11] Abel Stevens, writing anonymously in Pittsburgh *Christian Advocate*, June 21, 1848.

[12] Daily to Simpson, May 24, 1848.

[13] Larrabee to Simpson, May 22, 1848.

[14] Pittsburgh *Christian Advocate*, June 21, 1848.

[15] *Ibid.*, May 31, 1848.

[16] *Ibid.*

[17] *Ibid.*

[18] *Ibid.*

[19] *Ibid.*, June 7, 1848. Richmond *Christian Advocate*, June 15, 1848, as cited by Charles Baumer Swaney, *Episcopal Methodism and Slavery* (Boston, 1926), 178.

[20] William M. Wightman, *Life of William Capers* (Nashville, 1859), 441.

[21] Edward Thomson, *Life of Edward Thomson* (Cincinnati, 1885), 77.

[22] Daily to Simpson, May 24, 1848.

[23] L. W. Berry to Simpson, Apr. 15, 1846. John L. Smith to Simpson, June 23, 1848.

[24] William H. Allen to Simpson, June 5, 1848. Autobiography.

[25] Autobiography, Crooks, 255.

[26] John L. Smith to Simpson, June 23, 1848.

[27] Pittsburgh *Christian Advocate*, June 7, 1848. Autobiography.

Chapter XIV

CINCINNATI EDITOR

[1] Simpson Papers, Scrapbook [1848–1852]. Charles Cist, *The Cincinnati Miscellany, or Antiquities of the West* (Cincinnati, 1846), II, 153. Swaney, *Episcopal Methodism and Slavery*, 183.

[2] *Western Christian Advocate*, Aug. 2, 1848. Crooks, 258.

[3] Bishop Thomas A. Morris to Simpson, Aug. 16, 1848. Swaney, *Episcopal Methodism and Slavery*, 167. Autobiography.

[4] *Western Christian Advocate*, Aug. 2, 1848.

[5] *Ibid.*, Aug. 9, 16, 23, and Sept. 13, 1848, and Jan. 2, Feb. 20 and 27, 1850, and other issues. Simpson Papers, "Memo Book," Nov. 12, 1851.

[6] *Western Christian Advocate*, Dec. 26, 1849, Oct. 16, 1850, and Jan. 8, 1851.

[7] *Ibid.*, Dec. 26, 1849.

[8] L. W. Berry to Simpson, Dec. 3, 1849; E. House to Simpson, Apr. 24, 1852.

[9] Pittsburgh *Christian Advocate*, June 7, 1848. Daniel Curry to Simpson, Jan. 20, 1849.

[10] Autobiography.

[11] *Western Christian Advocate*, Nov. 1, 1848.

[12] *Ibid.*, Mar. 28, Apr. 11 and May 23, 1849.

[13] *Ibid.*, June 27, 1849.

[14] *Ibid.*, Feb. 7 and Nov. 14, 1849. Pittsburgh *Christian Advocate*, Dec. 18, 1848. *Missionary Herald*, XLV, 245–246 (July, 1849).

[15] *Western Christian Advocate*, May 30, 1849. Dr. Barnes wrote (*ibid.*, Sept. 26, 1849), protesting his admiration for the Methodists, and sent a copy of his sermon to prove his point: the account in the press had been badly garbled.

[16] *Ibid.*, Mar. 12, 19, and Apr. 23, 1851, and Mar. 3, 1852.

[17] *Ibid.*, Mar. 19, Apr. 16, May 7, June 11, Sept. 3, 10, and Nov. 26, 1851.

[18] *Ibid.*, Nov. 29, 1848.

[19] *Ibid.*, Mar. 6, 1850.

[20] *Ibid.*, Apr. 24, 1850.

[21] *Christian Advocate and Journal*, Mar. 14, 1850. *Western Christian Advocate*, Mar. 20, 1850.

[22] *Western Christian Advocate*, May 1, 1850. Reprinted in full in Crooks, 262–265.

[23] Autobiography. Salmon P. Chase to Simpson, quoted in Crooks, 265–266. J. L. Smith to Simpson, May 23, 1850. William M. Daily to Simpson, May 16, 1850.

[24] *Western Christian Advocate*, Sept. 25, Oct. 9, and Nov. 25, 1850.

[25] James Hill to Simpson, Oct. 2, 1850. L. W. Berry to Simpson, Nov. 23, 1850. Crooks, 259.

[26] *Indiana State Sentinel*, Nov. 5, 1850, quoted in full in *Western Christian Advocate*, Nov. 20, 1850.

[27] *Western Christian Advocate*, Nov. 20, 1850.

[28] William M. Daily to Simpson, Dec. 5, 1850. Berry to Simpson, Dec. 3, 1850.

[29] *Indiana Tri-Weekly State Journal,* Sept. 30, Oct. 18, and Nov. 26, 1850.

[30] David McDonald to Simpson, Jan. 9, 1851.

[31] *Indiana State Sentinel,* Jan. 7, 1851.

[32] *Western Christian Advocate,* Jan. 15, 1851.

[33] Autobiography.

[34] John L. Smith to Simpson, May 23, 1850. George Ames to Simpson, about Feb., 1850. Smith to Simpson, May 23, 1850. L. W. Berry to Simpson, July 1, 1850. J. F. Jaquess to Simpson, probably 1851. T. A. Morris to Simpson, Apr. 12, 1850. E. R. Ames to Simpson, Jan. 5, 1849, and June 19, 1851.

[35] L. W. Berry to Simpson, Oct. 14, 1848.

[36] *Western Christian Advocate,* Dec. 24 and 31, 1851, Jan. 7 and Feb. 4, 1852.

[37] E. House to Simpson, Apr. 24, 1852.

[38] Autobiography. *Western Christian Advocate,* June 19 and 26, 1850, and July 23, 1851. M. Marlay to Simpson, Mar. 18, 1852.

[39] James Hill to Simpson, Apr. 26, 1852.

[40] E. House to Simpson, Apr. 24, 26, 1852.

[41] Autobiography.

Chapter XV

AND SOME, BISHOPS

[1] Unsigned article by Abel Stevens in *Daily Zion's Herald,* May 22, 1852. Scrapbook A, Simpson Papers. Autobiography, in Crooks, 277.

[2] Advertisement in *Daily Zion's Herald,* Mar. 3, 1852, and succeeding issues.

[3] Autobiography, in Crooks, 277-278.

[4] Smith, *Indiana Methodism,* 205-206. L. W. Berry to Simpson, June 20, 1852, and July 22, 1854. Daily to Simpson, June 15, 1852.

[5] Autobiography, in Crooks, 277-278. William M. Daily to Simpson, June 15, 1852. L. W. Berry to Simpson, June 20, 1852. Thomson, *Life of Edward Thomson,* 79-80 (letter to Mrs. Thomson, May 27, 1852).

[6] Autobiography, in Crooks, 277-278. Thomson, *ibid.*

[7] *Daily Zion's Herald,* May 11, 1852.

[8] *Ibid.,* May 22, 27, 29, and 31, 1852.

[9] L. W. Berry to Simpson, June 20, 1852.

[10] Autobiography, in Crooks, 277-278. *Daily Zion's Herald,* May 26, 1852.

[11] Smith, *Indiana Methodism,* 205-206.

[12] Diary, May 25, 1852—quoted in Crooks, 276-277, with minor alterations and omissions.

[13] Unsigned article, "Bishop Ames," *National Magazine,* VII, 387 (Oct., 1855).

[14] Diary, May 30 and 31, June 1, 2, 3, 4, 5, and 6, 1852, in Crooks, 278. Autobiography.

[15] Simpson to Ellen Simpson, June 10, 1852, quoted in Crooks, 279-280.

[16] Diary, June 10, 17, and 18, 1852, in Crooks, 280.

[17] Allen Kramer to Simpson, June 28, 1852. W. C. P. Hamilton to Simpson, June 25, 1852. I. C. Sigler to Simpson, Mar. 12, 1852. Autobiography.

[18] Autobiography. Diary, Aug. 3, 1848, and undated entry, 1855. "Thoughts and Suggestions for 1859." William H. Kincaid to Simpson, Dec. 26, 1853.

[19] Autobiography. Diary, June 18, 1852, Apr. 17, 1855, and June 16, 1855.

[20] Diary, Nov. 26, 1852. Simpson to Ellen Simpson, Sept. 26, 1853, Dec. 23, 1854, and Apr., 1857.

[21] Simpson to Ellen Simpson, Apr., 1857, and Apr. 8, 1856. Diary, May 14, 1853.

[22] Undated "Thoughts for health and comfort necessary for health and action," probably in the early 1850's.

[23] Simpson to Ellen Simpson, May 1, 1853, quoted in Crooks, 289.

[24] *Ibid.*, Dec. 3, 1855.

[25] *Ibid.*, Oct. 8, 1852 (quoted in Crooks, 283), Sept. 1, 1854, and Oct. 2, 1855.

[26] Simpson to Ellen Simpson, June 8, 1852.

[27] G. C. Halstead to Simpson, undated (for the missionary rally, Nov. 2, 1853).

[28] Autobiography.

[29] John B. Wolff to Simpson, Feb. 19, 1853.

[30] Philadelphia *Press* and *Daily Evening Bulletin*, Jan. 4, 1861. Pittsburgh *Gazette*, Jan. 26, 1853. Pittsburgh *Christian Advocate*, Feb. 1, 1853.

[31] Philadelphia *Daily Evening Bulletin*, Jan. 4, 1861. Pittsburgh *Christian Advocate*, Feb. 1, 1853.

[32] Diary, Dec. 25 and 28, 1853, in Crooks, 284-285.

[33] *Ibid.*, Dec. 31, 1852, and Jan. 1, 1853, in Crooks, 286-287.

[34] Simpson, *Cyclopaedia of Methodism*, 691. Mrs. Phoebe Palmer to Simpson, undated, July 4, 1853. Diary, Jan. 1, 1854, in Crooks, 309.

Chapter XVI

TO CALIFORNIA AND OREGON

[1] L. W. Berry to Simpson, May 4, 1853.

[2] The materials for this chapter, unless otherwise noted, are derived from a long manuscript account of the trip to California and Oregon, fragments of which appear in Crooks, 301-321.

[3] William Ingraham Kip, *The Early Days of My Episcopate* (New York, 1892), 20.

[4] Crooks, 317. Simpson to Ellen Simpson, Feb. 14, 1854 (Crooks, 315).

[5] Ketturah Belknap, "Ketturah Belknap's Narrative," ed. Robert Moulton Gatke, *Oregon Historical Quarterly*, XXXVIII, 292 (Sept., 1937).

[6] Thomas Hall Pearne, *Sixty-one Years of Itinerant Life* (Cincinnati, 1898), 156-157.

[7] Belknap, 293.

[8] Crooks, 298. Belknap, 294. The printed account, in obvious error, transcribes "soared" as "scared."

Chapter XVII

THE OLD ORDER CHANGETH

1 Simpson, Scrapbook, clipping dated in pencil Feb. 24, 1854. *Ibid.*, an Indiana correspondent, probably to the *Western Christian Advocate.*

2 *Ibid.*, clipping dated in pencil Oct. 4, 1854—but names of persons in the account identify the exercises as those dated Nov. 17 in another account. *Ibid.*, clipping signed J. L. Crane, July 6, 1855.

3 *Ibid.*, two clippings—one unidentified, one probably written by J. V. Watson for the *Northwestern Christian Advocate.*

4 Diary, Dec. 23, 1856, Jan. 17 and 21, 1856, and May 8 and 12, 1857.

5 Scrapbook, address at Garrett Biblical Institute.

6 As quoted by *Methodist Quarterly Review*, XXXIX, 146–147 (Jan., 1857).

7 New York *Evening Post*, May 13, 1857, dedication of a bethel ship.

8 Simpson to Ellen Simpson, Apr. 8, 1856.

9 John S. Bayless to Simpson, June 4, 1850. Simpson to Charles Simpson, Dec. 19, 1857. Simpson to Ellen Simpson, May 13, 1856. James Harlan to Simpson, Nov. 17, 1856.

10 Simpson, *Sermons*, ed. George R. Crooks, 209.

11 Simpson, *Cyclopaedia of Methodism*, 722. E. M. Wood, *Peerless Orator: The Rev. Matthew Simpson* (Pittsburgh, 1909), 174–175.

12 Notes of Travel, Dec. 23, 1856.

13 *Ibid.*

14 Simpson to Ellen Simpson, Oct. 8, 1855.

15 "Address of the Bishops," *Christian Advocate and Journal*, May 15, 1856.

16 Henry B. Ridgaway, *The Life of Edmund S. Janes* (New York, 1882), 197. Simpson to Ellen Simpson, May 14, 1856.

17 Simpson to Ellen Simpson, May 21, 1856.

18 Lucius C. Matlack, *The Antislavery Struggle and Triumph in the Methodist Episcopal Church* (New York, 1881), 267–277.

19 *Ibid.*, 292–293.

Chapter XVIII

ENGLAND, THE CONTINENT, AND THE HOLY LAND

1 Swormstedt and Poe to Simpson, May 5, 1857. Daniel Ross to Simpson, May 15, 1857. Diary, May 14–22, 1857.

2 Simpson to Ellen Simpson, May 25, 1857.

3 Diary [1857]. Letter IV to the Pittsburgh *Christian Advocate*, July 28, 1857.

4 Materials for this chapter, unless otherwise indicated, are based on Simpson's narrative, Notes on a Trip to Europe, Syria, and Palestine. George R. Crooks, *Life and Letters of the Rev. John McClintock, LL.D.* (New York, 1876), 272–273.

5 Crooks, *Life of Bishop Simpson*, 335–336. *Christian Advocate and Journal*, Aug. 20 and Sept. 10, 1857.

6 "Letter from Dr. McClintock," *Christian Advocate and Journal*, Oct. 8, 1857. "Letter from Germany," *ibid.*, June 25, 1857.

7 Simpson, "Trip to Europe." "Letter from Europe," Nashville *Christian Advocate*, May 10, 1860. Crooks, *Life of Bishop Simpson*, 341–343, as derived from John McClintock and W. F. Warren, *Christian Advocate and Journal*, Oct. 8 and 15, 1857.

8 Crooks, *ibid.*

9 *Ibid.*

10 *Ibid.* Simpson to Ellen Simpson [1857].

11 Crooks, *ibid.*, 344, citing McClintock, *Christian Advocate and Journal*, Oct. 8, 1857.

12 *Ibid.*

13 Simpson to Ellen Simpson, July, 1857, Sept. 25, 1857. Crooks, 339, 347–348.

14 Simpson to Ellen Simpson, Aug. 21, 1857. Simpson to Charles Simpson, Sept. 27, 1857.

15 Simpson to Ellen Simpson, Aug. 21, 1857; "Trip to Europe . . ."

16 "Trip to Europe."

17 *Ibid.* Pittsburgh *Christian Advocate*, Nov. 24, 1857.

18 Simpson to Ellen Simpson, Oct. 21, 1857. Crooks, *ibid.*, 349. Pittsburgh *Christian Advocate*, Dec. 8, 1857.

19 Crooks, *ibid.*, 351.

20 *Ibid.*, 351–352. Simpson to Ellen Simpson, Nov. 3, 1857. Crooks, *ibid.*, 349–350. Diary, Oct. 29, 1857.

21 Simpson to Ellen Simpson, Nov. 5, 1857. Crooks, *ibid.*, 351.

22 Crooks, *ibid.*, 352–354. Sacramento *Daily Union*, July 19, 1862, report of lecture on Palestine.

23 Simpson to Ellen Simpson, n.d. (Dec. 1857), and Jan. 9, 1858.

24 *Ibid.*, Dec. 19, 1857. Crooks, *ibid.*, 355–356. Pittsburgh *Christian Advocate*, Feb. 9, 1858.

25 Crooks, *ibid.*, 352.

26 Simpson to Ellen Simpson, Jan. 9, 1858.

27 Simpson to Ellen Simpson, Feb. 12, 1858. Uncle Matthew to Simpson, Oct. 12, 1857.

28 Simpson to Ellen Simpson, Jan. 9, 1858. E. S. Janes to Simpson, Jan. 11, Feb. 3, and Mar. 10, 1858. John Durbin to Simpson, probably Mar., 1858.

29 Simpson to Ellen Simpson, Jan. 19, 1858. Crooks, *ibid.*, 356.

30 Simpson to Ellen Simpson, Jan. 24 and Feb. 5, 1858. Crooks, *ibid.*, 356–357. Simpson to Ellen Simpson, Feb. 12, 1858.

31 Simpson to Ellen Simpson, Feb. 5, 1858. Crooks, *ibid.*, 357.

Chapter XIX

FOR GOD AND COUNTRY

1 Diary, July 10, 1858. Cashbook, 1858 (2 entries). Alexander Cummings to Simpson, Dec. 1, 1858. Oliver Hoyt to Simpson, June 30, 1860.

2 E. R. Ames to E. S. Janes [Oct. 9, 1858], Correspondence of the Bishops of the Methodist Episcopal Church, Garrett Biblical Institute. Uncle Matthew to Simpson, Mar. 12, 1858.

3 Diary, 1858, flyleaf.

4 John McClintock to Simpson, June 4, 1858. Harper & Brothers to Simpson, Feb. 3, 1859. "Trip to Europe."

5 Diary, Jan. 25, 1859.

6 Simpson to Ellen Simpson, Dec., 1859, and Jan., 1860, Crooks, *Life of Bishop Simpson*, 358–360.

7 *Ibid.*

8 *Ibid.*, Sept. 28, 1860, Crooks, 361.

9 Simpson to Ellen Simpson, Jan. 9, 1858. John Evans to Simpson, Mar. 15, 1858. D. P. Kidder to Simpson, May 20 and June 8, 1859. C. P. Bragdon to Simpson, May 17 and 20, 1859.

10 Frances E. Willard, *A Classic Town: The Story of Evanston* (Chicago, 1892), 271. Estelle Frances Ward, *The Story of Northwestern University* (New York, 1924), 74, *et passim.*

11 *Liberator,* Oct. 7, 1859. Thomas Sewall to Simpson, Dec. 28, 1859. Resolutions of the Texas Conference of the Methodist Episcopal Church, South, Bonham, Texas, Mar. 11, 1859, as quoted by Charles Elliott, *South-Western Methodism* (Cincinnati, 1868), 128.

12 Simpson, Address to the Wesleyan Conference, Liverpool, as reported in the *Christian Advocate and Journal,* Sept. 10, 1857. *Liberator,* Apr. 30, 1858. Theodore Parker, "The Dangers of Slavery," *Old South Leaflets,* Vol. IV, No. 80, p. 11.

13 *Liberator,* July 31, 1857, Apr. 23 and 30, Oct. 22 and Nov. 19, 1858, July 15, 1859 (citing the Richmond *Christian Advocate,* n.d.), and Apr. 5, 1861. New York *Tribune,* Oct. 21, 1859 (letter from Hiram Mattison).

14 *Independent,* May 3, 1860. *Christian Advocate and Journal,* Nov. 21, 1867.

15 *Daily Christian Advocate,* May 7, 1860.

16 *Journal of the General Conference of the Methodist Episcopal Church, 1860* (New York, 1860), 258.

17 William Hirst to Simpson, Jan. 19, 1861.

18 "Border Methodist," in Baltimore *Sun,* June 5, 1860. John Lanahan to Simpson, Oct. 5 and Dec. 18, 1860, Feb. 18, Mar. 13 and 29, 1861.

19 L. F. Morgan to Simpson, Sept. 6 and Oct. 10, 1860. William Hirst to Simpson, Feb. 4, 1861. *Western Christian Advocate,* July 11, 1860.

20 Elliott, *South-Western Methodism,* 223, 283. (My analysis of the 1860 General Conference and the effect of its legislation will appear shortly under the auspices of the Speech Association of America in a volume of Debates on Slavery, 1860.) Charles Elliott, "The Martyrdom of Bewley," *Methodist Quarterly Review,* XLV, 626–628 (Oct., 1863).

21 Elliott, *South-Western Methodism,* 225 (quoting North Carolina *Christian Advocate* of Aug. 30, 1860), 228–229. *Northwestern Christian Advocate,* Jan. 2, 1861, quoted in *Southern Christian Advocate,* Jan. 31, 1861.

22 Swaney, *Episcopal Methodism,* 231.

23 New York *Tribune,* Feb. 18 and Mar. 11, 1861.

²⁴ *Ibid.*, Feb. 15, 21, and 22, 1861. Kenneth M. Stampp, *And the War Came* (Baton Rouge, 1950), 239.

²⁵ New York *Tribune*, Mar. 12 to Apr. 13, 1861. Montgomery *Telegraph*, Apr. 11, 1861, cited by New York *Tribune*, Apr. 15.

²⁶ New York *Tribune*, Apr. 13, 15, 16, and 18, 1861.

²⁷ William Warren Sweet, *The Methodist Episcopal Church and the Civil War* (Delaware, Ohio, 1912), 70, citing the *Minutes of the New York East Conference, 1861*, 14, 16.

²⁸ *Methodist*, May 4, 1861. Swaney, *Episcopal Methodism*, 300.

²⁹ Remarks to the New York East Conference, Apr. 24, 1865, as reported by *Methodist*, May 6, 1865.

³⁰ Reminiscences of Gen. Clinton B. Fisk, quoted by Crooks, *Life of Bishop Simpson*, 373.

³¹ Frances E. Willard, *Glimpses of Fifty Years* (Chicago, 1892), 131, citing diary of Apr. 21, 1861. Willard, *A Classic Town*, 266. Estelle Frances Ward, *The Story of Northwestern University*, 94.

³² Chicago *Evening Journal*, Apr. 27 and 29, 1861. Chicago *Tribune*, Apr. 29, 1861. *Northwestern Christian Advocate*, May 1, 1861.

³³ Simpson, Scrapbook, clipping [1876].

³⁴ *Methodist*, Oct. 12, 1861, and Mar. 8, 1862. Addresses at Rockport, Indiana, and St. Louis, Missouri.

Chapter XX

LINCOLN AND METHODIST POLITICS

¹ Crooks, 374. Address at the Chicago Wigwam, *Northwestern Christian Advocate*, May 1, 1861.

² Edgar C. MacMechen, *Life of Governor Evans*, 34–35. For a more detailed analysis of this problem see Robert D. Clark, "Bishop Matthew Simpson and the Emancipation Proclamation," *Mississippi Valley Historical Review*, XXXV, 263–271 (Sept., 1948).

³ Simpson to Thomas A. Morris, May 17, 1861.

⁴ *Ibid. Northwestern Christian Advocate*, Apr. 24, 1861. E. R. Ames to Simpson, May 27, 1861.

⁵ Osmon C. Baker to Simpson, May 28, 1861. E. S. Janes to Simpson, June 4, 1861. Levi Scott to Simpson, May 29, 1861. E. R. Ames to Simpson, June 10, 1861.

⁶ *Northwestern Christian Advocate*, Apr. 24, 1861. *Christian Advocate and Journal*, June 27, 1861. Simpson to Thomas A. Morris, June 24, 1861. "Copy of the Action of the Board of Managers of the Missionary Society," June 19, 1861, Simpson Papers.

⁷ Notes of Travel, June 6, 1862. *Methodist*, Nov. 1, 1862.

⁸ *Methodist*, May 6, 1865. Crooks, 375.

⁹ *Methodist*, Oct. 19, 1861. Carl R. Fish, *The Civil Service and the Patronage* (Cambridge, 1904), 169.

[10] William Hanneman to Simpson, Feb. 23, 1861. Jay S. Turney to Simpson, Feb. 26, 1861. William Nast to Simpson, Feb. 23, 1861. John Lanahan to Simpson, Mar. 11, 1861.

[11] Simpson to Simon Cameron, Abraham Lincoln Papers, Robert Todd Lincoln Collection, Library of Congress. John Lanahan to Simpson [Nov., 1861]. J. W. Marshall to Simpson, May 18, 1861. Carl Sandburg, *Abraham Lincoln: The War Years* (4 vols., New York, 1939), I, 310.

[12] James Harlan to Simpson, June 20, 1861.

[13] Simpson to Cameron, *ibid.*

[14] Charles A. Dana, *Recollections of the Civil War* (New York, 1898), 158. Simpson to Ellen Simpson, Jan. 20, 1863.

[15] B. Peyton Brown to Chase, Dec. 9, 1862.

[16] S. P. Chase to E. R. Ames, Apr. 6, 1863.

[17] Simpson to S. P. Chase, Apr. 23, 1863, Salmon P. Chase Papers, Library of Congress. John Lanahan to Simpson, May 13 [1863].

[18] Applications and recommendations for office, in National Archives, Records of the Department of State. Simpson to Abraham Lincoln [1861 and 1862]. John L. Smith, *Indiana Methodism* (Valparaiso, Ind., 1892), 284–285.

[19] Simpson to Montgomery Blair, May 16, 1867, Blair Family Collection, Library of Congress.

[20] Montgomery Blair to Simpson, May 30, and Simpson to Montgomery Blair, June 5, 1867, Simpson Papers. Montgomery Blair to C. A. Walborn, Jan. 22, 1870, Blair Family Collection. Blair's biographer, William Ernest Smith, in *The Francis Preston Blair Family in Politics* (2 vols., New York, 1933), II, 386, mistakenly accuses Simpson of spreading abroad a private conversation.

[21] D. H. Whitely to Simpson, May 20, 1863. William Warren Sweet, in *The Methodist Episcopal Church and the Civil War* (1912), 94–95, considers that 15 per cent would be a high estimate.

[22] J. H. Whallon to Simpson, Dec. 18, 1863.

[23] Johnson Brigham, *James Harlan* (Iowa City, 1913), 83, 185.

[24] Mitchell to Simpson, Oct. 31, 1864. John Evans to Simpson, Dec. 13, 1864.

[25] Simpson, Autobiography: "Not among the least of the arguments in favor of the righteousness of the present war . . . is the fact that the great leading denominations of the North have uttered a clear and decided testimony in its support. . . . Captains, lieutenants, and non-commissioned officers can be numbered by the thousand from the Methodist church." W. P. Strickland, in *Methodist Quarterly Review*, LV, 434, 435 (July, 1863). Bishops' address, General Conference of 1866, *Christian Advocate and Journal*, May 12, 1864. *Methodist*, Nov. 14, 1863. Two years later the amount was increased to $400,000 (*Independent*, Dec. 14, 1865). William W. Sweet, "The Methodist Episcopal Church and Reconstruction," *Journal of the Illinois State Historical Society*, VII, 147–165 (Oct., 1914).

[26] S. Reed to Simpson, Nov. 23, 1863.

[27] *Independent*, May 3, 1860. Letters Received, National Archives, War Department. Hawkins to Bishop E. R. Ames, Oct. 9 and 16, 1863.

[28] A[lexander] Cummings to Simpson, Nov. 23, 1863. Walter L. Fleming, ed., *Documentary History of Reconstruction* (2 vols., Cleveland, 1907), II, 221. E. E. Townsend to Rev. Bishop Ames.

²⁹ *Christian Advocate and Journal,* Feb. 4, 1864. *Methodist,* Dec. 19, 1863. Nashville *Christian Advocate,* July 17, 1869, citing *Northern Christian Advocate,* July 8, 1869.

³⁰ Knoxville *Whig and Rebel Ventilator,* Jan. 9, 1864.

³¹ James F. Rusling, *Men and Things I Saw in Civil War Days* (New York, 1899), 316-317. Simpson, fragment of letter addressed apparently to an editor of one of the Advocates [Jan., 1864]. Orders signed by Simpson Jan. 21, 1864.

³² Cramer to Simpson, Feb. 24, Mar. 18, and Apr. 2, 1864. Holman to Simpson, Feb. 1, 1864. H. A. Pattison to Simpson, Feb. 8, 1864. Joseph Jones to Simpson, Feb. 22, 1864. J. W. Hoover to Simpson, Apr. 22, 1864. Knoxville *Whig and Rebel Ventilator,* Apr. 30, 1864. E. Merton Coulter, *William G. Brownlow, Fighting Parson of the Southern Highlands* (Chapel Hill, 1937), 296-301.

³³ *Christian Advocate and Journal,* Feb. 18, 1864.

³⁴ Abraham Lincoln, *Complete Works,* ed. Nicolay and Hay (2 vols., New York, 1894), II, 480-481, 491.

³⁵ *Ibid.,* 481.

³⁶ Sweet, *The Methodist Episcopal Church and the Civil War,* 88-89.

³⁷ Crooks, 393-394.

Chapter XXI

YANKEE PURITAN

¹ Address at the meeting of the Christian and Sanitary Commissions, Philadelphia, Jan., 1863, as reported in Philadelphia *Press,* Jan. 30, 1863.

² *Ibid.*

³ Stuart to J. Field, Nov. 2, 1863, Simpson Papers.

⁴ Crooks, 386. Baltimore *Sun,* Nov. 19, 1862. Simpson to Ellen Simpson, Jan. 21, 1863.

⁵ Crooks, 378. *Methodist,* Nov. 12, 1864. Scrapbook clipping, citing the *Rochester Democrat,* n.d.

⁶ Washington *Daily National Intelligencer,* Jan. 26, 1865. John Eaton and Ethel O. Mason, *Grant, Lincoln, and the Freedmen* (New York, 1907), 181. Crooks, 372-373.

⁷ *Christian Advocate and Journal,* June 9, 1864, citing the Philadelphia *Press,* n.d.

⁸ Philadelphia *Press* and Philadelphia *Inquirer,* June 8, 1864.

⁹ J. G. Randall, *The Civil War and Reconstruction* (Boston, 1937), 569, 614 ff.

¹⁰ Crooks, 379 n., citing Mark Hoyt to Simpson, n.d.

¹¹ *Saturday Review,* XIX, 165 (Feb. 11, 1865).

¹² Detailed accounts occur in the Pittsburgh *Gazette* and the Pittsburgh *Commercial,* Oct. 19, 1864, and several New York papers, particularly the *Daily Tribune,* Nov. 7, 1864. Citations are from the *Tribune.*

¹³ Diary, Mar. 6, 1865. James Mitchell to Simpson, Mar. 6, 1865: "I rejoice that the effort to place Senator Harlan in the Cabinet has been successful."

¹⁴ New York *Daily Tribune,* Mar. 6, 1865.

¹⁵ *Ibid.* T. H. Pearne, *Sixty-one Years of Itinerant Christian Life in Church and State* (Cincinnati, 1898), 161.

Chapter XXII

HIGH PRIEST OF THE RADICAL REPUBLICANS

1 Carl Sandburg, *Abraham Lincoln: The War Years,* IV, 219–224, 413.

2 New York *Daily Tribune,* Apr. 15, 1865.

3 *Ibid.,* Apr. 15 and 17, 1865.

4 U.S. Government Archives, Treasury Records: Telegrams Sent, by order of Geo. Harrington, Apr. 18, 1865. Diary, Apr. 16, 1865.

5 New York *Daily Tribune,* Apr. 20, 1865.

6 *Ibid.,* Apr. 25 and 26, 1865.

7 Philadelphia *Press,* May 5, 1865.

8 *Our Martyr President: Abraham Lincoln* (New York, 1865), 393–410.

9 Chicago *Tribune,* May 5, 1865.

10 Diary, Mar. 4, 1865.

11 *Methodist,* May 6, 1865. *Zion's Herald,* May 10, 1865.

12 Philadelphia *Daily Chronicle,* May 19, 1865. *Christian Advocate and Journal,* Feb. 16, 1865.

13 Edgar C. MacMechen, *Life of Governor Evans,* 100, 133–136. Percy Stanley Fritz, *Colorado: The Centennial State* (New York, 1941), 178, 205–206. Simpson to John Evans, June 28 and Aug. 4, 1865, Governor John Evans Papers, Colorado Historical Society. J. M. Chivington to Simpson, Mar. 9, 1865.

14 Simpson to John Evans, Aug. 4, 1865, Gov. John Evans Papers.

15 Randall, *The Civil War and Reconstruction,* 718–730.

16 Baldwin to Simpson, Apr. 21, 1864. Baldwin to Andrew Johnson, June 5, 1865, Andrew Johnson Papers, Library of Congress.

17 Baldwin to Andrew Johnson, *ibid.*

18 Diary, June 12, Aug. 12 and 14, 1865. A. A. Gee to Simpson, Aug. 22, 1865.

19 E. R. Ames to Simpson, Jan. 2, 1865.

20 *Ibid.* E. S. Janes to Simpson, Dec. 28, 1865.

21 Diary, Jan. 17, 1866.

22 E. R. Ames to Simpson, Jan. 19, 1866. Memorandum, signed by E. D. Townsend, Jan. 18, 1866, in National Archives, War Department, Adjutant General's Office.

23 E. R. Ames to Simpson, Jan. 19, 1866. *Southern Christian Advocate,* Mar. 2, 1866, cited in Erasmus Q. Fuller, *An Appeal to the Records: A Vindication of the Methodist Episcopal Church* (Cincinnati, 1876), 311.

24 *Southern Christian Advocate,* Dec. 21, 1865.

25 Two excellent accounts of the northern church's activities in the South are William W. Sweet, "The Methodist Episcopal Church and Reconstruction," *Journal of the Illinois State Historical Society,* VII, 147–165 (Oct., 1914), and Hunter Dickinson Farish, *The Circuit Rider Dismounts: A Social History of Southern Methodism, 1865–1900* (Richmond, Va., 1938). "Disintegrate and Absorb" was openly espoused by the *Christian Advocate and Journal,* Feb. 22, 1866, April 25, 1867.

[26] *Southern Christian Advocate*, Sept. 6, 1867. St. Louis *Christian Advocate*, May 13 and 20, 1868. W. M. Leftwich, *Martyrdom in Missouri* (St. Louis, 1870), I, 257. *Christian Advocate and Journal*, Mar. 23, 1865. Enoch Marvin, "History of the Origin of the Methodist Episcopal Church, South," *Southern Review*, X, 415 (Apr., 1872).

[27] *Christian Advocate and Journal*, May 14, 1868.

[28] *Ibid.*, Feb. 18 and Mar. 4, 1869.

[29] *Ibid.*, Aug. 25, 1870.

[30] Nashville *Christian Advocate*, Oct. 24, 1867. Clipping from *Zion's Herald*, n.d., Scrapbook. William Coppinger to Simpson, Oct. 13, 1863. Ellis Yarnall to Simpson, Nov. 28, 1863. *American Freedman*, I, 4, 36 (Apr., 1866).

[31] C. C. Leigh to Simpson, Nov. 7, 1864. *Independent*, Jan. 4, 1866.

[32] Frank Abial Flower, *Edwin McMasters Stanton* (Akron, Ohio, 1905), 374 n.

[33] Simpson to L. L. Hamline, May 15, 1855. James Harlan to Simpson, Feb. 17, 1862.

[34] James Harlan to Simpson, Aug. 17, 1865; Charles Edward Russell, *Blaine of Maine* (New York, 1931), 95; Bliss Perry, *Walt Whitman, His Life and Work* (Boston and New York, 1906), 164–166.

[35] James Harlan to Simpson, Aug. 17, 1865.

[36] Harlan to Simpson, Oct. 28, 1865. Johnson Brigham, *James Harlan*, 217, citing the Muscatine *Daily Journal*, Jan. 3, 1866, and the Iowa City *Republican*, Jan. 17, 1856. George Fort Milton, *The Age of Hate: Andrew Johnson and the Radicals* (New York, 1930), 340.

[37] Scrapbook, newspaper clipping, Dec., 1865.

[38] Sweet, "The Methodist Episcopal Church and Reconstruction," *Journal of the Illinois Historical Society*, VII, 162 (Oct. 1914).

[39] Diary, Jan. 13 and 14, 1868. Flower, *Stanton*, 373.

[40] *Journal of the General Conference of the Methodist Episcopal Church, 1868* (New York, 1868), 147, 152. Milton, 316–317.

[41] Baltimore *Sun*, May 18 and 19, 1865. New York *Daily Tribune*, May 19, 1868. St. Louis *Christian Advocate*, June 10, 1868.

[42] *Journal of the General Conference . . . 1868*, 157. Milton, 601.

[43] Milton, *loc. cit.* Gideon Welles, *Diary* (3 vols., Boston, 1911), III, 358. Correspondence in the Waitman T. Willey Papers, University of West Virginia Library, suggests that pressure from his constituents was quite as strong a reason for his vote as the "badgering" of the Methodists.

[44] Charles V. Dyer to Simpson, May 16, 1868.

[45] Chicago *Republican*, May 21, 1868.

[46] Scrapbook, newspaper clipping.

[47] Sweet, "The Methodist Church and Reconstruction," *Journal of the Illinois State Historical Society*, VII, 153–154 (Oct., 1914). Farish, *The Circuit Rider Dismounts*, 140–143. Nashville *Christian Advocate*, Sept. 19, 1867, quoting the *Methodist*, n.d.

[48] St. Louis *Christian Advocate*, May 27, 1868, quoting the New York *Daily Tribune*, n.d.

[49] *Methodist*, Nov. 20, 1869, and Jan. 23, 1869. Scrapbook, clipping dated Jan. 22, 1867.

[50] *Christian Advocate and Journal*, Feb. 22, 1866, and Apr. 25, 1867. Crooks, 442. *Southern Christian Advocate*, May 10, 1867.

[51] *Methodist*, July 1, 1865.

[52] St. Louis *Christian Advocate*, Aug. 17, 1865.

[53] *Southern Christian Advocate*, Aug. 31, Sept. 21, and Oct. 12, 1865. St. Louis *Christian Advocate*, Nov. 2 and 23, 1865. Enoch Marvin, 417-418.

[54] St. Louis *Christian Advocate*, May 12, 1869.

[55] *Ibid.*, May 19 and July 21, 1869. Marvin, 417.

[56] St. Louis *Christian Advocate*, Aug. 17 and Nov. 2, 1865.

[57] Address at Church Extension Anniversary, *Christian Advocate and Journal*, Dec. 2, 1869. *Christian Advocate and Journal*, Feb. 18, 1869. *Methodist*, Oct. 23, 1869.

Chapter XXIII

THE VICTORY OF FAITH

[1] *Methodist*, May 3, 1879; *Zion's Herald*, Dec. 8, 1867. Resolutions unanimously adopted by the Philadelphia Annual Conference, March 18, 1863, MS. in Simpson Papers.

[2] *Zion's Herald*, Jan. 26, 1865.

[3] Manuscript of sermon at Muscatine, Iowa, in 1859.

[4] Simpson, *Sermons*, ed. George R. Crooks, 317, 318.

[5] *Ibid.*, 319, 101.

[6] *Ibid.*, 42, 323.

[7] *Ibid.*, 322, 323, 8.

[8] *Ibid.*, 228.

[9] *Ibid.*, 231-232.

[10] *Ibid.*, 51-52, 233, 237-238.

[11] *Ibid.*, 197-201.

[12] Willard, *A Classic Town*, 266-267.

[13] Joseph R. King, "Personal Reminiscences of Bishops Scott, Ames, and Simpson," *Christian Advocate*, LXXXI, 1249-1251 (Aug., 1906).

[14] James M. Buckley, "Editorial Letter: Bishop Simpson," *Christian Advocate*, LXXXVI, 791 (June 15, 1911).

[15] "A Great Modern Preacher," *Andover Review*, II, 186-193, contains a detailed account of the sermon.

[16] Simpson, *Sermons*, 193-205.

Chapter XXIV

"BISHOPS AS PARTISANS"

[1] *Christian Advocate and Journal*, Sept. 14, 1876.

[2] William C. Smith, *Pillars in the Temple* (New York, 1872), 216.

[3] Scrapbook C, newspaper clipping.

[4] J. R. Graves, *The Great Iron Wheel* (Nashville, 1855), 157.

[5] *Daily Christian Advocate,* May 19, 1860.

[6] *Ibid.,* May 7, 1860.

[7] Crooks, 412.

[8] *Ibid.,* 413.

[9] *Ibid.,* 414.

[10] *Christian Advocate and Journal,* Sept. 18, 1862.

[11] Ridgaway, *Janes,* 271–272.

[12] Crooks, 416.

[13] *Ibid.,* 418.

[14] Daniel Ross to George R. Crooks, June 26, 1863, George R. Crooks Papers, Drew University Library.

[15] Rev. James Cunningham, *A Review of Bishop Simpson's Address Before the Convention of Methodist Laymen* (Philadelphia, 1864).

[16] Crooks, 427.

[17] William Warren Sweet, *Indiana Asbury–DePauw University, 1837–1937,* 72.

[18] *Southern Christian Advocate,* Nov. 23, 1866. *Independent,* May 14, 1866.

[19] *Christian Advocate and Journal,* June 21, 1866.

[20] *Methodist,* Nov. 16, 1867.

[21] *Christian Advocate and Journal,* Nov. 21 and 28, 1867.

[22] *Zion's Herald,* Dec. 5, 1867.

[23] *Methodist,* May 23, 1867.

[24] *Christian Advocate and Journal,* July 15, 1869.

[25] *Ibid.,* Apr. 7, 1864.

[26] *Ibid.,* Jan. 30, Apr. 16, and June 18, 1868.

[27] *Ibid.,* Sept. 24, 1863.

[28] *Ibid.,* May 5, 1870.

[29] New York *Times,* Sept. 21, 1869. John Lanahan tells the story in great detail in *Era of Frauds in the Methodist Book Concern in New York* (Baltimore, 1896).

[30] *Christian Advocate and Journal,* Feb. 3, 1870. *Western Christian Advocate,* Jan. 26, 1870.

[31] *Christian Advocate and Journal,* Sept. 30, 1869, and Apr. 14, 1870.

[32] Lanahan, 165–166.

[33] B. F. Crary to George R. Crooks, Sept. 21, 1869, and Simpson to Crooks, Feb. 28, 1870—both in the George R. Crooks Papers.

[34] *Christian Advocate and Journal,* May 12, 1870.

[35] *Ibid.,* Apr. 14 and May 12, 1870.

[36] Simpson to Ellen Simpson, May 4 and 5, 1870.

[37] *Ibid.,* May 7, 9, and 10, 1870.

[38] *Christian Advocate and Journal,* June 9, 1870. Simpson to Ellen Simpson, Sept. 4, 1870.

[39] Simpson to Ellen Simpson, Jan. 8, 1871. Simpson to E. S. Janes, May 29, 1871 (Correspondence of the Bishops of the Methodist Episcopal Church, Garrett Biblical Institute).

[40] *Christian Advocate and Journal,* Feb. 9, 1871.

⁴¹ Simpson to Ellen Simpson, Feb. 19, 1871 (Crooks, 451). Simpson to E. S. Janes, May 29, 1871. Correspondence of the Bishops of the Methodist Episcopal Church, Garrett Biblical Institute.
⁴² *Christian Advocate and Journal,* July 20, 1871.
⁴³ Simpson to E. S. Janes, May 29, 1871.

Chapter XXV

EVEN THE EAGLE

¹ Diary, June 21, 1871.
² Smith, *Indiana Methodism,* 256. J. E. Parker to Simpson, Mar. 20, 1863. *Christian Advocate and Journal,* Sept. 22, 1870.
³ Smith, *Pillars,* 217.
⁴ *Christian Advocate and Journal,* Jan. 17 and Dec. 5, 1867. Untitled account written by Simpson [1868].
⁵ Scrapbook [1867]. Notes, Trip to Europe, June 19, 1870.
⁶ Simpson to Verner Simpson, Sept. 15, 1869. Diary, Feb. 12 and Aug. 28, 1873. Simpson to Libbie Simpson, Dec. 31, 1866. Helen A. Simpson, *Early Records of Simpson Families* (Philadelphia, 1937), 266.
⁷ Merle Curti, "A Great Teacher's Teacher," *Social Education,* XIII, 263–266 (Oct., 1949). Simpson to Ellen Simpson, Dec. 18, 1870. *Methodist,* Nov. 6, 1869.
⁸ Simpson to Ellen Simpson, Dec. 3, 1869.
⁹ Aug. 28, Oct. 14, and Nov. 27, 1870.
¹⁰ Dec. 18, 1870, and Feb. 12, 1871. In fact, he was thirty-three when he first crossed the mountains.
¹¹ *Christian Advocate and Journal,* Apr. 10, 1873 (Janes also received $4,500, other bishops $4,000, presumably because of the higher costs of living in New York and Philadelphia). Diary, May 23, 1873. *Christian Advocate and Journal,* July 24, 1873. Scrapbook D.
¹² *Methodist,* Nov. 16, 1867.
¹³ William B. Hesseltine, *Ulysses S. Grant, Politician* (New York, 1935), 305. Scrapbook, newspaper clipping [March, 1869]. Diary, Jan. 1, 2, and 4, 1869, Jan. 7, 1870, and Apr. 28, 1874. Simpson to Ellen Simpson, Jan. 8, 1871.
¹⁴ Wesley Prettyman to Simpson, Oct. 12, 1874. Oliver Hoyt to Simpson, May 26, 1874. F. B. Morgan to Simpson, Sept. 24, 1872.
¹⁵ Rutherford Birchard Hayes, *Diary and Letters* (Columbus, Ohio, 4 vols., 1925), IV, 91, 111, 630, and III, 578–579. R. B. Hayes to Simpson, Oct. 18, 1876. Simpson, Diary, Feb. 7, 8, 10, 1879, and Feb. 10, 1880.
¹⁶ Simpson to J. Allison, Mar. 3, 1880. "Methodism and Its Methods," *American Catholic Quarterly Review,* VII, 14 (Jan., 1882).
¹⁷ William Little to Simpson, Feb. 16, 1869. John H. Gull to Simpson, Jan. 24, 1873. Mrs. Rev. J. B. Henry to Simpson, Sept. 27, 1879. Addison C. Gibbs to Simpson, Dec. 15, 1879. Wesley Prettyman to Simpson, Oct. 12, 1874.
¹⁸ Simpson to J. Allison, Mar. 3, 1880. S. J. Kirkwood to Simpson, Mar. 10, 1881.

Wayne MacVeagh to Simpson, Apr. 11, 1881. Diary, Jan. 7, 1874. James Harlan to Simpson, Feb. 12, 1869. John A. Gosper to Simpson, Dec. 10 and 21, 1880, and Jan. 24, 1881. J. H. Whallon to Simpson, June 30, 1872.

19 Simpson to Libbie Simpson, Jan. 29, 1875.

20 Alexander Cummings to Simpson, Nov. 15 [1875]. James Harlan to Simpson, Apr. 4, 1876, and Dec. 28, 1872.

21 Scrapbook, clipping reporting Minneapolis address. Boston *Post* and Boston *Daily Advertiser*, Nov. 22, 1867.

22 Philadelphia *Press*, Feb. 8, 1873.

23 Lucy Stone to Simpson, Nov. 20, 1876.

24 Scrapbook, newspaper clipping, Mar. 8, 1874. *Ibid.*, n.d.

25 J. H. Vincent to Simpson [1870], quoting a Baptist preacher.

26 Scrapbook newspaper clipping reporting sermon at New Jersey Conference [1875].

27 Arthur M. Schlesinger, *The Rise of the City, 1878-1898* (Vol. X of *A History of American Life*—New York, 1933), 93.

28 Scrapbook C, clipping from *Indiana State Sentinel*.

29 Matthew Simpson, *Lectures on Preaching* . . . (New York, 1879), 9.

30 *Ibid.*, 75-85.

31 *Ibid.*, 220-222.

32 Ammi Bradford Hyde, *The Story of Methodism* (New York, 1888), 709.

33 San Francisco *Chronicle*, Sept. 2, 1878.

34 *Ibid.*

35 *Ibid.*, Sept. 16, 1878. William Norwood Brigance, *Jeremiah Sullivan Black* (Philadelphia, 1934), 150-155.

36 San Francisco *Chronicle* and *Morning Call*, Sept. 16, 1878.

37 London *Daily News* and *Times*, Sept. 26, 1881. Philadelphia *Inquirer*, Sept. 26, 1881. *Northwestern Christian Advocate*, June 25, 1884.

38 Simpson to J. L. Smith, Mar. 29, 1882.

39 Diary, Aug. 21 and Mar. 11, 1881.

40 Crooks, 464.

41 *Ibid.*, 465.

42 Philadelphia *Press*, May 2, 1884.

43 Crooks, 465-466.

44 Funeral Sermon by Bishop Randolph S. Foster, *Christian Advocate and Journal*, July 3, 1884. Crooks, 468.

45 Crooks, 468-469. *Western Christian Advocate*, June 25, 1884.

INDEX

INDEX

342

INDEX

Simpson, Matthew (*continued*)

At General Conferences: delegate, 112; trip to New York, 113, 116, 117-118; named to committee on education, 119; presents resolutions, 119; fears church will split, 123; opposes separation, 128; prepares compromise, 1848, 140; secretary, committee on state of church, 140; favors repudiation of plan of separation, 141-142, 144; opposes fraternal relations with South, 142; proposes California conference, 142; mentioned as bishop, 143; delegate, 1852, 161; addresses, 166

Editor, *Western Christian Advocate:* election, 145-147; policy, 148-150, 150-151; controversy with Episcopalians, 151; attacks Calvinism, 151-153; condemns exhibition of "Greek Slave," 154-155; criticizes Compromise of 1850, 155-160; controversy with William J. Brown, 158-160; involved in pew controversy, 162-163

As bishop: candidate, 138, 143; opposition to, 161-162, 162-163, 166; election, 165, 167; duties, 169, 170-171; first conference, 170; travel, 171-172; to California, 178-188; establishes new pattern, 190; supports theological school, 190-191; income, 191-192, 292-293; favors improved architecture, 192; favors liturgy, 192; to Europe, 196-206; at Evangelical Alliance, 198-201; illness, 202, 203, 204, 206, 207-208; second trip to California, 222, 223; final conference, 304-306

And slavery, 8, 54-55, 55-56, 67, 68, 69-70, 221, 236, 242; fears slavery will divide church and nation, 132; called abolitionist, 159; opposes change in Methodist discipline, 193-195; defends church in England, 197-198; moderates attempt to revise discipline, 210-215; and Emancipation Proclamation, 222-223

Temperance, morality, and reform, 27-28, 37, 153-155, 296-297, 298-299; praises John B. Gough, 153; condemns Jenny Lind, 153; opposes liquor licensing, 153-154; criticizes sculpture of Hiram Powers, 154-155; social effect of gospel, 270-271; women's rights, 298

As preacher: Indiana success, 76, 77-78; demands upon, 173-174; science and religion, 174-175; on Christian unity, 200-201; in the House of Representatives, 244; reputation enhanced by politics, 267-268; themes, 268-271; Victory of Faith, 271-274; six o'clock lectures, 283; endorses evolutionary hypothesis, 299-300; Yale lectures, 300-302; compared to Henry Ward Beecher, 302, 303; final sermon, 305

Eloquence, 102-103, 166, 169, 171, 188, 189, 190, 197-198, 199-201, 219, 219-220, 236, 237-238, 244, 248, 302, 302-303; Garfield Memorial Address, 303-304

And Providence: 150; and destiny of American people, 219, 236, 239, 240-242, 248-249, 268, 269-270, 271

And lay representation: 192-193; declares approval of, 277, 278; speaks in behalf of, 278-279, 279, 280, 281-282; attacked by opponents, 279; wins votes for, 286-287. See also Lay representation, Curry

And Lincoln: 210, 218, 244; calls for more troops, 218; protests discrimination against Methodists, 225; represents Lincoln at Philadelphia, 238-240; invited to preach funeral sermon, 246; memorial services at White House, 246; funeral sermon at Springfield, 247-248

And Civil War: calls for more troops, 218; prays for Union victory, 218-219; patriotic addresses, 219, 219-220, 237-243

And politics: office seekers, 224-229, 294-296; protests Wright's removal from Berlin, 225; suggests Evans for governorship, 227-228; quarrels with Montgomery Blair, 228; supports Harlan for Cabinet, 229; fails to prevent Evans's removal, 249-250; nominates Alexander Cummings for governorship, 250; sympathizes with Radical Republicans, 256, 257, 258; supports Harlan for Senate, 258

And Methodist Church in South:

230, 234, 264; occupies churches in East Tennessee, 230-231, 232-233; finds Johnson friendly to Methodists, 249; gives up Nashville chapel, 250-251; attempts to seize Virginia churches, 251-253; praises work of northern Methodists, 254-255; opposes mingling of Whites and Negroes, 255, 256; rights of Negroes must be secured, 258; refused southern pulpit, 263; favors reunion, 264

And Andrew Johnson, 248; praises Johnson's policies, 248-249; promises support, 249; alienated from Johnson, 256-258; supports Stanton against Johnson, 259; wins Methodist support for impeachment, 260-261

Simpson, Sarah Tingley, 3-4, 4, 5, 25-26, 29, 114, 291

Simpson, Verner, 218, 291

Slavery, 52-53, 54-55, 56, 69-70, 116, 120-122, 125-127, 130, 132, 181-182, 193-195, 210-213, 213-215, 221-222

Smith, John L., 104, 138, 139, 146, 161, 168, 227-228

Smith, William A., 120-122, 131

Soule, Bp. Joshua, 119, 127, 139, 145, 168

South Bend, Indiana, 102

Springfield, Illinois, 210, 218, 246, 247

Spurgeon, Charles, 272

Stanton, Edward M., 2, 226, 237, 244, 252, 257, 263; and possession of southern churches, 231, 234; praises Simpson's eloquence, 238; urges Simpson to organize Freedmen's Bureau, 255; barricades himself in office, 259

Stevens, Abel, 143, 166, 169, 194-195, 195, 210, 278

Stevens, Thaddeus, 222

Stockton, California, 185

Stone, Lucy, 298

Stuart, George H., 237

Sunderland, La Roy, 55, 56, 174

Talmage, T. De Witt, 272

Taylor, "Father" Edward, 166

Tefft, Benjamin, 100, 133, 134, 137, 167

Temperance, 27-28, 37, 153-154, 298-299

Tennessee, northern Methodists in, 230-233, 234, 251-252, 254, 259, 266

Terre Haute, Indiana, 71

Texas, 155, 211, 215, 256, 265-266

Thomas, George, 232

Thomas, Isaiah, 61

Thompson, L. G., 106

Thomson, Bp. Edward, 165-166, 167, 283-284, 285, 289

Thomson, Samuel, 24

Tingley, Joseph, 7, 8, 52

Tingley, William, 26, 52, 53, 54

Tyler, John, 110, 115, 216

Uncle Tom's Cabin, 164

Uniontown, Pennsylvania, 10, 11, 169-170

U.S. Sanitary Commission, 238-240

Verner, James, 35, 47

Voorhees, Daniel Webster, 157-158, 294

Wabash College, 72, 90, 101, 105, 105-106, 110-111

Wade, Benjamin F., 222, 229

Wallace, David, 79, 84

War Department, 231-232, 232, 233

Warren, William F., 198, 202

Washington, D.C., 115-116, 224, 237, 238, 243, 245-246, 249, 250, 252, 259, 267, 293, 294

Watson, Richard, 43, 54

Waugh, Bp. Beverly, 66, 165

Weakley, John W., 86

Weaver, James Riley, 291-292, 295

Webster, Daniel, 8, 156

Weld, Theodore, 53, 55-56

Welles, Gideon, 223, 229, 261

Wesley, John, 4, 25, 26, 32, 36, 37, 41-42, 43-44, 48, 51, 54, 66, 72, 77, 82, 112, 176, 192, 197, 202, 266, 268, 269, 276-277, 279

Wesleyan Conference, England, 196, 197-198

Wesleyan University, 125, 291

West Virginia College (University), 291

Western Christian Advocate, 57, 71, 73, 134, 145, 146-147, 148-149, 158, 159, 162, 163, 196, 298, 306

Wheeler, John, 92-93, 96, 133, 134, 135, 145, 290

Whigs, 156; Indiana gubernatorial campaign, 1843, 106-110

Whitcomb, James, 107-110, 110-111, 113, 135